Cool Colleges

SECOND EDITION

PETERSON'S
Publishing

About Peterson's Publishing

Peterson's Publishing provides the accurate, dependable, high-quality education content and guidance you need to succeed. No matter where you are on your academic or professional path, you can rely on Peterson's print and digital publications for the most up-to-date education exploration data, expert test-prep tools, and top-notch career success resources—everything you need to achieve your goals.

For more information, contact Peterson's Publishing, 2000 Lenox Drive, Lawrenceville, NJ 08648; 800-338-3282 Ext. 54229; or find us online at www.petersonspublishing.com.

Bernadette Webster, Managing Editor; Jill C. Schwartz, Editor; Ray Golaszewski, Publishing Operations Manager; Linda M. Williams, Composition Manager; Carrie Hansen, Christine Lucht, Bailey Williams, Fulfillment Team

Cover photos from left to right: Harding University, (AR), photo by Jeff Montgomery; Quinnipiac University (CT); Champlain College, Burlington (VT), photo by Kathleen Landwehrle. Divider page photos: Cool College Profiles: Monmouth University (NJ); Taking the SAT: Chestnut Hill College (PA); Getting Into College: Hillsdale College (MI)

ISBN-13: 978-0-7689-3439-7
ISBN-10: 0-7689-3439-7

Printed in the United States of America

10 9 8 7 6 5 4 3 2 1   14 13 12

Second Edition

Sustainability—Its Importance to Peterson's, a Nelnet company

What does sustainability mean to Peterson's? As a leading publisher, we are aware that our business has a direct impact on vital resources—most especially the trees that are used to make our books. Peterson's is proud that its products are certified by the Sustainable Forestry Initiative (SFI) and that this book is printed on paper that is 10 percent post-consumer waste.

Being a part of the Sustainable Forestry Initiative (SFI) means that all of our vendors—from paper suppliers to printers—have undergone rigorous audits to demonstrate that they are maintaining a sustainable environment.

Peterson's continually strives to find new ways to incorporate sustainability throughout all aspects of its business.

CONTENTS

TAKING THE SAT

GETTING INTO COLLEGE

WELCOME TO COOL COLLEGES!

Peterson's Cool Colleges is a new undergraduate guide featuring colorful, easy-to-read profiles of over a hundred "cool" colleges and universities across the United States and abroad. *Peterson's Cool Colleges* is designed for the ultimate decision maker—the student. It is not a typical four-year college guide: The layout reflects what *you* want—vibrant photos, essential information, and fast facts and figures— right at your finger tips!

Whether high school graduation is right around the corner or a year or two away, you need to consider which college or university is going to suit your needs and lifestyle best. After all, you're about to make one of the most important decisions of your life, and you need the best information possible.

Peterson's is here to help! For nearly fifty years, Peterson's has given students the most comprehensive, up-to-date information on undergraduate institutions in the United States and abroad. Now, we are offering this new, one-of-a-kind college search experience.

The profiles displayed in this guide serve as an introduction to the culture and lifestyle on college campuses throughout the United States and abroad. In each college profile, you'll find those attributes that make each school unique: its culture, tradition, social life, atmosphere, architecture, and environment. We hope that after reading *Peterson's Cool Colleges* you will have a richer sense of the experiences awaiting you at each individual college and university.

Cool College Profiles

Each profile appears on a two-page spread and contains vivid campus photos, an informative description, fast facts and figures, and contact information. The colleges appear in alphabetical order.

COLLEGE DESCRIPTIONS

All of the colleges featured in this guide have provided a fee to Peterson's to provide the brief description of what they have to offer you—the incoming student. Edited by Peterson's for consistency, the descriptions are designed to give students a better sense of the individuality of each institution in terms of campus environment, student activities, and college lifestyle. Peterson's believes that, in addition to the programs of study offered, these quality-of-life intangibles are often the deciding factors in the college selection process.

PHOTOS AND CAPTIONS

Throughout this guide you will find colorful photos that provide a visual preview of life on campus. The photos may feature school grounds, sports arenas, dining facilities, campus events, important buildings and monuments, and student life in general. The schools have provided captions to help contextualize the information in their photos and help students like you better understand what campus life may be like.

CONTACT INFORMATION

At the beginning of a college profile you will see the school name; school logo; the city, state (city, country in the International section); and the school's Web site and, in some cases, their social media sites. The name, title, phone numbers, and e-mail address of the person or department to contact for further information are given in a green box on the right-hand page of every profile. Toll-free numbers may also be included as well as numbers for in-state and out-of-state callers.

FAST FACTS AND FIGURES

Peterson's Cool Colleges offers fast facts and figures for prospective students who want basic data for quick review and comparison. At the end of the college description, you'll find bulleted information on school enrollment, selectivity, test scores, application deadlines, and expenses. Any item that does not apply to a particular college or for which no information was supplied is omitted from that college's profile.

Enrollment

The number of undergraduate and (if applicable) graduate students, both full-time and part-time, as of fall 2011 or spring 2012.

Selectivity

The five levels of entrance difficulty *(most difficult, very difficult, moderately difficult, minimally difficult,* and *noncompetitive)* are based on the percentage of applicants who were accepted for fall 2011 or 2012 freshman admission (or, in the case of upper-level schools, for entering-class admission) and on the high school class rank and standardized test scores of the accepted freshmen who actually enrolled in fall 2011. The colleges were asked to select the level that most closely corresponds to their entrance difficulty (according to the above guidelines) to assist prospective students in assessing their chances for admission.

Test Scores

The percentage of freshmen who took the SAT and received critical reading and math scores above 500, as well as the percentage of freshmen taking the ACT who received a composite score of 18 or higher. Some schools have provided additional or other pertinent test score information.

Application Deadline

Deadlines dates for both freshmen and transfer students are given as specific dates or as rolling or continuous. *Rolling* means that applications are processed as they are received, and qualified students are accepted as long as there are openings. *Continuous notification* means that applicants are notified of acceptance or rejection as applications are processed up until the date indicated or the actual beginning of classes. Some schools have also provided their *Early Action* and/or *Early Decision* dates.

Expenses

Tuition is the average basic tuition and fees for an academic year presented as a dollar amount. *Room & Board* is the average yearly room-and-board cost presented as a dollar amount. Most state-supported and state-related schools have provided figures for the cost of in-state resident tuition and fees as well as out-of-state nonresident tuition and fees.

DATA COLLECTION AND INCLUSION

The data contained in these college profiles were researched between winter 2011 and spring 2012 through *Peterson's Annual Survey of Undergraduate Institutions*. All data included have been submitted by officials at the colleges. Some of the institutions that submitted data were contacted directly by the Peterson's research staff to verify unusual figures, resolve discrepancies, or obtain additional data. Due to Peterson's comprehensive editorial review, we believe the information presented in this guide is accurate. However, you should check with a specific college or university at the time of application to verify such figures as tuition and room & board, which may have changed since the publication of this guide.

The absence of any college or university from this guide does not constitute an editorial decision on the part of Peterson's, nor do we attempt to portray one school as being "cooler" than any other. In essence, these profiles are an open forum for colleges and universities, on a voluntary basis, to communicate their particular message to a cool new generation of prospective students.

Taking the SAT

If you are prepping for the SAT, check out "Tips and Practice for the SAT," which offers expert tips as well as sample practice questions with detailed answer explanations. In this chapter, you'll find valuable information about the SAT format and scoring, helpful advice on what to do on the night before and the day of the exam, and great advice for each section of the

SAT. And don't miss our Top 10 Strategies to Raise Your SAT Score, which can definitely help your test-prep efforts. At the end of this chapter, we've provided practice test items taken from Peterson's *Master the SAT.* We hope that these sample questions, with their full answer explanations, will help you as you prepare to take this most important college-admissions test.

Getting Into College

For advice and guidance on searching for the right college, getting your application ready, or planning your education, or looking for those important scholarship dollars, check our this chapter with enlightening articles written for students like you. "Exploring Possible Career Paths in High School" shows you how you can test various career paths by exploring your interests. "Planning Your Education" can help you determine what you need to do to prepare for college. "The College Search" illuminates those resources at your disposal to locate the right school for you. "Applying to College" can help you figure out what's involved in the application process and what schools look for in prospective students. "What to Expect in College" can help answer some of the big questions, such as how to choose your classes or major and how you can make the most of your life outside the classroom. Need money for college or are you hoping to win a scholarship? Check out these articles: "Who Wants to Be a Scholarship Millionaire?," "Winning the Scholarship with a Winning Essay," "Tweet for Dollars: Use Your Fingertips and Social Media to Pay for College," How to Spruce Up Your Internet and Social Media Presence to Wow Scholarship Judges," and What to Do If You Don't Win a Scholarship, Grant, or Prize."

Find Us On Facebook®

Join the conversation at facebook.com/petersonspublishing and receive additional college search tips and advice.

Peterson's publishes a full line of books—education exploration, financial aid, and test and career preparation. Peterson's publications can be found at high school guidance offices, college libraries and career centers, and your local bookstore and library. Peterson's books are also available as eBooks.

We welcome any comments or suggestions you may have about this publication. Your feedback will help us make educational dreams possible for you—and others like you.

Colleges will be pleased to know that Peterson's helped you in your selection. Admissions staff members are more than happy to answer questions, address specific problems, and help in any way they can. The editors at Peterson's wish you great success in your college search!

Cool College Profiles

Students organize and lead over 100 clubs and organizations, including the popular Outing Club, which plans events throughout the year such as skiing, rock climbing, canoeing, and whitewater rafting.

ALLEGHENY COLLEGE

MEADVILLE, PENNSYLVANIA
http://www.allegheny.edu/unusualcombinations
http://www.allegheny.edu/distinctions

Allegheny College is the premier liberal arts institution where students with "Unusual Combinations" of interests, skills, and talents excel. The exploration of diverse perspectives and scholarly engagement with faculty members are at the heart of the experience. Students not only pursue an academic major, choosing from the humanities, social sciences, or natural sciences, but, each is also required to declare a minor in a separate academic division, developing the sort of "big picture" thinking that is in high demand in today's global economy. The required Senior Project further synthesizes students' academic experiences through mentored undergraduate research, demonstrating critical thinking and communication skills highly sought after by employers and graduate schools.

Students contact the Allegheny College Center for Experiential Learning (ACCEL) to seek out hands-on opportunities. This unique office combines community service, leadership development, career services, study abroad, and pre-professional advising to help students turn their unusual combinations into extraordinary outcomes. Whether volunteering at Hog Heaven Animal Rescue or developing an AIDS-prevention education program in Kenya, Alleghenians learn as much from hands-on experiences as they do from classroom instruction.

When not hitting the books, Gators explore their passions through more than 100 student organizations ranging from academic to political clubs, diversity organizations to service initiatives—all of which strengthen the campus and surrounding community. On any given day, a student may leave the biology lab and head to symphony practice only to end the evening at a night hike sponsored by the Outing Club. Allegheny is also a founding member of the NCAA, with 25 percent of students competing in 21 varsity sports at the Division III level. Another quarter participates in club sports, intramurals, and extensive outdoor adventures

throughout beautiful northwestern Pennsylvania.

As Allegheny approaches its Bicentennial Celebration in 2015, it maintains a commitment to incorporating environmental principles and ethics into everyday life. Allegheny pioneered campuswide composting, turning dining hall leftovers into organic fertilizer. In addition, Students for Environmental Action (SEA) proudly sponsors a "Trashion Show" each year, creating clothing from recycled materials.

The College sits just outside downtown Meadville, a cozy town and county seat with a rich arts culture and community. Students partner with business for internships and job shadowing, city

CONTACT INFORMATION

Office of Admissions
☎ 814-332-4351 or
   800-521-5293 (toll-free)
🖥 admissions@allegheny.edu

planning and collaboration, and enjoy food, fun, and the arts. Located just 1.5 hours from Pittsburgh and 2 hours from Cleveland and Buffalo, Allegheny and Meadville foster a home for students from around the country and the world.

- **Enrollment:** *2,123*
- **Selectivity:** *very difficult*
- **Test scores:** *ACT—over 18, 100%; SAT—critical reading over 500, 87%; SAT—math over 500, 87%*
- **Application deadline:** *2/15 (freshmen), 7/1 (transfer)*
- **Expenses:** *Tuition $34,810; Room & Board $8790*

Required research: Since 1821, Allegheny students have "comped" the Senior Project; topics range from regeneration in salamanders to the installation of solar panels to full theater productions.

Education on Location: Students admire one of Rome's many Baroque churches during Art of Rome, a course held entirely on-site. Students of all disciplines find face-to-face encounters with the rich art, history, and culture of Rome a highlight of their time at AUR.

THE AMERICAN UNIVERSITY OF ROME
1·9·6·9

ROME, ITALY

www.aur.edu

www.facebook.com/TheAmericanUniversityofRome

Founded in 1969, The American University of Rome (AUR) is one of the oldest private, independent, not-for-profit institutions of higher education in Europe, offering undergraduate liberal arts programs in English to degree and study-abroad students from over 40 countries. The mission of the University—to promote intellectual excellence, personal growth, and an appreciation of cultural diversity in an international environment—plays out in every sphere of University life. AUR students benefit from learning in every venue: in their classrooms, in their everyday life in the city, through academic work and practical internships, and on learning excursions in Italy and Europe. AUR also offers an orientation and a first year program designed to help students make a successful transition to the University's community of learners.

AUR offers 7 Bachelor of Arts degree programs in Archeology and Classics, Art History, Communication, Film and Digital Media, Interdisciplinary Studies, International Relations and Global Politics, and Italian Studies, as well as a Bachelor of Science in Business Administration, and there are more than 20 minors available. The

University provides small classes, with a student-faculty ratio of 16:1. The American University of Rome is accredited by the Middle States Commission on Higher Education.

The University is located on top of the highest hill of Rome, the Janiculum, and offers spectacular views of city. Three large city parks surround the AUR campus, which offers both the amenities and buzz of an urban setting and a quiet environment conductive to study and learning. The 30,000-square-foot campus provides computer labs, a student lounge and study areas, smart classrooms, a science lab, a multimedia lab, art studios, tutoring centers, an auditorium, a 12,000-volume library, and a wealth of electronic resources. Wi-Fi is available from locations on and around the campus.

AUR recognizes that learning and personal growth occur in all settings that allow students to develop their knowledge and skills. Students are encouraged to engage actively in clubs, excursions, performing groups, and student government and are represented on many of the University's governance committees. Students participate in athletic and recreational offerings: competitive university men's and women's soccer leagues, a coed running club, a yoga club, a men's basketball club, a rowing club, martial arts training, and cooking classes with authentic Italian chefs. Studying at AUR also gives students the opportunity to engage in the local culture through active participation in local events or to improve their Italian speaking skills through organized conversations with neighbors. All students opting for university housing are provided with furnished apartments in areas surrounding the campus for a "full immersion" experience in the Italian culture.

CONTACT INFORMATION

Melissa Abraham,
  Admissions Counselor
☎ +39.06.5833.0919
  888-791-8327 (toll-free in the United States)
🖳 admissions@aur.edu

- **Enrollment:** *500*
- **Selectivity:** *moderately difficult*
- **Application Deadline:** *rolling both for freshmen and transfer*
- **Expenses:** *Tuition €13,940, housing €7600*
- **Test scores:** *ACT—over 18, 100%; SAT—critical reading over 500, 100%; SAT—math over 500, 100%*

AUR prepares students from over 40 countries to live and work across cultures, combining the excellent academic attributes of higher education in the United States with the European and Italian Classical tradition education in the liberal arts.

AMC offers students the best of both worlds: a beautiful, New England campus in which to study and make friends, in proximity to the bustling college-town of Worcester, home to 10 colleges and universities.

AMC
ANNA MARIA COLLEGE
Prepare for Excellence

PAXTON, MASSACHUSETTS
www.annamaria.edu

Anna Maria College is a four-year, private, co-ed, Catholic institution accredited by the New England Association of Schools and Colleges. Founded by the Sisters of Saint Anne in 1946, the College is located in the heart of New England on a 192-acre campus in Paxton, Massachusetts, minutes from the vibrant college-town of Worcester. AMC provides quality academic programs that integrate a liberal arts education with career preparation.

AMC is a close-knit community offering 35 undergraduate degree programs and over 22 graduate and continuing education programs. Committed to a curriculum that fosters critical and integrated thinking, AMC offers academic excellence with respected faculty and class sizes averaging 15 students. Popular majors include art and music therapy, business, criminal justice, education, fire science, legal studies, nursing, paramedic science, psychology, social work, sport management, and more. AMC also offers an Honors Program and unique study-abroad opportunities.

Co-curricular programs abound, including 17 NCAA Division III sports teams: men's and women's basketball, cross-country, lacrosse, golf, soccer, and tennis, men's baseball and football, and women's field hockey, softball, and volleyball. The New England setting offers students the best of both worlds: a relaxed environment in which to live and study as well as proximity to Worcester, home to 10 other colleges and universities. AMC students can enjoy all that an AMC campus life has to offer and also partake in the excitement of the Worcester area, which includes concerts, skiing, art exhibits, and great restaurants in Worcester's growing downtown. AMC is also a short drive to Boston, Cape Cod, Connecticut, New Hampshire, Vermont, and Rhode Island.

The Office of Admission strongly encourages tours of the campus and attending

CONTACT INFORMATION

Nancy O'Dowd
☎ 508-849-3360
🖥 admission@annamaria.edu

open houses and accepted student day programs. Students can schedule a visit by calling 800-344-4586, Ext. 360.

Applications are accepted online at www.annamaria.edu/admission with a priority deadline of March 1 for full consideration of scholarships and housing. Requirements for the admission application include high school transcript (including first marking period), essay, and one recommendation. AMC is a test-optional college, with the exception of the paramedic science program.

- **Enrollment:** *1,500*
- **Selectivity:** *minimally difficult*
- **Application deadline:** *Rolling (freshmen), rolling (transfer)*
- **Expenses:** *Tuition $28,752; Room & Board $11,450*

Welcome to Anna Maria College, a vibrant, co-ed campus community where academic excellence, faculty support, 17 NCAA Division III athletic teams, an Honors Program, and an exciting living and learning environment await you.

AQUINAS COLLEGE
Makes all the difference in the world.

Aquinas' active student life, with more than 60 clubs and organizations, complements its location in a "Cool City" that features national events like "ArtPrize" and "LaughFest."

GRAND RAPIDS, MICHIGAN
www.aquinas.edu
https://www.facebook.com/
AQ.College
https://www.facebook.com/
AQ.Admissions

Aquinas College, located on a beautiful 107-acre campus in Grand Rapids, Michigan, was founded in 1886. Aquinas is a Catholic, co-educational, liberal arts college that embraces the inclusive Dominican charisms of prayer, study, service, and community and has an enrollment that exceeds 2,300 students.

The campus is a former estate, complete with an English Style Manor and Carriage House. The 90 species of trees, wooded paths, ponds, creeks, and terraced gardens clearly show why Aquinas has been called Michigan's "most beautiful small college."

At Aquinas, you'll discover many unique majors like Community Leadership, Sport Management, Conductive Education, and Sustainable Business. Students have over 60 majors to choose from including such traditional programs as Biology, Chemistry, Education, English, Psychology, Business, Communication, and Math. Internships abound, with hands-on learning experiences for any major.

At Aquinas, resources in terms of both facilities and faculty have been committed to ready students for a successful and rewarding future.

The new Sturrus Sports & Fitness Center provides a top-notch facility that benefits the entire student body in addition to Aquinas College's eleven-time "WHAC All-Sports Champions" athletic teams. The Grace Hauenstein Library and the

$7-million Performing Arts Center also provide modern-day structures to complement Aquinas facilities that have been deemed historical landmarks.

The Aquinas faculty members are both teachers and scholars. They provide an education that challenges students to think critically, and they instill a passion for learning that is second to none. The College's challenging core curriculum was designed to give students the critical foundation needed to be successful in an ever-changing world.

Outside the classroom, students travel overseas to countries such as Germany, France, Spain, Ireland, Costa Rica, Italy, and Japan. They also participate in numerous service learning opportunities in the Dominican Republic, Mexico, New York, Maine, and Mississippi—to just name a few.

In Grand Rapids, you'll discover a "Cool City" that is certain to entertain you. Annual events such as ArtPrize, LaughFest, and the Festival of the Arts and venues including the Van Andel Arena and Meijer Gardens are all found in one of the "best places to live in America."

Scholarship awards are available to students who not only excel academically but who are leaders, volunteers, activists, and athletes. Aquinas awards over $6 million in scholarships each year.

With a top-notch placement rate in jobs or graduate school after earning an Aquinas undergraduate degree, it's evident an Aquinas education makes all the difference in the world.

CONTACT INFORMATION

Admissions Office
☎ 616-632-2900 or toll-free 800-678-9593
⌨ admissions@aquinas.edu

- **Enrollment:** *2,327*
- **Selectivity:** *moderately difficult*
- **Test scores:** *ACT—over 18, 96%*
- **Application deadline:** *Rolling (freshmen), rolling (transfer)*
- **Expenses:** *Tuition $25,070; Room & Board $7810*

Founded in 1886, Aquinas is a Catholic liberal arts college that offers over 60 majors.

Arcadia University, Grey Towers Castle, Glenside, Pennsylvania.

ARCADIA
UNIVERSITY
GLENSIDE, PENNSYLVANIA
www.arcadia.edu/

Arcadia is a top-ranked private university that invites students to get their passports ready. Why? *U.S. News & World Report* ranks Arcadia University among the top tier of regional universities in the North. Students here can choose from over 120 programs in more than 22 countries from Tanzania to Ireland. Eligible first-year and transfer students are encouraged to participate in Preview, a fun and educational experience that features a week-long travel component abroad in locations such as London, Ireland, Italy, Mexico, Scotland, and Spain.

Arcadia students also choose from among 75 cutting-edge fields of study. Arcadia offers five 3-year accelerated under-grad programs in business administration, communications, international business and culture, international studies, and psychology—giving students a faster path to graduate school or a career.

Arcadia offers master's programs in business administration, counseling psychology, creative writing, education, English, forensic science, genetic counseling, health education, humanities, international film marketing, international peace and conflict resolution, international public relations, international relations and diplomacy, physician assistant, and public health—and *U.S. News & World Report* ranks Arcadia University among the top 25 master's universities in the North. Doctor of Physical Therapy (DPT) and Doctor of Education (EdD) in educational leadership and special education degrees are also offered.

Arcadia students may jump into the mix of more than 90 clubs and organizations or a variety of community service programs. Students volunteer on neighborhood improvement projects, work at literacy or gerontology centers, and assist disadvantaged or disabled children. Arcadia athletes participate in NCAA Division III intercollegiate sports in basketball, field hockey, golf, lacrosse, soccer, softball, swimming, tennis, and volleyball for women and baseball, basketball, golf, lacrosse, soccer, swimming, and tennis for men. Cheerleading and equestrian are offered as club sports, while a number of other students play intramurals like ultimate frisbee and flag football.

The Commons, a 62,000-square-foot student center opened in January 2012 and features a game room, fireplace lounge, dining area, flexible meeting rooms, an art exhibit space, and more. Arcadia features a beautiful rolling campus built around the historic landmark Grey Towers Castle.

The University is 12 miles from Center City Philadelphia and only 90 minutes from the Jersey shore and Pennsylvania's Pocono Mountains. Students have access to dozens of museums, galleries, performing arts centers, and nightspots, as well as historic, government, and commercial sites in the metropolitan area.

CONTACT INFORMATION

Collene Pernicello, Director of Undergraduate Admissions

☎ 215-572-2910 or toll-free 877-ARCADIA

🖳 admiss@arcadia.edu

- **Enrollment:** *3,932*
- **Selectivity:** *moderately difficult*
- **Test scores:** *ACT—over 18, 98%; SAT—critical reading over 500, 79%; SAT—math over 500, 80%*
- **Application deadline:** *3/1 (freshmen), 6/15 (transfer)*
- **Expenses:** *Tuition $35,620; Room & Board $12,150*

First Year Study Abroad Experience (FYSAE) students in London, England.

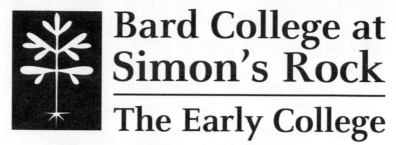

Bard College at Simon's Rock

The Early College

GREAT BARRINGTON, MASSACHUSETTS
www.simons-rock.edu/

Should you have to be 18 years old and finished with your senior year of high school in order to head off to college? Bard College at Simon's Rock doesn't think so. In fact, the average age of entering students is 16, and students typically begin at Simon's Rock after completing the tenth or eleventh grade. This is the only four-year college of liberal arts and sciences specifically designed to provide bright, highly motivated students with the opportunity to begin college when their interest, energy, and curiosity are at a peak. Students who complete the requirements receive the Associate of Arts (A.A.) degree after two years of study and the Bachelor of Arts (B.A.) degree after four.

There's something magical about people coming together from across the country and around the world, from incredibly diverse life experiences, eager to share and learn from each other. It changes you and expands your perspectives.

The academics are challenging and thought provoking, and philosophical debates in the dining hall and dorms are common; it's just plain fun to spend time with really bright, interesting, and creative peers.

For more than forty years, Simon's Rock has proven that exceptional students of high school age are fully capable of taking on college-level work, that these students learn best in a small-college environment with a faculty committed to excellence in teaching and scholarship, and that a general education in the liberal arts and sciences should be the foundation for early college students.

Simon's Rock students stay busy outside the classroom, too. Some start their own clubs; others join perennial favorites, such as the jazz ensemble or the Model UN. And all students get moving—part of the curriculum requires students to take at least one class in such activities as yoga, rock climbing, martial arts, scuba, or volleyball (just to name a few).

The College is built on over 200 rolling and wooded acres in the Berkshire Hills of western Massachusetts. Boston and New York City are 140 miles away; Albany and Springfield are 40 miles away. The Berkshires' natural beauty and wide variety of attractions make the area a great place in which to live. The countryside has excellent terrain for hiking, bicycling, cross-country and downhill skiing, canoeing, and climbing. The Tanglewood Music Festival, Jacob's Pillow Dance Festival, and a number of summer theaters take place annually in nearby towns.

- **Enrollment:** *400*
- **Selectivity:** *moderately difficult*
- **Test scores:** *ACT—over 18, 100%; SAT—critical reading over 500, 100%; SAT—math over 500, 100%*
- **Application deadline:** *5/31 (freshmen), 5/31 (transfer)*
- **Expenses:** *Tuition $44,075; Room & Board $12,260*

CONTACT INFORMATION

Steven Coleman, Director of Admissions

☎ 413-528-7228 or toll-free 800-235-7186

🖥 admit@simons-rock.edu

MIAMI SHORES, FLORIDA
www.barry.edu

Why choose Barry University? Its students will tell you because here they experience a high-quality education in a caring environment. Classes are small (14:1), so students receive personal attention from faculty members.

Find yourself at Barry University in Miami Shores, Florida, the second-largest Catholic university in the Southeast. Barry's tropical campus is a few miles from the ocean and the dynamic city of Miami.

The palm-tree-lined main campus is in Miami Shores. While Barry celebrates its Catholic roots, it remains a university where all are welcome. Students come from all age groups, ethnicities, and faiths and represent almost all fifty states and nearly 120 countries.

Barry offers more than 100 bachelor's, master's, and doctoral degree programs in the arts and sciences, business, education, health sciences, human performance and leisure sciences, law, podiatric medicine, public administration, and social work. Some programs allow students to earn a master's degree with just an extra year of study. No matter the program, Barry's academic advisors and career counselors are available every step of the way.

Barry's resident students live in ten residence halls and three apartment buildings. Each room has cable TV and high-speed Internet access. All students may keep cars on campus.

Students participate in twenty honor societies and more than 60 student organizations, including fraternities and sororities, student government, the WBRY radio station, Alternative Spring Break, and Habitat for Humanity.

When not in class, students can also hang out at Penafort Pool or the R. Kirk Landon Student Union, which houses a bookstore, dining room, snack bar, and game room. A fully equipped fitness center also offers free wellness classes such as yoga, kick-boxing, and circuit training.

The University fields twelve intercollegiate teams in the NCAA Division II Sunshine State Conference. The Buccaneers have won nine national championships.

Barry University is located just 5 miles from the ocean and minutes from Miami. Living near a unique, global city not only provides students with many profes-sional opportunities, but also exciting activities outside of the classroom. Students can dance their way through Calle Ocho, the largest Latin street festival in the nation; enjoy world-renowned contempo-rary art at Art Basel Miami Beach; or cheer on the Miami Dolphins, Miami Heat, and Miami Marlins. In addition, the natural beauty of the Florida Keys and Everglades are just a day trip away.

Barry University offers students an ideal location to broaden their horizons before making their mark in the world.

- **Enrollment:** *8,905*
- **Selectivity:** *moderately difficult*

CONTACT INFORMATION

Ms. Magda Castineyra,
   Director of Undergraduate
   Admissions
☎ 305-899-3100 or toll-free
   800-695-2279
💻 admissions@mail.barry.edu

- **Test scores:** *SAT—critical reading over 500, 29.6%; SAT—math over 500, 27.5%*
- **Application deadline:** *Rolling (freshmen), rolling (transfer)*
- **Expenses:** *Tuition $28,160; Room & Board $9440*

At Barry, learning comes from everything around you. The University offers more than 50 bachelor's degrees, an honor program, study-abroad opportunities, and personal career counseling to prepare you for the future you want.

Belmont's students have opportunities to learn, live, and serve in many settings—including studios on campus and on Nashville's Music Row.

BELMONT
UNIVERSITY
NASHVILLE, TENNESSEE
www.belmont.edu/

Nationally recognized liberal arts programs come alive on the Belmont University campus, which is located in the state capital of Nashville, known as Music City, U.S.A. and the Athens of the South (for its many colleges and universities). Belmont is a Christian university and the second-largest of Tennessee's private colleges and universities, and its goal is to be a leader among teaching universities. Working to make that happen are faculty members who believe that premier teaching is interactive, technology-supported, motivational, creative, and exciting. And these efforts have not gone unnoticed—in fact, Belmont was recently named one of two "Schools to Watch" in the nation by *U.S. News & World Report*. In addition, in 2012, Belmont won its second SIFE (Students in Free Enterprise) National Championship.

In addition to a number of bachelor's degrees, Belmont University offers 14 graduate degrees in 28 programs within the Master of Accountancy, Master of Arts in Teaching, Master of Business Administration, Master of Sport Administration, Master of English,

Master of Music, Master of Education, Master of Science in Nursing, Master of Science in Occupational Therapy, Doctor of Occupational Therapy, Doctor of Nursing Practice, Doctor of Pharmacy, Doctor of Physical Therapy, and the Juris Doctor programs.

The Belmont Bruins participate in varsity sports at the NCAA Division I level. Men and women compete in basketball, cross-country, golf, soccer, tennis, and track and field. Men also compete in baseball, and women also have softball and volleyball teams. In addition, Belmont has top-notch facilities to go with their top-ranked sports. The Curb Event Center has 5,000 seats in an oval configuration, three full-size basketball courts with maple hardwood floors, and three suites. Additional new facilities include multiple residence halls and academic complexes.

Belmont's beautiful campus reflects a long, rich history

that dates back to the 19th century when the grounds were Adelicia Acklen's Belle Monte estate. University buildings that were erected over the past 110 years surround the Italianate mansion, which is still used by the campus. On the way to classes that prep them for the 21st century, students walk by historic Victorian gardens, statuary, and gazebos.

With a metropolitan area of roughly a million residents, Nashville is a cultural, educational, healthcare, commercial, and financial center in the mid-South. The city's location halfway between the northern and southern United States makes it accessible

CONTACT INFORMATION

Brooke Dailey, Director of University Admissions
☎ 800-56ENROLL (toll-free)
🖥 brooke.dailey@belmont.edu

to students from across the country.

- **Enrollment:** *6,365*
- **Selectivity:** *moderately difficult*
- **Test scores:** *ACT—over 18, 100%; SAT—critical reading over 500, 90%; SAT—math over 500, 89.4%*
- **Application deadline:** *8/1 (freshmen), 8/1 (transfer)*
- **Expenses:** *Tuition $24,900; Room & Board $9020*

Life at Belmont includes cheering for the Bruins! Among the University's many successful athletic teams, Belmont's basketball teams have been regular participants in the NCAA Tournament.

Electronic Production and Design students at work.

Berklee College of Music

BOSTON, MASSACHUSETTS
http://www.berklee.edu
https://www.facebook.com/BerkleeCollege

Berklee College of Music was founded on the revolutionary principle that the best way to prepare students for careers in music is through the study and practice of contemporary music. For more than half a century, the college has evolved to reflect the state of the art of music and the music business. With more than a dozen performance and nonperformance majors, 15 minors, and 6 graduate programs, not to mention a diverse and talented student body representing more than 80 countries, and a music industry "who's who" of alumni, Berklee is the world's premier learning lab for the music of today—and tomorrow.

At Berklee, students acquire a strong foundation of contemporary music theory and technique and then build upon that foundation by learning the practical, professional skills needed to sustain a career in music. A range of majors leads toward either a fully accredited four-year baccalaureate degree or a professional diploma.

Berklee attracts a diverse range of students who reflect the multiplic-ity of influences in today's music, be it jazz, rock, hip-hop, country, gospel, electronica, bluegrass, Latin, or funk. The college is a magnet for aspiring musicians from every corner of the earth, which gives the school a uniquely international flavor. Of all U.S. colleges and universities, Berklee has one of the largest percentages of undergraduates from outside the United States—more than 25 percent.

The college's alumni form an ever-widening global network of industry professionals who use their openness, virtuosity, and versatility to take music in inspiring new directions. Notable alumni include BT, Gary Burton, Terri Lyne Carrington, Bruce Cockburn, Paula Cole, Juan Luis Guerra, Roy Hargrove, Quincy Jones, Diana Krall, Aimee Mann, Arif Mardin, Branford Marsalis, John Mayer, Danilo Perez, John Scofield, Howard Shore, Alan Silvestri, Luciana Souza, Susan Tedeschi, and Gillian Welch.

The college is located in Boston, Massachusetts, in the heart of the city's Fenway cultural district. Its neighborhood includes many of the world's other great colleges and universities, treasure-filled

museums and galleries, and world-class performing arts centers like Symphony Hall and the Berklee Performance Center.

Berklee has also launched an international campus in Valencia, Spain. The Berklee campus in Valencia aims to be a main hub for the study, evolution, and global proliferation of many musical genres, including flamenco, in European, Latin American, Middle Eastern countries, and all over the world.

CONTACT INFORMATION

Mr. Damien Bracken, Director of Admissions

☎ 617-747-2222 or toll-free 800-BERKLEE

🖳 admissions@berklee.edu

- **Enrollment:** *4,307*
- **Selectivity:** *Very selective*
- **Application deadline:** *1/15 (freshmen), 1/15 (transfer)*
- **Expenses:** *Tuition $35,450; Room & Board $16,950 (For current information, visit www.berklee.edu/cost)*

Located in the heart of Boston, Berklee presents students a vast array of cultural, academic, and athletic offerings.

BRIAR·CLIFF university

the catholic franciscan learning place

SIOUX CITY, IOWA
www.briarcliff.edu
www.facebook.com/BriarCliffUniversity

In the fall, incoming BCU freshmen experience the latest learning technology with BCU's Apple iPad Program.

Perched on a hilltop in Sioux City, Iowa, Briar Cliff University (BCU) is a private institution rooted firmly in the liberal arts and sciences. A Catholic Franciscan institution, BCU welcomes students of all faiths and offers a values-based experience that teaches students about personal integrity and social responsibility.

Briar Cliff is a vibrant campus where students become leaders and doers. Home for more than 1,150 students from 32 states and 11 countries, BCU provides a powerful sense of community, where students thrive in a supportive environment that fosters their personal growth and professional potential.

Ranked regularly in the top tier of the Midwest Best Colleges in the *U.S. News & World Report* survey of America's best colleges, BCU offers more than 40 areas of study in a challenging academic environment. Students receive a broad intellectual background with career development and hands-on approach to career preparation. Internships, field studies, and research are used in the curriculum.

Classes at BCU average about 17 students. With a student-to-faculty ratio of 14:1, BCU students enjoy individualized attention from professors. More than 93 percent of Briar Cliff students enter graduate school or begin working in their fields.

BCU is very affordable with numerous scholarships and other forms of financial aid to help pay for a student's college tuition. On average, 98 percent of Briar Cliff students receive grants, scholarships, and/or other forms of financial assistance.

Campus life is rich with a wide variety of competitive sports, social activities, cultural events, international travel, spiritual growth, service-learning, and mission experiences. BCU has several nationally recognized intercollegiate athletic teams, and varsity student-athletes enjoy NAIA action in the highly competitive Great

The focus of the entire faculty and staff at Briar Cliff University is on our students—even our president knows students by their names.

Plains Athletic Conference (GPAC). Briar Cliff Choirs have performed a wide variety of choral literature in regional, national, and international venues.

A dynamic metropolitan area of more than 140,000 residents, Sioux City is a great place to call home with a low crime rate, moderate cost of living, and Midwestern hospitality.

- **Enrollment:** *1,185*
- **Selectivity:** *moderately difficult*
- **Test scores:** *ACT—over 18, 91%*
- **Application deadline:** *Rolling (freshmen), rolling (transfer)*
- **Expenses:** *Tuition $23,388; Room & Board $7032*

CONTACT INFORMATION

Mr. Brian Eben, Assistant Vice President for Enrollment Management
☎ 712-279-5200
800-662-3303 (toll-free)
💻 admissions@briarcliff.edu

The M.Carey Thomas Library is home to classrooms and faculty offices as well as Thomas Great Hall, which is often used as a venue for large campus events.

BRYN MAWR

COLLEGE
BRYN MAWR, PENNSYLVANIA
www.brynmawr.edu/

Bryn Mawr women are leaders in the classroom, in the studio, in the laboratory, and on the field. They engage with the world beyond the campus, too, through advanced research projects, summer internships, and collaborative research with faculty members. The Katharine Houghton Hepburn Center, Office of Civic Engagement, and the Praxis Program provide many internship opportunities for students in Philadelphia and Washington, D.C.

The newest addition to Bryn Mawr College's innovative course offerings is 360°, a new interdisciplinary experience unique to Bryn Mawr in which a cohort of students takes several courses together to engage multiple aspects of a topic or theme, giving students an opportunity to investigate thoroughly and thoughtfully a multitude of perspectives. Typical 360°s focus on the history, economic concerns, cultural intersections, and political impact of an era, decision, event, policy, or important scientific innovation. 360° participants hone their arguments and insights through writing and research, develop strategies for teamwork that push the limits of their talents and creativity, and work with professors and scholars to promote big-picture thinking.

Students can choose from 36 majors and 38 minors and many students opt for independent and interdepartmental majors. Joint academic programs also exist with Haverford, Swarthmore, and the University of Pennsylvania.

Bryn Mawr ranks among the top ten schools in graduates going on to earn their Ph.D. Bryn Mawr's alumnae include the first woman president of Harvard University, one of the first women to receive the Nobel Peace Prize, and the first and only woman to receive four Academy Awards for acting. Above all else, Bryn Mawr women share a tremendous respect for individual differences, not just a passive tolerance of other lifestyles and points of view.

Bryn Mawr is home to 12 NCAA Division III varsity teams. Students compete in badminton, basketball, crew, cross-country, field hockey, lacrosse, soccer, swimming, tennis, indoor track and field, outdoor track and field, and volleyball.

A $7-million upgrade and renovation of the Bern Schwartz Gymnasium offers students and athletes enhanced spaces for training, fitness, and aquatics. Students live on campus in 12 unique halls; some rooms have fireplaces, window seats, and hardwood floors while others have private bathrooms and outdoor patios (two of the buildings are listed on the National Register of Historic Places). The $19 million renovation to the Goodhart Theater has created a hub for the performing arts on campus with facilities for music, dance, and theater.

Bryn Mawr College is located on a 135-acre suburban campus, 11 miles from Philadelphia. Students can hop on a train and find themselves in Philadelphia's funky art galleries or eclectic restaurants or music venues in just 25 minutes.

- **Enrollment:** *1,785*

- **Selectivity:** *most difficult*

- **Test scores:** *ACT—over 18, 100%; SAT—critical reading over 500, 97.67%; SAT—math over 500, 98.34%*

CONTACT INFORMATION

Ms. Laurie Koehler, Dean of Admissions

☎ 610-526-5152 or toll-free 800-BMC-1885

💻 admissions@brynmawr.edu

- **Application deadline:** *First-year applicants: –Early Decision I: 11/15; –Early Decision II: 1/1; –Regular Decision 1/15 Fall Transfer: 3/15; Spring Transfer: 11/1*

- **Expenses:** *Tuition $41,260; Room & Board $13,340*

Rhoads Dormitory is one of 12 residence halls on the Bryn Mawr Campus. Like all campus residences, it houses first-year students as well as sophomores, juniors, and seniors.

For your first year, you will be based at CCA's Oakland campus, a traditional college setting complete with residence halls and well-equipped studios.

CCA

CALIFORNIA COLLEGE OF THE ARTS

SAN FRANCISCO AND OAKLAND, CALIFORNIA
www.cca.edu
facebook.com/CaliforniaCollegeoftheArts

Students from all over the world come to California College of the Arts (CCA) to make art that matters. This internationally respected college has two campuses, in San Francisco and Oakland, and offers degrees in 21 undergraduate and 7 graduate programs in fine arts, architecture, design, and writing. In 2011, CCA was named one of the most environmentally responsible colleges in North America by The Princeton Review, and *Business Week* magazine has named CCA one of the world's best design schools. CCA's excellent studio facilities—from glass studios to 3D prototypers, animation labs to a full-scale production stage—enable students to realize almost any creative vision. CCA offers cross-disciplinary opportunities, innovative courses with real-world applications, an outstanding faculty, and strong connections to outside communities. CCA students and alumni have achieved success in a vast range of creative fields.

The college has a deep commitment to project-based learning, which is built on the idea that people learn best in the context of real-world problems and situations. ENGAGE at CCA, one of CCA's unique curricular initiatives, brings together students from all majors and connects them with outside organizations and experts to find solutions for clearly identified, actual issues.

CCA students and alumni are at the cutting edge of every creative field, from art to design, architecture, and writing. CCA students graduate with the tools and knowledge to be successful in their chosen fields as well as critical thinking skills that will be invaluable in any future pursuit. CCA alumni have designed graphics for MTV and VH1, created characters for animated films by Pixar, illustrated editorials for national magazines, created Emmy Award–winning motion graphics, and designed technology products such as HTC smartphones and the Jawbone JAMBOX. They have exhibited work at the Cannes and Sundance film festivals, and at major museums and galleries around the world.

Outside of class, CCA students join professional organizations or startup social groups. The San Francisco Bay Area is a great place to go to college, as it's known for creative and technological innovation, environmental leadership, and thriving art and design communities.

CCA's San Francisco campus spans a city block in the design district and the Oakland campus occupies 4 acres in the Rockridge neighborhood, just 2 miles from UC Berkeley. A free shuttle connects the campuses and residence halls. Napa Valley, Mendocino, Monterey, Lake Tahoe, and Yosemite National Park are all close by.

CONTACT INFORMATION

Ms. Robynne Royster, Director of Admissions

☎ 415-703-9523 or toll-free 800-447-1ART

💻 enroll@cca.edu

- **Enrollment:** *1,965*
- **Selectivity:** *moderately difficult*
- **Test scores:** *ACT—over 18, 96%; SAT—critical reading over 500, 63%; SAT—math over 500, 68%*
- **Application deadline:** *Rolling (first-year, transfer)*
- **Expenses:** *Tuition $38,448; Room only $7700*

At CCA, no single discipline, philosophy, or medium confines you. You can feel safe taking risks. While you major in one subject, you'll explore many.

CARROLL UNIVERSITY

WAUKESHA, WI
www.carrollu.edu
www.facebook.com/#!/carroll.university

Since its founding in 1846, the hallmarks of the Carroll educational experience have been teaching excellence and individualized attention. The institution draws upon its rich liberal arts tradition to prepare students to achieve their full potential in our ever-changing society. The University's educational philosophy is sustained by the four pillars of integrated knowledge, lifelong skills, gateway experiences, and enduring values. Carroll is a community for learning. Students bring distinctive perspectives, traditions, and experiences. They become participants in a community dedicated to the pursuit of academic excellence, personal fulfillment, and spiritual meaning.

Carroll University occupies a 50-acre campus in the center of Waukesha, Wisconsin, a city that boasts a population of more than 70,000 residents. The University offers proximity to Milwaukee (15 miles east), Madison (60 miles west), and Chicago (100 miles south). Carroll University draws upon the advantages of its location to offer students access to a wide range of internship and career opportunities.

Many opportunities exist for co-curricular involvement. A broad variety of organizations, including service, fraternities and sororities, and departmental clubs, provide many opportunities for student involvement. The University also offers an extensive intramural and recreation program. In addition, students have access to fitness classes, taught by professional instructors, and outdoor recreation activities, which include biking, hiking, rock climbing, and much more. Music and theater participation is available to all students, as well. Offering 18 intercollegiate sports at the NCAA Division III level, Carroll is a member of the Midwest Conference. Club sports include cheerleading, curling, dance, men's volleyball, and wrestling. With such an array of offerings, students are sure to find an opportunity to get involved.

Carroll University offers more than 80 areas of study, with the most popular including the health sciences (nursing, physical therapy, and exercise science), business and education. Students have an opportunity to be admitted to their chosen program as a freshman, and direct admission is offered in nursing, physical therapy, and athletic training. Opportunities for research are available through Carroll's Pioneer Scholars Program, which provides funding for student-led research. The University's location near several urban centers offers ample opportunity for internships. Study abroad can include a semester or year-long experience or participation in the New Cultural Experiences Program (NCEP), which provides short-term experiences. Together, Carroll students, faculty, and staff create the high-energy community for learning known as Carroll University.

CONTACT INFORMATION

Mr. James Wiseman, Vice President of Enrollment

☎ 262-524-7221 or toll-free 800-CARROLL

💻 info@carrollu.edu

- **Enrollment:** *3,385*
- **Selectivity:** *moderately difficult*
- **Test scores:** *ACT—over 18, 97%*
- **Application deadline:** *Rolling (freshmen), rolling (transfer)*
- **Expenses:** *Tuition $24,065; Room & Board $7371*

From rock-climbing and concerts to bike trips and ballgames, Carson-Newman students find many ways to get involved.

CARSON-NEWMAN

A Christian University

JEFFERSON CITY, TENNESSEE
www.cn.edu
http://www.facebook.com/cncollege

At Carson-Newman (C-N), there's a great sense of pride of where the university has been and where it's headed. Carson-Newman has a rich history that began in 1851 and continues along the banks of Mossy Creek, where it all started. Students are able to choose from 57 majors ranging from nursing and business to psychology and education. Inside the classroom, students find professors who are dedicated to knowing them by name and helping them find their potential. Small classroom learning environments and open door policies pave the way for mentorships that often continue long after graduation.

On paper, Carson-Newman looks good. It's celebrated in the pages of US News & World Report and The Princeton Review and by Forbes.com for its academic excellence and value. Newsweek/The Daily Beast champions Carson-Newman's commitment to service, listing the university as America's leading institution in community service and second overall among "Most Service-Oriented" schools.

Carson-Newman students learn the value of helping others through outreach programs and mission opportunities—here and abroad. The university's approach to nurturing students' minds as well as their hearts is recognized at the highest level: C-N is one of two universities to receive the Presidential Award in General Community Service as listed in the 2012 President's Higher Education Community Service Honor Roll. On paper, Carson Newman looks very good indeed!

But the Carson-Newman experience cannot be captured by a particular ranking or etched on a single award. It is seen and felt through late night study groups, evenings attending *Fellowship of Christian Athletes* (FCA), hiking with friends in the Great Smoky Mountains, or preparing for an exam over a latte from C-N's Java City. Students become part of a community that, quite frankly, makes college fun.

Carson-Newman has more than 70 different campus organizations, as well as an intramural program that features more than 40 offerings ranging from basketball and soccer to rock climbing and board games. Friendships are created daily at the Maddox Student Activities Center, Bible studies, theatre practice, study-abroad trips, outreach projects, cookouts, and concerts. This past year, students enjoyed campus events that included "Mudball," movies on the lawn, the first annual Hunger Games, and musical performances by Caleb, LeCrae, and country music legend Ricky Skaggs. For those who love the roar of the crowd, the C-N Eagles compete in 16 NCAA Division II sports, giving students the opportunity to play or show school pride by joining the "Mossy Creek Maniacs" in the stands.

Carson-Newman's campus is located within 10 minutes of Cherokee Lake and 45 minutes from the Great Smoky Mountains National Park, so students often take the opportunity to enjoy the great outdoors.

- **Enrollment:** *1,970*
- **Selectivity:** *moderately difficult*
- **Test scores:** *ACT —over 18, 94%*
- **Application deadline:** *8/1 (freshmen), 8/1 (transfer)*
- **Expenses:** *Tuition $20,562; Room & Board $5918*

CONTACT INFORMATION

Melanie Redding, Director of Admissions
☎ 865-471-3223 or toll-free 800-678-9061
🖳 cnadmiss@cn.edu

CASE WESTERN RESERVE
UNIVERSITY ___ EST. 1826

think beyond the possible™

CLEVELAND, OHIO
www.case.edu/

Case Western Reserve's location in University Circle provides students with access to more than 40 different arts, cultural, education, health, and human service organizations—all within walking distance.

Ranking consistently among the top private universities in the United States, Case Western Reserve University (CWRU) offers unlimited opportunities for motivated students. Its faculty members challenge and support students, and its partnerships with world-class cultural, educational, and scientific institutions guarantee that undergraduate education goes beyond the classroom. Co-ops, internships, and study abroad bring theory to life in amazing settings, and nearly every student completes some research or independent study. Although Case Western Reserve was formed in 1967 by the merger of Western Reserve University and Case Institute of Technology, it traces its roots back to the 1826 founding of Western Reserve College—this makes CWRU both a young university and one of the oldest private colleges in the nation.

Undergrads are enrolled in programs in engineering, science, management, nursing, the arts, the humanities, and the social and behavioral sciences. Students attend CWRU's graduate and professional schools in applied social sciences, dental medicine, graduate studies, law, management, medicine, and nursing. Several undergraduate programs and majors combine undergraduate and graduate and professional degrees and resources. Examples are five-year B.A./M.A. or B.S./M.S. degrees, including a five-year B.S./M.S. degree in engineering and management, and dual admission to undergraduate and professional school.

Collaborations with neighboring cultural and healthcare institutions enable the University to provide special opportunities in other fields. For example, a student can learn art history both in the classroom and in the world-renowned Cleveland Museum of Art.

Greek life (15 national fraternities and 8 sororities) is big here; about 30 percent of undergrads join. Through its NCAA Division III sports, CWRU has won championships in cross-country, football, softball, track and field, and wrestling. Twenty percent of undergraduates wear

the blue-and-white varsity uniform, and an amazing 70 percent join an intramural team. Club sports include archery, cheerleading, crew, cycling, fencing, ice hockey, kendo, kung fu, table tennis, taekwondo, ultimate, and volleyball.

CWRU is located in University Circle, a unique cultural district with 550 acres of parks, gardens, museums, schools, hospitals, churches, and human service institutions. The Cleveland Museum of Art, the Cleveland Museum of Natural History, and Severance Hall (home of the Cleveland Orchestra) are within walking distance; downtown Cleveland is

CONTACT INFORMATION

Mr. Robert McCullough, Director of Undergraduate Admission

☎ 216-368-4450

💻 admission@case.edu

10 minutes away by car or public transportation. Students get free access to many local attractions, including the Rock and Roll Hall of Fame and Museum.

- **Enrollment:** *3,882*
- **Selectivity:** *very difficult*
- **Test scores:** *ACT—over 18, 100%; SAT— critical reading over 500, 94.4%; SAT—math over 500, 99.7%*
- **Application deadline:** *1/15 (first-year), 5/15 (transfer)*
- **Expenses:** *Tuition $37,618; Room & Board $11,400*

A Case Western Reserve education combines outstanding classroom instruction from top notch faculty with ample opportunity to gain experience outside the classroom through internships, co-op, study abroad, or volunteering.

Champlain College students love living in Burlington, Vermont, a short walk from a lively downtown and the stunning Lake Champlain, of which the Miller Information Commons offers tremendous views (pictured). Ski resorts and other recreational opportunities abound nearby.

CHAMPLAIN
COLLEGE

BURLINGTON, VERMONT
www.champlain.edu

"I love Champlain! The school is big enough that there are so many people you don't actually know, but it's small enough that you don't have large classes, and you know the people you're around in your dorm and in classes," says first-year student Jamie Roberts from Newburyport, Massachusetts, a Business Administration major specializing in event management. "I know Champlain is the right school for me, because I feel like this is the place where I can get the right education that will help me be successful in the future."

Jamie, like so many talented students, was looking for an outstanding college experience and an education that will specifically prepare her to meet her life's goals. She found it at Champlain College. Champlain's personal approach and distinctive educational environment allow its students to enjoy extraordinary lives as college students, while equipping them to excel in their chosen career fields upon graduation.

Champlain offers majors in today's most promising career fields—like Game Design, Professional Writing, Computer & Digital Forensics, Environmental Policy, Graphic Design & Digital Media, Psychology, Accounting, and Marketing, to name a few. Through Champlain's Upside-Down Curriculum, students start taking courses in their major in their first semester, which allows them to take on internships as early as the summer after their first year and ensures that they take a wider and deeper range of classes in their career field than they could typically accomplish at any other institution.

Champlain's attentive faculty and career-focused approach have paid off handsomely for its graduates. In some of Champlain's academic divisions, more than 90 percent of 2011 graduates are in jobs related to their career goals.

In addition to Champlain's career-focused programs, its student-centered liberal arts Core Curriculum gives students excellent grounding in critical thinking and communication skills, and the four-year

Life Experience & Action Dimension (LEAD) program instructs students in important life skills such as career and financial management.

Champlain's stunningly beautiful campus located in the idyllic city of Burlington, Vermont—one of the country's most celebrated college towns—adds to the attraction for students looking to truly enjoy a fun, engaging, meaningful, and memorable college experience.

Since 1878, Champlain has provided a hands-on, relevant education that thoroughly prepares its students for the needs of emerging and changing career fields, as

CONTACT INFORMATION

Sarah Andriano, Director of Admission

☎ 802-860-2727 or toll-free 800-570-5858

🖳 admission@champlain.edu

well as public service organizations and graduate studies.

- **Enrollment:** *2,374*
- **Selectivity:** *moderately selective*
- **Test scores:** *ACT—over 18, 99%; SAT—critical reading over 500, 78%; SAT—math over 500, 79%*
- **Application deadline:** *2/1 (freshmen), rolling (transfer)*
- **Expenses:** *Tuition $29,765; Room & Board $13,095*

Students rate Champlain College's residential life experience and close-knit community highly. The Princeton Review included Champlain in The Best 376 Colleges: 2012 Edition.

CHAPMAN UNIVERSITY

ORANGE, CALIFORNIA
www.chapman.edu/

Chapman University is a comprehensive arts and sciences institution that is distinguished for its leadership in creativity, innovation, and collaborative education. Consistently ranked among the top universities in the West, Chapman offers a breadth of programs designed to develop global citizen-leaders who are distinctively prepared to improve their community and their world. The school boasts nationally recognized programs in film and digital media, business and economics, the performing arts, education, law, the humanities, and the natural and applied sciences.

Former Chapman dance student Stephen "Twitch" Boss, seen leaping through the air, was the male runner-up on the Fox hit TV series "So You Think You Can Dance?" (Photo by Tim Agler © 2005)

Chapman's park-like campus blends historic buildings with state-of-the-art learning environments and well-maintained residence halls. More than a dozen buildings have been built or renovated in just the last two decades, with four more on the drawing boards. Located in the center of the campus is Attallah Piazza, a gathering place for the University's 7,000 undergraduate and graduate students.

Chapman University comprises seven colleges: Wilkinson College of Humanities and Social Sciences, Dodge College of Film and Media Arts, Argyros School of Business and Economics, the College of Educational Studies, the School of Law, Schmid College of Science and Technology, and the College of Performing Arts. The University's curricula provide a uniquely personalized and interdisciplinary educational experience for highly qualified students.

Over the past years, Chapman students have been named Truman Scholars, Coro Fellows, *USA Today* All-USA College Academic Team members, NCAA All-Americans, and NCAA Academic All-Americans. Chapman student athletes compete within the Southern California Intercollegiate Athletic Conference in the NCAA Division III level, and the University fields teams in baseball, basketball (m/w), crew (m/w), cross-country (m/w), football, golf, lacrosse, soccer (m/w), softball, swimming (w), tennis (m/w), track and field (m/w), volleyball (w), and water polo (m/w).

More than 90 clubs and organizations are open to students, offering a range of activities stretching from intramural sports to academically oriented groups like the Student Sustainability Initiative or the Financial Management Association. The University also has a thriving Greek system, with numerous sororities and fraternities represented on campus.

Chapman is located in Orange County, California, known worldwide for its near-perfect climate as well as its cultural, recreational, educational, and career opportunities. Los Angeles is 35 miles to the north, and San Diego is 80 miles to the south. Nearby attractions include Disneyland, Knott's Berry Farm, the Segerstrom Center for the Performing Arts, and major-league baseball and hockey teams. Beautiful

CONTACT INFORMATION

Office of Admission
☎ 714-997-6711
    888-CUAPPLY (toll-free)
🖥 admit@chapman.edu

beaches are less than 10 miles from the campus, and ski spots are 90 minutes away.

---

* **Enrollment:** *7,155*
* **Selectivity:** *very difficult*
* **Test scores:** *ACT—over 18, 100%; SAT—critical reading over 500, 95%; SAT—math over 500, 94%*
* **Application deadline:** *1/15 (freshmen), 3/15 (transfer)*
* **Expenses:** *Tuition $41,040; Room & Board $12,957*

Chapman students produce and perform in the University's annual live song-and-dance revue, American Celebration, which raises millions for student scholarships.

Undergraduate Closing Convocation is one of Chatham's oldest traditions. Seniors wear their "Tutorial Hats" which represent their senior research project and memories at Chatham.

chatham
UNIVERSITY

PITTSBURGH, PENNSYLVANIA

www.chatham.edu

www.facebook.edu/chathamu

Chatham University provides students with a solid education built upon strong academics, public leadership, and global understanding. The University houses three distinctive colleges: Chatham College for Women offers academic and co-curricular programs for undergrad women; the College for Graduate Studies offers women and men master's- and doctoral-level programs; and the College for Continuing and Professional Studies provides online and hybrid degree programs for women and men as well as certificate programs and community programming.

Chatham College for Women offers more than 40 academic majors and experiential learning to supplement classroom learning. High-quality programming, leadership, and community service opportunities enrich students' out-of-classroom experience. Its innovative Accelerated Graduate Program allows students to earn bachelor's and master's degrees in as few as five years, saving time and money.

Students may also create their own interdisciplinary or double-major program.

Chatham fields NCAA Division III sports in basketball, cross-country, ice hockey, soccer, softball, swimming and diving, tennis, and volleyball. Chatham's Athletic and Fitness Center includes an eight-lane competition pool, a gym, squash courts, cardio rooms, a climbing wall, a running track, and exercise and dance studios.

All incoming undergrads receive Macbooks that can access the University's wireless network and are incorporated into the curriculum for in-class note-taking, research, and online learning. Students lease the computers, which they then own upon graduation.

Chatham's Shadyside Campus is located minutes from downtown Pittsburgh and features towering trees and century-old mansions that have been converted into residence halls. The Shadyside Campus includes Chatham Eastside, a new LEED Silver facility that houses the University's interior architecture, landscape architecture, occupational therapy, physical therapy, and physician assistant studies programs. The University's Eden Hall Campus is located north of the city in Richland Township, which will become the nation's first sustainable campus built from the ground up.

Pittsburgh is one of the safest and most dynamic green cities in the country and is headquarters to major businesses in finance, health care, and technology. Students ride free on public transportation within Allegheny County simply by flashing their Chatham ID. For sports enthusiasts, Pittsburgh has several professional sports teams: the Penguins, the Pirates, and the Steelers. Pittsburgh has also been rated "America's Most Livable City" by *Places Rated Almanac* and "Most Livable City in the United States" and the twenty-ninth "Most Livable City Worldwide" by *The Economist*.

CONTACT INFORMATION

Ms. Marylyn Scott, Director of Admissions

☎ 412-365-1295 or toll-free 800-837-1290

🖥 MSCOTT2@chatham.edu

- **Enrollment:** *2,220*
- **Selectivity:** *moderately difficult*
- **Test scores:** *ACT—over 18, 91.3%; SAT—critical reading over 500, 65.5%; SAT—math over 500, 48.9%*
- **Application deadline:** *8/1 (freshmen), rolling (transfer)*
- **Expenses:** *Tuition $29,100; Room & Board $8873*

Community service is integral to the Chatham experience, for undergraduates and graduates alike.

At Chestnut Hill College you will be able to take what you learn in the classroom and use it to make an impact in the world.

CHESTNUT HILL COLLEGE

PHILADELPHIA, PENNSYLVANIA
www.chc.edu
www.facebook.com/chcadmissions

Chestnut Hill College, founded in 1924 by the Sisters of Saint Joseph, is a private liberal arts college with a deep-rooted mission of holistic education. The College enrolls 950 students in the School of Undergraduate Studies, along with 700 students in the School of Continuing and Professional Studies and 750 students in the School of Graduate Studies. Currently, students come to the College from 21 states and 45 countries.

The beautiful 75-acre campus is located in the quaint Chestnut Hill section of Philadelphia and is surrounded by Fairmount Park, the largest city park system in the country. The campus is just a short train ride to Center City Philadelphia, where students can enjoy all of the social, cultural, and historical amenities that the city has to offer. Just a short walk up the hill to the cobblestones of Germantown Avenue leads students to the many shops, boutiques, and restaurants of downtown Chestnut Hill.

The College's four residence halls house nearly 80 percent of the undergraduate students, including an upperclassmen residence hall on the Sugarloaf Campus across the street from the main campus.

In the spirit of holistic education, students are encouraged to go beyond the classroom by attending faculty and guest lectures and be part of one (or many) of the student-run organizations on campus, such as the Mask and Foil Drama Club, the Hill Singers, or the African American Awareness Society. Also, the Campus Ministry office offers both spiritual and community service opportunities so that

students can take what they have learned at Chestnut Hill College and help others along the way.

Chestnut Hill College's 14 athletic programs participate in the Central Atlantic Collegiate Conference at the NCAA Division II level, and the state-of-the-art Gulati Complex allows all students the opportunity to be active on campus. The College also boasts Sorgenti Arena, home of the Griffin's basketball and volleyball teams along with six tennis courts, a softball field, and a soccer field that are available for recreational student use.

CONTACT INFORMATION

Ms. Stephanie Williams
☎ 215-248-7001 or toll-free 800-248-0052
⌨ williamss@chc.edu

While there are many colleges in Philadelphia, Chestnut Hill College truly is one of a kind.

- **Enrollment:** *2,309*
- **Selectivity:** *moderately difficult*
- **Test scores:** *ACT—over 18, 85%; SAT—critical reading over 500, 42.34%; SAT—math over 500, 36.94%*
- **Application deadline:** *Rolling (freshmen), rolling (transfer)*
- **Expenses:** *Tuition $28,200; Room & Board $9065*

Students enjoy Chestnut Hill College's geographic identity crisis—a city campus with a suburban feel.

Cheyney University's Biddle Hall.

Cheyney University of Pennsylvania

CHEYNEY, PENNSYLVANIA
www.cheyney.edu
www.facebook.com/cheyneyuniversitypa

Founded in 1837, Cheyney University is America's oldest historically Black institution of higher education. Today it leverages that rich history of providing access to higher education for all students and by producing visionary leaders and responsible citizens. Cheyney graduates are successful, talented individuals, and some of the most well-known include *60 Minutes* journalist, Ed Bradley, and NFL defensive back, Andre Waters. Cheyney University is in the business of developing human potential and talent and does so through an intellectually challenging environment and personal attention to every student—a hallmark of the Cheyney experience.

Cheyney University encourages prospective students to get to know its vibrant community. The University provides access to high-quality higher education, opportunities to help students realize their full potential and academic excellence—all in a friendly, caring, and collegiate environment. Cheyney's historic campus is located in one of the most scenic and developing suburban areas in Pennsylvania. When you walk around the campus, you will feel the pride of the Cheyney University community— its faculty, staff, alumni, and students.

The University's 275-acre campus of rolling hillsides in southeastern Pennsylvania is located only 25 miles from Philadelphia. The heart of the campus is its historic quadrangle with buildings dating back to the early 1900s. Cheyney University also has a location in Philadelphia, which houses the University's graduate degree programs and undergraduate degree completion programs and is also available for commuter

students to pursue their undergraduate degree.

Over 1,800 students choose from more than 30 undergraduate and graduate degree programs, and participate in more than 40 clubs, societies, and student organizations. Further, the University has implemented the University College Model for freshmen and sophomore students, enhancing student engagement and establishing a critical link between residence life and academics. The University is an NCAA Division II institution with 12 intercollegiate sports teams. Academics achievements in the classroom, together with the development of character, individual and team skills, the will to win, and a sense of fair play and sportsmanship in athletic competition determines distinction in

CONTACT INFORMATION

Dr. Eric Hilton, Executive Director of Enrollment Management

☎ 610-399-2275 or toll-free 800-CHEYNEY

🖳 admissions@cheyney.edu

intercollegiate athletics programs.

Cheyney University is part of the Pennsylvania State System of Higher Education and is regionally accredited by the Middle States Commission on Higher Education.

- **Enrollment:** *1,808*
- **Selectivity:** *minimally difficult*
- **Application deadline:** *3/31 (freshmen)*
- **Expenses:** *Tuition $8602; Room & Board $8910*

Cheyney University's Historic Quad.

Clemson University—Spirit & Determination.

CLEMSON® UNIVERSITY

CLEMSON, SOUTH CAROLINA
www.clemson.edu
www.facebook.com/clemsonuniv
www.twitter.com/BeAClemsonTiger
www.youtube.com/Clemson

Clemson University is a higher education hybrid: a major land-grant, science and engineering-oriented research university where undergraduates work alongside professors in award-winning research.

Clemson's 20,000 students can select from 80 undergraduate and 110 graduate degree programs. Despite record growth in applications, the University tightly manages undergraduate enrollment to ensure small classes, a low student-to-faculty ratio, and high retention and graduation rates. Over 50 percent of the students in Clemson's freshman class were in the top 10 percent of their high school classes.

Clemson is invested in the success of its students, providing supplemental instruction, tutoring and mentoring through its internationally recognized Academic Success Center. After graduation, Clemson students are finding jobs at twice the national average thanks to a career center that's been ranked No. 9 in the nation.

Professors frequently engage their students in service learning, challenging them to apply what they've learned in class to real-world situations. Examples of these projects include creating access to safe drinking water in Cange, Haiti; lowering bullying rates; and improving the chances of survival for newborns in Tanzania.

But it's not all about work at Clemson. The Tigers compete in the NCAA Division I Atlantic Coast Conference, and notoriously passionate fans support 17 varsity teams. There are more than 400 student clubs and organizations, including pre-professional chapters that network with and compete against students at other schools. Clemson is located on part of the +900-mile shoreline of Hartwell Lake, where sailing, swimming and fishing are just a few of the favorite pastimes. For indoor fun, the on-campus recreation

center has a bowling alley, arcade, and billiards room.

A wide variety of living options are available on campus. Clemson's award-winning living-learning communities are uniquely designed to facilitate meaningful connections among students, faculty, and staff. In fact, communities appeal to a wide range of student interests, such as service learning, academics, cultural exchange, class year, and much more. All freshmen live in university housing, and many other students choose to live on Clemson's picturesque, tree-lined campus.

Most classes are a 5-minute walk from any dormitory, but when students need to get around the 17,000-acre campus and other outlying areas, they catch a ride on the free bus system. The city

CONTACT INFORMATION

Ms. Audrey R. Bodell, Associate Director of Admissions
☎ 864-656-2287
✉ cuadmissions@clemson.edu

of Clemson is adjacent to the campus and offers numerous shopping, dining, and nightlife options.

- **Enrollment:** *19,914*

- **Selectivity:** *moderately difficult*

- **Test scores:** *ACT—over 18, 99%; SAT—critical reading over 500, 92%; SAT—math over 500, 96%*

- **Application deadlines:** *12/1 (preferred & for scholarship consideration), 5/1 (freshmen), 7/1 (transfer)*

- **Expenses:** *Tuition $13,076 (in-state); $29,720 (out-of-state)*

Clemson University's Landscape Architecture class—a unique major.

Students during Relay for Life on the campus lawn.

The College of Saint Rose

ALBANY, NEW YORK
www.strose.edu/

Academics and career preparation are top priorities at The College of Saint Rose. In fact, *Money* magazine and *U.S. News & World Report* have ranked Saint Rose as one of the top colleges in the Northeast and the nation, based on affordability and academic quality. Students dive into the College's 66 undergraduate programs, most of which incorporate a field experience or internship component—and finding internships is easy when you have the capital of New York as your location.

The College comprises eighty buildings that have the latest technology and are eco-friendly. The new, 46,000-square-foot Massry Center for the Arts (one of the most energy-efficient buildings in the region) has smart classrooms, practice and rehearsal rooms, and performance space—and students enjoy wireless Internet throughout the building. The $15-million Thelma P. Lally School of Education is entirely wireless, and each classroom is equipped with a multimedia station; it also has an educational and clinical services center with an onsite preschool and a speech and hearing clinic. The new William Randolph Hearst Center for Communications and Interactive Media has a full HDTV/photography studio, multimedia labs for Mac and PC, a viewing and projection room, and a high-tech music studio. Students of all faiths come to meditate and relax at The Hubbard Interfaith Sanctuary, which has a natural wood and interior garden and even a bubbling lily pond.

Campus housing includes traditional and suite-style residence halls and town houses as well as more than thirty Victorian homes. Each house has its own history and character, with unique wraparound porches and stained-glass windows. The 92,000- square-foot Centennial Hall is the college's newest addition to campus housing, opening in Fall 2012.

The College of Saint Rose participates in NCAA Division II and the Northeast-10 Conference. Intercollegiate teams include men's baseball and golf; men's and women's basketball, cross-country, soccer, swimming, tennis, and track and field; and women's softball and volleyball. Saint Rose students also belong to more than 30 groups and clubs from the Adventure Club to the student newspaper.

Saint Rose is located in the historic Pine Hills neighborhood of Albany. With more than 60,000 college students in the area, there are always things to do and people to meet. Off campus, students

CONTACT INFORMATION

Mr. Jeremy Bogan, Assistant Vice President of Undergraduate Admissions

☎ 518-454-5154 or toll-free 800-637-8556

⌨ admit@strose.edu

can walk or grab a bus to hit a ton of restaurants, shops, museums, malls, and theaters.

- **Enrollment:** *4,863*
- **Selectivity:** *moderately difficult*
- **Test scores:** *ACT—over 18, 96.5%; SAT —critical reading over 500, 62.9%; SAT—math over 500, 63.7%*
- **Application deadline:** *5/1 (freshmen), 5/1 (transfer)*
- **Expenses:** *Tuition $24,138; Room & Board $9880*

The Massry Center for the Arts at night.

The Main Campus of The College of New Rochelle is located on 20 beautiful acres in southeastern Westchester County, 16 miles from midtown Manhattan.

The College of New Rochelle

NEW ROCHELLE, NEW YORK
www.cnr.edu

The College of New Rochelle (CNR), founded in 1904 by the Ursuline Order, is an independent college that is Catholic in origin and heritage. Its primary purpose is the intellectual development of students through the maintenance of high standards of academic excellence.

The College is composed of four separate schools. The School of Arts and Sciences (women only) enrolls approximately 400 young women between the ages of 18 and 22 and offers baccalaureate degree programs in the liberal arts and sciences and in a number of professionally oriented fields. The School of Nursing (co-educational), founded in 1976 and accredited by the Commission on Collegiate Nursing Education (CCNE), offers baccalaureate and graduate-level professional nursing programs that combine clinical experience with a liberal arts background. The School of New Resources, which maintains six campuses in New Rochelle and New York City, offers a nontraditional baccalaureate program designed specifically for adults. The Graduate School offers professional degree programs in education, art, community/school psychology, gerontology, communication studies, career development, and guidance and counseling.

The College of New Rochelle is located on a 20-acre historic campus in New Rochelle, New York, a suburban community in southern Westchester County, just 16 miles from New York City and easily accessible by commuter trains. The area contains numerous parks and recreational areas, and the Long Island Sound, with its many beaches, is within walking distance of the campus. The main campus includes four residence halls that provide guaranteed housing for all undergraduates.

The College emphasizes the importance of a liberal arts background. Each

undergraduate in the Schools of Arts and Sciences and Nursing must complete a variety of courses focusing on philosophy and religious studies, social analysis, literature and the arts, foreign languages, and scientific inquiry. Interdisciplinary studies and dual-degree programs are available. Independent study options and seminars play important roles in undergraduate programs as well.

The College of New Rochelle offers an extensive internship program. Art students have opportunities to gain hands-on experience in art galleries and museums around the New York metropolitan area, such as the Metropolitan

CONTACT INFORMATION

Steven Chinni, Director of Admissions
☎ 914-654-5403 or toll-free 800-933-5923
🖥 admission@cnr.edu

Museum of Art and the Guggenheim Museum. Communication arts majors participate in internships at numerous radio stations, newspapers, film companies, advertising and public relations firms, and national and cable broadcasting networks. Business majors put theory into practice at companies such as Merrill Lynch and IBM, as well as at the New York Stock Exchange.

Students gathering in the new, state-of-the-art Wellness Center at The College of New Rochelle.

CSI CU NY

College of Staten Island

THE CITY UNIVERSITY OF NEW YORK
STATEN ISLAND, NEW YORK
www.csi.cuny.edu

The College of Staten Island (CSI) is a four-year senior college within the City University of New York (CUNY) and is Staten Island's only public college. Students may choose from over 80 exciting under-graduate programs and 25 graduate programs. During the summer, students may choose to enroll in a number of courses in order to accelerate their degree. CSI's magnificent campus consists of 204 park-like acres in the heart of Staten Island and is the largest single college campus (public or private) within New York City.

The College's state-of-the-art facilities include an Advanced Imaging Facility, complete with electron microscopy, live cell imaging system, and instruments for tissue processing. The College also has a High Performance Computing (HPC) supercomputer that supports inter-active and batch computing and visualization. The Astrophysical

Observatory (funded by NASA and the NSF) is an official Asteroid Tracking Station and is equipped with a powerful Meade 16-inch computerized telescope, open to the public. The two-story student-run Campus Center features study and multipurpose lounges, theater, performance/café space, game rooms with the latest game consoles, as well as the state-of-the-art broadcasting studios of WSIA 88.9FM (the only FM radio station on Staten Island).

CSI's Sports and Recreation Center boasts an Olympic-size eight-lane pool with diving tank, basketball arena, auxiliary gym, racquetball courts, cardio and weight-training rooms, and a full intramural schedule, including fitness classes. Outdoors, students enjoy tennis courts, FieldTurf® softball, track, and soccer fields and a semi-professional baseball field. The CSI Dolphins participate in NCAA Division III sports in the CUNYAC and ECAC Conferences. Men's and women's teams consist of baseball, basketball, cross-country, soccer, softball, swimming and diving, and tennis, as well as women's cheerleading and volleyball.

A new and exciting addition to the campus is on-campus luxury student housing, ready for the fall 2013 semester. Two buildings will feature apartment-style layouts with fully-equipped kitchens and amenities such as laundry, meeting spaces, study lounges, and fitness center.

CSI's location offers students the best of two worlds— the suburbs of Staten Island combined with Manhattan's city culture and nightlife, just 25 minutes away.

CONTACT INFORMATION

Mr. Emmanuel Esperance Jr.,
   Director of Recruitment and
   Admissions
☎ 718-982-2010
🖥 admissions@cuny.csi.edu

- **Enrollment:** *14,200*
- **Selectivity:** *moderately difficult*
- **Test scores:** *SAT—critical reading over 500, 42.86%; SAT—math over 500, 59.79%*
- **Application deadline:** *2/1 (freshmen), rolling (transfer)*
- **Expenses:** *Tuition $4978*

CSI's state-of-the-art facilities featuring electron microscopy offer prime research opportunities for students pursuing a career in the sciences or medicine. Students are trained from the ground-up to use the equipment as early as their sophomore year.

LIVE WHAT YOU LOVE

Columbia students
Live What They Love.

Columbia
COLLEGE CHICAGO

INNOVATION IN THE VISUAL, PERFORMING, MEDIA, AND COMMUNICATION ARTS

CHICAGO, ILLINOIS

http://www.colum.edu

Columbia College Chicago is the largest and most diverse, private, nonprofit, arts and media college in the nation. It offers a four-year liberal arts education specifically tailored for a community of highly motivated students who want to turn their creative talents into rewarding careers. The student body is composed of approximately 11,200 students who come from all 50 states and 41 foreign countries. The College uses a holistic review process of its applicants and bases admissions decisions on an examination of the entire student and provides them with the rigorous academics and unparalleled resources necessary to be successful in a highly competitive 21st century marketplace.

The College is located in Chicago's historic South Loop neighborhood. Close by are several other colleges, Lake Michigan, the Art Institute, Navy Pier, the Adler Planetarium, the Field Museum, the Chicago Symphony, the Museum of Contemporary Art, and the Theatre District.

Convenient public transportation allows Columbia's students to utilize the whole city as a social, cultural, educational, and professional resource—effectively turning the entire city into their campus.

Academics

Columbia College Chicago offers bachelor's degrees in more than 120 programs of study in the arts, media, and communications fields. The curriculum is designed to provide students with a real-world understanding of their field and to prepare them to meet its professional expectations. Columbia's faculty members are gifted, award-winning industry insiders who share their first-hand experience with students both in and out of the classroom. This interaction with a faculty of practicing professionals provides students with access to valuable expertise, insight, practices, and industry-current aesthetics.

Campus Life

The College hosts close to 700 events each year, and when students aren't showing at campus galleries, publishing in the College's award-winning newspaper, performing on stage, attending readings and screenings, freestyling at poetry slams, producing shows for

Columbia's television and radio stations, or taking an active role in the College's 85+ social and academic clubs, they're interacting with the larger Chicago community around them. The presence of Columbia's students can be felt in theaters, bookstores, nightclubs, concert venues, museums, and media outlets throughout the city.

Financial Aid and Scholarships

The College's Student Financial Services office is available to assist students with developing a financial plan to help pay for their education. Comprehensive information about grants, scholarships, and loans that are available to Columbia students can be found at www.colum.edu/sfs.

CONTACT INFORMATION

Mr. Murphy Monroe, Executive Director of Admissions
☎ 312-369-7130
📧 admissions@colum.edu

- **Enrollment:** *11,200*

- **Selectivity:** *moderately difficult*

- **Test scores:** *Not required for admission. Applicants who take the ACT or SAT are strongly encouraged to submit their scores.*

- **Application deadline:** *Rolling*

- **Expenses:** *Tuition $21,200; Room & Board $10,000*

Columbia College's campus is all of Chicago.

SciencesPo.
Columbia University
DUAL BA PROGRAM

NEW YORK, NEW YORK
www.gs.columbia.edu/sciences-po

Students will earn two bachelor's degrees in four years: one from Sciences Po in France and one from Columbia University in New York City.

The Dual BA Program Between Columbia University and Sciences Po re-envisions the college experience offering an undergraduate education with an international character.

As a Dual BA student, you'll have the opportunity to immerse yourself in two distinct academic, social, and cultural environments: a close-knit small college in a French regional setting and a research university in New York City.

Two Colleges, Two Degrees, Four Years

Drawing upon elements both traditional and innovative, the Dual BA Program combines the academic rigor of two world-renowned universities—all students complete the undergraduate curricula of both Columbia University and Sciences Po, alongside a uniquely diverse group of fellow students.

Sciences Po in France

By offering two distinct learning environments, the Dual BA Program seeks to present a variety of experiences in order to help students reach beyond familiar habits of mind and develop a richly textured understanding of an increasingly globalized world.

As a Dual BA student, you'll begin your college education at one of three Sciences Po campuses—situated on the French

Riviera, on the Normandy Coast, or in the Champagne region—each of which numbers 100–250 students and is devoted to a particular region of the world. At your regional campus, you'll be able to pursue numerous extracurricular activities and internship opportunities while completing Sciences Po's interdisciplinary social sciences curriculum, with instruction in economics, history, law, political science, and sociology, as well as in the living languages spoken in your campus's region of focus.

Columbia University in New York City

After two years in France, you'll matriculate at Columbia University School of General Studies, the undergraduate college at Columbia for students pursuing a rigorous education through a nontraditional path. At Columbia you'll pursue one discipline in depth by fulfilling the requirements for a major and cultivate intellectual breadth by completing core requirements in a variety of subjects. You'll be part of a vibrant campus community of 9,000 undergraduate students with access to abundant

extracurricular options as well as internship opportunities at the many industries that call New York City home.

Join a Global Network

Upon completion of the program, you'll graduate with two bachelor's degrees, one each from Sciences Po and Columbia, and you will be eligible for guaranteed admission to a Sciences Po graduate program in Paris. You'll also be a member of the global alumni networks of two of the world's leading universities and well prepared for your next challenging endeavor.

CONTACT INFORMATION

Mr. Curtis M. Rodgers, Dean of Enrollment Management

☎ 212-854-2772 or toll-free 800-895-1169

🖳 spo-dualba@columbia.edu

- **Selectivity:** *most difficult*
- **Application deadline:** *1/2 (freshmen)*
- **Expenses:** *Tuition & Fees vary by institution.*

While at Sciences Po, Dual BA students study at campuses located on the French Riviera, on the Normandy Coast, and in the Champagne region.

A passion for food is what brings students to the world's premier culinary college—The Culinary Institute of America (CIA). This private not-for-profit college provides the world's best undergraduate education in culinary arts and baking and pastry arts. At the CIA, students gain the general knowledge and specific skills they need to become leaders in the foodservice and hospitality industry, the largest private employer in the United States.

All CIA degree programs emphasize professional, hands-on learning in the college's kitchens, bakeshops, and restaurants—students typically log at least 1,300 hours in a kitchen or bakeshop. CIA classes span the culinary globe, exploring great cultures, cooking techniques, and cuisines—everything from sushi to Cuban sandwiches to strawberry Napoleons—CIA students prepare and eat amazing dishes every day. Classes are taken in a progressive sequence in order to build skills, food knowledge, and production experience. These studies culminate in operating courses that give students both kitchen and front-of-the-house experiences in the college's famous restaurants.

THE CULINARY INSTITUTE OF AMERICA®

THE WORLD'S PREMIER CULINARY COLLEGE
HYDE PARK, NEW YORK
www.ciachef.edu

On campus, students have access to 41 kitchens and bakeshops, five public restaurants, and a huge culinary library. Bachelor's degree students also focus on foodservice management development, with a broad range of business management and liberal arts courses.

CIA students enjoy an active campus life, with a variety of intramural and club sports, student clubs, and extracurricular activities such as ski and camping trips, live entertainment, presentations by leading chefs and industry executives, and cook-offs. The college's Student Recreation Center includes a six-lane pool, a gym, an aerobics studio, racquetball courts, a fitness center and free-weight room, a game room, outdoor tennis courts, and the Courtside Café and Pub. Freshmen live in air-conditioned residence halls on the banks of the Hudson River; upperclassmen can live in six Adirondack-style lodges with suites and private baths. All residence halls have wireless Internet access.

The CIA's 170-acre campus in Hyde Park is just 1½–2 hours from New York City and Albany. There are a number of state parks and historic sites throughout the area. Students can taste wines at local vineyards, visit farmer's markets, and pick apples at nearby orchards. To the west are the Catskill and Shawangunk Mountains, where CIA students go to hike, ski, rock climb, mountain bike, and sightsee.

CONTACT INFORMATION

Ms. Rachel Birchwood, Director of Admissions

☎ 800-CULINARY (285-4627) or 845-452-9430

🖥 admissions@culinary.edu

- **Enrollment:** *2,807*

- **Selectivity:** *moderately difficult*

- **Test scores:** *ACT—over 18, 94%; SAT—critical reading over 500, 59%; SAT—math over 500, 66%*

- **Application deadline:** *Rolling (freshmen)*

- **Expenses:** *Tuition $25,900; Room & Board $9160*

A 15:1 student-faculty ratio allows students to work with professors on a one-on-one basis.

DAEMEN COLLEGE

A World of Opportunity

AMHERST, NEW YORK
www.daemen.edu

Daemen College prepares students for life and leadership in an increasingly complex world. Daemen is a private, career-oriented liberal arts college. The College fosters an academic atmosphere that leads to open inquiry and debate.

At Daemen, the distinctive Core Curriculum takes an innovative approach to general education requirements. The Core Curriculum is based on achieving seven life and academic competencies. Daemen students learn beyond the classroom through experiential learning opportunities including collaborative undergraduate research with faculty members, internships for credit, clinical experiences, engaging service learning positions, and international education programs.

Assisted by a supportive faculty, Daemen students are encouraged to pursue goals beyond their initial expectations, to respond to academic challenges, and to develop habits that enrich their lives and their community. Small classes (15:1 student-faculty ratio) allow students to work with professors on a one-to-one basis. Daemen offers more than 50 majors including Accounting, Animation (NEW), Art, Arts Administration, Athletic Training, Biology, Business Administration, Education, English, French, Graphic Design, Health Care Studies, History, History and Government, Mathematics, Natural Sciences, Nursing, Paralegal (NEW), Physical Therapy, Physician Assistant, Political Science, Pre-med, Psychology, Social Work Spanish, Sustainability— Global and Local (NEW), and more.

Students enjoy intercollegiate athletics, intramurals, and over 50 clubs and organizations. On campus, the modern apartment-style residence halls provide separate housing for male and female students in addition to the existing five-story residence hall. A popular hangout is the Research and Information Commons, which houses a full-service library, RIC's Café, individual study rooms,

the Academic Computing Center, and plenty of comfortable state-of-the-art amenities to enhance the study experience.

The campus is located in suburban Amherst, New York, just minutes from Buffalo. Students enjoy the benefits of a city renowned for exceptional theater, music, art, restaurants, and major league sports. The campus is close to scenic Niagara Falls and Canada.

At Daemen, a personal admissions counselor helps guide students and families through the process from start to finish. Daemen creates individualized financial aid packages for students. Generous scholarships make attending Daemen very affordable. Over 92 percent of full-time undergraduate students receive some type of financial assistance.

CONTACT INFORMATION

Mr. Frank S. Williams, Dean of Admissions

☎ 716-839-8225 or toll-free 800-462-7652

💻 admissions@daemen.edu

Visit Daemen College—that's the best way to really get a feel for what Daemen has to offer.

- **Enrollment:** *2,177*
- **Selectivity:** *moderately difficult*
- **Test scores:** *ACT—over 18, 93.6%; SAT—critical reading over 500, 54.1%; SAT—math over 500, 60.9%*
- **Application deadline:** *Rolling (freshmen), rolling (transfer)*
- **Expenses:** *Tuition $22,620; Room & Board $10,700*

Daemen's beautiful suburban campus is located in Amherst, New York, near Buffalo.

A Denison education, grounded in the liberal arts, demands reflection, spirited debate, and active engagement with ideas. We expect to disagree, to surprise ourselves, and to discover new territory.

DENISON
UNIVERSITY

GRANVILLE, OHIO
www.denison.edu/

Denison University is a private, undergraduate liberal arts college that is committed to the Ideals of intellect, integrity, diversity, and respect for each other and the environment. Denison prepares students from across the country and around the world to be autonomous thinkers, discerning moral agents, and engaged citizens of a democratic society. A Denison education is delivered through an intentional process that combines the breadth and depth of a challenging academic program with an array of experiential learning programs and the transformative experience living and learning together as a diverse campus community. The proof of Denison's impact is witnessed among its 30,000 alumni, who thrive as thought and action leaders in all walks of life and show their loyalty to each other and the University in countless ways.

About 40 percent of Denison students take part in at least one of the University's summer internship programs by the time they graduate.

And more than half of Denison's graduates enroll in graduate or professional schools within ten years of graduation. Denison students are consistent finalists for a number of postgraduate awards, including the Rhodes and Marshal scholarships. In the past 17 years, the University has had 11 National Science Foundation Fellows, 11 Goldwater Science scholars, 2 Truman Scholars, 1 Udall Fellow, 1 recipient of the Charles B. Rangel International Affairs Fellowship, and 49 Fulbright Scholarship winners.

Virtually all students live on Denison's 900-acre Denison campus, which is located on a ridge overlooking the village of Granville, in central Ohio. Housing options range from traditional residence halls, to the special-interest housing of the North Quad, to apartment-style housing available for seniors.

Over the last 15 years, the campus has seen significant changes, with new and expanded facilities in the studio arts, biology, chemistry, senior housing, and athletics and recreation facilities—all of which have been conducted to meet the U.S. Green Building Council standards for Leadership in Energy and Environmental Design (LEED).

Denison is a member of NCAA Division III and the North Coast Athletic Conference (NCAC). Over the past 14 years, the 23 varsity sports teams have won a conference-high 12 NCAC All-Sports Trophies, as well as 104 conference championships since 1984, the NCAC's founding year. In addition, Denison athletes have earned 44 NCAA Postgraduate Scholarships—the third most among all Division III institutions.

CONTACT INFORMATION

Mr. Perry Robinson, Director of Admissions

☎ 740-587-6276 or toll-free 800-DENISON

🖥 admissions@denison.edu

- **Enrollment:** *2,275*

- **Selectivity:** *very difficult*

- **Test scores:** *ACT—over 18, 100%; SAT—critical reading over 500, 98%; SAT—math over 500, 99%*

- **Application deadline:** *1/15 (freshmen), 6/1 (transfer)*

- **Expenses:** *Tuition $38,220; Room & Board $9340*

Denison delivers to its students lifetimes of personal and professional success—as well as the knowledge, ability, vision, and resolve to bring coherence to a complex world.

DigiPen's 100,000-square-foot campus offers plenty of space for students to meet and collaborate, including a 250-seat game production lab designed to simulate a professional studio environment.

DigiPen
INSTITUTE OF TECHNOLOGY

REDMOND, WASHINGTON
www.digipen.edu
www.facebook.com/digipen.edu

DigiPen Institute of Technology is one of the top schools in the world for students interested in game development. Located in Redmond, Washington, a suburb of Seattle and a global hub of the software and technology industries, DigiPen offers an educational experience unlike any other four-year university. Students enroll directly into one of DigiPen's seven undergraduate or two graduate degree programs, specializing in disciplines like computer graphics programming, game design, 3D animation, computer hardware engineering, or sound design. From their first day of class onward, DigiPen students are immersed in a curriculum that combines rigorous study of the academic fundamentals of their field with applied team projects in a studio environment. These projects range from fully playable 2D and

3D video games to animated films and even proprietary handheld game consoles. Many DigiPen student games have won awards at international competitions like the Independent Games Festival, and a few have even laid the groundwork for professional titles like Valve Software's *Portal* series.

DigiPen's student body of roughly 1,000 enjoys close personal attention from faculty members who are deeply invested in their success. The student-to-faculty ratio is 12:1, and many faculty members have a wealth of experience in both academia and industry to share. Students also benefit from modern academic facilities: DigiPen's 100,000-square-foot campus, newly renovated in 2010, offers numerous spaces for students to meet and collaborate, including sculpture and drawing studios, a 250-seat game production lab, and an on-site café that provides students with access to fresh and healthy food options. Students don't stop learning when they leave campus, however. Because there are over 350 interactive media companies in the Seattle metro area, DigiPen students have an abundance of opportunities to intern for credit at local game companies such as Nintendo of America, PopCap Games, or ArenaNet.

Housing is available to a limited number of first-year students, and financial aid, including loans, grants, and scholarships, is available to those who qualify.

CONTACT INFORMATION

Ms. Danial Powers, Admissions Application Manager
☎ 425-558-0299
🖥 admissions@digipen.edu

- **Enrollment:** *Approximately 1,000*
- **Selectivity:** *minimally difficult*
- **Application deadline:** *Rolling (freshmen), rolling (transfer)*
- **Expenses:** *Tuition $20,760*

Students in DigiPen's Bachelor of Fine Arts in Digital Art and Animation program hone their skills in a 2D animation workshop.

Aerial shot of Dowling College.

DOWLING COLLEGE

OAKDALE, NY

www.dowling.edu
www.facebook.com/dowlingcollege

At Dowling College, students are not only the top priority, they are the mission. Located on the south shore of Long Island, just 50 miles from New York City and the Hamptons, and minutes from ocean beaches, Dowling believes education leads to important discoveries—each student will make many discoveries about the world as well as about themselves. By working with Dowling's renowned faculty, students will discover talents and abilities that they may not yet know they have.

Dowling College is extremely proud of the more than 120 academic offerings available through its schools of Arts and Sciences, Aviation, Business, and Education. And *U.S. News & World Report* lists Dowling's online graduate business degree as one of the top online programs in the nation. The College's faculty and staff members seek to inspire students to reach beyond their expectations, to prepare them for the challenges and opportunities for today, for tomorrow, and for life.

One thing students won't find on campus is a single lecture hall, which helps create a more personal learning environment. A new science laboratory, flight and air traffic control simulators, new classrooms, a newly converted Music House, and a newly redesigned library are just some of the exciting improvements around the Dowling College campus. Students have access to an extensive array of career services support including career development workshops and internships as early as their sophomore year. Dowling is proud that within a year of graduation, 96 percent of its graduates are either employed or attending graduate school. And like all of Dowling's more than 35,000 alumni, today's students will

also have lifetime access to Dowling's career services center.

The apartment-styles suites in the residence halls at the historic Rudolph-Oakdale campus and Brookhaven campus give students the opportunity to live on their own while learning how to manage their time between classes, working on or off campus, maintaining a comfortable living environment, and attending different school activities. With more than 40 clubs and organizations, 15 NCAA Division II sports, special events, and more, Dowling offers a vibrant community for students. If a student sees an opportunity for a new club, he or she is welcome to create one. *The Lion's Voice* student paper, online event calendars, the Weekly Roar, and a ticker

CONTACT INFORMATION

Ms. Ronnie Lee Macdonald,
   Vice President for Enrollment
   and Student Services
☎ 631-244-3480 or toll-free
   800-DOWLING
💻 macdonar@dowling.edu

on campus keep students informed of upcoming events. On-campus amenities include the Lion's Den student lounge, convenient fitness centers, and two cafeterias— one newly redesigned where students can dine overlooking the scenic Connetquot River.

- **Enrollment:** *4,416*
- **Selectivity:** *moderately difficult*
- **Application deadline:** *Rolling (freshmen), rolling (transfer)*
- **Expenses:** *Tuition $24,630; Room & Board $10,770*

Dowling College is home to the 2012 NCAA Division II National Champion Men's Lacrosse.

Koessler Administration Building,
D'Youville College Est. 1908.

D'Youville
COLLEGE
Educating for life

BUFFALO, NEW YORK

www.dyouville.edu

D'Youville College is internationally known as a leader in health care and teacher education and as having a friendly campus. It is where dedicated faculty members are committed to teaching, with personal attention, and preparing students on how to have not only a rewarding career but also compassionate, productive and responsible lives.

Sister Denise A. Roche, GNSH, Ph.D., President of D'Youville has said, "For more than a century, D'Youville has provided a quality environment for students seeking an education that translates into successful careers and personal satisfaction."

At D'Youville, experienced faculty members —not teacher aides or assistants— with advanced degrees teach all classes, labs, and seminars. Small classes, with a 14:1 student faculty ratio, ensure the highest level of individualized attention. The professors know each student and are always available to help. D'Youville's small classes are always ranked number one in student surveys.

A degree from D'Youville is widely respected in all the professional fields and can open many doors. The extensive offering of academic majors includes programs where a student can earn both bachelor's and master's degrees concurrently in just five years. Dual or interdisciplinary degrees in career fields with national shortages, such as health care, get D'Youville graduates into the workplace faster.

D'Youville provides opportunities for semester-abroad programs, internships, and

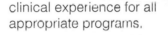

clinical experience for all appropriate programs.

Making education as affordable as possible is a priority at D'Youville. More than 90 percent of all incoming D'Youville freshmen receive financial aid. The scholarship programs for incoming students can cut the cost of tuition by as much as 50 percent. D'Youville believes that an investment in education will pay dividends over a lifetime and realize the practical aspects of paying for it.

Now in its second century, D'Youville continues its Catholic tradition and has established a reputation for providing a quality education, especially in the fields of health care and teacher education, which translates into a successful career

and satisfying life for its graduates.

The dedicated and devoted faculty and staff, small classes, friendly campus, and an opportunity to make life-long friends form the basis for a well-integrated education that provides exceptional job opportunities.

This all adds up to an institution where students are comfortable, have a great college experience, and are prepared for not only a great career but a great life as well.

Earlham students come from all over the United States and more than 80 other countries. They can choose from a wide range of academic programs, dozens of co-curricular activities, and off-campus study on six continents.

EARLHAM
C O L L E G E

RICHMOND, INDIANA
www. earlham.edu
facebook.com/earlhamcollege

Where will you begin your extraordinary life?

At Earlham College, students are prepared for lives of significant meaning, purpose and accomplishment. You will find opportunities for academic preparation and social engagement that transcend the ordinary. So what course will you set?.

Environmental Studies? Peace & Global Studies? Neuroscience? Maybe you've never heard of Border Studies or encountered a major in Human Development and Social Relations. At Earlham, you will. The College's diverse program offerings will introduce you to new concepts and information, expose you to new ideas and beliefs, and even carry you to new lands and continents. Along the way, you just may change your life and shape your world.

Earlham students come from 42 states and from more than 80 countries. As diverse as Earlham students are in their backgrounds and interests, they share a common aptitude for inquiry and an ability to meet rigorous intellectual challenge.

Earlham ranks 29th—ninth in life sciences—among 1,533 institutions of higher learning in the United States in the percentage of graduates who go on to receive Ph.D.s. Approximately one in every 10 Earlham graduates goes on to earn a Ph.D.

Established in 1847, Earlham College is a selective, private, liberal arts college, emphasizing profound academic inquiry in a challenging intellectual environment.

Of the 93 full-time faculty members, 96 percent hold a Ph.D. or the highest degree in their field. The student-faculty ratio is 12 to 1; 70 percent of classes have 19 or fewer students.

Earlham College students come from wide-ranging backgrounds. More than 30 percent are American minority or international students. Faith traditions from Islam to Catholicism to Judaism to Quakerism are represented in the student body.

Earlham's 16 women's and men's varsity teams compete in NCAA Division III as members of the Heartland Collegiate Athletic Conference.

New and renovated science facilities will provide more state-of-the-art research labs for undergraduates. New facilities for the fine arts, slated to open in the fall of 2014, will enhance opportunities for student participation in the arts.

With its emphasis on significant experiences and profound inquiry, an Earlham education is excellent preparation, not just for your first job, but a career, and a lifetime of rewarding involvement.

Every student studies a foreign language and completes a multicultural/intercultural curriculum component.

International study is common: nearly 70 percent of Earlham students study off campus, traveling to more than 20 different countries.

More than 50 percent of Earlham alumni graduating within the last 15 years enrolled in graduate or professional school, earning degrees from top universities.

As business leaders, entrepreneurs, teachers, authors and activists, Earlham alumni are global citizens making a difference in the world.

CONTACT INFORMATION

Nancy Sinex, Director of Admissions

☎ 765-983-1600 or toll-free 800-327-5426

🖳 admission@earlham.edu

- **Enrollment:** *1,181*
- **Selectivity:** *very selective*
- **Test scores:** *Optional*
- **Application deadline:** *2/15 (first-year), 4/1 (transfer)*
- **Expenses:** *Tuition $39,200; Room & Board $7400*

The average class size at Earlham is 15. Students have many opportunities to collaborate with their professors on research projects.

Students gather around one of the newest additions to our ever-growing campus to show their Edinboro University pride!

EDINBORO UNIVERSITY

EDINBORO, PENNSYLVANIA

www.edinboro.edu

www.facebook.com/edinboro

Surrounded by 40 campus buildings, 155-year-old Academy Hall—listed on the National Register of Historic Places—is symbolic of Edinboro University's beacon of knowledge, stretching back to its pioneering roots, yet beckoning and shining the way ahead for future generations of students.

Edinboro University—offering more than 100 associate, bachelor's, and master's degree programs in 24 academic departments to more than 8,000 students—serves as a modern paradigm of how a former community normal school of the mid-19th Century evolved into a major university of today. Where founders once sought only an education above the basic three Rs for their children, this sprawling, 585-acre center of knowledge could not have been envisioned 155 years ago; nor could it have foreseen many of this millennium's most popular courses, such as computer animation, cinema, astrophysics, and nuclear medicine.

Edinboro students from 22 countries and 39 states find their University is the place to pursue and attain their higher education aspirations. Even more, they're confident the "Edinboro Experience," on campus or online, is where they'll find paths leading to thousands of meaningful career opportunities, including journalism, education, health care, social work, criminal forensics, foreign languages, anthropology, psychology, music, industrial biochemistry, the environment, and multi-diversified areas of career interest. Add to that Edinboro's College of Arts and Sciences, Schools of Education, Business, and Graduate Studies, a dozen nationally accredited academic programs, internships and experiential learning in virtually every department, on-campus professional recruiting, and a networking alumni base of some 60,000 representing all leading professions, and one easily understands why Edinboro University is synonymous with success.

With a faculty and staff of over 800 individuals working as one dedicated team, Edinboro, part of the 14-university Pennsylvania State System of Higher Education, is one of America's "Military Friendly" schools and is

ranked in the top 5 for accessibility for students with physical disabilities.

With new suite-style residence halls, 17 NCAA men's and women's sports, world-class cultural events, and more than 150 student clubs and organizations, Edinboro University offers the complete college experience.

Edinboro has come a long way from its roots as the six-room Edinboro Academy of 1857. And now, Edinboro students know they'll go a long way, too. Under the leadership of President Julie E. Wollman, the University is well-positioned for continued growth, advancement in postsecondary educational opportunities, and service to its host community, the region, commonwealth,

CONTACT INFORMATION

Mr. Craig Grooms, Director of
   Undergraduate Admissions
☎ 814-732-2761 or toll-free
   888-846-2676
🖳 eup_admissions@edinboro.
   edu

nation, and the world for untold decades to come.

- **Enrollment:** *8,262*

- **Selectivity:** *moderately difficult*

- **Test scores:** *ACT—over 18, 65%; SAT—critical reading over 500, 36%; SAT— math over 500, 37%*

- **Application deadline:** *Rolling (transfer)*

- **Expenses:**
  Tuition $8577.60 (Pennsylvania residents); $12,315.40 (Non-residents); Room & Board $8068

With over 103 major programs across three campuses, Edinboro University has something for everyone!

Students at the flight line.

EMBRY-RIDDLE
Aeronautical University™

DAYTONA BEACH, FLORIDA
www.embryriddle.edu/

Embry-Riddle Aeronautical University is recognized worldwide as the leader in aviation and aerospace education. The University, which dates back almost to the time of the Wright brothers, offers programs in aviation, aerospace, engineering, business, and related fields, including its newest major in unmanned aircraft systems.

Residential campuses in Daytona Beach, Florida, and Prescott, Arizona, provide education in a traditional setting, while the Worldwide Campus provides instruction through more than 170 centers in the United States, Europe, Canada, and the Middle East as well as through online learning. Embry-Riddle's premier aeronautical science (professional pilot) program and award-winning aerospace engineering program are the largest on campus and among the largest of their type in the nation.

Embry-Riddle conducts applied research valued at approximately $30 million per year and is leading the development of the Next

Generation Air Transportation System along with the Federal Aviation Administration, Lockheed Martin, Boeing, and other high-tech organizations. Alumni are leaders in aviation and aerospace industries and serve as a strong network and resource for students.

At the Daytona Beach campus, students enjoy activities and clubs focused on aviation and aerospace, as well as fraternities, sororities, and recreational sports. Embry-Riddle's award-winning precision flight demonstration teams compete nationally in air and ground events. Embry-Riddle also has the largest all-volunteer Air Force ROTC detachment in the country and among the fastest-growing Navy ROTC units and Army ROTC battalions.

Embry-Riddle athletes participate in intercollegiate and intramural sports including baseball, basketball, crew, cross-country, golf, soccer, tennis, volleyball, and ice hockey. The 68,000-square-foot ICI Center contains two full-size NCAA basketball courts, a fitness center, and a weight room. The University sports complex also includes a soccer field, the Sliwa Stadium ballpark, the Ambassador William Crotty Tennis Center, and the Track

and Field Complex. The Tine Davis Fitness Center is adjacent to the pool and features fitness services and wellness programs.

The 5,300-square-foot interfaith chapel has a 140-seat nondenominational worship area and four prayer rooms (Catholic, Jewish, Muslim, and Protestant). The year-round clear flying weather surrounding Daytona Beach offers an excellent environment in which to study and fly. The campus, which is located adjacent to the Daytona Beach International Airport, is only 3 miles from what is called the world's most famous beach. The high-technology industries located in nearby Orlando provide Embry-Riddle students with

CONTACT INFORMATION

Mr. Robert J. Adams, Director of Undergraduate Admissions

☎ 386-226-6100 or toll-free 800-862-2416

🖳 dbadmit@erau.edu

an outstanding support base. In addition, the Kennedy Space Center is less than a 2-hour drive away.

- **Enrollment:** *5,205*
- **Selectivity:** *moderately difficult*
- **Test scores:** *ACT—over 18, 91%; SAT—math over 500, 78%*
- **Application deadline:** *Rolling (freshmen), 6/1 (transfer)*
- **Expenses:** *Tuition $29,728; Room & Board $8790*

Engineering lab—Helicopter project.

FIT is a creative community where talented students find their niche.

FASHION INSTITUTE OF TECHNOLOGY

NEW YORK, NEW YORK

www.fitnyc.edu

www.facebook.com/FashionInstituteofTechnology

The Fashion Institute of Technology (FIT) is New York City's college for creative and business talent. Occupying an entire block in Manhattan's Chelsea neighborhood, FIT's campus places students at the heart of the fashion, advertising, visual arts, design, business, and communications industries. A State University of New York (SUNY) college of art and design, business, and technology, FIT offers more than 45 programs leading to A.A.S., B.F.A., B.S., M.A., M.F.A., and M.P.S. degrees, all based on a solid liberal arts foundation.

FIT's mission is to produce well-rounded graduates: doers and thinkers who will become the next generation of business pacesetters and creative icons. Students can choose full- or part-time study, evening/weekend degree programs, and online studies. One of the things students like best is that they take courses in their majors right away, engaging the passions that brought them to FIT.

Campus life at FIT is dynamic and vital. The David Dubinsky Student Center houses a student radio station, the Style Shop (an FIT student-run boutique), student government and club offices, a state-of-the-art fitness center, and a counseling center. FIT has intercollegiate teams in tennis, cross country, half marathon, track and field, dance, swimming, women's volleyball, women's soccer, and table tennis. Students can choose from more than 60 clubs and organizations, from the Ad Group to the Snow Club to the Merchandising Society. They also have access to hip restaurants, museums, art galleries, and boutiques within walking distance of the campus.

In programs of study such as interior design, toy design, computer animation, and cosmetics and fragrance marketing, students get the tools they need for success in many in-demand careers. In fact, FIT's baccalaureate program in toy design was the first of its kind in the United States. Unique facilities include the only professionally outfitted fragrance development lab on a U.S. college campus and cutting edge knitting, lighting, screen printing, and toy design labs.

FIT's special brand of education reflects the college's close ties to industry. Students gain unparalleled exposure to their fields through internships and the college's professional connections; nearly one third of FIT student interns are offered employment on completion of their internships.

Among notable alumni in fashion are Calvin Klein, Reem Acra, Francisco Costa, Norma Kamali, Nanette Lepore, and Ralph Rucci. Other prominent graduates include Leslie Blodgett,

FIT's urban campus is convenient to the rich resources of New York City.

executive chairman of Bare Escentuals; international restaurant designer Tony Chi; Edward Menichocchi, vice president and publisher of *Vanity Fair*, and Joe Zee, creative director of *Elle*.

- **Enrollment:** *10,223*
- **Selectivity:** *moderately difficult*
- **Application deadline:** *1/1 (freshmen), 1/1 (transfer)*
- **Expenses:** *Tuition $5768; Room & Board $12,418*

CONTACT INFORMATION

Office of Admissions
☎ 212-217-3760
🖥 fitinfo@fitnyc.edu

At Felician, your college journey is a personal journey, tailored to your needs and interests.

The Franciscan College of New Jersey

LODI, NEW JERSEY
www.felician.edu/
http://www.facebook.com/
FelicianCollegeOfficeof
Admission

STUDENTS FIRST. It's the Felician College motto—words the College truly lives by. In fact, Felician believes in them so strongly that it has built an entire college around the idea of putting students first. Felician thinks a student's college experience should be a personal journey, one that's tailored to his or her needs and interests. And Felician is there with each student every step of the way—first to help discover their interests and then to work one-on-one to help build an exciting future.

Felician College is a Catholic college rooted in Franciscan values such as love, joy, compassion, and diversity. The College strives to develop more than just a student's intellect—it develops his or her whole character. Felician wants to make sure that students are prepared for life beyond college, and life is about more than getting good grades or writing essays. The College provides the right tools at the right time to help students every step of the way, like small class sizes and one-on-one tutoring in every discipline.

Felician College knows that choosing a career is a big step, and embarking upon that career is an even bigger one. The programs, which give students a solid footing for all the twists and turns life can throw at them, are among the top rated in the state. But that's not enough, which is why Felician's faculty members, advisors, and career counselors also assist students with finding internships.

Maybe you love the city. Or maybe you're more the small-town type. Most likely, you're somewhere in between. And so is Felician College. It's the kind of place that exemplifies the phrase, "the best of both worlds." Rutherford and Lodi are both suburban residential communities, featuring small-town charm and locally owned shops and restaurants. But just a quick train ride from the Rutherford station (or a 12-mile drive away) is one of the largest urban cultural and economic centers in the world—New York City. This proximity to New York City means proximity to internships and jobs at such companies as Bank of America, Johnson & Johnson, Pfizer, Madison Square Garden, ESPN and many, many more.

The College's residence halls are a lot of things. They're quiet places to study and exciting places to stage events. But above all, they're

CONTACT INFORMATION

College Admissions Office
☎ 201-559-6131
✉ admissions@felician.edu

home. Living in one of the residence halls means you'll be right on campus and won't have to worry about getting to and from class or any of Felician's NCAA Division II sporting events.

- **Enrollment:** 2,341
- **Selectivity:** moderately difficult
- **Test scores:** ACT—over 18, 47%; SAT—critical reading over 500, 21%; SAT—math over 500, 25%
- **Application deadline:** Rolling (freshmen), rolling (transfer)
- **Expenses:** Tuition $27,800; Room & Board $11,400

The average class size at Felician College is 15 students.

Russell Towers is one of seven residence halls and is home to students in the First Year Residential Experience program designed to help freshmen build a foundation for success at Fitchburg State.

FITCHBURG STATE UNIVERSITY

FITCHBURG, MASSACHUSETTS

www.fitchburgstate.edu

www.facebook.com/FitchburgStateAdmissions

Founded in 1894, Fitchburg State University was one of the first institutions of higher education in Massachusetts. The University is dedicated to integrating high-quality professional programs with strong liberal arts and science studies.

Enrolling over 3,500 full-time undergraduate students and 3,500 more in graduate, continuing education, and online programs, Fitchburg State is a vibrant center of learning in central Massachusetts. The University occupies 225 acres in a residential area of the city of Fitchburg, which has a population of over 42,000 residents. Fitchburg is about 1 hour northwest of Boston and only 4 hours from New York City. The area offers all sorts of things to do, including shopping, great restaurants, and many recreational and cultural activities.

The University stresses the importance of real-world experience in addition to classroom learning. Internships are required of Communications Media, Education, and Nursing students and are strongly recommended for all students. Students can choose from over 30 programs of study, 60 concentrations and minors, and four pre-professional tracks in several teaching formats such as evening and online. Fitchburg State's academic advisors and faculty members are an invaluable resource for its undecided students and those who have chosen their academic path. The low student-to-faculty ratio of 16:1 and the small average class size of 21 are key indicators of the personal attention Fitchburg State students receive.

About one half of the undergraduate students live on the campus in residence halls, apartments, or townhouses. The University's athletic teams participate in Division III sports, and "Falcon" athletes add much to the lively campus atmosphere. All students take advantage of the Recreation Center, which offers Fitchburg State students access to a world-class fitness center, including a swimming pool, dance studio, racquetball courts, and a wide variety of intramural sports and fitness classes. In addition, the University's Wallace Civic Center is the home of the ice hockey team and is a wonderful venue for exhibits, fairs, and events for the community—including a public ice rink where students can skate for free! The Hammond Dining Commons provides healthful and delicious meal options for both on campus and commuter students, and the North Street Bistro and McKay Café are also great places to grab a quick bite between classes.

With excellent academic programs, an active campus life, and myriad opportunities for personal growth, Fitchburg State University is an outstanding choice for higher education.

The Campus Quad provides an inviting outdoor setting on campus, whether you're studying, hanging out with friends, or playing Frisbee between classes.

- **Enrollment:** 6,891
- **Selectivity:** moderately difficult
- **Test scores:** ACT—over 18, 89%; SAT—critical reading over 500, 52%; SAT—math over 500, 60%
- **Application deadline:** Rolling (froshmen), rolling (transfer)
- **Expenses:** Tuition $8300; Room & Board $8340

CONTACT INFORMATION

Kay Reynolds, Director of Admissions

☎ 978-665-3144 or toll-free 800-705-9692

💻 admissions@fitchburgstate.edu

Professor Sol Negrin instructs his students using a Sony PMW EX-3 HD Camera in his Advanced Cinematography class.

FIVE TOWNS COLLEGE

When you're serious about Music, Business, Education, Media and the Performing Arts!

DIX HILLS, NEW YORK
www.ftc.edu

Students serious about music, business, education, media, and the performing arts look no further than Five Towns College. Located on Long Island's North Shore, this independent college lets students study in a suburban environment that is close to New York City.

The College offers a number of associate, bachelor's, master's, and doctoral degrees—notably, programs leading to the Master of Music (M.M.) degree in jazz/commercial music and in music education, the Master of Science in Education (M.S.Ed.), and the Doctor of Musical Arts (D.M.A.). The College's music programs are contemporary jazz in nature, although classical musicians are also part of this creative community. The most popular undergraduate degree programs are

Audio Recording Technology, Mass Communication in Broadcasting and Journalism (B.S.), Jazz/Commercial Music, Performance and Music Education (MUS.B.), Business and Music Business (B.P.S.), Elementary Teacher Education (B.S.), Theatre (B.F.A.), and Film/Video Production (B.F.A).

To support these two- and four-year programs, Five Towns is constantly upgrading its equipment and software; the campus has three audio recording studios, a film/television studio, a piano lab, a ProTools/MIDI lab, a PC lab, and a number of other music rooms and studios. The Dix Hill Performing Arts Center welcomes local and well-known musicians and comedians to campus.

The Five Towns College Living/Learning Center is a complex consisting of four modern residence halls. Each residence hall offers single- and double-occupancy rooms equipped with private bathrooms, climate control, high-speed Internet access, and cable television.

The College's beautiful 35-acre campus, located in the wooded countryside of Dix Hills, provides students with a quiet college setting. But just off campus is Long Island's bustling Route 110 corridor, home to national and multinational corporations—many places where Five Towns students can work and intern. Recently, students have interned at Sony, Def Jam, Cablevision, Disney, and Madison Square Garden. New York City, with everything from Lincoln Center to Broadway, is just a train ride away. The College is located within the historic town of Huntington, which is home to the Cinema Arts Center, Hecksher Museum, Vanderbilt

Museum, and numerous restaurants, coffeehouses, and shops. Nearby, students hit the white sand beaches of Jones Beach State Park and Fire Island National Seashore.

CONTACT INFORMATION

Undergraduate Admissions
☎ 631-656-2110
💻 admissions@ftc.edu

- **Enrollment:** *1,041*
- **Selectivity:** *moderately difficult*
- **Test scores:** *ACT—over 19, 80%; SAT—over 1350, 75%*
- **Application deadline:** *Rolling (freshmen), rolling (transfer)*
- **Expenses:** *Tuition $19,800; Room & Board $13,470*

A student mixes on the SSL 9000J 72-channel console in one of the College's four state-of-the art recording studios.

The 170-acre campus at Grove City College boasts gorgeous buildings like Hall of Arts and Letters and the Breen Student Union.

GROVE CITY COLLEGE

GROVE CITY, PENNSYLVANIA
www.gcc.edu/
https://www.facebook.com/GCCAdmissions

The campus of Grove City College (GCC) stretches more than 170 acres and includes twenty-nine neo-Gothic buildings valued at more than $100 million. The landscaped campus is considered one of the nicest in the nation. While the College has changed to meet business and societal needs, its basic philosophy has remained unchanged since its founding in 1876. It is a Christian liberal arts and sciences school dedicated to providing the highest-quality education at the lowest possible cost. Wanting to stay a private school governed by private citizens (trustees), it is one of the very few colleges in the country that does not accept any state or federal money.

Grove City College is informally affiliated with the Presbyterian Church (USA)—it believes that well-educated students should be exposed to the central ideas of the Christian faith. A 20-minute chapel program offered Tuesday and Thursday mornings, along with a Sunday evening worship service, challenges students in their faith. Students are required to attend sixteen out of the fifty scheduled chapel services per semester.

The Physical Learning Center is one of the finest among the nation's small colleges and includes an eight-lane bowling alley; two swimming pools; handball/racquetball courts; fitness rooms with free weights, aerobic equipment, and Cybex machines; a three-lane running track; and the basketball arena. The Grove City Wolverines participate in NCAA Division III sports. Men's teams are baseball, basketball, cross-country, golf, football, soccer, swimming and diving, tennis, and track and field. Women's teams are basketball, cross-country, golf, volleyball, soccer, softball, swimming and diving, tennis, and track and field. There are also more than 130 organizations, with 10 fraternities, 8 sororities, and 9 housing groups.

The College's placement services, ranked recently by *The Princeton Review* in the top 20 in the nation, help students obtain internships and jobs after graduation. A complete file of personal data, academic records, and recommendations is kept for each registrant, and potential employers who visit the campus have access to these files when interviewing graduating seniors.

Grove City is 60 miles north of Pittsburgh and only a day's drive from Chicago, New York City, Toronto, and Washington, D.C.

CONTACT INFORMATION

Director of Admissions
☎ 724-458-2100
🖥 admissions@gcc.edu

- **Enrollment:** *2,500*
- **Selectivity:** *very difficult*
- **Test scores:** *ACT—over 18, 100%; SAT—critical reading over 500, 95%; SAT—math over 500, 96%*
- **Application deadline:** *2/1 (freshmen), Rolling admission (transfer)*
- **Expenses:** *Tuition $14,212; Room & Board $7744*

Move-In Day Tradition—Grove City College students welcome incoming freshman by moving all their belongings from car to dorm room.

With men and women as welcoming as the campus they frequent, Harding students foster relationships that permeate the environment with a closeness and warmth you might not find anywhere else.

HARDING
UNIVERSITY

SEARCY, ARKANSAS
www.harding.edu
www.facebook.com/HUadmissions

Harding is more than just academics, spirituality, relationships, or community service. It's great to be at Harding because there is a balance of all these components—the integration of faith, learning, and living—and so much more. Since its beginning in 1924, Harding has striven to offer a challenging liberal arts curriculum taught from a Christian perspective—an education for both your heart and mind.

With approximately 100 majors, 14 preprofessional programs, and 20 postgraduate degrees, students are able to find a major that is a perfect fit for them. Harding's academic programs are designed by faculty members who hold the highest degrees in their fields and who continually develop themselves professionally. They are committed to providing a well-rounded, top-notch academic experience that includes hands-on learning, the latest research, effective professional preparation, and discipline-specific internships.

Students can further their out-of-classroom learning by participating in one of seven international programs located in Australia, Chile, England, France, Greece, Italy and Zambia. On campus, students may engage in a variety of activities, choosing from 118 academic and professional organizations and 29 social clubs. Ranging from the arts, music, politics, business, diversity, children, missions, service, and the environment, the clubs on campus offer a variety of interests to explore.

In addition, Harding provides lectures from such names as George W. Bush to Condeleezza Rice and concerts from Taylor Swift, the Avett Brothers, and Sara Bareilles. Along with student-produced shows such as the Homecoming musical and Spring Sing, Harding's campus is always providing exciting entertainment. A member of the NCAA Division II, Harding's sports teams compete within the Great American Conference. There are also a variety of intramural sports in which students may participate.

A residential campus, Harding provides 15 residence halls to give students a feeling of home away from home with a variety of accommodations, such as high-speed Internet, cable TV, ample parking, access to washers and dryers, storage, and TV/recreation/study lounges. There are also several apartment-style suites for upperclass students.

Harding is located in Searcy, Arkansas; it's about an hour away from Little Rock, Arkansas, and the Little Rock National Airport and about 2 hours from Memphis, Tennessee.

CONTACT INFORMATION:

Office of Admission Services

☎ 800-477-4407 (toll-free)

💻 admissions@harding.edu

- **Enrollment:** *7,200*

- **Selectivity:** *Moderately difficult*

- **Test scores:** *ACT—over 18, 92%; SAT—critical reading over 500, 77%; SAT—math over 500, 77%*

- **Application deadline:** *Rolling (freshmen), rolling (transfer)*

- *Expenses: Tuition, $11,700; Room & Board, $6192*

In the classroom, students are equipped for their future professions through solid classroom instruction and real-world application that gives Harding students an edge when joining today's highly competitive workforce.

Hillsdale College faculty and staff gather outside Central Hall to welcome returning students and incoming freshmen.

HILLSDALE COLLEGE

PURSUING TRUTH · DEFENDING LIBERTY SINCE 1844

HILLSDALE, MICHIGAN
www.hillsdale.edu/

Hillsdale College is a private college that values its academic excellence and its independence. In fact, Hillsdale does not accept any federal or state taxpayer subsidies. Students here can pick from a number of majors leading to a Bachelor of Arts or Bachelor of Science degree, and an impressive 97 percent of Hillsdale students are either employed or attending graduate school within six months of graduation.

Hillsdale students live in dorms, fraternity and sorority houses, and off-campus apartments. Recent campus upgrades include a new music hall, a new dorm, the newly built Grewcock Student Union, and renovations to the Strosacker Science Center.

Hillsdale's Charger athletes compete in 12 intercollegiate NCAA Division II varsity sports as part of the Great Lakes Intercollegiate Athletic Conference (GLIAC). In the past 20 years, the College has produced 196 athletic and academic All-Americans, 28 conference champions, and 18 teams that have finished tenth or better nationally. Men's teams are baseball, basketball, cross-country, football, and track. Women's teams are basketball, cross-country, softball, swimming, tennis, track, and volleyball. An active intramural program is also available.

Four national fraternities, three national sororities, and more than 70 other social, academic, spiritual, and service organizations provide Hillsdale students with a ton of co-curricular opportunities. A resident drama troupe and dance company, a bagpipe and drum corps, a concert choir and chamber chorale, a jazz program with big band and combos, instrumental chamber ensembles from string quartets to percussion ensemble, and a College-community orchestra and band round out the College's performing arts organizations.

Special student services provided by the College include career planning and placement counseling, academic advising and tutoring, and a health service staffed by a physician and a resident nurse.

Hillsdale College is surrounded by the hills, dales, and lakes of south-central Michigan. The College is close to Detroit, Chicago, Cleveland, Toledo, Ft. Wayne, and Indianapolis. Stores, churches, restaurants, and movie theaters are all within walking distance of the campus.

CONTACT INFORMATION

Mr. Jeffrey S. Lantis, Director of Admissions

☎ 517-607-2327

💻 admissions@hillsdale.edu

- **Enrollment:** *1,457*
- **Selectivity:** *very difficult*
- **Test scores:** *ACT—over 18, 100%; SAT—critical reading over 500, 100%; SAT—math over 500, 100%*
- **Application deadline:** *2/15 (freshmen), 2/15 (transfer)*
- **Expenses:** *Tuition $20,500; Room & Board $7990*

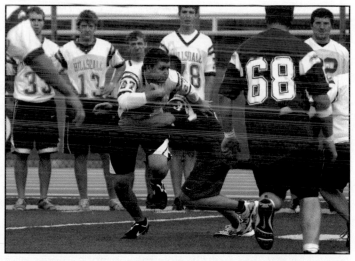

Hillsdale's men compete in the students' annual Residence Hall Football Tournament.

Hofstra offers the appeal of a large university along with all the comforts and amenities of a close-knit campus community.

HOFSTRA
UNIVERSITY®

prideandpurpose

HEMPSTEAD, NEW YORK

www.hofstra.edu

At Hofstra University, you can learn and grow on a campus that offers engaging classes, exceptional facilities and resources, dedicated faculty members, and a supportive network of peers and mentors. Hofstra's students discover their strengths and find their passions in about 140 undergraduate and 150 graduate program options. In addition, Hofstra offers students more than 100 dual degree programs, providing the opportunity to earn both a graduate and undergraduate degree in less time than if each degree was pursued separately.

On Hofstra's vibrant campus, which blends longstanding traditions with 21st-century resources, students find exceptional and technologically advanced classrooms, six theaters, a state-of-the-art fitness center, an accredited museum, modern athletic facilities, and an impressive 10-floor library that offers 1.2 million print volumes and 24/7 electronic access to more than 95,000 journals and books.

Here at Hofstra, it's all about choice. You may choose to live and learn in one of the 37 residence halls, each with a unique flair, community, and life of its own. Hofstra also offers 8 living/learning communities, which give students the opportunity to live with many of the same students they are in classes with, as well as students who share the same passion for political and civic issues, health sciences, and the arts. In addition, Hofstra students can choose from 20 on-campus dining facilities, including California Pizza Kitchen, Starbucks, Subway, and Au Bon Pain, as well as sushi and vegetarian and kosher options.

At Hofstra, students join a network of nearly 121,000 graduates. In addition, each year the University is visited by more than 400 employers who recognize just how much Hofstra's students have to offer. In addition to these plentiful networking opportunities on campus, students may choose to do an internship at a top company on

Long Island or in New York City, thus gaining critical work experience that can give them an edge in today's competitive job market.

Hofstra University hosts more than 500 cultural events each year, drawing together scholars, business leaders, authors, celebrities, healthcare professionals, politicians, and journalists from across the nation and around the world. These events help foster that connection between in-classroom work and extracurricular interests.

Hofstra also offers 17 intercollegiate athletic programs that compete at the NCAA Division I level; sports clubs; and more than 200 academic, fraternal/sororal, media, multicultural, performance, preprofessional, religious, and social/political organizations.

CONTACT INFORMATION

Sunil Samuel, Director of Admission

☎ 516-463-6700 or toll-free 800-HOFSTRA

🖳 admission@hofstra.edu

- **Enrollment:** *11,404*

- **Selectivity:** *moderately difficult*

- **Test scores:** *ACT—over 18, 99%; SAT—critical reading over 500, 91%; SAT—math over 500, 95%*

- **Application deadline:** *Rolling (freshmen)*

- **Expenses:** *Tuition $34,000; Room & Board $12,370*

On our 240-acre campus, students find an educational experience that is second to none.

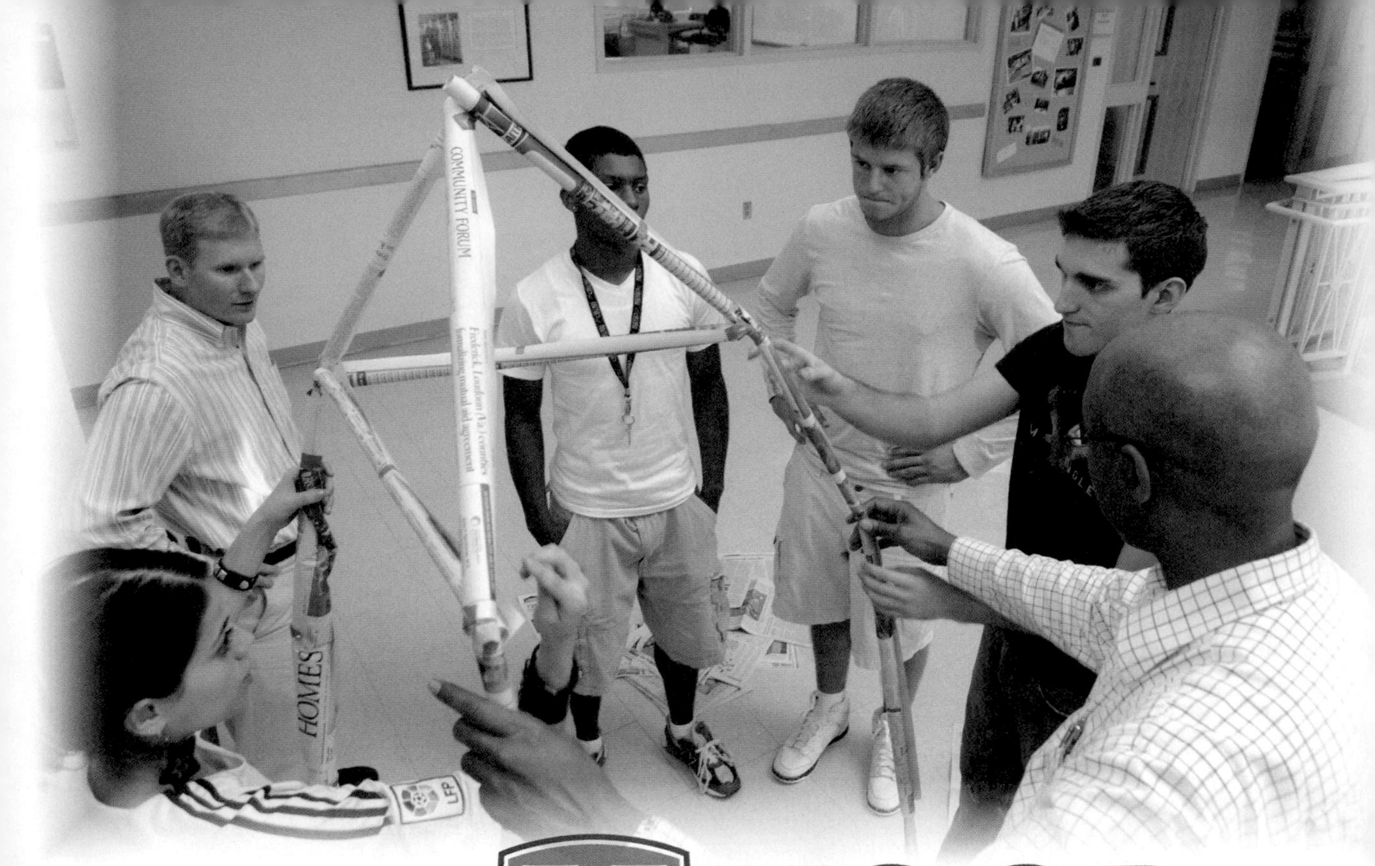

Classes at Hood often involve team-building and hands-on activities.

HOOD COLLEGE ®

FREDERICK, MARYLAND

www.hood.edu

www.facebook.com/hoodcollege

Hood College, founded in 1893, is an independent, co-educational liberal arts college. Hood's notably small class sizes, extraordinary faculty, outstanding student-to-faculty ratio, and attractive and friendly campus contribute to an exceptional learning experience.

Located on a 50-acre campus in the historic district of Frederick, Maryland, Hood offers Bachelor of Arts and Bachelor of Science degrees in 30 major fields of study, 14 master's degrees, and five certificate programs and certification programs in education. Hood, noted for its success in preparing students for careers and professions while providing a broad and rigorous liberal arts education, offers study-abroad programs, a unique coastal studies semester, and an honors program. Academic facilities feature a science and technology center with modern science and computing laboratories, an outstanding library and information center, advanced computing laboratories, a child education laboratory, and a language laboratory.

Hood's career center professionals help students find volunteer positions or internships in all fields of study. They're also experts in résumé writing and interview coaching and have numerous connections with employers throughout the Washington-Baltimore-Frederick area.

Five residence halls and three language residences give students the chance to learn together and create friendships that last a lifetime. First-year students can apply to live in themed, living learning communities, where students with similar interests live, study, and participate in field trips and community-related activities that add depth and breadth to their topics of study. Upperclass students can form their own living-learning communities designed around self-selected educational topics.

There are more than 60 student-led organizations that cover every interest—social, academic, governing, creative, service, spiritual, and cultural—and new ones, based on student interests, are formed every semester. Students can work out in Hood's new state-of-the-art,

two-level fitness center and athletes participate in 18 Division III varsity teams and three club sports, most of which are played in the new state-of-the-art athletic center or turf field.

Numerous scholars and world-renowned personalities—Khalid Hosseini, author of A Thousand Splendid Suns; Mary Robinson, former president of Ireland; and Rebecca Skloot, author of The Immortal Life of Henrietta Lacks, to name a few—come to campus each semester to speak on an array of topics, and guest artists specializing in every visual and performing genre showcase their works in the college's galleries and on its stages. In addition, students have the opportunity to share their talents in art exhibits; dance, instrumental and vocal concerts; and theater productions.

CONTACT INFORMATION

Mr. David Adams, Director of Admissions

☎ 301-696-3400 or toll-free 800-922-1599

💻 admissions@hood.edu

- **Enrollment:** *2,435 (fall 2011)*
- **Selectivity:** *moderately difficult*
- **Test scores:** *ACT—over 18, 94%; SAT—critical reading over 500, 71%; SAT—math over 500, 64%*
- **Application deadline:** *2/15 (freshmen), rolling (transfer)*
- **Expenses:** *Tuition $31,840, Room & Board $10,910*

The Brodbeck Music Hall cupola is visible throughout campus.

Houghton College's 1,300-acre campus provides plenty of space to study, contemplate, and play.

HOUGHTON
COLLEGE

HOUGHTON, NY

www.houghton.edu

www.facebook.com/houghtoncollege

As one of a select number of Christian colleges to receive widespread national recognition, Houghton is a clear choice for students desiring an academically rigorous Christ-centered college. Of all member institutions of the Council for Christian Colleges and Universities, Houghton College is ranked 4th highest in the national liberal arts category by *U.S. News & World Report*. Forbes ranks Houghton in the top 3 percent of schools nationwide in terms of quality of teaching, career prospects for alumni and graduation rates. The Princeton Review names Houghton a "Best College in the Northeast" and also lists Houghton in their Green College Guide.

Up for a challenge? Houghton offers more than 70 areas of study, meaning students can choose to study anything from applied physics to writing. No matter what major you select—or double major or major and minor—Houghton asks you to look deeply, consider carefully, and question diligently. With a student-faculty ratio of 11:1, Houghton professors serve a critical role—as teachers, mentors, role models, and guides. Involved and engaged, they help students tackle matters academic and spiritual. Over 85 percent hold a doctorate or the highest degree in their field.

What's different at Houghton? Looking for opportunities beyond a traditional classroom setting? Over 50 percent of Houghton students study off campus in places as diverse as Australia, Croatia, Israel, Morocco, Tanzania, and Thailand. Students can work side-by-side with faculty in Houghton's Summer Research Institute, participate in development work in Sierra Leone, or challenge themselves in the interdisciplinary honors program. Houghton's top-notch facilities support and enhance a student's education. Master the art of digital video in Houghton's brand new media commons. Conduct research in the recently updated science center. Strategize stock purchases in the College's state-of-the-art business investment center. Study and enjoy the environment throughout Houghton's 1,300-acre wooded campus.

Students let their competitive side out with Houghton's expanding slate of NCAA Division III athletic teams. Choose from more than 30 official campus clubs and organizations like the Artists' Guild, Climbing Club, Encore Theatre Group, or Global Christian Fellowship.

The future. Houghton helps develop thoughtful, generous, and responsible human beings—people with open minds, deep faith, and compassionate hearts; people who will make an impact on the world.

CONTACT INFORMATION

Mr. Matthew Reitnour, Director of Admission

☎ 585-567-9353 or toll-free 800-777-2556

🖥 admission@houghton.edu

- **Enrollment:** *1,287*
- **Selectivity:** *moderately difficult*
- **Test scores:** *ACT—over 18, 97%; SAT—critical reading over 500, 82.5%; SAT—math over 500, 79.7%*
- **Application deadline:** *Rolling (freshmen), rolling (transfer)*
- **Expenses:** *Tuition $25,460; Room & Board $7330*

There's certainly no shortage of things to do at Houghton, from NCAA D-III athletics to over 30 campus clubs and organizations.

At Hunter we believe the study of studio art is a multi-faceted enterprise of studio practice and courses in the history and theory of art.

HUNTER

The City University of New York

NEW YORK, NEW YORK
www.hunter.cuny.edu/

Hunter College has once again been named one of the "Best 376 Colleges" as determined by an annual survey conducted by *The Princeton Review*. Hunter also made the cut in a number of "Top 20" category lists, including "Lots of Race/Class Interaction" and "Great Financial Aid."

Hunter College has also gone up five slots in one year—to #34—in *U.S. News & World Report*'s annual college rankings of Best Regional

Universities in the North. This continues Hunter's upward trend; the college has gone up a full 18 slots in the rankings in just three years, more than any other CUNY college. Hunter was also recognized in other categories, including "Least Debt" and "Most Diverse."

How did it earn this distinction? For starters, Hunter offers top-notch academic programs that cover more than 100 fields ranging from anthropology to nursing, women's studies to Arabic. Hunter is also the home of world-renowned research centers, including the Center for Study of Gene Structure and Function, the Center for Puerto Rican Studies, and the Brookdale Center on Aging, to name a few.

For fun, students join special interest clubs (Animal Rights Team, Gay Men's Alliance), recreational clubs (Billiards Club, Ultimate Frisbee), and visual and performing arts groups (Hip Hop-ology, Jazz Improv Club). The Hunter Hawks compete in NCAA Division III sports. Men and women have teams in basketball, cross country, fencing, indoor and outdoor track, tennis, and volleyball. Men also compete in soccer and wrestling, and women have swimming and softball teams. The Hunter College Sportsplex is the premier athletic and recreational center in the New York City area. It lies completely underground on the corner of 68th and Lexington and is the deepest building in NYC. The Sportsplex is completely climate controlled and has multiple gyms, racquetball courts, a weight room, and a training room.

Hunter students get to live and study in the heart of Manhattan. Many of the

CONTACT INFORMATION

Welcome Center
☎ 212-772-4490
🖥 admissions@hunter.cuny.edu

world's finest museums, libraries, concert halls, and theaters are just a quick walk away.

- **Enrollment:** *22,407*
- **Selectivity:** *moderately difficult*
- **Test scores:** *SAT—critical reading over 500, 70%; SAT—math over 500, 92%*
- **Application deadline:** *2/1 (freshmen), 2/1 (transfer)*
- **Expenses:** *$5500*

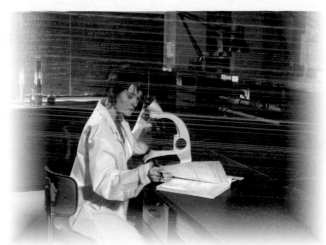

Hunter's newly developed biochemistry program will provide a solid stepping stone for biochemistry students to dive into the exciting field of biomedical research.

Kendall College

RIVERWORKS CAMPUS • CHICAGO

CHICAGO, ILLINOIS
www.kendall.edu/

Kendall College, located near the heart of downtown Chicago, prepares its graduates for exciting opportunities in the fields of business, culinary arts, hospitality management, and early childhood education. Whether choosing Kendall's acclaimed School of Culinary Arts, distinctive School of Hospitality Management, innovative School of Business, or its well-established School of Education, students are encouraged to explore their talents and passions.

Kendall's School of Culinary Arts has prepared outstanding culinary professionals for more than twenty-five years. Its bachelor's and associate degree programs are intensive, hands-on, and cutting-edge—utilizing twelve commercial-grade kitchens, an onsite fine-dining restaurant, and an equally well-regarded cafeteria. Chicago Michelin Guide Restaurants ranked Kendall College the No. 1

Chicago program for preparing students for culinary arts careers.*

Kendall's School of Hospitality Management combines European customer-focused expertise with American management skills. The Bachelor of Arts (B.A.) program offers a variety of concentrations including asset management, casino management, club management, events management, hotel and lodging management, restaurant and foodservice management, and sports and leisure management. Chicago's leading hotels rank Kendall College the No. 1 Chicago program for preparing students for hospitality management careers.*

Kendall's School of Business offers a B.A. program with four concentrations: management, food service management, psychology, and small business management. The curriculum uses situation-based challenges, actual case studies, management simulations, and integrative projects to produce employment-ready graduates.

The School of Education at Kendall offers a B.A. in Early Childhood Education program, with optional Illinois Type 04 Teacher Certification preparation, as well as concentrations in childhood nutrition, English as a second language (ESL), infants and toddlers, and special education.

Kendall College is a member of Laureate International Universities, a global network of more than 60 institutions in 29 countries offering undergraduate and graduate degree programs to 675,000 students worldwide. Through this partnership, students have access to study-abroad programs, internships, and professional opportunities in Asia, Australia, Europe, and Latin America. The school is minutes from some of the country's best restaurants, hotels, and companies, providing students prime access to internships and work experiences. The campus also has amazing views of the Chicago skyline, access to newly developed areas on the Chicago River, and all benefits of being in the third-largest city in the United States.

*(ORC International Survey, 2011; www.kendall.edu)

CONTACT INFORMATION

Ross Rosenberg, Director of Enrollment

☎ toll-free 888-90-KENDALL

🖳 admissions@kendall.edu

- **Enrollment:** *2,050*
- **Selectivity:** *minimally difficult*
- **Test scores:** *ACT—over 18, 77%*
- **Application deadline:** *Rolling (freshmen), rolling (transfer)*
- **Expenses:** *Tuition: Business—$13,545; Culinary Arts—$22,095; Education—$7,500; Hospitality Management—$19,608 Room & Board $10,950*

Any university will take you places.
Kettering will take you farther.

Kettering
UNIVERSITY

FLINT, MICHIGAN
www.kettering.edu/

Kettering University is a nationally ranked institution with programs in engineering, mathematics, business, and science that are richly integrated with hands-on and cooperative learning opportunities. Kettering students graduate with an extraordinary ability to link what they learn in the classroom to real-world, hands-on experiences. It gives Kettering graduates the knowledge to be globally competitive and the soft skills they need to be truly successful.

Kettering offers 14 in-demand undergraduate degrees and 12 graduate degrees, including an MBA. Most classes have fewer than

20 students and are taught by Ph.D.–level professors, not teaching assistants. This combination of small class size and highly qualified faculty members guarantees a personalized learning experience.

Kettering University's innovative cooperative education and experiential learning program provides students with hands-on experiences in both the classroom and the workplace. Students alternate between on-campus study terms and full-time work terms where they are paid professionals at businesses and organizations related to their major. Kettering students have done everything from testing ballistic systems for the U.S. government to re-engineering crowd management at Disney World.

Kettering University has the only co-op and experiential learning program of its kind where students begin working as early as their freshman year. By graduation, students have up to 2½ years of professional experience and impressive resumes. Historically, Kettering students graduate with job offers or graduate school acceptances in hand.

Kettering students also bring a wide range of hobbies and interests to campus. Kettering offers more than 50 student organizations, including 13

fraternities and 6 sororities, student government, and competitive intramural sports. Recreation facilities include athletic fields, an Olympic-size pool, aerobics rooms, a full line of Nautilus equipment, and basketball, tennis, and racquetball courts.

Kettering's home city of Flint is located 60 miles west of Lake Huron and 60 miles north of Detroit. Flint's Cultural Center, just 10 minutes from campus, includes the Sloan Museum, The Whiting Auditorium (home of the Flint Symphony and host to leading shows and entertainers), the Longway Planetarium (Michigan's largest and best-equipped sky show facility), the Flint Institute of Arts, The F.A. Bower Theater, the Flint Institute of Music, Mott Community College, and the Flint Public Library. Within a

CONTACT INFORMATION

Ms. Karen Full, Director,
 International and
 Undergraduate Admissions
☎ 810-762-7496 or toll-free
 800-955-4464 Ext. 7865
⌨ admissions@kettering.edu

few minutes of campus are skiing spots, lakes, public golf courses, indoor and outdoor skating rinks, and many shops and restaurants.

- **Enrollment:** *2,079*

- **Selectivity:** *very difficult*

- **Test scores:** *ACT—over 18, 100%; SAT—critical reading over 500, 87.5%; SAT—math over 500, 95.83%*

- **Application deadline:** *Rolling (freshmen), rolling (transfer)*

- **Expenses:** *Tuition $33,946; Room & Board $6760*

Learn more. Experience more. Achieve more. That's the Kettering Advantage.

LAFAYETTE · COLLEGE

EASTON, PENNSYLVANIA
www.lafayette.edu

Located 70 miles from Manhattan and 60 miles from Center City Philadelphia, Lafayette provides powerful university-size resources in a student-centered, exclusively undergraduate college. All the experiences students need to create their edge are built into their four years. Their rallying cry is the Marquis de Lafayette's family motto, Cur Non ("Why not?"). It means anything is possible here! With Lafayette's muscle and energy, no dream is too wild or ambitious to make happen. It's an unparalleled platform from which students can find their way forward into a complex, rapidly changing world.

One of the nation's highest endowment-per-student rates means powerful resources to provide remarkable academic opportunities. Students cross disciplinary, cultural, and international boundaries to connect in meaningful and valuable ways with faculty members, with each other, and with the world. This high-impact education—with a distinctive cross-disciplinary orientation, high-level research, rigorous small-class discussion, field experiences, community-based learning projects, and global studies—attracts active, engaged learners who achieve a career advantage. In recent years, 94 percent or more of Lafayette's graduating classes have been employed, enrolled in graduate school, or pursuing an internship within six months of graduation.

What do you want to accomplish in the next four years? Lafayette has the muscle and energy to make it happen. The College's university-size resources include a beautiful, historic, high-tech campus.

Students choose from nearly 50 majors in the humanities, social sciences, natural sciences, and engineering. Many work with Lafayette's dedicated professor-mentors to design their own customized major. One of the nation's most academically competitive colleges, Lafayette has recently invested more than $200 million in new and renovated academic, residential, and recreational facilities and provides more than $600,000 each year for collaborative student-faculty research projects that expand the boundaries of knowledge.

Life on College Hill starts with some of the most involved, focused, and active students anywhere. Lafayette has the big energy of 23 NCAA Division I sports, the big variety of many clubs and organizations, the big heart of community service, and the big thrill of the arts. The proximity to New York and Philadelphia means that world-class speakers, artists, and performers visit campus often—and students have phenomenal access to career-shaping internships and externships in an unparalleled variety of professions and industries.

Easton, a picturesque, historic small city in Pennsylvania's third-largest metro area, has a distinctive and beautiful setting at the confluence of the Delaware and Lehigh Rivers. The College Hill neighborhood is a tree-lined residential community, and downtown Easton, with restaurants, shops, galleries, and more, is a short walk from campus.

CONTACT INFORMATION

Mr. Matthew Hyde, Director of Admissions

☎ 610-330-5100

🖥 hydem@lafayette.edu

- **Enrollment:** *2,478*
- **Selectivity:** *most difficult*
- **Test scores:** *ACT—over 18, 100%; SAT—critical reading over 500, 96.95%; SAT—math over 500, 98.57%*
- **Application deadline:** *1/15 (freshmen), 5/1 (transfer)*
- **Expenses:** *Tuition $41,920; Room & Board $12,708*

All the experiences you need to create your edge are built into your four years at Lafayette. It's a powerful platform from which to launch your life.

The experiences you have at LVC should sharpen your intellect, build your skill set, and increase your options for the future.

Lebanon Valley College

ANNVILLE, PENNSYLVANIA
www.lvc.edu
www.facebook.com/LebanonValleyCollege

Founded in 1866 and located just minutes from Hershey, Pennsylvania, Lebanon Valley College (LVC) is an exciting place to be! LVC boasts a remarkable student body, an exceptional faculty, and academic programs that emphasize experience-based education. LVC's 1,630 undergraduates are taught by full-time faculty members, not graduate assistants. A 13:1 student-faculty ratio ensures that students have direct access to their faculty and mentors. Students enjoy a beautiful campus with more than 340 acres of award-winning academic and athletic facilities.

LVC has received national recognition for its generous and distinctive merit-based scholarship program, which rewards strong high school performance with automatic merit scholarships. Students who graduate in the top 30 percent of their high school class qualify for an LVC scholarship worth up to one-half the cost of tuition. Need-based financial assistance and additional merit awards are also available. Overall,

98 percent of LVC students receive some form of financial assistance.

The College is well-known for its collaborative research. Many LVC students co-author articles or present their work at professional conferences. This experiential learning supports independent student research, internships, and student-faculty research across all disciplines. The College offers 34 undergraduate majors, individualized majors, and a range of minors and concentrations; graduate programs in physical therapy, business, music, and science education; and pre-professional programs in dentistry, law, medicine, ministry, pharmacy, and veterinary medicine.

Students can study abroad in 11 countries or in Philadelphia or Washington, D.C.; participate in more than 90 organizations and clubs; or compete on one of the 24 intercollegiate athletic teams.

LVC's strong advising, straightforward requirements, and outstanding student support services mean that its students are able to graduate in four years at rates far above national averages. LVC's Career Services' staff members help students with career research, establish contacts with potential employers, and offer seminars on resume writing and interviewing skills.

The LVC admission process is selective, and the applicant's academic record is the most important factor in admission decisions. The College seeks students from a variety of backgrounds as well as those who display leadership abilities, a commitment to community involvement, and special talents or interests that might benefit or enrich the LVC community.

CONTACT INFORMATION

William J. Brown Jr.

☎ 866-LVC-4ADM (866-582-4236, toll-free)

💻 admission@lvc.edu

To apply, students should visit www.lvc.edu/admission.

- **Enrollment:** *1,630*
- **Selectivity:** *selective*
- **Application deadline:** *Rolling*
- **Expenses:** *Tuition and Fees $34,470; Room & Board $9180*

At LVC, you will find a campus community that is close knit and welcoming.

*Dolphy Day, the College's
annual spontaneous
celebration of spring, means
music, games, and spending
time relaxing with friends.*

LE MOYNE

SPIRIT. INQUIRY. LEADERSHIP. JESUIT.

SYRACUSE, NEW YORK

www.lemoyne.edu/

https://www.facebook.com/LeMoyne

Le Moyne College is the perfect choice for undergrads who know
what they want to do with their lives and for those who are still deciding what they want their contribution to the world to be. One of only
twenty-eight Jesuit colleges and universities in the United States,
Le Moyne College uniquely balances a comprehensive liberal arts
education with preparation for a career or graduate study.

Students choose from more than 30 bachelor's degree programs in
the humanities, science, nursing, business, and education. Master's
degrees are offered in business administration, education, nursing,
and physician assistant studies. The College's newest facility, a state-
of-the-art science center, opened in 2012. The 48,000-square-foot
facility includes cutting-edge facilities for faculty-mentored student
research as well as spaces for students and faculty members to

gather informally; the science building was carefully designed and constructed to minimize its environmental impact.

Out of the classroom, Le Moyne students participate in more than 70 clubs and organizations on campus. Le Moyne is home to a student newspaper, *The Dolphin*, and a student-run television and radio station. Most undergraduates live in residence halls, apartments, and townhouses on campus. The Residence Hall Councils and the Le Moyne Student Programming Board organize a variety of activities, including concerts, dances, a weekly film series, student talent shows, and off-campus trips

Le Moyne is home to 17 intercollegiate sports—8 for men and 9 for women. Intramural sports are very popular with Le Moyne students, too; nearly 85 percent of the students play wallyball, basketball, indoor soccer, and more. Athletic facilities include softball and baseball fields and soccer and lacrosse fields; tennis, basketball, and racquetball courts; a weight-training and fitness center; practice fields; and two gyms. The College's recreation center houses an Olympic-size indoor swimming pool, a jogging track,

indoor tennis and volleyball courts, and additional basketball, racquetball, and fitness areas.

Le Moyne's 160-plus acre, tree-lined campus is located 10 minutes from downtown Syracuse, which offers year-round entertainment in the form of rock concerts at the Landmark Theatre, movies at the Bristol Omnitheatre, professional baseball and hockey, and the Everson Museum of Art—as well as one-of-a-kind restaurants, pubs, and coffeehouses in Armory Square. Just a few miles outside the city are hills and miles of open country for swimming, boating, hiking, skiing, snowboarding, and golf.

CONTACT INFORMATION

Mr. Dennis J. Nicholson, Dean of Admission

☎ 315-445-4300 or toll-free 800-333-4733

🖳 admission@lemoyne.edu

- **Enrollment:** *3,533*
- **Selectivity:** *moderately difficult*
- **Test scores:** *ACT—over 18, 96%; SAT—critical reading over 500, 70%; SAT—math over 500, 77%*
- **Application deadline:** *2/1 (freshmen), 8/1 (transfer)*
- **Expenses:** *Tuition $27,340; Room & Board $10,480*

*One of the first two buildings at Le Moyne, Grewen Hall today houses classrooms, faculty and administrative offices, and the Dolphin Den, a place for students to relax or have a bite to eat between classes. It is also the home to the College's student newspaper, **The Dolphin,** and radio station, WLMU.*

Members of the Fashion Show Production Club pose with Phillip Bloch after the annual Spring Fashion Show at Roseland Ballroom.

LIM COLLEGE

NEW YORK, NEW YORK
www.limcollege.edu
www.facebook.com/LIMCollege

LIM College focuses on the business aspects of the fashion industry. LIM offer four majors: Fashion Merchandising, Marketing, Management, and Visual Merchandising, so it is safe to say that the business of fashion is its specialty. LIM's "concrete campus" is nestled in the Midtown East section of Manhattan, and 5th Avenue is a student's hallway as he or she moves from building to building. This fabulous location provides LIM's students with opportunities galore including showrooms, major fashion magazines, and the garment district—all within walking distance. LIM College's luxury, state-of-the-art, residence hall is located on the Upper East Side, just a few blocks from Central Park. Move-in-ready rooms feature flat screen televisions, private bathrooms, and many more extravagant amenities.

LIM College is a small private school and prides itself on the mentorship its faculty and staff members are able to provide its students. The average class size is 17, and the student-to-teacher ratio is 9:1. So, if you are looking for a school where you are going to be a name and not just another number, look no further.

LIM College has a diversified curriculum that keeps students engaged in their learning experience. The in-class learning provides an excellent balance of business, fashion, and liberal arts classes. The most distinctive features of LIM's academic programs are the opportunities for hands-on learning and the College's ability to bring all of the networking advantages of New York City to its students. Many schools give their students the opportunity to take an internship. At LIM College, all students are *required* to take at least three internships. Students graduate from LIM College with a degree in one hand and a resume in the other, which definitely gives students a leg up in today's competitive job market. If you are a business savvy student who likes to learn in the field, LIM College will be a great fit for you.

Networking opportunities extend both inside and outside of the classroom. Every LIM College student is provided with business cards from day one to help them form connections with today's industry leaders. LIM's Career Development Office tweets daily volunteer opportunities within the city, such as fashion shows, product launches, and much more, to help students build their resumes and meet the people in the industry they need to meet. LIM's Fashion Insiders series brings luminaries

CONTACT INFORMATION

Ms. Kristina Ortiz, Assistant Dean of Admissions

☎ 212-752-1530 Ext. 217 or toll-free 800-677-1323

🖳 admissions@limcollege.edu

from the industry to speak on campus and share their insight with students.

You don't have to wait to get some of this great experience. LIM's Fashion Lab pre-college programs, which allow high school students to take classes, on weekends or over the summer, are a fun and informative way to explore the industry.

New students relax during a spring welcome back party.

Want to have lunch with your Dean of Students? Happens at Lynchburg all the time!

LYNCHBURG
C O L L E G E EST. 1903

LYNCHBURG, VIRGINIA
www.lynchburg.edu/

Lynchburg College—included in *Princeton Review*'s "*The Best 376 Colleges: 2012 Edition*"—offers 39 majors and 45 minors in the liberal arts, sciences, and professional disciplines and graduate programs in English, history, music, business, education, and nursing. A Doctorate of Physical Therapy program began in the fall of 2010, followed by a Doctorate in Educational Leadership in 2011.

The 214-acre campus has long been considered one of the most beautiful in the South with the majestic Blue Ridge Mountains as a backdrop. The Claytor Nature Study Center, a 470-acre farm in nearby Bedford County, is used as an environmental and educational learning laboratory and is home to the Belk Astronomical Observatory, a 700-square-foot facility with an RC Optical Systems 20-inch (0.51 meter) Truss Ritchey-Chretien telescope. There is also a 384-square-foot observation deck equipped with twelve piers for mounting smaller telescopes. An observatory control room has instrumentation that allows LC to conduct research in conjunction with other colleges and universities. The Annual Student Scholar Showcase is an opportunity for students to present their research in many academic areas. Each student has a faculty mentor who advises them throughout the process. Student projects may include scholarly papers, creative writing projects, scientific or historical research projects, or performance arts projects and may be presented in a variety of formats, including oral presentations and poster presentations.

Many activities are open to the Lynchburg College community: service and honor groups; more than 100 clubs and organizations; fraternities and sororities; student publications, and musical groups. Community service is an important part of the Lynchburg experience—students and staff and faculty contributed more than 70,000 hours to the community last year through projects like Habitat for Humanity, Camp Jaycees, and Special Olympics. Nearly 30 percent of the 2012 graduating class participated in a variety of study-abroad programs. The College has set a strategic goal that 50 percent of students will participate in a study-abroad experience to broaden their knowledge and intelligence of global society and understanding. Study-abroad programs vary in lengths of time, which also allows students to have more than one abroad experience.

The varsity athletic program (NCAA Division III) includes baseball, basketball, cheerleading, cross-country, equestrian sports, golf, indoor/outdoor track and field, lacrosse, soccer, and

tennis for men and basketball, cheerleading, cross-country, equestrian sports, field hockey, lacrosse, soccer, softball, tennis, indoor/outdoor track and field, and volleyball for women. Other students join club sports, including cycling, skiing, snowboarding, and karate.

The Turner Athletic Facility includes state-of-the-art exercise and fitness areas, a dance studio, and one of the top exercise physiology labs in Virginia. Shellenberger Field boasts a brand new artificial turf field, an eight-lane track, 3,000-spectator capacity including chair and bleacher seating, and night lighting. Also included are Moon Field upgrades—a permanent softball outfield fence and new areas for track and field events. The baseball field, Fox Field, was updated recently to include seating for up to 1,000 fans, batting cages, and a press box.

CONTACT INFORMATION

Ms. Sharon Walters-Bower, Director of Admissions

☎ 434-544-8300 or toll-free 800-426-8101

🖳 admissions@lynchburg.edu

Lynchburg College is located in central Virginia, 100 miles from Richmond, 180 miles southwest of Washington, D.C., and 50 miles east of Roanoke. The city of Lynchburg is noted for its climate, culture, and historic landmarks.

- **Enrollment:** *2,828*
- **Selectivity:** *moderately difficult*
- **Test scores:** *ACT—over 18, 85%; SAT—critical reading over 500, 52%; SAT—math over 500, 51%*
- **Application deadline:** *Rolling (freshmen), rolling (transfer)*
- **Expenses:** *Tuition $29,905; Room & Board $8020*

Have a group project to work on or want to take a break from studying? The Westover Room patio is a great place!

Manhattan College students enjoy some downtime in Cafe 1853.

MANHATTAN COLLEGE

RIVERDALE, NY
www.manhattan.edu
http://www.facebook.com/ManhattanCollegeEdu

Manhattan College is a private, independent, co-educational Catholic college in the Lasallian tradition. The College offers some 40 major fields of study within five undergraduate schools, guided by an internationally recognized faculty, sought-after leaders, and real-world consultants in their fields, 96 percent of whom hold doctoral degrees. Students have opportunities to study abroad in more than 30 countries.

The student body of 3,000 consists of students from 39 states and 59 countries. With a four-year guarantee of resident housing, 82 percent of freshmen choose to live on campus. Throughout the academic year, there are many activities offered at the College, which creates a community atmosphere for the entire student body.

Manhattan College is located in the Riverdale section of New York City, giving students a beautiful tree-lined neighborhood, just a short distance from the heart of midtown. The campus' 22 acres provide students with a peaceful environment, with the knowledge that all cultural, business, and educational experiences New York City has to offer is a quick subway, bus, or car ride away.

Each year more than 300 students find internships in their field of study. Students participate in internships throughout the metropolitan area, gaining experience in the fields they are studying. With so many college alumni living in the tri-state area, networking opportunities are in every academic offering.

Manhattan College is one of the few American colleges to have chapters of all five of these distinguished national honor societies: Beta Gamma Sigma, Kappa Delta Pi, Phi Beta Kappa (nation's oldest and most widely know

academic honor society), Sigma Xi, and Tau Beta Pi.

Both commuters and residents can take advantage of the campus life, including the Fitness Center, newly renovated cafeterias, and the O'Malley Library. There are various dining options, as well as spaces to relax while watching flat screen televisions. Manhattan's O'Malley Library is a state-of-the-art facility featuring modern accommodations for study and research. There are over 80 different clubs and organizations students take part in. In addition, the college has 19 Division I sports teams.

The College is currently in the building phase of a new student center, which will include a 1,200-square-foot fitness center, cafeterias, lounges, offices for student clubs, and much more.

CONTACT INFORMATION

William J. Bisset
Vice President for Enrollment
    Management
Manhattan College
Riverdale, New York 10471
United States
☎ 718-862-7200
    800-MC2-XCEL (toll-free)
💻 admit@manhattan.edu
    http://www.manhattan.edu

Manhattan College offers many financial aid programs including academic scholarships, athletic awards, endowed scholarships, grants, campus employment, state and federal grants, loans, and work-study programs.

Manhattan College students often cross paths in the quad as they head to class.

Manhattanville College's NCAA Division III Men's and Women's Hockey Teams are nationally ranked.

Manhattanville
COLLEGE

PURCHASE, NEW YORK
www.manhattanville.edu/

On its 100-acre campus 30 minutes north of New York City, Manhattanville College has created a small global village. This private college offers more than 50 bachelor's degree programs, ranging from Liberal Arts to Environmental Science, and professional concentrations in areas such as Business and Museum Studies. Many students pursue their studies in Manhattanville's competitive performing arts programs, which range from dance therapy and studio art to music management and musical theatre. In addition, many students choose to continue their education at Manhattanville, earning masters degrees in Sports Management, Education, and Creative Writing. Finally, many students choose to spend a "semester abroad" living, interning, and studying in the city; others head a bit farther away to explore South Africa, Spain, Germany, or Japan.

Back home on campus, students enjoy the many clubs (Irish Step Dancing to Rugby), as well as the chocolate fountain in the dining hall and the cheese fries in the pub. In between classes, students meet up with friends in the Game Zone, Manhattanville's own arcade and rec center that underwent a complete renovation in 2012. With its Olympic-size ping-pong table, arcade games, foosball table, Jukebox, gaming kiosk, and video wall with seven TV monitors, this is truly a gamer and techie paradise.

Manhattanville students know how to have fun, but they also have a sense of purpose. Last year, undergrads logged 30,000 hours of community service through the College's close ties with organizations such as the American Cancer Society, local Humane Societies, and Habitat for Humanity. Manhattanville's global perspective is enriched by its role as a Non-Government Organization of the United Nations. Select

students have an opportunity to intern at the UN and to study with an ambassador on Manhattanville's faculty. In addition, the College offers a Meet the Ambassadors Series on campus, where students attend lectures by leading ambassadors followed by dinner at the home of the College's president.

Manhattanville's campus lies in the heart of Westchester County, bordered on the east by Long Island Sound and on the west by the Hudson River. From the roof of the castle that serves as the campus' main hall, students have a clear view of Manhattan's skyline. The College provides transportation to the city on weekends and to Manhattan-bound commuter trains during the week so students can take advantage of all New York City has to offer.

CONTACT INFORMATION

Kevin O'Sullivan, Director of Admissions
☎ 914-323-5464 or toll-free 800-328-4553
💻 admissions@mville.edu

- **Enrollment:** *2,796*

- **Selectivity:** *moderately difficult*

- **Application deadline:** *3/1 (freshmen), 3/1 (transfer)*

- **Expenses:** *Tuition $34,350; Room & Board $13,920*

Reid Castle, a beautiful replica of a 19th century Norman castle, is the centerpiece of Manhattanville College.

Forty percent of Menlo College students participate in NAIA sports. The Department of Athletics complements the Menlo College experience by developing leaders who take initiative in their teams.

MENLO
C O L L E G E
Silicon Valley's Business School
ATHERTON, CALIFORNIA
www.menlo.edu/

Menlo College stands out among colleges and universities in five exciting ways: programs, location, small size, sports, and alumni. Rather than offer a traditional set of majors as many schools do, Menlo provides excellent programs in business management with a strong foundation in the liberal arts. The College is small enough to be a real community but large enough to support a ton of intercollegiate sports, student organizations and internship opportunities. Menlo's distinguished alumni provide a strong base of support for graduates, which helps students make the transition from college to career with great success.

A Menlo education is a process that trains and cultivates leaders. This process begins with a broad-based liberal arts education in the humanities, mathematics, sciences, and social sciences. Next, students take on major programs with faculty members who are experts in their respective fields. The advantage is a cutting-edge curriculum that equips students to succeed. Menlo's superior business program is renowned throughout the world and has produced generations of dynamic and successful business, industrial, and civic leaders.

The learning process does not end in the classroom. Students are encouraged to participate in internships and study-abroad programs that bridge the gap between theory and practice. These opportunities range from Fortune 500 companies to innovative start-up enterprises, from San Francisco to South America, Asia, and Europe.

Students join a variety of clubs or organizations, ranging from the Alpha Chi National Honor Society and the Poetry, Art, and Music Society to the newspaper and the Outdoor Club. Menlo offers NAIA sports in men's baseball, basketball, cross-country, football, golf, soccer, and wrestling and in women's basketball, cross-country, soccer, softball, volleyball, and wrestling. Menlo also offers Competitive Cheerleading.

Menlo College is located on the San Francisco peninsula, near the cities of Menlo Park and Palo Alto. The area ranks among the most attractive and exciting in the world, with a wide range of outdoor activities to do in a mild climate. The campus is in the heart of Silicon Valley, where high-tech companies in the electronics, computer, aerospace, biotechnology, and pharmaceutical industries are literally transforming the world in which we live and work. Surrounding the San Francisco Bay Area is the great natural beauty of northern California, extending from the spectacular California coast to the majestic Sierra Nevada Mountains. Favorite spots such as Big Sur, Monterey Bay, Lake Tahoe, Napa Valley, and Yosemite National Park are just a few hours' drive from Menlo.

CONTACT INFORMATION

Office of Admissions
☎ 800-55-MENLO (toll-free)
✉ admissions@menlo.edu

- **Enrollment:** *642*

- **Selectivity:** *moderately difficult*

- **Test scores:**
  Minimum ACT: 16
  Minimum Combined SAT: 1200

- **Application deadline:** *Rolling (freshmen), rolling (transfer)*

- **Expenses:** *Tuition $35,510; Room & Board $11,111*

Menlo College provides students with the knowledge, skills, and abilities that ensure graduates an effective leading edge in a global business environment where the only constant is change.

Fall Fest and Family Weekend.

MERCYHURST UNIVERSITY

ERIE, PENNSYLVANIA
www.mercyhurst.edu
www.facebook.com/HurstU

Now is the perfect time to look at Mercyhurst University. This past year, Mercyhurst went from being a college to being a University! Why is that important? You'll get the same top-notch education, from the same internationally-renowned professors, in the same small school setting, but you'll now have more opportunities for research and international travel.

Mercyhurst University students choose from more than 100 academic majors, minors, and concentrations in a variety of areas, including art, business, education, forensics (real applied forensic science), humanities, intelligence studies (want to work for the FBI or CIA?), interior design, fashion merchandising, sciences, sports medicine/athletic training, and much more. The new Center for Academic Engagement is scheduled to open in fall 2012 and will house the University's intelligence, hospitality management, and applied politics programs. Regardless of your major, you are guaranteed a hands-on education experience—you'll apply what you learn in the classroom to real-world situations and have access to the outstanding members of Mercyhurst's faculty.

The Mercyhurst Laker athletes are champions on and off the playing field. In 2011, 17 teams qualified for conference tournaments (3 won the title), 11 qualified for the NCAA playoffs, and one captured the national title (men's lacrosse). Mercyhurst University had 67 All-Conference athletes, 14 All-Americans, 6 Players of the Year, and, most importantly, 2 ESPN The Magazine Academic All-Americans.

In addition to sports, there are more than 80 student clubs and organizations. Most students live on campus in one of several residence halls, including upperclassmen

apartments and townhouses. The Student Activities Council organizes a variety of campus events, including concerts, comedians, formal dances, Spring Fest, off-campus trips, and guest lecturers.

Mercyhurst's 75-acre residential campus is located 3 miles from downtown Erie, which offers a wide variety of entertainment options, including concerts, professional sports, performing arts events at the historic Warner Theatre, and the Erie Art Museum, as well as several dining and shopping options. Erie is conveniently located within 2 hours of three major metropolitan cities: Buffalo, New York; Cleveland, Ohio; and Pittsburgh, Pennsylvania.

CONTACT INFORMATION

Christopher Coons, Associate Vice President, Enrollment Management
☎ 814-824-2202 or toll-free 800-825-1926
🖥 ccoons@mercyhurst.edu

- **Enrollment:** *4,298*
- **Selectivity:** *moderately difficult*
- **Test scores:** *ACT—over 20, 94%; SAT—critical reading over 500, 67%; SAT—math over 500, 69%*
- **Application deadline:** *Rolling (freshmen), rolling (transfer)*
- **Expenses:** *Tuition $27,150, Room & Board $10,104*

Old Main, the signature building on campus, at night.

Michigan Tech offers more than 130 degree programs in engineering; forest resources; computing; technology; business; economics; natural, physical, and environmental sciences; arts; humanities; and social sciences.

Create the Future

HOUGHTON, MICHIGAN

www.mtu.edu/admissions

At Michigan Technological University, students can be crazy—building 30-foot snow statues, tearing up fresh powder on the University's ski hill, or spending all night embattled in a group gaming competition.

And they are definitely smart—they have created a prosthetic knee joint for amputees in developing countries, invested more than $1 million of real money through the School of Business and Economics' Applied Portfolio Management Program, and designed and built a newer and more aerodynamic solar car.

The best part is that at Michigan Tech, they can be both. Michigan Tech is where the crazy and the smart come together.

Michigan Tech is a leading public research university, offering more than 130 degree programs in arts; business; computing; economics; engineering; forest resources; humanities; natural, physical, and environmental sciences; social sciences; and technology—all with a reputation for extraordinary hands-on learning.

Research is a big deal at Michigan Tech. The university's undergraduate students get involved from the beginning, helping with new developments, working with industry sponsors—even getting their names included on patents. Michigan Tech's Enterprise program allows students to manage their own real-world research projects and business ventures. Students work in teams alongside faculty members and corporate sponsors to create products and develop solutions to some of industry's—and the world's—most vexing problems.

When class is over, students at Michigan Tech find plenty to keep themselves busy. There are more than 200 student organizations to choose from—everything from intramural sports to Greek life to Engineers Without Borders—plus campus leadership positions; outdoor adventures like skiing, hiking, and biking; Division I and II athletics; great theater and live music; and that legendary ski hill—not to mention the largest freshwater lake in the world (Lake Superior), just miles from campus.

Head to www.mtu.edu/admissions, and you can learn all about Michigan Tech. Better yet, schedule a visit and see for yourself what a crazy smart student—and campus—looks like.

- **Enrollment:** *7,034*

- **Selectivity:** *moderately difficult*

- **Test scores:** *ACT—over 18, 99.82% (average ACT score is 26.4); SAT—critical reading over 500, 90.09%; SAT—math over 500, 91.08%*

CONTACT INFORMATION

Ms. Allison Carter, Director of Admissions

☎ 906-487-1888 or toll-free 888-MTU-1885

🖥 mtu4u@mtu.edu

- **Application deadline:** *Rolling (freshmen), rolling (transfer)*

- **Expenses:** *Tuition $13,095; Room & Board $8865*

Michigan Tech is located in Houghton, Michigan, in the heart of the Upper Peninsula. Surrounded by natural beauty, Tech students understand the importance of balancing sustainability, technology, and innovation.

Find your purpose at MNU.

MIDAMERICA
NAZARENE UNIVERSITY

OLATHE, KANSAS
www.mnu.edu
https://www.facebook.com/MNUPioneers

MidAmerica Nazarene University (MNU) understands that a life lived to its fullest is a life filled with purpose. It is for that reason that MNU students are encouraged to explore their talents, pursue their interests, serve the global community, and celebrate their faith.

MNU students live and learn in a Christ-Centered community located within easy commuting distance of Kansas City. Students not only study with faculty members who are experts in their respective fields, but they also intern at some of the best known companies in corporate America. Whether your interests lead you to the KC Royals, Hallmark,

Waddell & Reed Investments, the American Heart Association, or the Chamber of Commerce, you will find opportunities to apply what you learn in the classroom to real life.

MidAmerica's graduates are recognized locally, regionally, and nationally for their accomplishments. No matter which of MNU's more than 35 majors you choose, you can be assured that you will join a community of engaged students and successful graduates. MidAmerica Nazarene's nursing graduates exceed both state and national averages for first time passing rates on their licensure examination. Education majors average a 99 percent pass rate on state content exams.

And no matter what their major, students find opportunities to serve through mission trips. Recently MNU students traveled to Guatemala, Australia, Peru, Kenya, Bulgaria, Haiti, and Romania.

MidAmerica students understand that the questions they ask are as important as the answers they receive. They fully embrace life both in and out of the classroom. They recognize how to lead and when to follow. You will find them on the athletic field and in the theater. You will meet fellow students who respect one another's talents. You will discover lifelong friends and colleagues. You will discover the difference that is MidAmerica Nazarene University.

CONTACT INFORMATION

Office of Admissions
☎ 913-971-3380 or toll-free 800-800-8887
🖳 admissions@mnu.edu

- **Enrollment:** *895 traditional undergraduate*
- **Selectivity:** *Moderately difficult*
- **Test scores:** *ACT—over 18, 71%*
- **Application deadline:** *Rolling*
- **Expenses:** *Tuition $20,500; Room and Board $7000*

A calling or a career? How about both! Find them at MNU.

Health science majors, including nurses, find excellent resources and personal attention at Misericordia University.

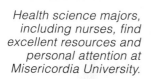

MISERICORDIA UNIVERSITY

DALLAS, PENNSYLVANIA

www.misericordia.edu/
www.facebook.com/misericordiauniversity

Misericordia University is a high-quality liberal arts and professional studies university set on a beautiful suburban campus in Northeast Pennsylvania. With 37 degree programs including health sciences, business, natural sciences, and education, Misericordia is highly personalized to help students succeed both professionally and personally. In the National Survey of Student Engagement, Misericordia students say they are more involved in learning and have better relationships with faculty members and peers than students at other similar institutions. Misericordia is also ranked in the top tier of *U.S. News & World Report*'s "Best Colleges 2012" in the Master's North category.

Misericordia has comfortable residence halls and townhouses right on campus—including a brand new residence facility for 2012 with integrated classrooms. The new dining hall is located in the Banks Student Life Center, which also houses the Cougar's Den coffeehouse and the newly renovated Student Union.

Cultural events, Campus Ministry, intramural and inter-collegiate athletics (includ-ing a new football team for 2012), performing arts shows, and art exhibits in the Pauly Friedman Art Gallery all add to the academic experience. In keeping with the Sisters of Mercy Catholic tradition of mercy, justice, service, and hospitality, the University engages students in the development of lifelong civic responsibility through course work. On spring break, students have served those in need in dozens of locations in the United States and around the world.

As part of Misericordia's "learn to succeed" promise, the University offers a guar-anteed career placement program. If a student fulfills the requirements of this program and is not employed in his or her field or enrolled in graduate or professional school within six months of graduation, a paid internship is assured.

Misericordia has bachelor's, master's, and doctoral programs for adults, including Expressway, an accelerated degree program; Women with Children, which provides housing and support for single women with children; and evening, online, and weekend formats for people with families and full-time jobs. Master's degrees are avail-able in education, nursing, occupational therapy, physician assistant, speech-language pathology, busi-ness administration, and organizational management. A doctoral program in physi-cal therapy is available to students, and a doctoral program in occupational therapy is available for gradu-ate students via part-time study.

Misericordia University is 9 miles from the city of Wilkes-Barre. The area offers shop-ping centers, malls, skiing, and professional sports. Pennsylvania's largest natural lake and two state parks are nearby, as are the Pocono Mountains.

Students find many spaces to relax on Misericordia's beautiful suburban campus.

- **Enrollment:** *2,830*
- **Selectivity:** *moderately difficult*
- **Test scores:** *ACT— over 18, 99%; SAT—critical reading over 500, 69%; SAT—math over 500, 76%*
- **Application deadline:** *Rolling (freshmen), rolling (transfer)*
- **Expenses:** *Tuition $24,990; Room & Board $10,410*

CONTACT INFORMATION

Mr. Glenn Bozinski, Director of Admissions

☎ 570-675-6264 or toll-free 866-262-6363

💻 admiss@misericordia.edu

The Mitchell College experience offers the personal attention of a small college with emphasis on practical experience. Regardless of the length of their time on campus, Mitchell graduates leave prepared to make a contribution in the workplace.

The First-Year College is a program that facilitates a smooth transition to campus life. Mentored by Mitchell's best professors, freshman learning communities engage in projects centered on a common theme—for example, sports, global studies, or arts and entertainment.

A member of the NCAA Division III New England Collegiate Conference (NECC), Mitchell has a history of athletic excellence. Its teams have won both regional and national championship titles. Men's teams include baseball, basketball, cross-country, golf, lacrosse, soccer, and tennis; women's teams include basketball, cross-country, golf, soccer, softball, tennis, and volleyball. Sailing is a co-ed intercollegiate sport.

Mitchell's academic programs prepare students for careers in

Main gate and Duques Center, campus center.

NEW LONDON, CONNECTICUT
http://www.mitchell.edu

many fields, including business, health sciences, law enforcement, hospitality, and homeland security. The vast majority of students have an internship in their field of study, which, in many instances, leads to a full time position after graduation.

Bordered on one side by sandy beaches of the Thames River, Mitchell College is just minutes from downtown New London, Connecticut, a small but sophisticated city, located between New York and Boston. The city is well known for an active and eclectic music scene and is a center of arts and entertainment. Opportunities for shopping, dining, and fun abound. The waterfront, adjacent to the campus, is used for both recreational and educational purposes.

The traditional campus facilities, such as the gymnasium and fitness center, the dining hall and café, the athletic fields, and campus center, are located on a 68-acre campus. In addition to traditional residence halls, upper class students have the option to live off campus or in one of three historic houses on the waterfront.

The Career Center, which gets involved with students from the moment they step on campus, has sponsored a chapter of The National Society of Leadership and Success. Through that organization, Mitchell College has hosted such speakers as Nigel Barker, Al Duncan, Dr. Bertice Barry, and Josh Linkner on campus.

CONTACT INFORMATION

Ms. Susan Bibeau, Vice President of Enrollment Management

☎ 800-443-2811 (toll-free)

🖥 admissions@mitchell.edu

- **Enrollment:** *800*
- **Selectivity:** *moderately difficult*
- **Application deadline:** *Rolling, until the class is filled.*
- **Expenses:** *Tuition $26,774; Room & Board $12,492; Fees $1,720*

Students observe the results of their experiment.

Molloy College

Molloy College, an independent Catholic college based in Rockville Centre, Long Island, serves a student population of approximately 4,400 undergraduate and graduate students. Molloy students can earn degrees in a variety of outstanding academic programs, including nursing, business, education, social work, criminal justice, music therapy, and many more.

For more than fifty years, Molloy has encouraged critical thinking and creative exploration in a personal community setting. Molloy combines the strengths of academic excellence and leadership with personal, compassionate mentoring to bring out the best in every student.

The College has expanded its global learning program, where students travel from Rockville Centre to study abroad in such countries as Belgium, India, Italy, France, Spain, Thailand, and Australia. By immersing themselves in cultures in other parts of the world, students gain knowledge while learning acceptance and understanding.

Closer to home, Molloy College students make a difference in Rockville Centre as well as other nearby local communities. For example, as part of

Molloy's global learning program enables students to study abroad in such countries as Belgium, India, England, Italy, France, Spain, Thailand, and Australia.

Molloy's tradition of service, students become involved in a number of service projects that include BoxTown, a program to raise social consciousness about the issue of homelessness.

Athletics and academics go hand-in-hand at Molloy College, where students are known for both their athletic and scholastic success. The Long Island school has a winning tradition in a number of NCAA Division II athletic programs, and the women's softball team recently made it to the NCAA Super Regionals.

Campus life in Rockville Centre, New York, is alive and vibrant, with more than 40 student clubs and honor societies. In addition, in fall 2011, Molloy opened its first residence hall, which houses more than 150 students. A new student center (which also opened in the fall of 2011) provides opportunities for Molloy students to study, interact with their fellow students, or simply relax.

In recent years, Molloy College has become a focal point for civic discourse with key community forums.

Top regional, national, and international leaders, including former Secretary of State Colin Powell and *New York Times* best-selling author Malcolm Gladwell, have come to Rockville Centre to visit the College to address critical and timely issues.

Through Molloy College's diversity of programs, personal attention from faculty members, and commitment to improving both Long Island and the world, students develop an "I will" attitude that prepares them to enter the professional world— ready and able to make a difference.

CONTACT INFORMATION

Ms. Marguerite Lane, Director of Admissions

☎ 516-678-5000 Ext. 6240 or toll-free 888-4MOLLOY

🖥 admissions@molloy.edu

- **Enrollment:** *4,434*
- **Selectivity:** *moderately difficult*
- **Test scores:** *ACT—over 18, 100%; SAT—critical reading over 500, 63%; SAT—math over 500, 72%*
- **Application deadline:** *Rolling (freshmen), rolling (transfer)*
- **Expenses:** *Tuition $22,130*

Molloy students can join more than 40 clubs or compete in a variety of sports. In 2010, the Molloy softball team became one of only 8 schools in the country to earn a spot in the College World Series.

Personalized education is a hallmark of the Monmouth University experience.

MONMOUTH UNIVERSITY

WHERE LEADERS LOOK *forward*

WEST LONG BRANCH, NEW JERSEY
www.monmouth.edu
www.facebook.com/MonmouthUniversity

With top-tier academic programs in a great location, Monmouth University offers students multiple opportunities to succeed and grow as future leaders. Monmouth students are able to experience the vibrant life of a large university while receiving the individual attention typical of a small college.

Monmouth offers a comprehensive array of undergraduate and graduate degree programs in areas that are in demand in the workplace, including software engineering, healthcare management, music industry, and homeland security. The University is sensitive to the needs of the market and ensures that students have the best opportunity for employment. Classes are taught by experienced faculty members, not teaching assistants, and students receive academic support from special services on campus, such as First Year Advising and Tutoring and Writing Services.

The school's location—approximately 1 hour from both New York City and Philadelphia—makes it equipped to help students link classroom academics with real-world experiences. Students can pursue internships and other opportunities in various offices and settings, including local high-tech firms and financial institutions. Monmouth's ideal location also allows students to have a fun, enriching college experience. The University is 1 mile from the beaches of the Atlantic Ocean, and many restaurants, shops, and theaters are nearby.

At Monmouth, students enjoy one of the most beautiful campuses in New Jersey. The centerpiece of the 156-acre campus is Woodrow Wilson Hall, a National Historic Landmark that was used as Daddy Warbucks' mansion in the film *Annie*. Another unique building is the Jules L. Plangere Jr. Center for Communication, which provides state-of-the-art studios and editing facilities. In addition, depending on academic level, students can live in comfortable, air-conditioned residence halls or off-campus apartment complexes with full kitchens across the street from the beach.

Throughout the year, students and employees cheer on Monmouth's Division I athletics teams. The school fields 21 teams for men and women, including men's lacrosse (new for 2014). Many teams are housed in the 153,200-square-foot Multipurpose Activity Center (MAC), which features a 4,100-seat arena with premium suites, as well as

a fitness center and a 200-meter, six-lane indoor track. Outdoor facilities on campus include tennis courts; an all-weather track; and baseball, football, soccer, and softball fields.

When not attending a Monmouth Hawks game, students can participate in many popular activities, including the campus newspaper *(The Outlook)*, the FM radio station (WMCX), the television station (Hawk TV), intramurals, open mike nights, sororities and fraternities, the Student Government Association, and more than 75 student-run clubs and organizations. Special events run throughout the year, such as the SpringFest outdoor carnival; the International Student Festival; kayaking and whitowater-rafting trips; concerts and movie screenings; student art exhibits; and day trips to museums, theaters,

CONTACT INFORMATION

Office of Undergraduate Admission

☎ 732-571-3456 or toll-free 800-543-9671

🖥 admission@monmouth.edu

and sporting events in New York City and Philadelphia.

- **Enrollment:** *6,568 (Fall 2011)*
- **Selectivity:** *moderately difficult*
- **Test scores:** *ACT— over 18, 100%; SAT— critical reading over 500, 59%; SAT—math over 500, 73%; SAT—writing over 500, 71%*
- **Application deadlines:** *Early Action, 12/1 and Regular Decision, 3/1 (freshmen); Fall Semester, 7/15 and Spring Semester, 12/1 (transfers)*
- **Expenses:** *Tuition & Fees $29,710; Room & Board $10,802*

Monmouth students enjoy a challenging learning environment on a campus that offers classical beauty and the latest technology.

The Mount's 195-acre campus sits atop the beautiful Southern Allegheny Mountains.

CRESSON, PENNSYLVANIA
www.mtaloy.edu
www.facebook.com/mountaloysiuscollege

Mount Aloysius College—close to Pittsburgh, State College, and tons of four-season outdoor fun—is an affordable, private, Catholic liberal arts college welcoming students of all faiths. Established in 1853 by the Sisters of Mercy, the College offers undergraduate and graduate education and lists nearly 14,000 alumni. Committed to small class sizes, 2,500 enrolled students benefit from accessible faculty and staff members. Students come mostly from throughout Pennsylvania and the mid-Atlantic region, but many states are represented.

A member of NCAA Division III, athletic programs include basketball, cross-country, golf, soccer, tennis, men's baseball, women's softball, and volleyball. Athletes benefit from the Walker Athletic Field Complex including a softball and soccer field, and the Calandra-Smith baseball complex. The Mountie Stables were recently opened, adding dugouts, lockers, showers, storage, and concession facilities. A 90,000-square-foot Athletic Convocation and Wellness Center is under construction on the western edge of the beautiful and expansive campus. This facility will open in early 2014, taking Mount Aloysius athletics to a new level and adding a welcomed special events venue to the Southern Allegheny Mountains.

The Mount's iconic main building dates to 1897 and houses admissions, financial aid, the President's Office, classrooms, the region's premiere nursing simulation center, and the Wolf-Kuhn Art Gallery. Cosgrave Center is the hub of campus life and contains the dining hall, snack bar, bookstore, child-care center, lounges, recreation rooms, student affairs, and meeting rooms. The College's Health and Physical Fitness Center is the main athletic arena. Ihmsen Halls are key housing facilities for residential students. Misclayna Residence is a state-of-the-art dormitory providing 25 suites and private baths. McAuley Hall features double and single rooms, a large multipurpose room, and study lounges throughout. Pierce Hall is the campus science center. Alumni Hall is a historic, multipurpose facility used for drama, musicals, lectures, and other performing arts. Smart classrooms

are used throughout, and the campus is 100 percent wireless.

Mount Aloysius is accredited by the Middle States Association of Colleges and Schools and approved by the Pennsylvania Department of Education. Nursing and health studies programs are accredited by their professional accrediting bodies, including the National League for Nursing Accrediting Commission, the Commission on Accreditation for Programs of Diagnostic Medical Sonography, the Commission on Accreditation in Physical Therapy Education, the American Association of Medical Assistants, and the Joint Commission on Accreditation for Programs of Surgical Technology.

- **Enrollment:** *2,500*

- **Selectivity:** *minimally difficult*

- **Test scores:** *ACT—over 18, 71%; SAT—critical reading over 500, 32%; SAT—math over 500, 28%*

- **Application deadline:** *Rolling (freshmen), rolling (transfer)*

- **Expenses:** *Tuition $18,000; Room & Board $8500*

CONTACT INFORMATION

Mr. Frank C. Crouse Jr., Vice President for Enrollment Management/Dean of Admissions

☎ 814-886-6383 or toll-free 888-823-2220

🖥 admissions@mtaloy.edu

Mount Aloysius competes in NCAA Division III sports.

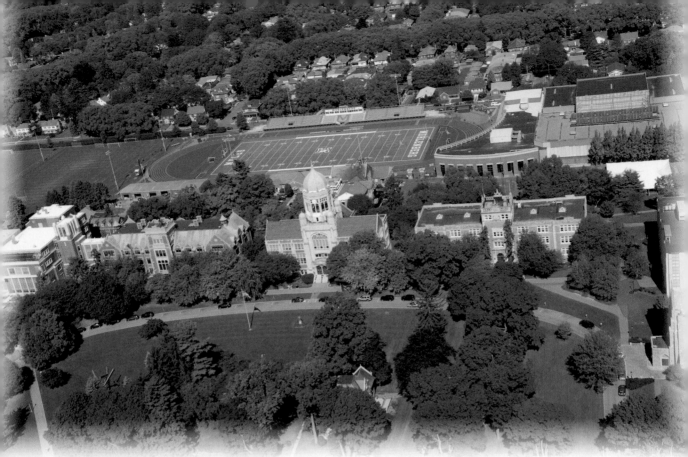

A bird's eye view of Muhlenberg College's 81-acre, scenic suburban campus in Allentown, Pennsylvania.

MUHLENBERG

COLLEGE

ALLENTOWN, PENNSYLVANIA
www.muhlenberg.edu/

Muhlenberg College is a highly selective, private college that attracts independent critical thinkers. Students here choose from 40 majors (and just as many minors) in the humanities, fine arts, social sciences, and natural sciences. Muhlenberg's cutting-edge pre-professional programs prep students interested in pursuing pre-medicine and allied health, pre-law, business, education, and pre–theological studies. About one third of Muhlenberg's graduates head immediately to graduate or professional school.

Muhlenberg is big on service learning (academically based community service projects); in fact, there are service learning courses available in nine different departments.

For fun on the Muhlenberg campus, students jump right into the more than 100 student clubs and organizations from the special interest (Gaming Society) to the academic (History Club) and from media (WMUH Allentown 91.7 FM) to club sports (women's rugby, men's ice hockey). Muhlenberg fields twenty-two intercollegiate teams at the NCAA Division III level. Men compete in baseball, basketball, cross-country, football, golf, lacrosse, soccer, tennis, indoor/outdoor track and field, and wrestling. Women compete in basketball, cross country, field hockey, golf, lacrosse, soccer, softball, tennis, indoor/outdoor track and field, and volleyball. Even more students play intramural or club sports ranging from air hockey to co-ed volleyball. Muhlenberg's state-of-the-art sports facilities include the solar-heated Life Sports Center with basketball, racquetball, and squash

courts; an all-weather outdoor track with AstroTurf Gameday Grass 3D (resurfaced in 2008); and tennis courts built in 2003.

Students are aided by an active Career Planning and Placement Service in relating academic and personal knowledge and skills to appropriate career goals and obtaining positions upon graduation.

Muhlenberg College makes its home in suburban west Allentown. The downtown area of Allentown is a 10-minute ride from the campus. The College is located 90 miles west of New York City and 60 miles north of Philadelphia. The College also maintains a 60-acre arboretum and a 40-acre environmental field station/wildlife sanctuary.

CONTACT INFORMATION

Christopher Hooker-Haring,
Dean of Admission &
Financial Aid
☎ 484-664-3200
🖥 admissions@muhlenberg.edu

- **Enrollment:** *2,483*

- **Selectivity:** *very difficult*

- **Test scores:** *ACT—over 18, 100%; SAT—critical reading over 500, 94.5%; SAT— math over 500, 94.2%*

- **Application deadline:** *2/15 (freshmen), 6/15 (transfer)*

- **Expenses;** *Tuition $38,380; Room & Board $8735*

Students stroll down picturesque academic row.

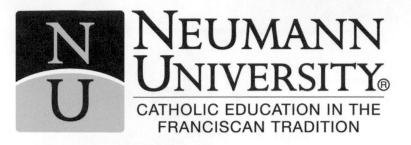

NEUMANN UNIVERSITY®

CATHOLIC EDUCATION IN THE FRANCISCAN TRADITION

ASTON, PENNSYLVANIA
www.neumann.edu

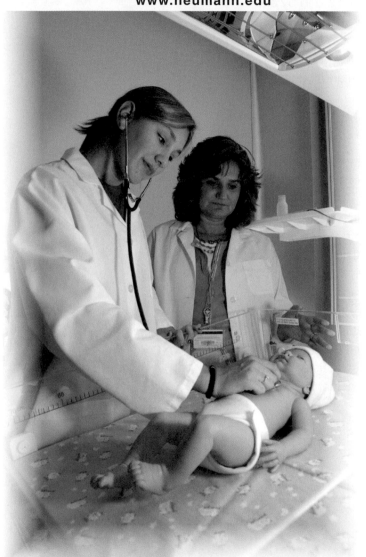

Majors like nursing, biology, athletic training, and clinical laboratory science prepare Neumann students for careers.

Neumann University offers a uniquely personal experience for students, in a campus culture that emphasizes respect for individuals, concern for the environment, and social responsibility.

Located just a half hour outside Philadelphia, Neumann University is committed to first-rate academic instruction and real-world career preparation. This promise reflects Neumann's core philosophy, which is that knowledge is a gift to be shared in the service of others and that learning is a lifelong process.

The University offers degrees in a broad range of subjects and had an enrollment of 2,144 full-time undergraduates in fall 2011. There are internships, co-op placements, or clinical experiences in every field. Some of Neumann's most popular majors are Athletic Training, Business

Administration, Criminal Justice, Education, Nursing, Psychology, and Sport and Entertainment Management. A student-faculty ratio of 13:1 allows professors to provide personal attention to each student.

Neumann is committed to making private higher education affordable through financial aid packages, scholarships, and work-study opportunities. More than 92 percent of Neumann's students receive some kind of financial assistance.

More than 800 students live on campus in residence halls that are air conditioned and provide wireless Internet access. Each suite has its own bathroom accommodations. Campus life is active and welcoming, offering opportunities to form life-long friendships here. Arts and culture are nurtured at Neumann with organizations such as the Neumann University Players, Art Gallery,

Jazz Band, and Concert Chorale.

Athletics are also a central part of the Neumann experience. The Knights field 21 intercollegiate teams that compete in NCAA Division III as members of the Colonial States Athletic Conference (CSAC) and the Eastern Collegiate Athletic Conference. In 2009, the men's ice hockey team won the NCAA Division III national championship, and the University opened the Mirenda Center for Sport, Spirituality and Character Development, a new athletic arena.

Neumann fields 21 NCAA teams and offers health & fitness facilities in the new Mirenda Center.

- **Enrollment:** 3,087
- **Selectivity:** minimally difficult
- **Application deadline:** Rolling
- **Expenses:** Tuition $23,262; Room & Board $11,070

CONTACT INFORMATION

Mr. Dennis J. Murphy, Vice President for Enrollment Management
☎ 610-558-5616 or 800-9NEUMANN (toll-free)
🖳 neumann@neumann.edu

Entrance to East 70th Street building on Manhattan's Upper East Side.

New York School of Interior Design
founded 1916

NEW YORK, NEW YORK
www.nysid.edu

Throughout its history, the New York School of Interior Design (NYSID) has been devoted to a single field of study—interior design—and has played a significant role in the development of the profession. NYSID's curriculum reflects the complex yet sophisticated world of interior design—everything from designing homes to commercial spaces such as offices, hotels, and hospitals.

Courses stress the health, safety, and welfare of the public while also focusing on functionality and beauty. The college offers three undergraduate degree programs: a **Bachelor of Fine Arts (B.F.A.) in Interior Design,** an **Associate in Applied Science (A.A.S.) in Interior Design,** and a **Bachelor of Arts (B.A.) in the History of the Interior and Decorative Arts.**

NYSID also offers five graduate programs to satisfy the creative and professional needs of people aspiring to practice interior design and those well established within the profession. NYSID offers a professional level **Master of Fine Arts (M.F.A.)** degree in Interior Design, a **post-professional level M.F.A.** degree in Interior Design, and **Master of Professional Studies (M.P.S.) degrees in Sustainable Interior Environments, Interior Lighting Design,** and **Healthcare Interior Design.**

Whether learning the importance of historic preservation or the latest programs in computer-aided design, NYSID students gain a wide range of skills and techniques taught by faculty members who work in the field. Because of its esteemed professional faculty and established reputation, the School continues to maintain a close relationship with the interior design industry. This translates into phenomenal internship opportunities and valuable contacts for after graduation.

The New York School of Interior Design is located on Manhattan's Upper East Side, where several major interior design studios are located. Many of the world's finest galleries, museums, and showrooms are within walking distance. The new LEED-Platinum certified Graduate Center, located in the Gramercy/Flatiron area of Manhattan, is also well situated in the design district, nearby the famous New York Design Center and hundreds of showrooms representing leading manufacturers in interior furnishings.

CONTACT INFORMATION

Office of Admissions
☎ 212-472-1500 Ext. 204
💻 admissions@nysid.edu

- **Enrollment:** *707*
- **Selectivity:** *moderately difficult*
- **Test scores:** *SAT—critical reading over 500, 31%; SAT—math over 500, 23%*
- **Application deadline:** *2/1 (freshmen), 2/1 (transfer)*
- **Expenses:**
  Undergraduate tuition plus fees $27,166; Graduate tuition plus fees $23,334–$20,850

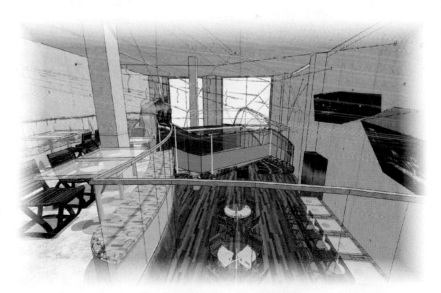

View from the mezzanine level of GoGi Bar, a design project by BFA student Ho Youn Yi.

Overlooking the Niagara River Gorge, Niagara University is located just a few miles north of the world famous Falls and a few minutes from the quaint village of Lewiston, New York. Nearby metropolitan areas include Buffalo, New York, and Toronto, Canada.

NIAGARA UNIVERSITY

Education That Makes a Difference

NIAGARA UNIVERSITY, NEW YORK

www.niagara.edu

www.facebook.com/niagarau

www.twitter.com/NiagaraUniv

Situated high above the Niagara River Gorge in Lewiston, New York, and within a few miles of Niagara Falls, Niagara University (NU) possesses one of the most picturesque campuses in the United States.

And with more than 80 majors, 7 preprofessional options, and combined master's programs, NU students can design a course of study that meets their career goals. All four of the University's academic colleges—Arts and Sciences, Education, Business Administration, and Hospitality and Tourism Management—have received the highest rankings from the top accreditation boards in their fields. The University also offers an award-winning Academic Exploration Program for students entering college without a declared major.

Now is a great time to enroll at Niagara, as the University recently completed a transformational $80-million capital campaign that has significantly upgraded the University's facilities and programs. Within the last six years, major capital improvement projects have been undertaken on NU's scenic campus, each catering to students' varied interests and talents.

Inspired by St. Vincent de Paul, the patron saint of charitable societies, NU students take great pride in helping those less fortunate. In 2011, undergraduates performed more than 56,000 hours of community service, prompting Niagara's inclusion on the President's Higher Education Community Service Honor Roll for a sixth straight year. This is precisely the type of hands-on, practical experience that today's employers crave.

Outside of class, Niagara students can take advantage of dozens of clubs, organizations, and intramural sports teams. There's always something to do on or off campus, including trips to sporting events, local landmarks, and restaurants in the United States and across the border in Canada.

NU student-athletes compete in 18 Division I athletics programs, giving the entire campus community numerous opportunities to put its "Purple Pride" on full display. In addition, the Kiernan Center, Niagara's well-equipped fitness and recreation complex, features an indoor track, swimming pool, weight room, cardio equipment, basketball courts, and an aerobic dance area.

Niagara's cultural community is thriving as well, thanks to a professional-quality theatre program and a nationally renowned art museum residing on campus. Students in search of a more casual outing can stop in the Gallagher Center for a coffee and a muffin or head off for a bike ride along the Niagara Gorge.

Finally, Niagara continues to strengthen the financial aid packages that it offers to students. From merit-based scholarships, achievement awards, and grants to generous monetary assistance for veterans and nurses, Niagara is doing all that it can to help students attain a well-rounded, world-class education.

A recently-completed $80-million capital campaign has furnished Niagara students with several new state-of-the-art facilities, including Bisgrove Hall, home to NU's College of Business Administration.

- **Enrollment:** *4,182*
- **Selectivity:** *moderately difficult*
- **Test scores:** *ACT—over 18, 90%; SAT—critical reading over 500, 50%; SAT—math over 500, 59%*
- **Application deadline:** *8/1 (freshmen), 8/15 (transfer)*
- **Expenses:** *Tuition $26,100; Room & Board $11,300*

CONTACT INFORMATION

Ms. Christine M. McDermott, Associate Director of Admissions

☎ 716-286-8700 Ext. 8715 or toll-free 800-462-2111

🖥 admissions@niagara.edu

NKU students outside Griffin Hall, the home of NKU's new College of Informatics.

NORTHERN KENTUCKY UNIVERSITY

HIGHLAND HEIGHTS, KENTUCKY
www.nku.edu
https://www.facebook.com/#!/nkuedu

Northern Kentucky University (NKU), founded in 1968, is the newest of Kentucky's eight state universities. Students can choose from 70 bachelor's degrees, 6 associate degrees, 20 graduate programs, a Juris Doctor, and a Doctor of Education in Educational Leadership. The most popular bachelor's degree programs are in teacher education, nursing, human resources management and services, psychology, and marketing.

The atmosphere of the campus is futuristic, emphasizing a high-quality education by supporting the liberal arts. Campus buildings are of modern, contemporary design and are set on 300 acres of rolling countryside. NKU opened its $37 million student union building in 2008; it houses a mulitpurpose room for concerts and comedians, a fully equipped game room, seven dining spots (including a Starbucks), and outdoor areas for lounging and studying. The state-of-the-art, $60 million Bank of Kentucky Center also opened in 2008. This arena is the home of the NKU basketball teams; it seats 9,400 fans and also has a study lab, media room, and top-of-the-line workout and physical therapy rooms.

There are more than 200 student organizations to pick from at NKU—from the Wiffle Ball Club to the Students for 9/11 Truth. Student athletes compete in the NCAA Division I Atlantic Sun Conference. Men and women play intercollegiate sports in basketball, cheerleading, cross-country, golf, soccer, tennis, and track. Men also

NKU men's soccer team clinches the NCAA championship.

compete in baseball, and women also compete in fast pitch softball and volleyball. Intramurals include basketball, dodgeball, field hockey, flag football, ice hockey, racquetball, soccer, softball, Tae Kwan Do, and volleyball.

NKU is located in the largest metropolitan area of any state university in Kentucky. It is located 8 miles southeast of Cincinnati, Ohio, and only 60 miles from Dayton, 79 miles from Lexington, 93 miles from Louisville, and 114 miles from Indianapolis. While the immediate area is suburban, NKU is part of the metropolitan area of greater

Cincinnati—where many students find internships through the United Way, the Kentucky Symphony Orchestra, the U.S. Secret Service, and so many other organizations.

- **Enrollment:** *15,724*
- **Selectivity:** *moderately difficult*
- **Test scores:** *ACT—over 18, 92.80%, SAT—critical reading over 500, 48.02%; SAT—math over 500, 46.18%*
- **Application deadline:** *7/15 (freshmen), 8/1 (transfer)*
- **Expenses:** *Tuition $7872; Room & Board $6650*

Two students from the Corps of Cadets walk along the Upper Parade Ground.

Norwich University

NORTHFIELD, VERMONT
www.norwich.edu
www.facebook.com/
NorwichUniversity

Norwich University was established in 1819 as the first private military college in America. It was at Norwich that the idea of the citizen-soldier developed and eventually evolved into the Reserve Officer Training Corps (ROTC) program. Norwich was the first private college to offer civil engineering, and in 1974, it became one of the first military colleges to admit women into its Corps of Cadets, preceding the federal academies.

Norwich University offers a diverse blend of disciplines, teaching styles, and viewpoints. Students enrolled in the Corps of Cadets have a more disciplined, challenging, and structured path through college, while their civilian student classmates lead a more traditional collegiate lifestyle. However, both groups are coeducational and attend classes and participate in sports and other activities together. In keeping with its mission, Norwich provides opportunities for all of its students to develop leadership skills with a strong commitment to community service.

Norwich University has an enrollment of 2,300 students from more than 45 states and 20 countries. The University's minority enrollment is consistently higher (by percentage) than that of any other Vermont university or college.

The athletic facilities at Norwich are comparable to the best at any of New England's Division III universities. The main athletic complex, Andrews Hall, features a gymnasium, a modernized athletic training room, racquetball courts, an equipment room, and laundry facilities. Kreitzberg Arena is a multipurpose facility with a seating capacity of 1,500 and a fully equipped weight room. Plumley Armory has a gym, an indoor track, weight and aerobics rooms, a wrestling room, and an indoor swimming pool. Shapiro Field House has 50,000 square feet of floor space and includes a 200-meter indoor track, tennis courts, and a climbing wall. The newly developed Shaw Outdoor Center at the base of Paine Mountain offers students a variety of outdoor recreational activities including trails for hiking, snowshoeing, cross-country skiing, and mountain biking. Equipment to participate in these activities is available to students free of charge.

There are numerous playing fields for baseball, football, rugby, soccer, and softball. Paintball, obstacle, and confidence courses along with a rappel tower are also part of the 1,200-acre campus.

Norwich has the only professional five-year Master of Architecture program in northern New England. The University also offers online graduate degrees in business administration, diplomacy, information assurance, nursing, public administration, business continuity, organizational leadership, civil engineering, history, and military history.

CONTACT INFORMATION

Ms. Sherri Gilmore, Director of Admissions

☎ 802-485-2001 or toll-free 800-468-6679

💻 nuadm@norwich.edu

- **Enrollment:** *2,300*
- **Selectivity:** *moderately difficult*
- **Test scores:** *ACT—over 18, 95%; SAT— critical reading over 500, 69%; SAT—math over 500, 74%*
- **Application deadline:** *Rolling (freshmen), rolling (transfer)*
- **Expenses:** *Tuition $30,048; Room & Board $10,976*

Corps and civilian students work together in Chaplin Hall.

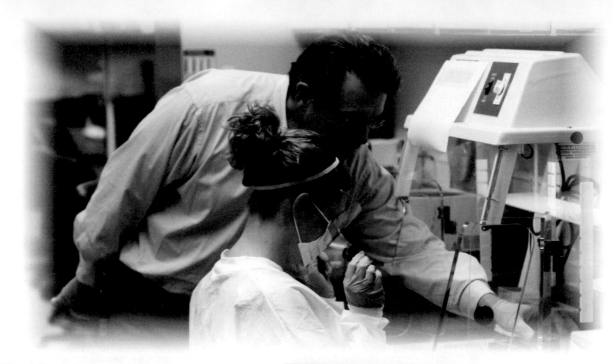

[True] Opportunity: Ohio Northern students work closely with faculty members, preparing for top-notch internships, conducting research, and applying what they've learned in the classroom. This hands-on experience makes Ohio Northern graduates strong candidates when applying for jobs.

OHIO NORTHERN UNIVERSITY

ADA, OHIO

www.onu.edu/

www.facebook.com/OhioNorthern

Ohio Northern University (ONU) is a selective, comprehensive school and one of the few private universities to offer nationally ranked liberal arts and professional programs in its five colleges: Arts & Sciences, Business Administration, Engineering, Pharmacy, and Law. The University's motto—*Ex diversitate* vires, which means "out of diversity, strength"—illustrates ONU's mission to provide experiences and programs that prepare graduates to live in a world that embraces difference. Ohio Northern is a student-centered, service-oriented, values-based university. Education is a collaborative process at Ohio Northern. Students work side-by-side with faculty members. The result is serious research and meaningful learning experiences that extend to both sides of the classroom.

Students can choose from a variety of campus activities including nearly 200 student organizations, four national sororities, and six national fraternities, music and theatre, and intramural and club sports. There are ten residence halls on campus as well as seven campus apartment complexes and an Affinity Housing complex, which usually houses juniors and seniors.

The University participates in NCAA Division III athletics and is a member of the Ohio Athletic Conference. The eleven men's teams are baseball, basketball, cross-country, football, golf, indoor/outdoor track and field, soccer, swimming and diving, tennis, and wrestling. Women compete in basketball, cross-country, fast-pitch softball, golf, indoor/outdoor track and field, soccer, swimming and diving, tennis, and volleyball.

Ohio Northern is strongly committed to creating an environmentally friendly campus. The use of geothermal technology to heat and cool recently built or renovated buildings is the most recent example of this commitment. The campus of Ohio Northern University is located on 342 beautiful acres in the friendly, rural village of Ada. Located in northwestern Ohio, ONU is not far from Columbus, Dayton, Toledo, and Fort Wayne, Indiana. And family and visitors can stay at Ohio Northern University's own hotel right on campus. The Inn at Ohio Northern University offers 72 deluxe guest rooms, a beautiful courtyard area, a comfortable pub, and large meeting spaces—all within walking distance to the Freed Center (performing arts), Presser Recital Hall, Elzay Gallery of Art, and the ONU Dial-Roberson Stadium (home of ONU football).

CONTACT INFORMATION

Ms. Deborah Miller, Director of Admissions

☎ 419-772-2260 Ext. 2464 or toll-free 888-408-4ONU

🖳 admissions-ug@onu.edu

- **Enrollment:** *3,611*

- **Selectivity:** *moderately difficult*

- **Test scores:** *ACT—over 18, 100%; SAT—critical reading over 500, 83%; SAT—math over 500, 88%*

- **Application deadline:** *8/1 (freshmen), 8/1 (transfer)*

- **Expenses:** *Tuition $35,678; Room & Board $10,220*

[True] Experience: Ohio Northern students have very active social lives. With nearly 200 student organizations, there is truly something for everyone. Above, students enjoy a "Movie on the Tundra" sponsored by the Student Planning Committee. Watch more at **experience.onu.edu**.

Ohio Wesleyan University

DELAWARE, OHIO

http://choose.owu.edu
http://www.facebook.com/OhioWesleyanUniversity
http://twitter.com/ohiowesleyan

Wherever you are at Ohio Wesleyan, you can see the bell tower at University Hall, one of the 11 campus buildings listed on the National Register of Historic Places.

Ohio Wesleyan is a national liberal arts university with a major international presence. It is remarkable for the depth of its academic and preprofessional programs, the international dimension of its curriculum, its focus on community through leadership and service, and its unwavering commitment to linking theory and practice in a global context and in every field of study.

Ohio Wesleyan University (OWU) is home to approximately 1,850 undergraduates, with a nearly equal number of men and women. Students come to Ohio Wesleyan from more than 40 states and more than 50 countries, lending a rich diversity to the campus community; most students live on the attractive 200-acre campus in residence halls, fraternity houses, or a variety of themed Small Living Units (SLUs).

This small, close-knit community provides amazing opportunities for study throughout the world. Competitive, university-funded Theory-to-Practice Grants allow students to propose and conduct original research, carry out internships, and participate in service and cultural immersion in countries ranging from Brazil to Bangladesh to Borneo. Travel-learning courses augment classroom work, taking students far from campus as they travel with professors and classmates for practical experiences related to on-campus study of issues and cultures ranging from Bolivia to Italy to Greece.

OWU offers more than 90 majors, sequences, and courses of study, far more than the number usually available at an institution of its size.

Service is a significant part of life at OWU. From 2009 to 2012, the school has been on the Presidential Honor Roll for Community Service, with Distinction, and in 2009–10, the University earned the President's Award for Excellence in General Community Service, one of only three colleges in the country to be so honored that year. The University also boasts nearly 100 clubs and organizations, offering students ample opportunity to develop leadership skills.

OWU is home to 23 Division III varsity athletic teams. In 2011, the men's soccer team took the Division III National

OWU's new Meek Aquatics and Recreation Center is LEED®-Certified. The plaza offers a place for relaxation, study, and conversation.

Championship for the second time; men's coach Dr. Jay Martin is the all-time winningest coach in collegiate men's soccer across all NCAA divisions. OWU also has more conference championships and Academic All-America® scholar-athletes than any other member of the North Coast Athletic Conference.

Only 20 miles from Columbus, Ohio's capital city, OWU provides the best of small-town living and the internship and cultural opportunities available in the nation's 16th-largest city.

- **Enrollment:** *1,829*
- **Selectivity:** *very difficult*
- **Test scores:** *ACT—over 18, 97.87%; SAT—critical reading over 500, 80.08%; SAT—math over 500, 81.58%*
- **Application deadline:** *3/1 (freshmen), rolling (transfer)*
- **Expenses:** *Tuition $38,890; Room & Board $10,310*

CONTACT INFORMATION

Ms. Rebecca Eckstein, Vice President for Enrollment
☎ 740-368-3025 or toll-free 800-922-8953
🖳 rreckste@owu.edu

Dixon Rec Center is home to the Northwest's largest indoor climbing wall and elliptical machines that power the campus grid.

OSU

Oregon State

UNIVERSITY

CORVALLIS, OREGON

http://oregonstate.edu

https://www.facebook.com/ osubeavers

Oregon State is a leading research university located in one of the safest, smartest, greenest, small cities in the nation. Situated 90 miles south of Portland, and an hour from the Cascades or the Pacific Coast, Corvallis is the perfect home base for exploring Oregon's natural wonders.

Founded in 1868, Oregon State is the state's Land Grant university and one of only two universities in the United States to have Sea Grant, Space Grant, and Sun Grant designations. Oregon State is also the only university in Oregon to hold both the Carnegie Foundation's top designation for research institutions and its prestigious Community Engagement classification.

As Oregon's largest public research university, with $261.7 million in external funding in the 2011 fiscal year, Oregon State's impact reaches across the state and beyond. With 12 colleges, 15 Agricultural Experiment Stations, 35 county

Extension offices, the Hatfield Marine Sciences Center in Newport, and OSU-Cascades in Bend, Oregon State has a presence in every one of Oregon's 36 counties, with a statewide economic footprint of $1 billion.

Oregon State welcomes a diverse student body of nearly 25,000 students from across Oregon, all 50 states, and more than 100 countries. Students can choose from more than 200 undergraduate and more than 80 graduate degree programs, including over 20 degrees offered online. Oregon State increasingly attracts high achieving students, with nationally recognized programs in areas such as conservation biology, agricultural sciences, nuclear engineering, forestry, fisheries and wildlife management, community health, pharmacy, and zoology. The average GPA for entering first-year students in 2011 was 3.55.

Oregon State also ranks high in sustainability, fourth among universities nationwide for using renewable energy and first in the PAC-12 Conference, and it's considered one of the greenest universities in the United States. And Oregon State's students literally help power the University: 22 exercise machines at Dixon Recreation Center are connected to the grid.

The 400-acre main campus in Corvallis includes a Historic District, making Oregon State one of only a handful of U.S. university campuses listed on the National Register of Historic Places. The district includes such icons as Weatherford Hall, the Memorial Union, and Benton Hall, the oldest building on campus.

Oregon State is located in Corvallis, a vibrant college town of 53,000 in the heart of Western Oregon's Willamette Valley. Corvallis consistently ranks among the best and safest cities to live in the United States, as well as among the most environmentally responsible.

CONTACT INFORMATION

Noah Buckley, Director of Admissions

☎ 541-737-4411 or toll-free 800-291-4192

💻 osuadmit@oregonstate.edu

- **Enrollment:** *24,977*

- **Selectivity:** *moderately difficult*

- **Test scores:** *ACT—over 18, 92%; SAT— critical reading over 500, 63%; SAT—math over 500, 73%*

- **Application deadlines:** *2/1 (freshmen priority) 8/1 (freshmen regular) 5/1 (transfer)*

- **Expenses:** *Tuition $8091 (Resident), &22,212 (Nonresident)*

The Memorial Union is the centerpiece of the Oregon State University campus, which is a registered Historic District and one of the top student unions nationwide.

Nestled in the heart of the Allegheny Mountains and just 45 miles from the University Park campus, Penn State Altoona's 167.5-acre campus is the perfect setting for students to pursue their educational goals and gain the knowledge and skills for future success.

Penn State Altoona

ALTOONA, PENNSYLVANIA
www.altoona.psu.edu
www.facebook.com/PSAltoona

Make no mistake—size does matter, and at Penn State Altoona, students receive the high-quality education synonymous with the Penn State name, in a welcoming, supportive environment. The small campus allows for a comprehensive learning experience while combining the high standards of a major research university. Penn State Altoona, with one of the largest enrollments of the twenty locations making up the Pennsylvania State University undergraduate system, is a full-service, four-year, residential campus located less than 45 miles from the research campus at University Park. Penn State Altoona offers 20 baccalaureate degree programs, 8 associate degree programs, 19 minors, and the first two years of course work for more than 180 Penn State majors that can be completed at other Penn State campuses. In addition to undergraduate studies, Penn State Altoona affords its students study-abroad and internship opportunities. Further, students can collaborate with faculty members on original research and creative projects. There is also an honors program at the college with challenging and exciting course work and the opportunity for scholarships.

In addition to its Ivyside campus, Penn State Altoona boasts a downtown campus that includes state-of-the-art nursing labs and communications suites. The nursing labs offer high-tech simulation mannequins and a low-fidelity lab, while the communication suites afford students use of sound booths, editing bays, a control room, and a television news studio complete with cameras, lighting, and a green screen. Also located at the downtown campus is a business and entrepreneurship center that opened in fall 2011 and includes a trading room and business incubator.

Penn State Altoona offers more than 100 student groups and organizations, fraternities and sororities, and volunteer opportunities. There are theatre, musical, and pre-professional groups of which to be a part, plus intramural sports and 17 varsity athletic teams to join. Spring Run Stadium, home of Penn State Altoona's men's and women's soccer teams, features a regulation soccer field, an eight-lane track, and a 2,000-seat grandstand.

Four on-campus residence halls provide comfortable living quarters close to the dining hall and classrooms. Bus service is offered between campuses, to and from off-campus housing, as well as various local shopping centers.

The college sits between Pittsburgh and Harrisburg, in the home of a minor league baseball team, the Altoona Curve. Nearby are two local amusement parks, several ski resorts, Rails to Trails hiking and biking, shopping, and fine dining.

Penn State Altoona's goal is to help you reach your goals—educational, personal, and professional.

- **Enrollment:** *4,105*
- **Selectivity:** *Very difficult*
- **Test scores:** *SAT—critical reading over 500, 46.99%; SAT—math over 500, 58.47%*
- **Application deadline:** *Rolling (freshmen), rolling (transfer)*
- **Expenses:** *Tuition $13,250; Room & Board $8370*

Students can experience the full collegiate experience at Penn State Altoona, with student clubs, organizations, internships, research opportunities, and athletics.

CONTACT INFORMATION

Admissions Office
☎ 814-949-5466 or toll-free
  800-848-9843
🖥 aaadmit@psu.edu

Taking a break outside the Kanbar Campus Center.

PhilaU
PHILADELPHIA UNIVERSITY

PHILADELPHIA, PA
www.PhilaU.edu
http://www.facebook.com/PhilaU.Undergrad

Founded in 1884, Philadelphia University is a private institution of higher learning for students with high motivation and academic ability. Philadelphia University is professionally oriented and offers undergraduate and graduate degree programs in the areas of architecture, business, design, engineering, fashion, general sciences, health sciences, and textile materials technology. The University's enrollment of approximately 2,800 undergraduates represents a diverse and talented group of students from 38 states and 42 countries. With an average class size of 18 and a 14:1 student-faculty ratio, students receive the personal attention so important to social and professional growth.

Through a unique blend of liberal and specialized education with an interdisciplinary focus, the University prepares students for today's complex, global workplace. Recognized as a premier professional university, Philadelphia University has established a phenomenal record of career success for its graduates. PhilaU has always believed it needed to create the professional of the future—and has been doing this since 1884. PhilaU's method? NEXUS LEARNING—its signature approach that is making the University a transformative force in higher education. Nexus Learning is the PhilaU "X Factor," crossing active, collaborative, real-world learning and infusing it with the liberal arts like no other university.

At PhilaU, students work hard but also have fun. With over 60 clubs in which to join, there is sure to be something of interest. PhilaU athletes compete in NCAA Division II sports, with the

men's teams consisting of baseball, basketball, cross-country/track, golf, soccer, and tennis. Women compete in basketball, cross-country/track, lacrosse, rowing, soccer, softball, tennis, and volleyball. Students may also participate in intramural or club sports, such as field hockey, lacrosse, and Ultimate Frisbee.

Located on a 100-acre, park-like campus, only minutes away from Philadelphia, PhilaU provides the best of both worlds.

CONTACT INFORMATION

Mr. Greg W. Potts, Director of Admissions

☎ 215-951-2800

💻 admissions@philau.edu

- **Enrollment:** *3,579*
- **Selectivity:** *moderately difficult*
- **Test scores:** *SAT—critical reading over 500, 64.9%; SAT—math over 500, 76.8%*
- **Application deadline:** *Rolling (freshmen), rolling (transfer)*
- **Expenses:** *Tuition $31,874; Room & Board $10,178*

Nexus Learning in action.

Residence halls at Pitzer.

PITZER COLLEGE

A MEMBER OF THE CLAREMONT COLLEGES

CLAREMONT, CALIFORNIA
www.pitzer.edu/

Pitzer is located in the city of Claremont, about 35 miles east of Los Angeles. The College is a short drive from rock climbing at Joshua Tree National Park, ski resorts, the beaches of Southern California, and Los Angeles County museums and attractions.

Pitzer's focus on social responsibility, student engagement, environmental sustainability, interdisciplinary studies, and intercultural understanding sets it apart from other colleges. Flexible general education requirements allow students more freedom to choose the courses they want to take.

Pitzer's governance structure is also distinctive; students are represented on all standing committees of the College, including those that deal with the most vital and sensitive issues of the College community. Pitzer offers its students membership in a close-knit academic community as well as access to the resources of a midsize university through Pitzer's partnership with The Claremont Colleges. The Claremont Colleges are a consortium of five undergraduate colleges and two graduate schools. Each college has its own personality, but all share major facilities such as the library, bookstore, campus security, health services, counseling center, ethnic study centers, and chaplains' offices.

Pitzer offers 40 majors in the arts, humanities, sciences, and social sciences. Students are also able to enroll in courses offered by the other Claremont Colleges. The most popular majors are art, biology, English, environmental studies, media studies, organizational studies, political studies, psychology, and sociology.

The student-faculty ratio at Pitzer is 11:1, and faculty members are readily available for academic advising and support. In line with

Pitzer's focus on interdisciplinary learning, most faculty members are conversant in at least one other field of study in addition to the area of their degrees, and they may teach in more than one area.

The majority of Pitzer students live on campus for all four years of college. In keeping with the College's commitment to environmental sustainability, three Gold LEED- certified residence halls opened in the fall of 2007, and in fall 2012, the College is opening a Platinum LEED-certified residence hall.

Student life also includes a wide variety of sports, clubs (more than 150!), community service programs, and social

CONTACT INFORMATION

Office of Admission
☎ 909-621-8129 or toll-free
   800-748-9371
🖳 admission@pitzer.edu

activities. Pitzer partners with Pomona College to field 13 NCAA Division III teams. In addition to the many on-campus opportunities, Pitzer currently offers 12 exchanges with U.S. institutions and over 40 international study options. Approximately 74 percent of Pitzer students participate in study abroad programs.

Students in front of Pitzer's clock tower.

The Queens College campus is spread over 77 green acres just minutes away from midtown Manhattan.

QUEENS
COLLEGE

FLUSHING, NEW YORK

www.qc.cuny.edu

Often referred to as "the jewel of the City University of New York (CUNY) system," Queens College has a national reputation for its liberal arts and sciences and pre-professional programs. Students come from more than 170 different nations; the result is a diverse education and experience that gives Queens College graduates a competitive edge in today's global society.

The 77-acre campus surrounds a quad that has a fantastic view of the Manhattan skyline. The campus also blends the old with the new. Still standing are original Spanish-style stucco and tile buildings from the early 1900s, including Jefferson Hall, which houses the Welcome Center. Powdermaker Hall has state-of-the-art technology throughout its classrooms, and the college's science labs recently underwent a $30-million renovation. The entire campus has Wi-Fi capability, and students may relax and meet friends in the Student Union and the college's many cafes, lounges, and dining areas. With the opening of the college's first residence hall, The Summit, Queens College shed its commuter school identity. The low-rise building has individually climate-controlled single- and double-room suites with shared kitchen and lounge areas. It also has its own exercise room. Queens College goes to great lengths to accommodate its many commuter students; the professionally staffed Child Development Center, provides inexpensive childcare services to students with children.

There are more than 100 clubs on campus, from the Accounting Honors Society and Alliance of Latin American Students to clubs for theater, fencing, environmental science, science fiction, and the fine arts. Queens, the only CUNY college that participates in Division II sports, has 19 men's and women's teams. Ongoing cultural events include readings by such well-known authors as Margaret Atwood, Toni Morrison, and Salman Rushdie; concerts by world-famous artists; and theater and dance performances. Queens College is home to the Godwin-Ternbach Museum, the only comprehensive museum in the borough of Queens, with art from ancient times to the present.

Queens College has had a chapter of Phi Beta Kappa since 1950 (fewer than 10 percent of U.S. liberal arts colleges are members of Phi Beta Kappa, the nation's oldest and most respected undergraduate honors organization). In 1968, Queens College became a member of Sigma Xi, the national science honor society.

Queens College offers its students numerous opportunities to study abroad and to intern in some of New York City's top businesses and institutions. The College is located in a residential area of Flushing and is only 20 to 30 minutes from Manhattan.

CONTACT INFORMATION

Mr. Vincent Angrisani, Executive Director of Enrollment Management and Admissions

☎ 718-997-5600

🖥 vincent.angrisani@qc.cuny.edu

- **Enrollment:** *20,993*
- **Selectivity:** *very difficult*
- **Test scores:** *SAT—critical reading over 500, 73%; SAT—math over 500, 91%*
- **Application deadline:** *5/15 (freshmen)*
- **Expenses:** *Tuition $5430; Room & Board $11,125*

Queens College students have opportunities to meet and study on the Quad, located centrally on campus.

Quinnipiac students develop critical thinking skills through hands-on learning, collaborative projects, and independent research.

QUINNIPIAC UNIVERSITY

HAMDEN, CONNECTICUT

www.quinnipiac.edu

www.facebook.com/QuinnipiacUniversity

Quinnipiac University is big enough to support a wide variety of people and programs but small enough to keep students from getting lost in the shuffle. This coed university offers four-year and graduate-level degree programs leading to careers in health sciences, nursing, business, engineering, communications, liberal arts, natural sciences, education, and law.

Life on campus is exciting with more than 100 student clubs and organizations, a host of intramural sports and activities, 21 intercollegiate NCAA Division I athletic teams, an award-winning student newspaper, plus a student-run TV station and radio station.

The University has three distinct settings to accommodate academic and campus life: The 250-acre Mount Carmel campus is home to the Arnold Bernhard Library, academic buildings, a student center, administrative offices, and a 24,000-square-foot recreation facility with a fully-equipped fitness center; aerobics/dance studios; basketball, volleyball and tennis courts; an indoor track; and playing fields. The residential village consists of 25 residence halls with traditional rooms, suites, and multilevel suites with kitchens, for freshmen and sophomores. The nearby 250-acre York Hill campus includes the TD Bank Sports Center with twin 3,500-seat arenas for ice hockey and basketball; new apartment- and suite-style residence halls for juniors and seniors; and the lodge-like Rocky Top Student Center, which includes a 500-seat dining hall, meeting and study space, a fitness center and Spinning® studio, and magnificent views of the surrounding area. Less than 6 miles away is the 104-acre North Haven campus with state-of-the-art facilities for graduate and doctoral programs in the Schools of Health Sciences, Nursing, Education, and Medicine (opening fall 2013).

Academic advising and career counseling are offered through each of the academic schools. Approximately 30 percent of Quinnipiac undergraduates remain at Quinnipiac to earn graduate degrees in education, business, nursing, molecular and cell biology, occupational therapy, physician assistant,

and physical therapy (DPT). Several graduate degree programs are offered online. The Quinnipiac University School of Law offers programs leading to a JD degree or the JD/MBA degree.

Quinnipiac provides the best of the suburbs and the city—the University is only 8 miles from New Haven and less than 2 hours from New York City and Boston. Bordering the campus is the 1,700-acre Sleeping Giant State Park, for walking and hiking. The free campus shuttle takes students to nearby shopping and restaurants. The University encourages students and families to visit for a campus tour, individual interview, group information session, or open house. You can also take Quinnipiac's virtual tour at www.quinnipiac.edu/tour.

CONTACT INFORMATION

Ms. Joan Isaac Mohr, Vice President of Admissions & Financial Aid

☎ 203-582-8600 or toll-free 800-462-1944

💻 admissions@quinnipiac.edu

- **Enrollment:** *8,352*

- **Selectivity:** *moderately difficult*

- **Test scores:** *ACT—over 18, 100%; SAT—critical reading over 500, 82%; SAT—math over 500, 87%*

- **Application deadline:** *2/1 (freshmen), 4/1 (transfer), Physical Therapy, Nursing, & Physician Assistant programs: 11/15, Early Decision: 11/1*

- **Expenses:** *Tuition $38,000; Room & Board $13,800 (freshmen)*

Quinnipiac's Mount Carmel campus, adjacent to Sleeping Giant Mountain in Hamden, Connecticut, is an architectural gallery of modern brick buildings and sweeping lawns, with a stately clock tower above the library.

Randolph College—big enough to give you a global perspective, small enough to know everyone cares.

RANDOLPH COLLEGE

LYNCHBURG, VIRGINIA
www.randolphcollege.edu

Randolph College is a place for original thinkers coming from 36 states and more than 30 countries. Students choose Randolph for its unique blend of academic rigor, individualized instruction, research, a strong and active Honor System, career-oriented experiential learning, and intercultural experiences (off campus through study abroad and on campus through interaction with a highly diverse student body that is 13 percent international). The College has also been recognized as a "best value" by The Princeton Review—one of only two private colleges in Virginia so designated. The beautiful, historically significant campus is situated on 100 rolling acres in the historic district of Lynchburg, Virginia, a suburban college town within easy driving distance of Washington, D.C. The student-faculty ratio is 8:1, with an average class size of 10.

Randolph College offers more than 50 majors, concentrations (minors), and programs of study leading to a Bachelor of Arts (B.A.),

Bachelor of Science (B.S.), or Bachelor of Fine Arts (B.F.A.) degree. The double major is a popular option. Also, students may select up to two minors in addition to the major. Randolph has 3-2 programs in engineering and nursing and pre-professional programs in law, medicine, and veterinary studies, as well as teacher education.

Most students are involved in at least one of the more than 40 clubs or organizations and activities. The $6-million Student Center renovation, expected to be complete in 2012, will offer a two-level fitness center on the top floor; a 90 coat theater; a student grill; an outside deck; an entertainment floor with pool tables, ping-pong, foosball, and other activities; a glass-enclosed student radio station studio, WWRM; and new student government and publications offices. Nearly 30 percent of Randolph's students compete on one of the College's 13 NCAA Division III teams, including a nationally recognized riding program with its own 100-acre indoor/outdoor riding facility.

The academic program is enhanced throughout the year by visiting speakers, performers, and artists. In recent years, these have included former Governor of Vermont and DNC Chairman Howard Dean; aquatic filmmaker and oceanographic explorer, Fabien Cousteau; John Dau, a Lost Boy of Sudan known for his memoir and Sundance Film Festival award-winner *God Grew Tired of Us;* educator, poet, writer, Civil Rights activist Nikki Giovanni; Frances Mayes, alumna of the College and author of several works including *Under the Tuscan Sun;* and political strategist Karl Rove. In addition, the College sponsors numerous plays, awards, and exhibitions.

Ms. Margaret Blount, Director of Admissions
☎ 434-947-8100 or toll-free 800-745-7692
💻 admissions@randolphcollege.edu

- **Enrollment:** *Less than 600*
- **Selectivity:** *moderate*
- **Test scores:** *ACT—over 18, 100%; SAT—critical reading over 500, 95%; SAT—math over 500, 90%*
- **Application deadline:** *3/1*
- **Expenses:** *Tuition $31,030; Room & Board $10,790*

Randolph College students value and appreciate a strong history of honor, community, and a celebration of originality.

"Green" before it was trendy—you'll always find the perfect chill spot on Stockton's stunning 2,000-acre, environmentally protected campus, minutes from Jersey Shore beaches, 1 hour from Philadelphia, and 2 hours from New York City.

STOCKTON COLLEGE

THE RICHARD STOCKTON COLLEGE OF NEW JERSEY

GALLOWAY, NEW JERSEY
www.stockton.edu
http://www.facebook.com/richardstocktoncollege

The personal attention and hands-on opportunities of a private college at a public price, Richard Stockton College is New Jersey's DISTINCTIVE public college.

At Stockton, thinking always translates into doing. Gain hands-on experience in nursing, public health, or physical therapy at the two hospitals on campus. Conduct computational science or information systems research in Stockton's high-powered computer labs or at the nearby technology centers. "Live" a hospitality and tourism management internship 24/7 at the Seaview, Stockton's world-class resort. Study artistic techniques firsthand through Stockton's partnership with the nearby Noyes Museum of Art—southern New Jersey's only fine arts museum—mere minutes from campus, and at the Philadelphia Museum of Art, just an hour away. Bask in Stockton's beautiful,

2,000-acre campus in the Pinelands Natural Reserve just minutes from the ocean—also a natural lab perfect for Stockton's nationally recognized marine science and environmental studies programs.

A selective, medium-sized, highly-ranked, public college with a strong liberal arts focus, Stockton provides interdisciplinary opportunities for in-depth study in every chosen field. This means that every major is based on a student's own interests.

More than 80 percent of Stockton students engage in some type of independent study with a faculty mentor. Small classes allow for discussion, debate, and discovery—guided by Fulbright scholars, the most-published scientist in the world, and other professors who care as much about teaching as research. Stockton has always drawn students and professors with a deep social and environmental consciousness, those willing to get involved. That's why Stockton offers extensive service learning and human rights opportunities and has become an international leader in alternative energy research and conservation efforts.

On the lighter side, over 10,000 events, more than 130 clubs and organizations, Greek life, academic societies, intramural and club sports, and study-abroad options enhance the college experience. Being winners in two of the nation's most competitive NCAA Division III conferences generates plenty of Osprey spirit for 17 varsity sports.

The perfect size, the perfect place, at a public cost: Stockton College—as distinctive as YOU.

CONTACT INFORMATION

Mr. John Iacovelli, Dean of
  Enrollment Management
☎ 609-652-4261
📧 admissions@stockton.edu

- **Enrollment:** *8,108*

- **Selectivity:** *very difficult*

- **Test scores:** *ACT—over 18, 86%; SAT—critical reading over 500, 64%; SAT—math over 500, 73%*

- **Application deadline:** *5/1 (freshmen), 6/1 (transfer)*

- **Expenses:** *Tuition $11,303; Room & Board $10,281*

Independent thinking is what Stockton is all about. Classes are small to allow for discussion, debate, and discovery, with unbelievable faculty/student interaction—both in and out of the classroom!

The Richmond Hill campus is situated near the River Thames in one of London's most attractive areas. The impressive neo-Gothic structure was constructed in 1843.

RICHMOND
THE AMERICAN INTERNATIONAL
UNIVERSITY
IN LONDON

LONDON, ENGLAND

www.richmond.ac.uk/

Richmond, The American International University in London, is a comprehensive American liberal arts and professional university. Richmond offers a strong academic program with many fields of study, an exceptional faculty, a fun campus life, and fellow students

from all over the world. In addition to its undergrad programs, Richmond offers Master of Arts degrees in art history and international relations.

Freshmen and sophomores study and live at the Richmond campus, 7 miles from central London. Junior and senior years are spent at the Kensington campus in one of London's most beautiful residential and historic districts. As part of their four-year B.A. degree program, students may spend a semester or a year studying at one of the University's two international study centers in Florence and Rome, Italy.

Approximately 45 percent of the degree students are from North America, and 38 percent are from Europe and the United Kingdom. The remaining students are from the Middle East, Africa, Asia, and South America. About 350 study-abroad students from various universities are enrolled for a semester or a year at Richmond.

Outside the classroom, many Richmond students get involved in extracurricular activities such as student government, the Green Project (an environmental group), Model United Nations, Gay Straight Alliance, RTV (Richmond Television), and sports and business clubs.

The Richmond Hill campus has a ton of nearby entertainment, shopping, cultural and recreational opportunities. Only yards from the University campus is Richmond Park, more than 2,200 acres of rolling hills and woodland, where students can ride horses, play tennis, jog, or simply relax. The trip from Richmond into Central London takes about 30 minutes. The Kensington campus has fine museums, libraries, theatres, concert halls, and historic buildings.

CONTACT INFORMATION

Mr. Nick Atkinson, Director of United States Admissions

☎ 617-450-5617

💻 usadmissions@richmond.ac.uk

The University takes full advantage of London's resources through selected academic courses, internships with multinational corporations, and special visits to museums, art galleries, theatres, and concert halls.

- **Enrollment:** *over 1,000*
- **Expenses:** *Tuition: $27,000 Room & Board: $13,740.*

Richmond students.

Located in Nashua, New Hampshire, Rivier University is just an hour away from the mountains, the seacoast, and Boston.

Rivier
UNIVERSITY

NASHUA, NEW HAMPSHIRE
www.rivier.edu/

Rivier University invites students to take a closer look. What they will see is a small, Catholic university committed to its students that's located in one of the most beautiful areas of the United States. Rivier University offers more than 60 undergraduate, graduate, and post-graduate degrees—and the only Doctor of Education degree in the state of New Hampshire.

Global initiatives are a vital component of the University's offerings including two new bachelor's degrees in global studies and transnational security beginning in fall 2012.

Academic advisers, staff members at the Writing and Resource Center, and peer tutors help students meet their academic goals.

The Regina Library and Educational Resource Center include 91,000 volumes and access to more than 3 million volumes in twelve area libraries.

Life on campus is relaxed and comfortable. Students can choose from four modern residence halls that have suites, Internet connections in each room, and lounges. All students can have cars on campus. Rivier University also has more than 25 active clubs and organizations from the Riviera Dance Team to the Psychology Club. The University hosts concerts, live entertainment, films, sporting events, and many trips. One weekend students may be visiting the museums of Boston or New York; the next weekend they may be building a house for Habitat for Humanity in Kentucky.

Rivier competes in NCAA Division III men's baseball, basketball, cross-country, lacrosse, soccer, and volleyball; and women's basketball, cross-country, field hockey, lacrosse, soccer, softball, and volleyball. Rivier is a member of the ECAC, the Great Northeast Athletic Conference (GNAC) and the North Atlantic Conference (NAC) for field hockey. The men's volleyball team has been nationally ranked every year since 2001. In 2012, the team finished 7th in the nation in Division III and was one of 8 teams competing in the inaugural DIII National Championship Tournament. The Muldoon Health and Fitness Center is home to the Rivier Raiders varsity athletics as well as intramural sports and activities that include volleyball, floor hockey, basketball, weight training, aerobics, and self-defense. Also on campus are a lighted turf soccer field and softball field, a beach volleyball court, and a cross-country trail.

Nashua is located in southern New Hampshire. The city of Boston lies just 40 miles to the south. Students have easy access to nearby lakes and ski areas in the White Mountains to the north and at the coast, which is just an hour's drive to the east.

CONTACT INFORMATION

Karen Schedin, Vice President of Enrollment

☎ 603-897-8507 or toll-free 800-44RIVIER

🖳 rivadmit@rivier.edu

- **Enrollment:** *2,289*
- **Selectivity:** *moderately difficult*
- **Test scores:** *SAT—critical reading over 500, 30%; SAT—math over 500, 32%*
- **Application deadline:** *Rolling (freshmen), rolling (transfer)*
- **Expenses:** *Tuition $26,430; Room & Board $10,118*

Rivier offers hands-on learning in all its academic programs; students build confidence and knowledge that will help them in their future careers.

RMU students showing their school spirit during athletic events.

The **Experience** University®

ROBERT MORRIS UNIVERSITY
ILLINOIS

CHICAGO, ARLINGTON HEIGHTS, BENSENVILLE, DUPAGE, ELGIN, LAKE COUNTY, ORLAND PARK, PEORIA, SCHAUMBURG, AND SPRINGFIELD, ILLINOIS

www.robertmorris.edu

"I knew I was in the right place."

That's a comment from a Robert Morris University graduate who looked beyond the traditional undergrad experience to learning, living, and enjoying college in the heart of downtown Chicago. Housed in a 110-year-old landmark building that has been completely renovated with the latest in design, educational technology and student-centered spaces, Robert Morris University (RMU) holds a prime position in Chicago's "education corridor." RMU is in the center of the city and all it offers: theaters, museums, restaurants, clubs, festivals, and thousands of students from the neighborhoods of Chicago and all around the world.

As an affordable, highly ranked, nonprofit private university, Robert Morris provides professional, career-focused undergraduate and graduate education. With the lowest tuition of any private university in the state of Illinois, RMU awarded more than $22 million in scholarships in 2011.

Professional faculty members are key to the education that has built RMU's reputation as the Experience University, with fields of study in economics, business administration, nursing, organizational writing, culinary arts, graphic design, and technology and media, to name a few. The faculty's active involvement in the workplace ensures that classes are current, relevant, and continually improving, meeting the needs of both graduates and employers. RMU has been nationally recognized for an outstanding graduation rate—in the top 10 percent of schools—and its high student retention.

RMU prepares students for their professional lives with required internships, Innovation Center projects and career management course work through which students experience authentic work settings, all while earning credit toward their degree and valuable professional experience.

For students who choose to live on campus, housing is available at the vibrant University Center. With several floor plans, the University Center is home to students from different institutions, creating a unique and diverse community. In addition, RMU's Passport Chicago introduces students to the city through fun, free activities—turning every student into a true Chicagoan.

Extracurricular activities round out the college experience. RMU has great variety: Sigma Beta Delta and Lambda Epsilon Chi promote academic and professional excellence; service organizations recruit students for RMU community projects; and for those with artistic flair, show choir, drumline, the painting guild, and graphic arts clubs always welcome new members.

CONTACT INFORMATION

Office of Admissions
☎ 312-935-4100 or toll-free
   800-762-5960
💻 enroll@robertmorris.edu

- **Enrollment:** *1,120*
- **Selectivity:** *minimally difficult*
- **Test scores:** *ACT—over 18, 57%*
- **Application deadline:** *Rolling (freshmen), rolling (transfer)*
- **Expenses:** *Tuition $22,200; Housing $10,500*

Robert Morris University Men's Soccer Team.

Colonials mascot RoMo at the opening of the $8 million business school complex.

MOON TOWNSHIP, PENNSYLVANIA

www.rmu.edu
www.facebook.com/RMUpgh

A private university in the suburban hills of Pittsburgh, Robert Morris University (RMU) is just a short drive from the social, cultural, and professional opportunities of a major city. RMU offers more than 60 undergraduate programs and 20 graduate programs, both on the 230-acre campus and online. For more than 90 years, the University has provided academic excellence with a professional focus and personal attention that truly changes lives.

RMU built its reputation in business, and that tradition continues with a new $8 million School of Business complex and accreditation from AACSB International–The Association to Advance Collegiate Schools of Business, a designation placing RMU at the top tier of business schools. The University continues to grow and offers acclaimed programs in communications, information systems, engineering, mathematics, science, education, social sciences, and nursing.

Engaged learning is a highlight of an RMU education, and the University provides graduating seniors not only an academic transcript but also a Student Engagement Transcript, which shows potential employers the student's internships, service-learning activities, study abroad, leadership roles, and other learning that's occurred outside the classroom. This focus on engaged learning contributes to the 93 percent placement rate of RMU's graduates in careers or graduate school within six months of graduation.

More than 80 percent of freshmen live in campus housing, creating a close-knit community and a chance to make new friends. Visiting international scholars and

a variety of opportunities to study abroad—for a semester or a few weeks—enrich students' global perspectives. Students also can choose to join any of RMU's nearly 100 clubs and organizations. In addition, nearby Pittsburgh is a full of attractions of all kinds, from culture to night life to internship opportunities.

RMU's competitive athletics program fields 23 NCAA Division I teams. The Colonials have won titles and championships in nearly every sport they participate in. The football and basketball teams draw enthusiastic crowds to Joe Walton Stadium and the Charles Sewall Center, while the region's only Division I men's and women's ice hockey teams play at 84 Lumber Arena in the RMU Island Sports Center, a 32-acre sports and recreation complex. Students can also

CONTACT INFORMATION

Kellie L. Laurenzi, Dean of Admissions
☎ 800-762-0097 (toll-free)
💻 admissionsoffice@rmu.edu

participate in a number of club and intramural sports.

Robert Morris University is committed to the mission of changing the lives of its students and empowering them to go into the world to change the lives of others.

- **Enrollment:** *5,000*

- **Selectivity:** *minimally difficult*

- **Test scores:** *ACT—over 18, 98%; SAT—critical reading over 500, 50%; SAT—math over 500, 80%*

- **Application deadline:** *Rolling (freshmen and transfer)*

- **Expenses:** *Tuition & fees $24,185; Room & board $9730*

RMU's suburban Pittsburgh campus spreads across 230 scenic acres that were once the grounds of a country estate.

RIT's modern, well-equipped campus has many park-like settings.

R·I·T
ROCHESTER INSTITUTE OF TECHNOLOGY

ROCHESTER, NEW YORK

http://www.rit.edu

http://www.facebook.com/RITfb

http://twitter.com/RITAdmissions

No matter what your passion, you can master it at RIT. It is a place where brilliant minds assemble and collaborate, where they pool together their individual talents across disciplines in service of big projects and big ideas. It is a vibrant community teeming with students collaborating with experts and specialists: a hub of innovation and creativity. It is a unique intersection of disciplines in science, engineering, technology, visual arts, business, and social sciences.

As one of the world's leading technological, career-focused universities, RIT's unmatched array of academic programs attract designers, artists, photographers, journalists, and filmmakers on the one hand, and scientists, engineers, computing scientists, social scientists, and entrepreneurs on the other. RIT attracts students from every state and over 1,500 international students from more than 100 countries. Embodying RIT's commitment to diversity, more than 2,500 students of color have elected to study at the university. Adding a social and educational dynamic not found at any other university are more than 1,300 deaf and hard-of-hearing students supported by RIT's National Technical Institute for the Deaf.

RIT is a world-leader in experiential education. The cooperative education program is the fourth oldest and one of the largest in the world, and it is the most extensive and intensive of RIT's experiential education opportunities. Other opportunities to apply your education to real-world problems and projects include internships, undergraduate research, and study abroad. Accelerated degree programs, the Honors Program, and more than 100 minors are prominent among the many opportunities to enrich and expand a student's undergraduate experience.

Each year, RIT demonstrates its leadership in innovation and creativity by sponsoring the Imagine RIT: Innovation and Creativity Festival, a campuswide event that showcases the innovative and creative spirit of its students, faculty, and staff. This year, more than 350 exhibits, many of them interactive, were viewed by more than 32,000 awed, enlightened—and sometimes astonished—spectators.

Students take their studies seriously, but they'll be the first to tell you that they are passionate about life outside of the lectures and labs. RIT is alive with energy and excitement 24/7, and it won't take long to find your niche because there are so many ways to be involved.

RIT is a launching pad for a brilliant career and a highly unique state of mind. It is a perfect environment in which to pursue your passion. Here, the future is envisioned each day—and remade each day after.

CONTACT INFORMATION

Dr. Daniel Shelley, Assistant Vice President

☎ 585-475-6631

🖥 admissions@rit.edu

- **Enrollment:** *17,397*
- **Selectivity:** *moderately difficult*
- **Test scores:** *ACT—over 18, 100%; SAT—critical reading over 500, 88.6%; SAT—math over 500, 81.2%*
- **Application deadline:** *2/1 (freshmen)*
- **Expenses:** *Tuition $32,784; Room & Board $10,800*

Fans love to come out and cheer for both Men's and Women's Division I hockey teams.

Friendships, faculty interaction, research, and outcomes—the only thing missing is you.

Roger Williams University

Learning to Bridge the World

BRISTOL, RHODE ISLAND

www.rwu.edu/

Roger Williams University (RWU) prepares students for life as 21st century citizen-scholars through a curriculum that pairs the essence of a liberal arts education with the best of what the professions have to offer. Personal attention is a guarantee, and professors (not graduate assistants) teach all of the courses—even the intros. RWU's student-to-faculty ratio is 14:1, and the average class size is just 19 students—so when RWU says personal attention, it means it.

But, the college experience is about more than what you learn in the classroom. Interested in community service? All entering freshmen participate in Community Connections, an annual day of service that sends 1,500 students and faculty and staff members to volunteer at more than 80 local organizations, such as animal shelters, the food bank, area beaches, and wetlands. Perhaps travel is more your speed? The University encourages all students to study abroad, whether it's for a year, a semester, a summer session, or even a mini-mester. Maintain a 3.0 GPA and the University will give you your passport for free!

On campus, students enjoy cultural programs at the Intercultural Center, home to international student life, spiritual life, the Multicultural Student Union, and LGBT initiatives. Global Heritage Hall is the eco-friendly academic center at the heart of campus, complete with a three-story atrium, outdoor terrace, and high-tech Mac labs. Students live on- and off-campus in RWU's various residence halls (shuttle service is available). The newest addition, North Campus Residence Hall, combines living space, classroom and study space, and a café to create a modern living and learning community.

RWU students can choose from more than 70 clubs and organizations—everything from the Ski & Snowboard Club to the radio station. Students can also join one of the University's 20 varsity teams or an intramural team. At the modern Dining Commons, students eat locally grown, organic foods. They work out in the state-of-the-art Campus Recreation Center, complete with swimming pool, basketball and squash courts, weight lifting and cardio room, jacuzzi, and a sauna. And the campus' waterfront location is perfect for sailing and kayaking.

Roger Williams University is located in Bristol, a quaint seaside town that is home to stores, gourmet restaurants, ice cream shops, and spas, and it's just 30 minutes from both Providence—Rhode Island's capital and cultural center—and Newport—home to some of the state's best beaches and nightlife.

CONTACT INFORMATION

Office of Admission
☎ 401-254-3500 or toll-free 800-458-7144
🖥 admit@rwu.edu

- **Enrollment:** *3,785*

- **Selectivity:** *moderately difficult*

- **Test scores:** *Submission of standardized test scores for admission consideration is now optional.* However, if accepted, RWU will use your standardized test scores for academic placement and advising. *Students applying for elementary and secondary education programs must submit test scores for admission.*

- **Application deadline.** *2/1 (freshmen), rolling (transfer)*

- **Expenses:** *Tuition $29,976; Room & Board $13,600*

Yes…we're on the water.

SACRED HEART UNIVERSITY

SACRED HEART UNIVERSITY

FAIRFIELD, CONNECTICUT
www.sacredheart.edu

Sacred Heart University attracts students who are committed to academic excellence, cutting-edge technology, career preparation and community service. Founded in 1963, Sacred Heart University (SHU) is the second-largest independent Catholic university in New England and the first in America to be led and staffed by lay people. With endless opportunities for hands-on education through research, internships, independent study, work-study, and study-abroad programs worldwide, Sacred Heart University students are consistently challenged to apply their skills outside the classroom.

These learning opportunities are enhanced by an active student life program that includes Division I athletic teams and more than 80 student organizations. Students can join fraternities and sororities, student government, the newspaper, the yearbook, radio and television stations, academic clubs, political organizations, community service organizations, multicultural organizations, the performing arts, intramural programs, and 18 competitive sports programs. Sacred Heart University has 31 NCAA Division I men's and women's sports, making it one of the largest Division I programs in the country. Varsity teams include baseball, basketball, bowling, crew, cross-country, equestrian, fencing, field hockey, football, golf, ice hockey, indoor/outdoor track and field, lacrosse, soccer, softball, swimming, tennis, volleyball, and wrestling. Students also participate in the University's 24 intercollegiate teams, competing against teams from top schools in the Northeast, including Ivy League schools.

In addition to the more than 30 undergraduate degree programs, SHU offers numerous graduate degree programs, including Master of Science in computer science and information science (with a concentration in computer game design and development), a nationally ranked Master of Science

in Occupational Therapy, a Master of Science in exercise science and nutrition, and a Doctor of Physical Therapy program ranked first in the State of Connecticut and among the five best in the Northeast, according to *U.S. News & World Report*.

Located on 71 acres along the coast in Fairfield, Connecticut, Sacred Heart University is just 1 hour north of New York City and 2 hours south of Boston, with international campuses in County Kerry, Ireland, and in Luxembourg.

CONTACT INFORMATION

Mr. Jamie Romeo, Executive Director of Undergraduate Admissions

☎ 203-365-7560

✉ romeoj@sacredheart.edu

- **Enrollment:** *6,407*
- **Selectivity:** *moderately difficult*
- **Test scores:** *ACT—over 18, 98%; SAT—critical reading over 500, 77%; SAT—math over 500, 83%*
- **Expenses:** *Tuition $33,780; Room & Board $13,230*

Sacred Heart University's Linda E. McMahon Commons.

Founded in 1858, St. Bonaventure's campus is one of the most beautiful in the Northeast.

ST. BONAVENTURE
U N I V E R S I T Y

ALLEGANY, NEW YORK

www.sbu.edu

www.facebook.com/bonaventure

The ceremony that welcomes you as a freshman to St. Bonaventure is the same as the ceremony that sends you into the real world four years later: a simple candlelight procession on the steps of De La Roche Hall.

Only one thing is noticeably different—you. Four years at this uniquely indescribable university change the people who come here forever. They become members of a passionate alumni base who flock back a thousand strong each summer to the picturesque campus in Western New York for Reunion Weekend.

What inspires the rabid devotion? Plenty of things, to be sure—from distinguished academic programs to St. Bonaventure's remarkable legacy of service. But relationships are at the core of each one—relationships students develop with nurturing professors who guide their development every step of the way; relationships with the townspeople who embrace the Bonaventure family; relationships with members of the Bonaventure community on a disaster-relief trip to a tornado-stricken town or at the nation's oldest student-run soup kitchen; relationships with basketball teams at one of the smallest Division I colleges, playing in one of the nation's best leagues, the Atlantic 10 (both teams went to the 2012 NCAA Tournament); and relationships with friends they'll never forget.

Academically, there are more than 50 programs to choose from, including exciting new programs in Sport Studies, Strategic Communication and Digital Media, and International Studies. St. Bonaventure's hallmark programs are Business, Journalism and Mass Communication (featuring a remote TV production studio), Education, Psychology, Biology, English, and History. And the University's acclaimed Franciscan Health Care Professions combined-degree program has attracted medical, dental, pharmacy, and physical therapy students from all over the country.

From the moment a student steps foot on St. Bonaventure's beautiful 500-acre campus, he or she begins preparation for college life through the First-Year Experience program, and for post-college life through the innovative Career

and Professional Readiness Center (CPRC).

New and upgraded facilities are all around, from the state-of-the-art Richter Recreation Center and Café La Verna, to brand-new homes for St. Bonaventure's Sciences departments and School of Business (opening in fall 2013).

If getting involved is a priority, there's an array of extracurriculars, highlighted by award-winning student media, nationally recognized SIFE, BonaResponds disaster relief, Warming House soup kitchen, and fitness opportunities that never end—a 6-mile recreation trail with its own spur on campus; vibrant intramurals and club sports (featuring nationally ranked men's and women's rugby); Holiday Valley ski resort just 20 miles away; and 14 Division I sports.

CONTACT INFORMATION

Monica Emery, Director of Recruitment

☎ 716-375-2400 or toll-free 800-462-5050

🖳 memery@sbu.edu

- **Enrollment:** *2,460*
- **Selectivity:** *moderately difficult*
- **Test scores:** *ACT—over 18, 93%; SAT—critical reading over 500, 63%; SAT—math over 500, 68%*
- **Application deadline:** *7/1 (freshmen), 8/15 (transfer)*
- **Expenses:** *Tuition $26,805; Room & Board $9071*

Opened in 1927, Devereux Hall is St. Bonaventure's most historic residence hall.

Off-campus housing affords students the opportunity to live in one of the most desirable neighborhoods in NYC—Brooklyn Heights. Stroll or take a run on the Promenade, and capture the Manhattan skyline.

ST.FRANCIS COLLEGE
THE SMALL COLLEGE OF BIG DREAMS

BROOKLYN HEIGHTS, NEW YORK

www.sfc.edu

www.facebook.com/SFCNY

For more than 150 years, the mission of St. Francis College has been to provide an affordable, high-quality education to students of all racial, ethnic, and religious backgrounds. Offering more than 70 programs and majors, the College's well-rounded core curriculum gives students the skills they need to succeed in the workplace and in life. Graduates of St. Francis College go on to a wide variety of careers—from working at Top Four accounting firms to teaching in a classroom and from Wall Street to public service. And if graduate school is on the horizon, St. Francis College students have an excellent track record at some of the top programs in the country.

St. Francis College consistently makes the grade when it comes to college rankings. U.S. News & World Report classifies St. Francis as one of the "best regional colleges in the North," while Forbes.com just placed St. Francis on its America's Top Colleges list for the fourth year in a row.

With the College's generous scholarship and financial aid program, more than 80 percent of St. Francis' last incoming class qualified for academic grants and institutional awards based on their grades, making the already reasonable tuition even more affordable. If you are looking for a greater academic challenge, the Honors Program offers s an interdisciplinary approach, inspiring tudents academically while encouraging intellectual exploration.

Students have several opportunities to continue their studies outside of the United States. Many take advantage of this every year, studying in places as diverse as The Sorbonne in Paris, Madrid, Rome, Prague, Costa Rica, Australia, and even a Semester-at-Sea. Students also have an opportunity to study in Cortona, Italy, learning through a faculty-led program in the beautiful region of Tuscany. In addition, students can apply for the Student Franciscan Pilgrimage to Assisi, Rome, and other places associated with Saint Francis and Saint Clare. This free pilgrimage affords students a wonderful Franciscan experience.

Participating in an internship related to one's goals offers a most valuable hands-on experience. The College provides an up-to-date listing of New York metropolitan-area companies that offer internships, services, and tools needed to help students fill positions of their choice.

Students participate on 19 Division I athletic teams, including men's basketball, cross-country, golf, indoor/outdoor track, soccer, swimming & diving, tennis, and the nationally ranked water polo team, which made the NCAA Final Four last season. Women compete in basketball, bowling, cross-country, golf, indoor/outdoor track, swimming & diving, tennis, volleyball, and water polo.

Whether you commute or live in the newly renovated off-campus residence hall, St. Francis College offers a supportive educational environment that helps develop the whole person. Only one subway stop away, all the wonder and opportunity of New York City—your extended campus—is right at your doorstep, but you will always be able to step out of that fast-paced world and return home to a community that believes in social responsibility and mutual respect.

CONTACT INFORMATION

Office of Admissions
☎ 718-489-5200
🖥 admissions@sfc.edu

No matter what your dream, St. Francis College is here to help you achieve it. With small classes taught by top professors, successful alumni who actively mentor current students, and a strong Franciscan tradition that guides the community, your future is full of limitless possibilities.

- **Enrollment:** *2,600*
- **Selectivity:** *Moderate*
- **Test scores:** *ACT 17 (min); SAT critical reading and math combined: 800 (min.)*
- **Application deadline:** *Rolling (Freshmen & Transfers)*
- **Expenses:** *Tuition $19,200; (Rooms start at $11,900)*

St. Francis College provides a personalized experience, with small classes taught only by professors who know you by name.

Golisano Academic Gateway.

ST. JOHN FISHER COLLEGE

ROCHESTER, NEW YORK

www.sjfc.edu/freshman

www.facebook.com/StJohnFisherCollege

St. John Fisher College—an independent, liberal arts institution in the Catholic tradition of American higher education—enjoys a strong reputation in New York State. Fisher offers outstanding undergraduate and graduate education in the traditional arts and sciences, in addition to highly successful professional programs in business, education, nursing, and pharmacy. The College offers 32 undergraduate majors, 9 pre-professional programs, 12 master's programs, and 3 doctoral programs. The academic departments of the College are organized into five schools: School of Arts and Sciences; Bittner School of Business; Ralph C. Wilson, Jr. School of Education; Wegmans School of Nursing; and Wegmans School of Pharmacy.

Fisher's mission is to equip its students to become active members of a diverse society and to prepare them to serve the community. Founded by the Congregation of St. Basil in 1948, the College retains the educational philosophy of the Basilian Fathers, whose motto, "Teach me goodness, discipline, and knowledge," expresses the College's traditions and values.

Located just minutes outside of Rochester, New York, in the picturesque town of Pittsford, the campus is situated on 154 park-like acres—a beautiful setting for 24 modern buildings and a warm, friendly campus community of 2,700 full-time undergraduates, 200 part-time undergraduates, and 1,100 graduate students. Fisher is also the home of the Buffalo Bills NFL Summer Training Camp.

Faculty members are selected for their teaching excellence, scholarly initiatives, and commitment to students. Fisher boasts experts in international business, comparative politics, organizational behavior, women and gender studies, and leadership development, among others. With a student-faculty ratio of 13:1, Fisher students receive personal instruction in small classes.

All of Fisher's first-year students receive some form of financial assistance. In addition to its merit-based awards, the College offers a number of unique scholarships, including the Service Scholars Program, the First Generation Scholarship and the Foreign Language Scholarship.

The College, a Division III member of the NCAA, the Eastern College Athletic Conference, and the Empire 8, offers 23 varsity sports, as well as club/intramural sports. In addition to athletics, students may choose from a wide range of campus clubs and organizations, including student government, music groups, language clubs, cultural organizations, student publications, and intramural sports. Many academic departments also sponsor clubs.

Fisher students enjoy living and learning in a community that values them as individuals, challenges them as students, and prepares them to be leaders in the community.

CONTACT INFORMATION

Office of Freshman Admissions
☎ 585-385-8064 or toll-free 800-444-4640
⌨ admissions@sjfc.edu

- **Enrollment:** *3,977*

- **Selectivity:** *moderately difficult*

- **Test scores:** *ACT over 18, 100%; SAT—critical reading over 500, 66%; SAT—math over 500, 81%*

- **Application deadline:** *Rolling (freshmen), rolling (transfer)*

- **Expenses:** *Tuition $26,810; Room & Board $10,720*

Kearney Hall, Fisher's main administration building.

Founded in 1696 as the King William's School and chartered as St. John's College in 1784, we are the third oldest college in the country.

St JOHN'S
College

ANNAPOLIS · SANTA FE

ANNAPOLIS, MARYLAND AND SANTA FE, NEW MEXICO
www.stjohnscollege.edu/

St. John's College students are inquisitive, eclectic, thoughtful, articulate, passionate, self-disciplined, and serious about the joys of a profoundly fundamental liberal education. They love to read, and they love to think about things. They examine questions, big and small, about all aspects of the world, in extended and in-depth conversations, often on a very personal level, without distrust or disrespect for those who don't agree with them.

At St. John's, there are no lecture classes, no written exams, no conventional textbooks, no academic departments, no elective classes, and no majors. The all-required four-year course of study is based on reading and discussing original texts, the so-called "Great Books"; the focus, however, is not on novels and literature but on the great works across the spectrum of human thought, from science and mathematics to philosophy and music.

Conversations—in the classroom and across the campus—are both disciplined and imaginative, both logical and whimsical, and both rational and heartfelt. The students question assumptions that they've made their whole lives. They explore ideas they never knew they were interested in. They drill down deep into meaning. They experiment. They create. They revel in subtlety and become bold thinkers. They read as if their lives depended on it. They're also serious about living those lives, devoting themselves to non-academic pursuits as wholeheartedly as they read Sophocles or Einstein.

Sports, music, theater, publications, community service, parties, the arts, whatever: Johnnies play as energetically as they study. And they have the opportunity to experience this intense educational odyssey and fulfilling community life in two very different locations: one campus is a classic cameo of academia, with colonial red brick buildings and stately shade trees, in Annapolis, Maryland; the other is a desert mountain paradise, a breathtaking world of sun, snow, art, and peace in Santa Fe, New Mexico. In both places, students longing to take on the full challenge of a life-changing education come together and find plenty to talk about.

CONTACT INFORMATION

Annapolis: Ms. Sarah Morse, Director of Admissions
☎ 410-626-2522 or toll-free 800-727-9238
🖳 admissions@sjca.edu
Santa Fe: Mr. Larry Clendenin, Director of Admissions
☎ 505 984-6060 or toll-free 800-331-5232
🖳 admissions@sjcsf.edu

- **Enrollment:** *858*
- **Selectivity:** *moderately difficult*
- **Test scores:** *ACT—over 18, 100%; SAT—critical reading over 500, 98%; SAT—math over 500, 98%*
- **Application deadline:** *Early Action I: November 15; Early Action II: January 15; Rolling (after February 15)*
- **Expenses:** *Tuition $44,544; Room & Board $10,644*

Seminars take place on Monday and Thursday evenings.

Students benefit from state-of-the-art instructional technology, engaged faculty members, and a caring staff. Saint Leo gives every student the tools they need to love the person they become here!

SAINT LEO, FLORIDA

www.saintleo.edu
https://www.facebook.com/officialsaintleo

Founded in 1889, Saint Leo University is now recognized as one of the nation's leading Catholic teaching universities and a school of international consequence. The University Campus in Saint Leo, Florida, serves the education needs of just under 2,000 traditional-age undergraduate students. The University also offers a variety of dynamic graduate programs, a weekend and evening program for working adults, and both undergraduate and graduate degree programs through 17 education centers in seven states and through the Center for Online Learning, which houses the University's cutting-edge online degree programs.

The diverse University College student body represents 39 states and territories, as well as 58 countries. International students make up 13 percent of the student population. Minority students represent 34 percent of the University College enrollment. Approximately 62 percent of traditional full-time students live in one of 13 residence halls, with two more residence halls slated to come online for the 2012–13 academic year.

Saint Leo University offers 43 traditional majors, pre-professional studies, specializations, endorsements, and programs. Students can participate in the nationally recognized honors program and also elect to double major.

Students can choose from the more 60 sixty different clubs and organizations on campus, including national fraternities and sororities. The Student Government Union and various campus organizations also sponsor movies, concerts, art exhibits, lectures, dances, and other special events throughout the academic year.

Saint Leo is a member of the Sunshine State Conference and competes in NCAA Division II intercollegiate athletics for men and women. Men's sports include baseball, basketball, cross-country, golf, lacrosse, soccer, swimming, and tennis. Women compete in basketball, cross-country, golf, lacrosse, soccer, softball, swimming, tennis, and volleyball. Students can also participate in a wide variety of intramurals. Campus

recreational facilities include lighted racquetball and tennis courts; soccer, baseball, and softball fields; a weight room/fitness center; and a heated outdoor Olympic-size swimming pool. The campus is bordered by a 154-acre lake and an eighteen-hole golf course.

Saint Leo is committed to giving its students an education that prepares them for the future. The goal of the University is to develop the whole person, both academically and personally, by providing a values-based education in the Benedictine tradition. In a recent satisfaction survey, 93 percent of respondents said they would recommend Saint Leo to a friend. The University has been honored as a Best

CONTACT INFORMATION

Mr. Reggie Hill, Director of Admission

☎ 352-588-8283 or toll-free 800-334-5532

💻 admissions@saintleo.edu

University–South Region by *U.S. News & World Report* for the past two years.

- **Enrollment:** *1,926*

- **Selectivity:** *minimally difficult*

- **Test scores:** *ACT—over 18, 79%; SAT—critical reading over 500, 34%, SAT—math over 500, 31%*

- **Application deadline:** *8/15 (freshmen), 8/1 (transfer)*

- **Expenses:** *Tuition $18,700; Room & Board $9394*

Saint Leo University is located on a picturesque lakefront campus in beautiful west central Florida.

SAIC's diverse faculty are practicing artists, designers and scholars who will help you acquire and refine your technical and conceptual abilities.

SAIC School of the Art Institute of Chicago

CHICAGO, ILLINOIS
www.saic.edu

The School of the Art Institute of Chicago (SAIC) the most influential art school in the United States educates artists and designers in a highly professional, studio-oriented environment. And *U.S. News & World Report* just ranked SAIC's Master of Fine Arts program second among fine arts graduate programs in the nation.

SAIC stands apart from other art and design schools in its comprehensive curriculum, with more than 900 courses offered each semester. Instead of declaring a major, students are free to design a path of study that suits their creative needs. A student may choose to do all their course work in one area of study or among multiple department areas. Liberal arts and art history are central to the life of SAIC; the School has one of the largest art history departments in the nation and is the only college in the country that offers courses on the history, theory, and philosophical bases of art criticism.

SAIC students live in loft-style rooms with individual bathrooms, kitchens, voice mail, and Internet. The residence halls have 24-hour security, well-lit studios, lounge rooms with big screen TVs, and computer labs.

Students have unique access to SAIC's sister institution – The Art Institute of Chicago—its Modern Wing and Ryerson & Burnham Libraries, the largest art and architecture research libraries in the country. The Gene Siskel Film Center screens about 1,500 cutting-edge independent and international films every year and hosts guest appearances (Robert Downey, Jr., recently stopped by). SAIC's Video Data Bank houses more than 1,600 titles and is the leading resource in the

United States for videotapes by and about contemporary artists.

SAIC is located in the heart of downtown Chicago, home to the nation's second-largest art scene with its world-class museums, galleries, alternative spaces, and organizations that support the arts. Students have plenty of places to go: ballet, opera, theater, libraries, blues and jazz clubs, parks, ethnic restaurants, professional sports venues, and street festivals. SAIC is located across the street from an extraordinary space. Millennium Park is a 21st-century mix of art, architecture and nature,

CONTACT INFORMATION

Larry Lee, Associate Director, Undergraduate Admissions
☎ 312-629-6100 or toll-free 800-232-SAIC
💻 ugadmiss@saic.edu

and SAIC, its faculty, and its students played a key role in the realization of the Crown Fountain with 1,000 video portraits that are screened continuously on the fountain's twin video towers.

A Christ-centered university, Shorter offers a wonderful blend of faith and learning. Shorter's aim is to help students become fully prepared to embrace God's plan for their lives.

Shorter University

ROME, GEORGIA
www.shorter.edu

Shorter University combines a high-quality education with an intentionally Christian atmosphere. The University is a pioneer in both traditional semester programs and innovative continuous programs for working adults. And Shorter is proud of its statistics—an overall graduate school acceptance rate of 80 percent and an impressive 82 percent acceptance rate to medical colleges over the past twenty-two years.

Each year, the campus is visited by Christian leaders, scholars and outstanding musicians. The campus minister works to provide a wide range of opportunities for spiritual growth. The largest religious organization on campus is the Baptist Collegiate Ministries (BCM), which includes Christians of many denominations.

Music and drama groups are an important part of life at Shorter. They include the Shorter Chorale, the Shorter Chorus, the Shorter Theater Company, the Opera Workshop, and the Shorter Marching Band. The Shorter Chorale was selected to represent the United States in choral festivals held in Yugoslavia, France, and Austria, and it performed in St. Petersburg, Russia, to represent the University. Shorter has also been the home of numerous National Metropolitan Opera Audition winners and finalists.

The University has three fraternities and three sororities as well as chapters of two national music fraternities and honor societies for majors in biology, communication, English, music, religion, and social sciences. Student publications include a newspaper, a yearbook and a literary magazine.

Shorter University finished the 2011–12 year ranked No. 2 in the Learfield Directors Cup in the NAIA. Shorter is transitioning to membership in the NCAA Division II and has recently joined the National Christian College Athletic Association (NCCAA). Varsity teams compete in men's baseball, basketball, cross-country, football, golf, lacrosse, soccer, tennis, track and field, and wrestling and in women's basketball, cheerleading, cross-country, fastpitch softball, golf, lacrosse, soccer, tennis, track and field, and volleyball.

The University has 150 acres atop Shorter Hill, in Rome, Georgia. It's located just 65 miles northwest of Atlanta and 65 miles south of Chattanooga, Tennessee. In Rome, students can enjoy the Symphony Orchestra, Rome Little Theatre, Rome Area Council for the Arts events, popular concerts and attractions at The Forum, and the 334,859-volume modern library.

CONTACT INFORMATION

Office of Admission
☎ 706-233-7319 or toll-free 800-868-6980
🖳 admissions@shorter.edu

- **Enrollment:** *1,500*
- **Selectivity:** *moderately difficult*
- **Test scores:** *ACT—over 18, 76.8%; SAT—critical reading over 500, 43.5%; SAT—math over 500, 48%*
- **Application deadline:** *6/1 (freshmen), 6/1 (transfer)*
- **Expenses:** *Estimated Tuition $19,300; Estimated Room & Board $9400*

Freshmen thrive in Learning Communities that combine 3 core courses around a theme, building connections between classwork and understanding.

SIMPSON COLLEGE

INDIANOLA, IOWA

www.simpson.edu

http://www.facebook.com/SimpsonCollege

Simpson College is dedicated to your success. Personalized attention, a cutting-edge curriculum, and a great location are just some of the benefits of a Simpson education that will help you reach your goals. Since its founding in 1860, the College has guided students to the next stage in their lives, be that a successful career or graduate school.

Simpson professors are as dedicated to their fields of study as they are to teaching, and it shows in the classroom. When this type of passion is combined with well-prepared and motivated students, the potential for success is unlimited. Simpson's 1,500 students benefit from a student to faculty ratio of 14:1. More than 90 percent of Simpson faculty members hold the highest degree in their field, and they also are dedicated to nurturing each student's growth. They work side by side with students and promote hands-on learning, equipping students with the skills demanded by today's employers and graduate schools.

The beautiful, tree-lined campus is ideally located in Indianola, Iowa. Recent renovations to campus facilities include a state-of-the-art performing arts center, updated athletic facilities, and the new Kent Campus Center opening fall 2012. The setting is intimate enough to offer a personalized education, but close enough to the Des Moines metropolitan area to take advantage of internship and career opportunities. In fact, Des Moines was ranked the #1 place for business and careers by Forbes.

Simpson offers 81 majors and minors, highlighted by a cutting-edge curriculum that is gaining national attention. As part of this, students take advantage of community partnerships, hold internships, study abroad, and conduct independent research. Simpson also offers a guaranteed internship program to qualified students, and the popular 4-4-1 academic calendar includes a three-week May term for academic and career exploration.

Extracurricular activities at Simpson range from award-winning fine arts programs to nationally recognized NCAA Division III teams. Students participate in more than 75 clubs and organizations, including student government, campus publications, fraternities and sororities, religious life, intramurals, and departmental clubs. Community service is also part of Simpson's DNA,

and Newsweek magazine ranked Simpson as one of the nation's top 25 service-minded colleges.

Simpson students are engaged in the classroom and in the world. They continue to find success on campus as well as the years following graduation. Simpson students have watched whales off the coast of Madagascar, conducted research at the Institute of Genetic Medicine at Johns Hopkins, created a fast check Web site to analyze the claims of 19 presidential candidates, visited boardrooms with top executives, and performed monologues at the 4th Street Theatre. Simpson College is filled with student success stories. Let us help you find yours!

CONTACT INFORMATION

Deborah Tierney, Vice President for Enrollment
☎ 515-961-1624 or toll-free 800-362-2454
💻 admiss@simpson.edu

- **Enrollment:** *1,485*
- **Selectivity:** *moderately difficult*
- **Test scores:** *ACT—over 18, 100%*
- **Application deadline:** *Rolling admissions—Applications are accepted up to two weeks before the start of the term.*
- **Expenses:** *Tuition $29,529; Room & Board $7963*

Simpson's tree-lined campus in spring.

Fostering Community to Build Communities.

SCC
SOMERSET CHRISTIAN COLLEGE
SOMERSET COUNTY AND NEWARK, NJ
www.somerset.edu

Somerset Christian College (SCC) is a new college being built on an old foundation. For over a century, the College has offered biblically sound courses teaching men and women how to serve God, society, and the church in a wide variety of fields. Since 2001, SCC has been the only evangelical college chartered by the State of New Jersey, operating with educational sites in Newark and suburban areas of central New Jersey.

SCC offers a unique blend of spiritual enrichment, academic excellence, and social fulfillment. The student body is a wide-spread spectrum of ages, races, interests, and personalities, reflecting the wide diversity of the metropolitan corridor of the Northeast. Through godly instructors, rich curricula in career-shaping majors, spiritually enthusiastic students, valuable enriching internships, and global learning experiences, SCC offers students all they need to be equipped for their best future.

SCC offers Bachelor of Arts (B.A.) degrees—a four-year, 120 credit-hour course of study. The B.A. is awarded upon successful completion of all requirements, which includes a core curriculum consisting of Biblical Studies, General Education, and Major Requirements. Majors include Business Administration/Management, Psychology/Counseling, and Biblical Studies. Areas of concentration include Organizational Leadership, Family and Marriage Counseling, Communications, and Worship/Music/Media.

Among its many course selections, SCC offers a Life Enhancing Accelerated Degree (LEAD) for adult students to complete their baccalaureate degree so they can advance in their professional careers. These students form a small group, or cohort, that creates a supportive relationship among its members to facilitate learning and collective completion of the program. To accommodate working students, SCC has scheduled 16 modular courses one night a week/one course at a time, for the duration of the program.

SCC operates a full student financial aid program, including grants, scholarships, loans, and employment, allowing any student a realistic opportunity to finance his or her college education. More than 95 percent of all SCC students who apply for financial assistance to further their education receive it. The College is aware that each family offers a unique financial situation and the Financial Aid staff is available to work with students to find the resources to fund their education at SCC.

Somerset Christian College admits all qualified students of any race, color, disability, and national or ethnic origin to all the rights, privileges, programs, and activities available through the College. SCC does not discriminate on the basis of gender, race, color, disability, or national or ethnic origin in administration of its educational policies, admission policies, financial aid, or other school-administered programs.

CONTACT INFORMATION

Keyla Pavia, Director of Admissions
☎ 973-803-5000 or toll-free 800-234-9305
🖳 info@somerset.edu

- **Enrollment:** *300*
- **Application deadline:** *Open enrollment*
- **Expenses:** *Tuition & fees: $8181 per semester*

Transforming Minds for Career Callings.

Student life at Southern integrates classroom learning with extracurricular experience to foster a climate in which each student can achieve higher levels of intellectual, personal, and social growth.

Southern Connecticut State University

SC
SU

NEW HAVEN, CONNECTICUT
www.southernct.edu/

The academic and social environment at Southern Connecticut State University encourages students to discover who they are, who they want to be, and how to realize their dreams. This public, coed university offers 117 undergraduate and graduate programs, fascinating internships, unique research opportunities, a challenging faculty, and an energetic campus.

Southern has five academic schools: Arts and Sciences; Business; Education; Health and Human Services, including nursing, public health, recreation and leisure studies and social work; and Graduate Studies. Southern offers several honors programs for highly motivated students. The Honors College is a four-year alternative program featuring team-taught interdisciplinary courses, symposia, and a written thesis.

The Office of Student Supportive Services provides tutoring support and includes services and programs for veterans, international students, and students with learning, physical, and emotional/psychiatric disabilities. The student body represents diverse ethnic and socioeconomic groups; students from 38 states and 39 countries enroll at Southern. Students live on campus in nine modern residence halls and townhouses.

Competitive athletes and eager amateurs enjoy the unique sports programs at Southern. Intramural and club sports include coed basketball, cheerleading, flag football, coed floor hockey, a golf tournament, ice hockey (men), karate, rugby (men and women), skiing and snowboarding, coed softball, Ultimate Frisbee, coed soccer, a tennis tournament, Wiffle ball, and coed volleyball. A member of the National Collegiate Athletic Association (NCAA), the Eastern College Athletic Conference, and the Northeast-10 Conference, Southern has a long tradition of athletic excellence. It ranks among the top 10 NCAA Division II colleges and universities with its 9 NCAA team championships and 67 individual championships. Southern offers

intercollegiate competition in men's baseball, basketball, cross-country, football, soccer, swimming, and track and field. Southern holds 6 national championships in men's soccer and 3 in men's gymnastics. Intercollegiate programs for women include basketball, cross-country, field hockey, gymnastics, lacrosse, soccer, softball, swimming, track and field, and volleyball. Outstanding facilities are available to all athletes in Moore Fieldhouse, Pelz Gymnasium, and the Jess Dow Field outdoor sports complex.

New Haven, Connecticut, is a sophisticated city of 130,000 people and a classic college town; about 35,000 students attend its half-dozen universities and colleges. Only 75 miles from New York City and 3 hours from Boston, New Haven provides students

CONTACT INFORMATION

Ms. Paula Kennedy, Associate Director of Admissions

☎ 203-392-5656

💻 cronek1@southernct.edu

with easy access to movies, restaurants, clubs, concerts, seaside activities, sports, museums, and world-famous theater at the Yale Repertory, the Shubert, and Long Wharf.

- **Enrollment:** *11,533*

- **Selectivity:** *moderately difficult*

- **Test scores:** *ACT—over 18, 71%; SAT— critical reading over 500, 35%; SAT—math over 500, 34%*

- **Application deadline:** *4/1 (freshmen), 8/1 (transfer)*

- **Expenses:** *Tuition $8541; Room & Board $10,686*

Southern's School of Business, the University's third most popular major, opened its new building in August 2012.

The state-of-the-art Richard B. Flynn Campus Union serves as the hub of campus life. It features a food court with a two-story atrium.

SPRINGFIELD, MASSACHUSETTS

www.springfieldcollege.edu

Springfield College students are leaders who are committed to helping others. Serving a unique mission to "educate students in spirit, mind, and body for leadership in service to humanity," the college is known for its Humanics philosophy. This philosophy creates an environment where learning, both inside and outside the classroom, is valued and respected. Academic and co-curricular programs are integrated, and majors include traditional course work, enhanced by applied internships, fieldwork experiences, and many other experiential learning activities. The focus on leadership development and community service adds to this learning experience by engaging students in volunteer service activities and service-learning initiatives on campus and in the community. Graduates are prepared for leadership roles in both their professions and in their communities.

Campus life is exciting. There are more than 40 special interest clubs and organizations. Students can be featured in dance and Broadway productions, DJ at the student-run radio station WSCB, write for the

Springfield Student newspaper, serve on a class board, or even help plan weekend activities, concerts, or Sti-Yu-Ka (spring week). Students are encouraged to get involved in campus activities.

Springfield College offers four-year and graduate-level degree programs leading to careers in health sciences, business, communications, education, physical therapy, physical education, sport and exercise science, human services, and social work. The student-to-faculty ratio is 14-to-1.

Stellar individuals have made indelible marks on society, science, and health and wellness, including student and instructor James Naismith's invention of basketball in 1891. From groundbreaking studies in exercise to wellness education and research, Springfield College students continue to transform lives and communities.

The award-winning Wellness and Recreation Complex includes a 49,000-square-foot Wellness Center, featuring two floors of exercise machine space, a climbing wall, four group/exercise/ aerobics studios, and fitness testing labs, and the 94,000-square-foot Field House, containing a six-lane, 200-meter Mondotrack—the

same surface used in the 2008 Beijing Olympics—and four large multipurpose courts.

The Springfield College athletic program is regularly recognized as one of the top Division III athletic programs in the country. The men's volleyball team won the inaugural Division III National Championship in 2012.

Springfield College is located in western Massachusetts, a thriving and exciting environment in which to live, work, and study. The Berkshire Hills are an hour away. Boston is just 1½ hours away, and New York City is 2½ hours away.

CONTACT INFORMATION

Richard K. Veres, Director of Undergraduate Admissions
☎ 413-748-3136 or toll-free 800-343-1257
💻 admissions@ springfieldcollege.edu

- **Enrollment:** *2,300 full-time undergraduates*
- **Selectivity:** *moderately difficult*
- **Application deadline:** *4/1 (freshmen), 8/1 (transfer)*
- **Expenses:** *Tuition $30,660; Room & Board $10,280*

Springfield College has been a leader in providing a broad and balanced educational experience, earning an international reputation as an educational institution of exceptional quality.

Students celebrate in front of Oriskany Residence Hall, SUNYIT's new suite-style residence for first-year students.

UTICA, NEW YORK

www.sunyit.edu

www.facebook.com/sunyit

A SUNYIT education challenges students to engage the future, offering dynamic opportunities that empower them to change the world.

At New York's only public institute of technology, SUNYIT students can choose from a variety of programs in technology and professional studies at an especially affordable cost. Undergraduate and graduate studies prepare students for a wide range of career opportunities, many in fields with increasing demand. New and recently launched SUNYIT programs include biology, civil engineering, community & behavioral health, electrical & computer engineering, and network & computer security.

Centrally located in the foothills of the Adirondack Mountains, the SUNYIT campus has the convenience of being near a city and the charm of a woodland setting. A $100-million campus expansion has included the addition of three new buildings: the Student Center, the Wildcat Field House, and, for freshmen only, Oriskany Residence Hall. The Campus Center's residential dining hall has undergone a multi-phase, $4.5-million transformation into a modern, two-story, station-style eatery. Construction on a new technology complex will begin later this year.

A wide-ranging nanotechnology partnership with the University at Albany's College of Nanoscale Science & Engineering, and the development of the Marcy NanoCenter at SUNYIT, a 300-acre campus site intended for high-tech manufacturing, has furthered SUNYIT's unique reputation as an academic innovator— and a college of opportunity for tomorrow's students.

Apart from an enriching academic experience, students enjoy campus life in highly rated residence halls. The campus's three residential complexes offer popular amenities and comfortable living in townhouse-style suites. Student athletes participate in NCAA Division III athletics, which include men's and women's basketball, cross country, lacrosse, soccer, and volleyball; men's baseball; and women's

CONTACT INFORMATION

Jennifer Phelan Ninh
☎ 315-792-7500 or toll-free 866-2-SUNYIT
💻 admissions@sunyit.edu

softball. Intramural offerings, entertainment, activities, and community-building experiences support and sustain a unique campus culture.

SUNYIT's new Student Center, a unique gathering place for students, includes an eatery, a theater, a 20-foot media wall, a café, and student club offices.

Mustang fans have a lot to cheer about! Among Stevenson's Division III teams are the nationally top-ranked men's lacrosse team and a new football team which competed for the first time in 2011.

STEVENSON
UNIVERSITY

Imagine your future. Design your career.®

STEVENSON, MARYLAND
www.stevenson.edu/

Stevenson University (SU) doesn't just focus on the four years students spend on campus. It prepares undergraduates to survive and thrive in the working world after graduation. Stevenson University (SU) offers a career-focused, liberal arts education. With a student-faculty ratio of 16:1, it is easy to understand why students often cite the easygoing, personal relationship with faculty members as one of the University's strong points.

Through Stevenson University's concept of Learning Beyond, students step outside of the class-room to take their learning to the next level. Experiential learning opportunities include study abroad, service learning, field placements, and independent research. In addition, through an approach known as Career Architecture[SM], each student develops a professional career plan based on their values, skills, and strengths. Stevenson's graduates maintain a placement rate that tops 95 percent each year, with students landing jobs or going on to graduate school within six months of graduation.

At Stevenson University, students enjoy more than 45 clubs and organizations, multiple honor societies, and NCAA Division III athletics. The following sports are offered: men's and women's basketball, cross-country, golf, lacrosse, soccer, tennis, track and field, and volleyball; men's baseball and football; and women's field hockey, ice hockey, and softball. Cheerleading, dance, and intramural sports are also extremely popular.

In addition to its undergraduate programs, the University offers the master's degree programs, some of which

At Stevenson, the classroom is only the beginning. From clubs and organizations to opportunities in the performing and visual arts, there is something here for everyone.

offer a five-year B.S. to M.S. option.

Stevenson University (formerly Villa Julie College) has two beautiful campuses in the heart of Maryland, in Stevenson and Owings Mills, and the University continues to expand. The original Greenspring Campus sits among the rolling hills in Stevenson, Maryland. The Owings Mills Campus, opened in 2004, offers top-notch facilities for learning and for living, including 13 residence halls, Mustang Stadium, the Brown School of Business and Leadership, and a state-of-the art gymnasium. The University is expanding its campus facilities in 2013 with the opening of a 28-acre addition to the Owings Mills Campus, which will become the new home for the School of Design and the School of the Sciences. Classes are held on both

campuses, and the University provides a free shuttle service that runs between the locations.

- **Enrollment:** *4,317*
- **Selectivity:** *moderately difficult*
- **Test scores:** *ACT—over 18, 68.12%; SAT—critical reading over 500, 45.82%; SAT—math over 500, 50.12%*
- **Application deadline:** *Rolling (freshmen), rolling (transfer)*
- **Expenses:** *Tuition $23,562; Room & Board $11,894*

CONTACT INFORMATION

Mrs. Kelly Farmer, Director of Freshman Admissions
☎ 410-486-7001 or toll-free 877-468-6852
🖥 admissions@stevenson.edu

With close to 350 clubs and organizations, 20 red hot Seawolves varsity teams, unique traditions like the Roth Pond Regatta, and dining options open as late as 3 a.m., Stony Brook University has fun on the menu 24/7.

Cheer your heart out for NCAA Division I football and lacrosse teams under the bright lights of Stony Brook's 8,300-seat Kenneth P. LaValle Stadium, or catch a home run at the new Joe Nathan Field. You also can whoop it up at basketball, soccer, cross-country, swimming, tennis, and indoor and outdoor track and field events.

One-of-a-kind Stony Brook traditions include the annual Roth Pond Regatta, where students, faculty, and staff get soaked as they race across Roth Pond in boats constructed only of cardboard, duct tape, and paint. Springtime Strawberry Fest and Diversity Day celebrations bring everyone together on the Academic Mall to enjoy mouth-watering strawberry treats and a day of live music, dancing, and student performances that highlight their different heritages. Earthstock, Homecoming, the Festival of Lights, and Chillfest

Students and faculty and staff members design and build boats made of only cardboard, duct tape, and paint. Then they race them across the pond at the annual Roth Pond Regatta.

Stony Brook University

STONY BROOK, NEW YORK

www.stonybrook.edu

www.facebook.com/stonybrooku

are other traditions you won't want to miss.

On more than 1,000 acres of woodland, including bicycle paths and a nature trail, the University is ideally located 60 miles east of New York City, with a Long Island Rail Road station right on campus for easy access to Manhattan. Close to both the ocean and Long Island Sound, Stony Brook also is just a short bicycle ride away from North Shore beaches and shopping areas. The campus boasts a fine arts center with discounted performance tickets for students, six residential quads, and a centrally located academic mall with plenty of outdoor seating for lunch or people watching. An 85,000-square-foot Campus Recreation Center opened in fall 2012.

Academic programs of note include Stony Brook University's School of Journalism, featuring one of the nation's first courses in news literacy; the College of Engineering and Applied Sciences, with seven ABET-accredited programs; and the School of Marine and Atmospheric Sciences, with waterfront research facilities and vessels. Stony Brook offers more than 200 majors, minors, and combined-degree programs, including the Fast Track MBA Program in which students can complete their bachelor's and master's degrees in five years. Stony Brook also offers 11 majors and minors in sustainability studies, leading to green careers.

Study abroad for a year, a semester, summer, or winter session in locations as diverse as a rain forest of Madagascar, Turkana Basin Institute in Kenya, and the coral reef of Discovery Bay, Jamaica, West Indies. Internships and research opportunities abound on and off campus and around the world through Stony Brook's Career Center and Undergraduate Research and Creative Activities program.

CONTACT INFORMATION

Ms. Judith Burke-Berhanan,
  Director of Undergraduate
  Admissions

☎ 631-632-6868

💻 enroll@stonybrook.edu

- **Enrollment:** *24,061*
- **Selectivity:** *very difficult*
- **Test scores:** *ACT—over 18, 99%; SAT—critical reading over 500, 86%; SAT—math over 500, 95%*
- **Application deadline:** *1/15 (freshmen), 3/1 (transfer)*
- **Expenses:** *Tuition $6580; Room & Board $10,142*

Seawolves fans get their red on in the Kenneth P. LaValle Stadium. Go, Seawolves!

Imani Dickerson '15 on the first day of pottery class. The College's historic dairy barns were converted into modern studio art spaces—one of the many ways Sweet Briar has preserved and repurposed its original architecture.

SWEET BRIAR COLLEGE

SWEET BRIAR, VIRGINIA

www.sbc.edu/

Sweet Briar College is consistently ranked as one of the top liberal arts and sciences colleges in the country. Its excellent academic reputation and beautiful campus attract ambitious, self-confident women who want to excel. Small classes (averaging 12 students per class) ensure personal attention and academic interaction.

Most students are enrolled at Sweet Briar's Virginia campus; about 120 students are enrolled in Sweet Briar's coed Junior Year in France and Junior Year in Spain programs. The College offers more than 35 majors, minors, and certificate programs and two graduate degree programs: the Master of Arts in Teaching and the Master of Education. The College is also one of two women's colleges in the country to offer a degree-granting, ABET-accredited engineering program.

More than 50 campus organizations are open to students, including honor societies, community service groups, political groups, drama and dance clubs, a radio station, and singing groups. Recent speakers on campus include journalist and local food advocate Michael Pollan, author and founder of the Afghan Women's Writing Project Masha Hamilton, and activist and commentator Reza Aslan. Each academic year, the Babcock Season brings in national theater, music, and dance acts to perform in addition to a full slate of visual and performing arts events presented by students and faculty.

Sweet Briar is the only college in the United States with a residential artists' colony on campus. Known as the Virginia Center for the Creative Arts, the colony is a working retreat for international writers, visual artists, and composers. Sweet Briar is also home to the Blue Ridge Summer Theatre Festival, an annual production of the College's resident Endstation Theatre Company, and to BLUR: The Blue Ridge Summer Institute for Young Artists, an intensive three-week camp for high school students.

A 53,000-square-foot fitness and athletic center has a three-lane elevated track, a field house, an aerobics/spinning room, and racquetball and squash courts. The on-campus equestrian center, one of the largest and best college facilities in the country, attracts competitive and recreational riders. The 100-acre Rogers Riding Center has a 120-foot by 300-foot indoor arena with Perma-Flex footing, stables for about 90 horses, outdoor rings, paddocks, and miles of hacking trails—all within walking distance of the main campus.

The academic buildings and many common spaces are equipped for wireless connection to the campus network. Ongoing classroom and library improvements take advantage of the latest in instructional technology, including resource-sharing and mobile platforms. Varsity athletes compete in NCAA Division III field hockey, lacrosse, soccer, softball, swimming, and tennis. Club sports include cross-country, fencing, and riding.

Sweet Briar's 3,250-acre campus in the foothills of the Blue Ridge Mountains includes hiking, biking, riding trails, and two lakes. The College is centrally located on the outskirts of Lynchburg, southwest of Washington, D.C., and Charlottesville and Richmond, Virginia.

CONTACT INFORMATION

Ms. Gretchen Gravley-Tucker, Director of Admissions

☎ 434-381-6142 or toll-free 800-381-6142

🖳 admissions@sbc.edu

- **Enrollment:** *760*

- **Selectivity:** *moderately difficult*

- **Test scores:** *ACT—over 18, 93.3%; SAT—critical reading over 500, 71.1%; SAT—math over 500, 50.6%*

- **Application deadline:** *2/1 (freshmen), 5/1 (transfer)*

- **Expenses:** *Tuition $31,850; Room & Board $11,440*

Each spring, professors take their classes outdoors to enjoy the warm weather. The lawn in front of the Mary Helen Cochran Library is a favorite gathering spot.

Syracuse University's residential campus features historical and modern architecture. Students enjoy diverse academic and extra-curricular opportunities, along with a community-oriented campus.

SYRACUSE UNIVERSITY

SYRACUSE, NEW YORK
www.syracuse.edu/

Explore, discover, break boundaries, and leave your mark at Syracuse University (SU). This private university with an international reputation draws students from every state and from more than 100 other countries. The University offers a unique mix of academic programs—more than 200 majors and 90 minors—through its nine liberal arts and professional colleges. With one of the oldest study-abroad programs in the nation, Syracuse sends students to study and live in more than 30 amazing places around the globe—Hong Kong, Madrid, Istanbul, Florence, Beijing, and London, to name a few.

Students at SU live in modern residence halls, apartments, and town houses and all are connected to the University's wireless networks.

Social life is centered on the campus through the more than 300 extracurricular groups and clubs and a full events calendar that is regularly updated online.

The Syracuse Orange dominate in the classroom and on the playing fields in NCAA Division I sports. Men's intercollegiate sports are basketball, cross-country, football, lacrosse, rowing, soccer, and track and field. Women have teams in basketball, cross country, field hockey, ice hockey, lacrosse, rowing, soccer, softball, tennis, track and field, and volleyball. The 50,000-seat world-famous Carrier Dome is the site of concerts and sports events. It's the only domed stadium in the Northeast and the country's largest structure of its kind on a college campus.

The city of Syracuse is the business, educational, and cultural hub of central New York. The 200-acre campus sits on a hill overlooking the downtown area of Syracuse. The city offers professional theater and opera, as well as visiting artists and performers. Highlights of the downtown area include the Everson Museum of Art, the Milton J. Rubenstein Museum of Science and Technology (MOST), the impressive Civic Center, and the Armory Square shopping area. Syracuse is within easy driving distance of Toronto, Boston, Philadelphia, Montreal, and New York City,

CONTACT INFORMATION

Office of Admissions
☎ 315-443-3611
💻 orange@syr.edu

- **Enrollment:** *17,493*
- **Selectivity:** *moderately difficult*
- **Test scores:** *ACT—over 18, 98.1%; SAT—critical reading over 500, 81.1%; SAT—math over 500, 89.3%*
- **Application deadlines:** *Early Decision: 11/15 Regular Decision: 1/1 Spring Admission: 11/15 (freshman & transfer)*
- **Expenses:** *Tuition $37,610; Room & Board $13,692*

SU's vision of Scholarship in Action allows academic exploration to extend far beyond the classroom. Above, current students apply their knowledge in meaningful ways within the Syracuse community.

Trine continually makes national headlines because of the success of some of its 21 NCAA Division III teams and 600 student-athletes. Will you be cheering with Storm and your friends in the stands?.

TRINE
UNIVERSITY

ANGOLA, INDIANA

www.trine.edu/

Trine University endeavors to provide an affordable, career-oriented, project-based education. With a worldwide reputation for being "job-ready," Trine graduates are in demand. That is why 91 percent of Trine graduates are employed in major-related positions or graduate school within six months of graduation. Trine offers associate, bachelor's, and master's degrees in more than 35 programs in engineering, mathematics, science, informatics, business administration, teacher education, communication, criminal justice, and more.

With 2,339 students, small class sizes ensure one-on-one attention with faculty members who bring their own workplace experience into the classroom. The focus is on active participation through more than 60 student organizations, competitive intercollegiate athletics, and extensive co-op and internship opportunities. In 2011, 98 percent of students received $20 million in institutional aid in the form of grants and scholarships.

The University's 450-acre campus includes an 18-hole championship golf course. In 2009, Trine's Golf Course Village, four student apartment buildings, opened on Zollner Golf Course. The Rick L. and Vicki L. James University Center has become the focal point of the campus and features a gourmet dining hall, bookstore, climbing wall, sports and wellness center, Fabiani Theatre, post office, radio station, and library.

Trine is a member of the NCAA Division III and the Michigan Intercollegiate Athletic Association (MIAA), the nation's oldest athletic conference. Men's sports include baseball, basketball, cross-country, football, golf, lacrosse, soccer, tennis, track, and wrestling. Women's sports include basketball, cross-country, golf, lacrosse, soccer, softball, tennis, track, and volleyball. Intramural sports are also a big part of life at Trine. The Steel Dynamics Inc. Athletic and Recreation Center (ARC), which has a 200-meter indoor track and training and practice facilities for other sports, opened in 2009. The Fred Zollner Athletic Stadium opened in the summer of 2010, and the adjacent, iconic Ryan Skywalk opened in 2011.

Student organizations include the student senate, honor societies, professional organizations, the campus newspaper, the FM radio station, the drama club, music ensembles, pep and marching band, and fraternities and sororities. Trine is located in Angola, in the heart of northeast Indiana's scenic lake resort region and about halfway between Chicago and Cleveland, Ohio. Just a 45-minute drive from Fort Wayne, Indiana, Trine offers the safety and ease of a small-town environment, near some of the nation's most exciting cities. Pokagon State Park provides year-round recreation and is just 5 miles north of Trine's campus.

CONTACT INFORMATION

Scott Goplin, Dean of Admission
☎ 260-665-4365 or toll-free
   800-347-4878
⌨ admit@trine.edu

- **Enrollment:** *2,339*
- **Selectivity:** *moderately difficult*
- **Test scores:** *ACT—over 18, 98%; SAT—critical reading over 500, 55%; SAT—math over 500, 77%*
- **Application deadline:** *8/1 (freshmen), 8/1 (transfer)*
- **Expenses:** *Tuition $$27,000 (Engineering $29,750) Room & 19 meal plan: $9200*

The central focus part of Trine's transforming campus, the Rick L. and Vicki L. James University Center, is named in honor of a couple that has become a central part of the continued success of Trine University. Trine is the fastest-growing private institution in Indiana and has job-placement rates above 90 percent.

JACKSON, TENNESSEE
uu.edu
Facebook.com/UnionUniversity

"Jesus Christ is Lord of this place." What does it look like when a top-tier, highly recognized university makes this confession? It looks like faculty and students pursing Christian intellectual discipleship in order to engage the pressing issues of our day. It looks like community—a diverse people all pulling in the same direction, united by a heart for Christ as they learn and work together. It looks like purpose, inspiring young leaders to live in God's truth while equipping them to make our world better.

In addition to *U.S. News & World Report* ranking Union among the top 15 master's universities in the South, independent research by America's 100 Best College Buys ranks the University among the nation's best for combining academic quality and affordable price. Founded in 1823, Union University offers bachelor's, master's, and doctoral degrees. Union graduates enjoy a high acceptance rate at top graduate schools. Nearly 100 percent of faculty-recommended health science students have been accepted to medical school or professional graduate study.

The University provides each resident student with a private bedroom within apartment-style complexes, most of which

Union University faculty members are leaders in their fields who challenge their students to integrate Christian faith and learning in more than 100 programs of study.

were built in recent years. These units have four bedrooms with Internet connection, a kitchen, living room, washer/dryer unit, and one or two bathrooms. A new student commons building has two fireplaces, TV and game rooms, music practice rooms, two kitchens, a gymnasium, and a walking track. The University coffeehouse is another favorite location for concerts, conversation and study. In all, the campus has seen more than $120 million in new construction in the last ten years.

Students participate in more than 60 campus clubs, societies, fraternities and sororities, and intramural sports such as sand volleyball and water polo. In addition, students and faculty members set aside one day a year to serve the local community though more than 50 different volunteer projects. Union's 11 intercollegiate athletic teams compete in baseball, basketball, cross-country, golf, soccer, softball, and

volleyball. The University has achieved candidacy status in the NCAA Division II membership process.

The 290-acre campus is located in suburban Jackson, located 80 miles east of Memphis and 120 miles west of Nashville along the I-40 corridor. *Forbes* magazine recently named Jackson one of America's top 150 cities for business and careers.

Union is committed to its four core values of being excellence-driven, Christ-centered, people-focused, and future-directed in everything it does.

CONTACT INFORMATION

Mr. Robbie Graves, Assistant Vice President for Undergraduate Admissions
☎ 731-661-5100 or toll-free 800-33-UNION
💻 rgraves@uu.edu

- **Enrollment:** *4,200*
- **Selectivity:** *moderately difficult*
- **Test scores:** *ACT—over 18, 97%; SAT—critical reading over 500, 88%; SAT—math over 500, 83%*
- **Application deadline:** *Rolling (freshmen), rolling (transfer)*
- **Expenses:** *Tuition $24,940; Room & Board $8430*

In a friendly, close knit learning community, Union University faculty members invest in their students through award-winning classroom teaching, mentoring, and collaboration on research.

Findlay ranks in the top tier of U.S. News & World Report's "America's Best Colleges in the Midwest" and has been named a "Best Midwesten College" by the Princeton Review *for the past four years.*

FINDLAY, OHIO
www.findlay.edu/

The University of Findlay is a private, liberal arts university that prides itself on being flexible and forward-looking. In today's fast-paced world, Findlay is continually adapting programs and teaching methods to meet the needs of current students who are preparing for tomorrow's careers.

The University of Findlay has nearly 60 majors leading to bachelor's degrees. Unusual and well-recognized programs include equestrian studies, pre-veterinary medicine, nuclear medicine technology, physical therapy, as well as environmental, safety and occupational health management, and sport and event management.

The University also offers master's degrees in athletic training; business administration; education; environmental, safety, and health management; health informatics; occupational therapy; physician assistant studies; teaching English to speakers of other languages (TESOL);

and bilingual education. The University's two doctoral programs are the Doctor of Pharmacy (Pharm.D.) and Doctor of Physical Therapy programs.

The University is driven by a focus on experiential learning and providing real-world skill development opportunities for students in any program. Opportunities abound for learning leadership and interpersonal skills outside the classroom. Students participate in any of nearly 100 organizations, including special interest clubs, student government, performing arts groups, service clubs, spiritual life groups, and Greek sororities and fraternities. Club sports and 28 intramural sports keep the competitive spirit alive on campus.

Findlay offers 10 intercollegiate sports for men: baseball, basketball, cross-country, football, golf, indoor and outdoor track, soccer, swimming and diving, tennis, and wrestling. Women compete in basketball, cheerleading, cross-country, dance team, golf, indoor and outdoor track, lacrosse, soccer, softball, swimming and diving, tennis, and volleyball. There are two mixed sports, western and English equestrian riding.

The University of Findlay is located in Findlay, Ohio, a

Be active! Findlay offers 60 student organizations and intercollegiate, club and intramural sports, allowing you to learn leadership and interpersonal skills outside the classroom.

small city that is known for having a progressive business industry and high quality of life. Findlay has been designated a "dreamtown" by Demographics Daily, and it has been repeatedly named one of the top 10 "micropolitan" areas (small cities) in the United States by Site Selection magazine. Findlay has also been named one of the 100 Best Communities for Young People three consecutive times by America's Promise Alliance..

The University's campus consists of more than 388 acres on several sites. A campus-owned farm houses the pre-veterinary medicine and Western equestrian studies programs, including a 31,000-square-foot animal science center. A second facility houses the English equestrian program. Approximately 450 horses

are stabled and trained at the equestrian facilities, which offer barns and indoor and outdoor riding arenas.

- **Enrollment:** *4,999*
- **Selectivity:** *moderately difficult*
- **Test scores:** *ACT—over 18, 93%; SAT—critical reading over 500, 68%; SAT—math over 500, 66%*
- **Application deadline:** *Rolling (freshmen), rolling (transfer)*
- **Expenses:** *Tuition $26,798; Room & Board $8810*

CONTACT INFORMATION

Dr. Donna Gruber, Director of Undergraduate Admissions

☎ 419-434-4540 or toll-free 800-548-0932

💻 admissions@findlay.edu

Built on excellence, scholarship and original thought are strongly encouraged, engaging the entire campus community at the University of La Verne in beautiful Southern California.

LA VERNE, CALIFORNIA
www.laverne.edu

The city of La Verne is ideally located. One can go to the beach, the mountains, or "the City" all in the same day! The campus is only 35 miles east of Los Angeles, 30 miles from Orange County beaches, and 20 minutes north of Disneyland. Students get involved in research projects and internships and take advantage of local cultural, intellectual, and recreational resources while based in a safe, homey, and undistracted environment.

The University of La Verne is composed of four colleges: College of Arts and Sciences, College of Business & Public Management,

College of Education & Organizational Leadership, and the College of Law.

La Verne features top-notch faculty members who invite students to challenge themselves intellectually, be open to new experiences, and most of all, fully engage in their own personal and academic growth. Students benefit from small class sizes and have a choice of over 55 undergraduate majors.

In addition to an outstanding academic environment, La Verne students participate in their choice of over 50 student clubs and organizations including 18 varsity sports (NCAA Division III), fraternities, and sororities. The Campus Activities Board sponsors and coordinates year-round events, lectures, concerts, and other activities enjoyed by the campus and community at large.

Diversity is an integral component of life at La Verne and makes it stand out from other institutions. More than 50 percent of enrolled undergraduate students identify themselves as Hispanic, African American, or Asian American. In addition,

international students from all over the globe enhance the campus community. Students learn from people of different backgrounds, perspectives, and experiences, preparing them to live and work in an increasingly complex and diverse society and world.

The University is ranked by *Forbes* magazine among the top 15 percent of "America's Best Colleges." *U.S. News & World Report* heralds La Verne as one of the top 20 most diverse universities in the nation.

CONTACT INFORMATION

Ms. Ana Liza V. Zell, Associate Dean of Undergraduate Admission

☎ 909-593-3511 Ext. 4026 or toll-free 800-876-4858

🖳 admission@laverne.edu

- **Enrollment:** *2,172*
- **Selectivity:** *moderately selective*
- **Test scores:** *ACT—average 22 Composite; SAT—critical reading average 513; SAT—math average 530*
- **Application deadline:** *2/1 (freshmen), 4/1 (transfer)*
- **Expenses:** *Tuition $33,350; Room & Board $11,660*

La Verne's president with students.

At the University of Maine, learning isn't confined to a classroom, lecture hall, or laboratory. UMaine students take advantage of Maine's natural environment as a living laboratory. On campus and off, undergraduates have opportunities to participate in research as part of their academic experience.

1865 THE UNIVERSITY OF MAINE

ORONO, MAINE
go.umaine.edu
facebook.com/umaineadmissions
twitter.com/goumaine

When students start at the University of Maine, they can end up anywhere—like Honduras, engineering a water sanitation project for a rural village, or Antarctica, retrieving ice cores with scientists from UMaine's Climate Change Institute. But students also don't need to leave campus to find inspiration. At UMaine, they're surrounded by groundbreaking innovation, inspiring scholarship, and some of the most cutting-edge research anywhere. In other words, the world comes to them.

The University of Maine provides Maine's most comprehensive academic experience, with more than 90 majors and programs across five colleges, and the Maine Business School. UMaine's Honors College, one of the country's oldest and most prestigious honors programs, offers qualified students in any discipline a chance to explore topics outside their major and delve deeply into their areas of interest through senior theses projects.

UMaine is one of the National Science Foundation's top 100 public research universities. The University prides itself on providing opportunities for undergraduates to publish, travel, and work alongside its world-class scholars and scientists. Students also have extraordinary opportunities to gain real-world, hands-on experience in their fields. SPIFFY, UMaine's student investment club, manages a $1.6-million real-money portfolio. Wildlife ecology majors learn about black boar behavior by going out and tagging cubs. Engineering majors take advantage of co-ops and internships that often lead to employment after graduation. Education majors take advantage of urban, rural, and international student-teaching opportunities.

At UMaine, students find the academic opportunities and state-of-the-art facilities they'd expect from a major university with the friendly, close-knit feel of a small college. The majority of undergraduate classes are taught by professors—and many of those faculty members go on to become friends and mentors to their students. Here,

professors are known for having an open-door policy, whether they're hammering out physics equations after class or talking civil engineering over dinner at Pat's Pizza.

UMaine is located in Orono, a classic college town bounded by the Stillwater and Penobscot rivers. The campus is 10 minutes from the state's third-largest city, Bangor, and its international airport. Students can get involved in more than 200 clubs and organizations—academic and social—as well as one of 17 fraternities or 7 sororities, Student Government, community service–oriented groups, intramural sports and much, much more. UMaine is the state's only Division I school, and athletic

CONTACT INFORMATION

Ms. Sharon Oliver, Director of Admissions

☎ 207-581-1561 or toll-free 877-486-2364

🖳 um-admit@maine.edu

events—especially hockey—are a big part of student life here.

- **Enrollment:** *11,168*

- **Selectivity:** *moderately difficult*

- **Test scores:** *ACT—over 18, 94%; SAT—critical reading over 500, 62%; SAT—math over 500, 67%*

- **Application deadline:** *Early Action: 12/15; Rolling (freshmen & transfer)*

- **Expenses:** *Tuition $10,168; Room & Board $8766*

Founded in Orono in 1865, the University of Maine is among the most comprehensive higher education institutions in the Northeast, attracting students from across the U.S. and more than 80 countries. As Maine's flagship university, UMaine offers more than 90 undergraduate majors and academic programs, 75 master's programs, and 30 doctoral programs. Top students are invited to join UMaine's Honors College, one of the country's oldest honors programs.

The University of Maine at Machias' location along the Bold Coast of Maine provides endless opportunities for hands-on learning and outdoor recreation.

THE UNIVERSITY OF MAINE AT
MACHIAS
Naturally!

MACHIAS, MAINE
www.machias.edu/
www.facebook.com/umainemachias

Where you learn has great impact on what you learn. That's the philosophy of the faculty at the University of Maine at Machias. Located on the spectacular Bold Coast of Maine, the University of Maine at Machias (UMM) is a small, Environmental Liberal Arts university that lends itself to amazing out-of-classroom experiences. Small classes (the average is 17 students) and a faculty-student ratio of 1:13 contribute to an academic atmosphere that is intimate and intense and where independent thinking is encouraged.

The University's environmental emphasis, unique programs and desirable location draw students from all parts of the United States. Students come here for courses they won't find anywhere else—Book Arts, Adventure Recreation, and Wildlife Biology to name a few. They also enjoy the numerous ways to get involved in clubs and organizations; choices range from Greek life to the Ukulele Club.

Machias, Maine, is a classic New England town located on the tidal Machias River, with a town center that includes retail stores, restaurants, a natural foods store, and churches of various denominations. The area is a popular outdoor destination because of its ocean beaches, inland lakes, and streams and miles of mountains, forests, and trails. Downeast Maine has been a source of inspiration for generations of artists, outdoorsmen, mariners, and environmentalists. UMM's coastal location offers excellent opportunities for fieldwork, hands-on learning, and cooperative education and internship experiences.

CONTACT INFORMATION

Director of Admissions
☎ 207-255-1318 or toll-free
    888-GOTOUMM (in-state);
    888-468-6866 (out-of-state)
🖥 ummadmissions@maine.edu

- **Enrollment:** *951*
- **Selectivity:** *moderately difficult*
- **Test scores:** *ACT—over 18, 53.9%; SAT—critical reading over 500, 36.7%; SAT—math over 500, 27.5%*
- **Application deadline:** *8/15 (freshmen), rolling (transfer)*
- **Expenses:** *Tuition & Fees: $7480 (in-state); $19,300 (out-of-state); Room & Board $7900*

Dr. Kevin Athearn, Associate Professor of Environmental and Community Economics, discusses Maine's fishing industry with a University of Maine at Machias business student.

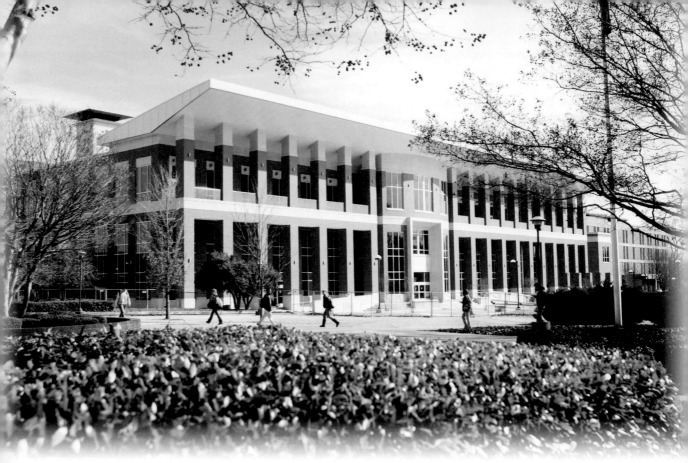

The University Center is the place to be at the University of Memphis. Opened in 2010, the UC is where students gather for dining, socializing, studying, and organizing student activities.

THE UNIVERSITY OF MEMPHIS®

MEMPHIS, TENNESSEE
www.memphis.edu/

Located on a beautifully landscaped campus in the heart of one of the South's largest and most progressive cities, the University of Memphis (U of M) is the flagship institution of the Tennessee Board of Regents System. The University of Memphis is recognized regionally and nationally for its academic, research, and athletic programs.

The University offers more than 254 areas of study from which to choose and is spread across a total of 1,160 acres at eight sites. In addition to the main campus, the Park Avenue campus has modern graduate and student family housing, a research park, and outstanding varsity athletic training facilities. The University of Memphis also owns the Meeman Biological Field Station, a 623-acre tract used for biological and ecological studies. The Chucalissa Archaeological Museum in southwest Memphis is often used as a research and training facility for archaeology and anthropology students.

The Memphis Tigers participate and win in NCAA Division I sports. Men and women compete in basketball, cross-country, golf, rifle, soccer, tennis, and track and field. Men also play baseball and football, and women also compete in softball and volleyball.

The outstanding facilities include the $3.2-million Larry O. Finch Center, with $50,000 worth of weight and cardio equipment and a fully equipped training room. The Liberty Bowl Memorial Stadium is one of the finest football stadiums in the nation. And the amazing FedExForum, home to the basketball teams, is a $250-million, state-of-the-art arena. It has a 35,000-square-foot outdoor plaza, four full-service restaurants, a massive center-hung scoreboard with live video and instant replays, and luxury suites.

The greater Memphis area has a population of approximately 1.1 million, making it the 18th-largest in the country. Centrally located on the Mississippi River, Memphis is an active hub for business, agriculture, and transportation industries. The city has the Mid-South's largest medical center. Major museum exhibits, sporting events, concerts, art shows, lectures, and even barbecue contests take place throughout the year. The AAA baseball team, the Redbirds, and

CONTACT INFORMATION

Kate Howard, Senior Associate Director of Admissions
☎ 901-678-2111 or toll-free 800-669-2678
💻 mkhoward@memphis.edu

the NBA team, the Grizzlies, both make their homes in Memphis. Memphis provides students with employment and internship opportunities in a variety of fields.

- **Enrollment:** *22,735*
- **Expenses:** *Tuition $7390; Room & Board $8330*

About 23,000 students attend the University of Memphis from 49 states and 99 countries. With over 190 active student organizations, there is something for everyone.

UNLV's unique location offers students a living laboratory where they can get hands-on experience in their future careers while living in one of the most exciting cities in the world.

UNLV
University of Nevada, Las Vegas

LAS VEGAS, NEVADA
unlv.edu
facebook.com/UNLVOfficialSite

The University of Nevada, Las Vegas (UNLV), is recognized nationally as a comprehensive teaching and research university that provides students with an excellent education at a reasonable cost. Since its first classes were held on campus in 1957, UNLV has transformed itself from a small branch college into a thriving urban research institution of more than 27,000 students and 3,100 faculty and staff members. Along the way, UNLV has become an indispensable resource in one of the country's fastest-growing and most enterprising cities.

Recently ranked the 10th Most Diverse University and the 12th Most Popular University by *U.S. News & World Report*, UNLV attracts students from 84 different countries. With over 200 areas of study, UNLV offers innovative academic programs and research in fields such as hospitality management, entertainment engineering and design, entrepreneurship, and much more. UNLV's Las Vegas location offers students a living laboratory where they can get hands-on experience in their future careers while making a difference in a thriving community.

UNLV is a NCAA Division I university and offers full-time students free tickets to all home sporting events including basketball, soccer, football, and much more. Known as the Runnin' Rebels, the UNLV basketball team boasts the third-best winning percentage in Division I history, has been to four Final Fours, and won the national championship in 1990.

UNLV students have access to endless ways to be involved on campus. More than 300 clubs and organizations offer students an active social life, including intramural sports, Greek organizations, ethnic and religious clubs, a student newspaper, community service organizations, outdoor adventures, and more. Numerous productions are performed throughout the year by UNLV's student music groups, choirs, dance companies, and theatre ensembles. In addition, the student government sponsors lectures, films, concerts, and entertainment throughout the year.

The Las Vegas metropolitan area is a rapidly growing community of more than 2 million residents with a strong sense of family and community pride. The surrounding area is one of the Southwest's most picturesque, offering residents outdoor recreation year-round. Within a 50-mile radius lie the shores of Lake Mead, Hoover Dam, and the Colorado River recreation area; the snow-skiing and hiking trails of 12,000-foot Mount Charleston; and a panoramic view of rugged rock mountains. Las Vegas has an average of 320 days of sunshine per year.

CONTACT INFORMATION

Office of Admissions
☎ 702-774-UNLV (8658)
🖳 admissions@unlv.edu

- **Enrollment:** *27,378*

- **Selectivity:** *moderately difficult*

- **Test scores:** *ACT—over 18, 86.4%; SAT—critical reading over 500, 50.4%; SAT—math over 500, 53.2%*

- **Application deadline:** *7/1 (freshmen), 7/1 (transfer)*

- **Expenses:** *Tuition $5368; Room & Board $9880*

The new Science and Engineering Building's innovative design supports collaboration among faculty in the sciences, engineering, health sciences, and other university research units.

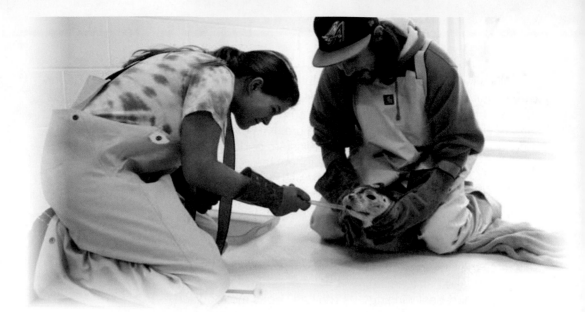

UNE academic programs ensure that students have plenty of opportunities for extensive fieldwork, clinical experiences, research, global study, and internships through University partnerships.

UNE UNIVERSITY OF NEW ENGLAND

BIDDEFORD AND PORTLAND, MAINE

www.une.edu/

The University of New England (UNE) is an innovative health sciences university grounded in the liberal arts, where students enroll in more than 40 undergraduate programs. UNE has six colleges: the College of Arts and Sciences, the Westbrook College of Health Professions, the College of Pharmacy, the College of Dental Medicine, the College of Osteopathic Medicine (Maine's only medical school), and the College of Graduate Studies.

At UNE, students focus on business management, education, health sciences, the humanities, the natural sciences, and social sciences. Internships, co-ops, clinicals, and student teaching allow UNE students to apply skills learned in the classroom to real job situations.

In addition to academics, the University encourages students to get involved in activities, clubs, and sports. Popular interests include scuba diving, skiing, surfing, hiking, biking, swimming, theater, music, and community service programs.

The University of New England Athletic Department participates in NCAA Division III varsity sports. Men's teams are basketball, cross-country, golf, lacrosse, soccer, and ice hockey. Women's teams are basketball, cross-country, field hockey, ice hockey, lacrosse, soccer, softball, swimming, and volleyball. Intramural teams in basketball, floor hockey, softball, skiing, and volleyball are also popular.

The Biddeford Campus contains a fitness center, bookstore, gym, pool, racquetball courts, and an indoor track. Academic facilities include the Harold Alfond Center for Health Sciences with biology and chemistry labs as well as lecture halls, a gross anatomy lab, and UNE's medical school facilities; the state-of-the-art Pickus Center for Biomedical Research; the Peter and Cecile Morgane Hall with laboratories for biology, chemistry, and physics; and the George and Barbara Bush Center where students study and socialize on the outdoor terraces of Windward Cafe. The Marine Science Education and Research Center features wet labs, aquaculture labs, and a marine mammal rehabilitation wing. A new addition to the Biddeford campus in 2012 is the 105,000-square-foot Harold Alfond Athletics Complex, which includes an NHL-size hockey rink and a basketball court, as well as classroom space, a cyber café, and student study space.

The 550-acre Biddeford Campus sits on a beautiful coastal site where the Saco River flows into the Atlantic Ocean. Located 20 miles to the north is the 41-acre Portland Campus where many graduate programs are housed. Students at both campuses can enjoy the social life of nearby Boston or Portland and the dynamic outdoor activities that have made Maine a prime tourist destination.

- **Enrollment:** 5,587
- **Selectivity:** *moderately difficult*
- **Test scores:** *ACT—over 18, 92.6%; SAT—critical reading over 500, 64%; SAT—math over 500, 68.2%*
- **Application deadline:** *2/15 (freshmen), rolling (transfer)*
- **Expenses:** *Tuition $30,750; Room & Board $12,500*

The coastal area of southern Maine is a beautiful, livable part of the country, and the people are friendly and welcoming.

University of New Haven, Maxcy Hall, West Haven, Connecticut.

University *of* New Haven

WEST HAVEN, CONNECTICUT

www.newhaven.edu

www.facebook.com/visitUNH

The University of New Haven's (UNH) mission is to prepare career-ready graduates for meaningful roles in today's global economy and to nurture the pursuit of lifelong learning. Founded in 1920, the University of New Haven is a private, independent institution focused on combining professional education with liberal arts and sciences. UNH is committed to educational innovation, continuous improvement in career and professional education, and support of scholarship and professional development. UNH became a four-year college in 1958. Moving to its present location in West Haven in 1960, UNH rapidly expanded its programs, facilities, and faculty, attracting a student body that now stands at over 6,300—including the current enrollment of over 4,300 full-time day students among its undergraduates.

The University is fully accredited by the New England Association of Schools and Colleges (NEASC). Individual programs, departments, and schools hold various forms of national professional accreditation. Four of the University of New Haven's bachelor's degree programs—chemical, civil, electrical, and mechanical engineering—are fully accredited by the Engineering Accreditation Commission of the Accreditation Board for Engineering and Technology, Inc. (EAC/ABET). The computer science program is fully accredited by the Computing Accreditation Commission of the Accreditation Board for Engineering and Technology, Inc. (CAC/ABET).

Despite a broad academic program, UNH is small enough to accommodate individualized educational needs. Programs evolve and adapt to meet changing career interests as well as the requirements of business, industry, and professional fields. Small classes foster close student-faculty relationships. Accelerated weekend and evening programs in business and convenient evening hours provide access for part-time students in engineering, computers, public safety, and the arts and sciences.

The main campus is in West Haven, Connecticut, on a hillside close to Long Island Sound. UNH also operates a satellite branch, the Southeastern Center in New London, Connecticut. Main campus administrative and classroom buildings support the University's four academic colleges: the College of Arts and Sciences, the College of Business, the Tagliatela College of Engineering, and the Henry C. Lee College of Criminal Justice and Forensic Sciences. Following the addition of the Graduate School in 1969, New Haven College was designated a university. Thirty master's degree programs attract full- and part-time graduate students, while nearly 100 associate and bachelor's degree programs are available to entering freshmen and transfer students in a great variety of academic disciplines. UNH also offers evening, accelerated, cohort, and executive degree programs.

CONTACT INFORMATION

Undergraduate Admissions
☎ 203-932-7319
💻 adminfo@newhaven.edu

- **Enrollment:** *6,385*
- **Selectivity:** *moderately difficult*
- **Test scores:** *ACT—over 18, 93.79%; SAT—critical reading over 500, 63.1%; SAT—math over 500, 70.28%*
- **Application deadline:** *Rolling (freshmen), rolling (transfer)*
- **Expenses:** *Tuition $30,750; Room & Board $12,778*

University of New Haven, Henry C. Lee Institute, West Haven, Connecticut.

Nursing Professor Dr. Tammy Haley guides a student in Pitt-Bradford's nursing suite.

University of Pittsburgh Bradford™

BRADFORD, PENNSYLVANIA
www.upb.pitt.edu/

The University of Pittsburgh at Bradford (Pitt-Bradford) can take students beyond—beyond the classroom by offering internships and research opportunities; beyond the degree by providing a helpful Career Services Office and an informal alumni network; beyond 9 to 5 with its active student life and excellent athletic facilities; beyond place by exposing students to the world through study-abroad programs; and beyond students' expectations by giving them a college experience that changes them for the better. So it's no surprise that *The Princeton Review* has named the University of Pittsburgh at Bradford one of the Best Colleges in the Northeast every year since 2006 and in 2012 named it a Best Value College.

At Pitt-Bradford, students live and learn on a safe, intimate campus where they receive individual attention from committed professors who work at their side. In addition, students earn a degree from the University of Pittsburgh, which commands respect around the world. Students here choose from 40 majors and more than 50 minors, concentrations, and pre-professional programs.

Pitt-Bradford students can take a yoga class in the dance studio, play a game of pickup basketball in the McDowell Fieldhouse, or swim in the six-lane swimming pool in the state-of-the-art Sport and Fitness Center. They can grab a bite in the Frame-Westerberg Commons or head back to their comfortable townhouse or apartment to study—there are no cramped dorm rooms here.

There are more than 40 clubs and organizations—from the campus radio station and newspaper to academic clubs, honor societies, and fraternities and sororities. Pitt-Bradford competes in Division III of the NCAA and fields seven men's teams in baseball, basketball, cross-country, golf, soccer, swimming, and tennis and seven women's teams in basketball, cross-country, soccer, softball, swimming, tennis, and volleyball.

Pitt-Bradford stretches across 317 acres in the foothills of the Allegheny Mountains, only steps from the Allegheny National Forest. The campus is a short drive from larger cities such as Buffalo, New York (80 miles north); Pittsburgh (160 miles southeast); and Erie, Pennsylvania (90 miles west). Pitt-Bradford students go off campus to enjoy cross-country and downhill skiing, snowboarding, snowshoeing, ice skating, biking, fishing, hiking, and hunting.

CONTACT INFORMATION

Mr Alexander P Nazemetz,
   Director of Admissions

☎ 814-362-7555 or toll-free
   800-872-1787

🖥 nazemetz@pitt.edu

- **Enrollment:** *1,565*

- **Selectivity:** *minimally difficult*

- **Test scores:** *ACT—over 18, 87%; SAT—critical reading over 500, 44%; SAT—math over 500, 49%*

- **Application deadline:** *Rolling (freshmen), rolling (transfer)*

- **Expenses:** *Tuition $11,970; Room & Board $8088*

These Pitt-Bradford students take a minute in between classes to enjoy the beautiful campus surroundings.

The $9.7 million Wellness Center is a state-of-the-art facility featuring strength-training equipment, a cardiovascular area, multipurpose athletic courts, a three-lane elevated running track, and a 30-foot climbing wall.

University of Pittsburgh Johnstown

JOHNSTOWN, PENNSYLVANIA
www.upj.pitt.edu

Founded in 1927, the University of Pittsburgh at Johnstown is the first and largest regional campus of the University of Pittsburgh. A vital knowledge center and a foremost contributor to the region's educational, social, cultural, and economic development, Pitt-Johnstown provides a high-quality educational experience that is purposefully designed to prepare students for the real world of the 21st century. Pitt-Johnstown's record of excellence is reflected, in part, by the accomplishments of its students, faculty, and staff; the record of achievements of more than 19,000 alumni; the satisfaction of area employers; and the commendations of many external organizations. Pitt-Johnstown's supportive living-learning environment is grounded in the liberal arts and sciences, is current, and is responsive to both its students' personal and professional needs and to its communities' needs.

Pitt-Johnstown is known for excellent faculty teaching, scholarship, and service; enriching faculty-student mentorships and collaborations in scholarship, research, and creative activity; and a dedicated, attentive, and supportive staff.

The University offers personalized instruction in state-of-the-art classrooms; an 18:1 student-to-faculty ratio, and 46 undergraduate majors including 3 University of Pittsburgh graduate degrees. Pitt-Johnstown has received national recognition for its wide selection of majors—some of the most popular include engineering technology, business, education, nursing, and natural sciences.

Pitt-Johnstown has 95 active student organizations and a tradition of athletic excellence with nationally recognized, award-winning NCAA Division II (11 teams) athletics.

The campus, located on 655 picturesque acres in the Laurel Highlands of Pennsylvania, 70 miles east of Pittsburgh, features a nature preserve with scenic hiking trails. It also offers a state-of-the-art performing arts center and a leading conference center.

Pitt-Johnstown's student graduation and success rates exceed the national average. Graduates are expanding the workforce capacity by enhancing problem-solving skills, linking theory-to-practice through experiences such as internships and service-learning projects.

Pitt-Johnstown offers a comprehensive New Dimension of Excellence Strategic Plan for accomplishing its Mission and a unique Real World Action Program that empowers students to design a customized personal and professional action plan to develop as agents of positive change in their communities and the world.

CONTACT INFORMATION

Office of Admissions
☎ 814-269-7050 or toll-free
    800-765-4875
🖳 upjadmit@pitt.edu

- **Enrollment:** *3,000*
- **Selectivity:** *moderately difficult*
- **Test scores:** *ACT – over 20, 90%; SAT – critical reading over 500, 92%; SAT – math over 500 91%*
- **Application deadline:** *Rolling (freshmen), rolling (transfer)*
- **Expenses:** *Tuition $11,970; Room & Board: $7255*

Pitt-Johnstown is located on 655 picturesque acres in the scenic Laurel Highlands of Pennsylvania.

*University of Redlands
Memorial Chapel.*

UNIVERSITY OF
Redlands

REDLANDS, CALIFORNIA
www.redlands.edu

University of Redlands places significant value on the connection between learning and doing. At Redlands, you'll find faculty members who are far more than interesting lecturers; they push, cajole, and listen, and they thrive on the give and take of a good argument. The University's international study programs have placed students in British universities, Kenyan villages, and everywhere in between— experiences as uncommon and life-changing as any class you can imagine. When you find yourself synthesizing what you've learned in a senior research paper on the economics of deforestation or organizing a community service project for battered women, you'll see what it's like to produce original work that matters to others. Redlands is looking for students who want more than a series of courses taken in a vacuum but are looking for an education that is linked to the world we live in.

Redlands is a private, liberal arts and sciences and pre-professional university. Its 2,500 students major in over 40 undergraduate programs in the College of Arts and Sciences and the School of Music. In addition, about 10 percent of students at Redlands are involved in the Johnston Center for Integrative Studies, a progressive student-driven program and community that enables them to negotiate their own course of study with a faculty/peer committee, receiving narrative evaluations instead of grades.

The University is located on 160 acres in the city of Redlands (population 70,000), 65 miles east of Los Angeles and 40 miles west of Palm Springs. Overlooking the campus are the two highest mountains in Southern California. While Los Angeles and the beaches are just over an hour away, Redlands remains a city with the feel of a small town, still a place where people say hello to each other on the street. Miles of hiking trails, skiing, and back country campsites are 15 minutes north in the magnificent San Bernardino Mountains—home to Big Bear Lake and Lake Arrowhead resorts and the San Gorgonio wilderness. The University's residential campus encourages personal involvement and promotes a genuine sense of community where friendships are easily made and last well beyond the college years. Redlands also fields one of the most competitive NCAA Division III athletic programs on the west coast, with 21 men's and women's varsity teams.

Redlands encourages every student to consider a semester studying abroad. More than 100 programs, covering every inhabited continent, provide an opportunity to experience the sounds, smells, language, politics, and people of another culture. The 4-4-1 academic calendar of two semesters followed by a one-month term was designed to allow concentration on a single subject, travel-study trips, community service, research, or independent projects. While many colleges view community service as an extracurricular activity, University of Redlands believes that it is one more important experience that helps students achieve academic goals and learn about the world and themselves. Redlands students are deeply committed to making a difference.

CONTACT INFORMATION

Mr. Paul Driscoll, Dean of Admissions

☎ 909-748-8074 or toll-free 800-455-5064

💻 admissions@redlands.edu

- **Enrollment:** *2,500*

- **Selectivity:** *moderately difficult*

- **Test scores:** *Middle 50% ACT Composite: 22–27; Middle 50% SAT Critical Reading: 510–610; Middle 50% SAT Math: 510–610*

- **Application deadlines:** *Fall: 3/1 (freshmen), 5/1 (transfer)*

- **Expenses:** *Tuition $39,038; Room & Board $11,924*

University of Redlands Administration Building and Garden.

With an average daily temperature of 73 degrees, six professional sports teams, numerous cultural amenities, and gorgeous beaches, the Tampa Bay area is the perfect home away from home.

USF UNIVERSITY OF SOUTH FLORIDA

TAMPA, FLORIDA

www.usf.edu/admissions

www.facebook.com/newstampede

Located on Florida's sunny and warm Gulf Coast, the University of South Florida (USF) is one of the United States' top 50 public research universities. Serving more than 39,000 students from every state and more than 150 countries, USF offers 232 degree programs at the undergraduate, graduate, specialist, and doctoral levels. Such a wide variety of programs means students have the freedom to choose and develop their precise academic passion.

No matter what course of study chosen at USF, students find talented professors, extensive resources, and fascinating opportunities to conduct research and apply their classroom learning in real-world settings—in the United States and around the globe. Research is conducted in all academic disciplines, allowing opportunities for students to work alongside many of the world's leading experts. USF faculty and students make a difference in both the local and global community by finding solutions to problems, volunteering, and by partnering with organizations and agencies.

Outside the classroom, students can take part in more than 500 organizations and endless activities. USF fields 17 varsity athletic teams that compete in the exciting Big East Conference. The University's men's basketball team advanced to the second round in the 2012 NCAA tournament, and USF's men's soccer team advanced to the Elite Eight in the 2011 NCAA tournament. USF also boasts an extensive intramural program, and the brand new campus recreation center was called "one of the highest tech fitness centers in the nation" by NBC's *Today* show.

With one of the lowest tuition rates in the country, USF is an excellent value. In addition, the university's location in Tampa means students have access to rich professional, cultural, and recreational resources. The city has been ranked by *Forbes Magazine* as "15th Best in the Nation for Business and Careers," and it is located in the 12th largest media market in the United States. USF has built internship partnerships with a number of Tampa businesses and organizations ranging from JPMorgan Chase to Tampa General Hospital.

Cultural and recreational opportunities include numerous musical venues, a thriving art scene, three professional sports teams, and world-famous beaches. Ybor City, an area of Tampa that reflects Cuban, Spanish, and Italian history, offers live entertainment, outdoor cafes, and great ethnic restaurants. The Tampa Bay area attracts millions of tourists each year who appreciate its mild winter climates, tropical summers, spectacular sunsets, and beautiful beaches.

CONTACT INFORMATION

Office of Undergraduate
   Admissions
☎ 813-974-3350
💻 admissions@usf.edu

- **Enrollment:** *39,629*
- **Selectivity:** *moderately difficult*
- **Test scores:** *ACT—over 18, 99.87%; SAT—critical reading over 500, 85.9%; SAT—math over 500, 90.09%*
- **Application deadline:** *3/1 (freshmen), 6/1 (transfer: fall term); 10/1 (transfer: spring term); 3/1 (transfer: summer term)*
- **Expenses:** *Tuition: $5800 (in-state) $14,990 (out-of-state) Room & Board $9190*

USF students learn by doing in a dynamic, modern city and gain practical experience through access to career-enhancing internships, service-learning opportunities, and community partnerships.

University of the Arts is located in the heart of downtown Philadelphia, one of the nation's most culturally vibrant cities.

THE UNIVERSITY OF THE ARTS
in Philadelphia
PHILADELPHIA, PENNSYLVANIA
www.uarts.edu
www.facebook.com/UArts.Admissions

Established in 1876, the University of the Arts is dedicated to educating students in the visual, performing, and communication arts—and to being the catalyst for students' innate creativity. Students and faculty connect, create, and collaborate across disciplines and traditional boundaries in the heart of downtown Philadelphia, one of the nation's most culturally vibrant cities.

With 22 undergraduate and 13 graduate programs in 6 areas of study (Design, Visual Arts, Film, Dance, Theater, and Music), its 2,200 students immerse themselves in a rigorous and well-rounded curriculum with a strong liberal arts component that prepares them to be the creative leaders of tomorrow, no matter what field they choose. UArts' 500 faculty members are all practicing artists, bringing the latest techniques and knowledge into their classrooms.

As one of the nation's only comprehensive arts universities, and with an innovative new approach to educating artists, the University of the Arts offers a unique environment where students from across disciplines—artists, performers and media makers—interact in a dynamic community of creativity. University of the Arts graduates are prepared to live, work, and lead in a world in which art, creativity, and imagination are the engines for social and economic change.

Life as a student at the University of the Arts is a unique, transformative process. Living in the center of an exciting city among a supportive community, students become flourishing artists and creative entrepreneurs, while making the most of all that UArts has to offer. That includes a steady stream of some of the nation's leading artists, performers, and innovative thinkers visiting the campus as lecturers and master-class teachers.

UArts students are collaborators and boundary-crossers able to help design their own educational paths— problem solvers, innovators, and entrepreneurs, they imagine and create things that don't yet exist and point to new possibilities for change.

University of the Arts students enjoy the benefits of a dynamic urban setting and easy access to world-class theaters, museums, and art galleries, as well as the resources of the nation's cultural capitals, New York and Washington, D.C., both within a 2-hour drive. Philadelphia is UArts' campus, and students are just steps away from the Kimmel Center for the Performing Arts, home to the world-renowned Philadelphia Orchestra and Pennsylvania Ballet; the Academy of Music; UArts' own historic Merriam Theater; and six regional theaters.

CONTACT INFORMATION

Eileen Grabosky, Director of Enrollment Management
☎ 215-717-6049 or toll-free 800-616-ARTS
🖳 admissions@uarts.edu

- **Enrollment:** *2,246*
- **Selectivity:** *moderately difficult*
- **Test scores:** *ACT—over 18, 82%; SAT—critical reading over 500, 58%; SAT—math over 500, 48%*
- **Application deadline:** *Rolling (freshmen), rolling (transfer)*
- **Expenses:** *Tuition $34,040; Room only $8200*

The Merriam Theater stands as a monument to Philadelphia's active performing arts culture. Centrally located on the Avenue of the Arts, the Merriam functions as the hub of the College of Performing Arts' School of Music.

State-of-the-art labs in the new Correll Science Complex provide students hands-on learning and research opportunities. A 16:1 student-faculty ratio ensures small classes and individual attention.

UNIVERSITY
of the
CUMBERLANDS

WILLIAMSBURG, KENTUCKY

www.ucumberlands.edu

https://www.facebook.com/ucumberlands

Chartered in 1888, University of the Cumberlands (UC) is one of Kentucky's largest private universities and is consistently listed as a "Top Tier" institution by U.S. News & World Report. The University's broad curriculum includes 36 majors and pre-professional programs, as well as graduate degrees in business, education, physician assistant studies, psychology, and religion. UC remains keenly aware of the importance of a traditional liberal arts education, which provides the foundation for a deeper understanding of advanced studies.

The acceptance rate of UC students into business, dental, law, medical, seminary, and other graduate programs is excellent. In fact, within five years of graduation, 66 percent of UC graduates are pursuing or have completed advanced degrees.

Recent additions to campus include the state-of-the-art Correll Science Complex, the Hutton School of Business, and a women's residence hall. UC is home to more than 1,500 full-time undergraduate students who represent 40 states and 30 countries. About 75 percent of UC students live in one of the University's 10 residence halls and enjoy free laundry facilities, air-conditioned rooms (in all dorms but one), and cable television. All dorms and academic areas are connected wirelessly, as well as public areas like the library and dining hall. Students enjoy varied dining options, which include the T. J. Roberts dining hall (TJ's), the Cybernet Café, and The Patriot Steakhouse.

UC students are involved in all aspects of campus life from stimulating academic programs, internships, and research opportunities to ministry programs, marching band, and student government. Many students are involved in the University's extensive intramural program—everything from flag football and volleyball to corn hole and basketball and avidly compete for the coveted I-M championship t-shirt. University of the Cumberlands is proud of its competitive athletic program, which fields 22 varsity sports for men and women, many of which are consistently nationally ranked.

Conveniently located in southern Kentucky, between Lexington, Kentucky, and Knoxville, Tennessee, students often take advantage of UC's location, which is known for its lakes, rivers, and waterfalls. The Patriot Adventure Club plans day excursions for whitewater rafting, hiking, spelunking, horseback riding, skydiving, and more!

UC's well-kept campus blends stately old antebellum-style buildings with new ones and has a panoramic view of the Cumberland River Valley. To quote Southern Living magazine, the University of the Cumberlands' campus "looks as if it came straight out of central casting….. bricks, columns and all".

- **Total Enrollment:** *3,748*

- **Selectivity:** *moderately difficult*

CONTACT INFORMATION

Erica Harris, Director of Admissions

☎ 606-539-4241 or toll-free 800-343-1609

🖳 admiss@ucumberlands.edu

- **Test scores:** *ACT—over 18, 92%; SAT—critical reading over 500, 30%; SAT—math over 500, 34%*

- **Application deadline:** *Rolling (freshmen)*

- **Expenses:** *Tuition $19,900; Room & Board $7000*

UC students enjoy a beautiful campus. The fountain is a focal point of the campus and is located in the Quad.

University of Washington Bothell—Inspiring Innovation and Creativity.

UNIVERSITY *of* WASHINGTON

BOTHELL

BOTHELL, WASHINGTON

www.uwb.edu

The University of Washington Bothell opens the door to an internationally and nationally ranked university experience that inspires innovation and creativity. Faculty members are passionate about the knowledge they bring to the classroom. UW Bothell promotes a spirit of innovation and creativity where big ideas are born and tested. With 3,377 (FTE) students and approximately 200 faculty members, UW Bothell offers modestly sized classes, perfectly suited for meaningful interaction and critical thinking. Students at UW Bothell take on an active role in their educational experience, discover their own strengths and abilities, and ultimately learn how to fulfill their dreams—academic and otherwise.

UW Bothell offers access to a prestigious, student-centered education in a collaborative learning environment. UW Bothell is one of three

University of Washington campuses. Though providing distinctive offerings, its graduates earn a fully accredited UW degree.

UW Bothell combines the benefits of modest class sizes with the resources of a world-renowned university. The curriculum emphasizes close student-faculty interactions, collaboration among students, and hands-on learning. Outstanding regional connections present students with unique opportunities for projects, internships, and research with leading businesses and organizations. At UW Bothell, students earn a University of Washington degree while building a solid foundation of relevant knowledge, practical skills, and professional preparation.

UW Bothell offers more than 30 degrees through a variety of programs as well as the UW Bothell School of Business and the UW Bothell School of Interdisciplinary Arts & Sciences. UW Bothell is proud of its reputation for innovative, specialized degree options.

Students can choose from an array of undergraduate disciplines including: American studies; applied computing; biology; business; business administration; community psychology; computing and software systems;

culture, literature and the arts; electrical engineering; environmental science; environmental studies; global studies; interdisciplinary arts; interdisciplinary studies; science, technology and society; society, ethics and human behavior; and nursing.

Post-baccalaureate courses include K–8 teacher certification as well as professional certification.

UW Bothell also offers several graduate programs in disciplines including business, computing and software systems, cultural studies, education, nursing, policy studies, and fine arts.

UW Bothell takes advantage of the regions' extraordinary capacity for creativity and innovation by connecting students to career-building experiences. Committed to the greater good, UW Bothell builds regional partnerships, inspires change, creates knowledge, shares

CONTACT INFORMATION

Molly Ormsby, Associate Director of Admissions

☎ 425-352-5244

🖳 mormsby@uwb.edu

discoveries, and prepares students for leadership in the state of Washington and beyond.

- **Enrollment:** *3,759*
- **Selectivity:** *moderately difficult*
- **Test scores:** *ACT—over 18, 81%; SAT—critical reading over 500, 53%; SAT—math over 500, 63%*
- **Application deadline:** *1/15 (freshmen), 1/15 (transfer)*
- **Expenses:** *Tuition $8619; Room & Board $6075*

UW Bothell students enjoy working together in a unique learning environment provided by a world-class faculty.

UW Outdoor Adventure
rock climbing belay class.

UNIVERSITY
OF WYOMING

LARAMIE, WYOMING

www.uwyo.edu/

www.facebook.com/discoveruw

As a student at the University of Wyoming (UW), you will benefit from a first-rate education complemented by more than 200 areas of study offering academic adventure and intellectual challenge. The University of Wyoming has the personality of a small school with all the attributes of a larger university—awesome research facilities, state-of-the-art technology, extensive clubs and organizations, and NCAA Division I athletics. Research currently completed by UW professors and students pushes the boundaries of science and technology resulting in UW's classification as a Carnegie Doctoral/High Research Activity institution.

Wyoming, unique among the fifty states, has only one university. UW offers bachelor's degree programs through six undergraduate colleges: the Colleges of Agriculture, Arts and Sciences, Business, Education, Engineering and Applied Science, and Health Sciences. UW also offers graduate and professional programs, including the Doctor of Pharmacy and the Juris Doctor.

There are more than 200 campus clubs and organizations including fraternities and sororities, honor and professional societies, political and religious organizations, and special interest groups. Students can also participate in more than 60 different intramural and club sports. UW is a Division I member of the NCAA and competes in 17 men's and women's sports. On-campus facilities are nothing short of amazing. Students have complete access to Half Acre Gym, an indoor climbing wall, an 18-hole golf course, tennis and racquetball courts, weight rooms, two swimming pools, rifle and archery ranges, indoor and outdoor tracks, softball and baseball fields, and a hockey rink. UW houses students in six residence halls with a number of unique living environments, such as special interest floors, freshman interest groups, honors floors, and single-gender floors.

UW's 785-acre campus is located at the foot of the Rocky Mountains in Laramie, a scenic town in southeastern Wyoming. Students enjoy easy access to Alpine and Nordic skiing, snowboarding, snowmobiling, hiking, backpacking, camping, hunting, fishing, rock climbing, and mountain biking. Laramie—with its blue skies, clean air, and 320 days of sunshine a year—is a friendly and supportive university town, conveniently located 45 miles west of Wyoming's capital, Cheyenne, and only 130 miles northwest of Denver, Colorado.

- **Enrollment:** 13,922

- **Selectivity:** moderately difficult

- **Assured Admission Requirements:** ACT score 21+ or SAT score 980+ (Math/ Critical Reading), 3.0+ GPA

CONTACT INFORMATION

Shelley Dodd, Director of Admission

☎ 307-766-5160 or toll-free 800-342-5996

🖳 admissions@uwyo.edu

(4.0 unweighted scale), and completion of UW success curriculum. Visit: www.uwyo.edu/admissions for complete details.

- **Application deadline:** Rolling admission, separate admission application deadlines for UW's scholarships. For details, visit: www.uwyo.edu/scholarship

- **Expenses:** Wyoming resident tuition $4278; Nonresident tuition $13,428, Room & Board $9084

Exciting Cowboy athletics action as part of the Mountain West Conference.

The Economic Crime, Justice Studies, and Cybersecurity Building— Phase II of UC's Science and Technology Complex.

UTICA COLLEGE

UTICA, NEW YORK

www.utica.edu

www.facebook.com/UticaCollegeAdmissions

A private, independent college founded in 1946, Utica College (UC) is known for its excellent academic programs, outstanding faculty, personal attention, and diverse student population. The hallmarks of Utica College's academic programs are the integration of liberal and professional studies and a strong emphasis on internships, research, and other experiential learning opportunities. But UC is best known for the close, personal relationship students have with both faculty and staff members. Approximately 3,600 undergraduate and graduate students attend UC, including men and women from a wide variety of socioeconomic and cultural backgrounds as well as older students, veterans, and students with disabilities. While most students come from New York, New England, and the Middle Atlantic States, students are drawn to UC from all parts of the United States, and there is a growing international student population.

Utica College offers 37 majors, a broad selection of minors and special programs, and 21 graduate programs. UC also offers a robust selection of study-abroad opportunities as well as pre-professional programs and an honors program. Utica College is located on a modern, 128-acre campus on the southwestern edge of Utica, New York. Its facilities include a recently completed science and technology complex that comprises state-of-the-art learning and research facilities for health professions and justice studies, the Frank E. Gannett Memorial Library, a fully equipped high-definition television studio and convergence media center, the Ralph F. Strebel Student Center, seven residence halls, an athletic center, a 1,200-seat stadium, and numerous athletic fields.

Half of UC's students live on campus in residence halls that feature a variety of housing options, modern amenities, and lounges for studying or relaxing with friends. Students enjoy a range of dining venues, from the main dining commons in Strebel Student Center to the new Pioneer Café with seven large-screen flat panels, convenient coffeehouses in the Library and academic buildings, and a Subway sandwich shop on campus. Whether they live on or off campus, students can take advantage of more than 80 student organizations, focusing on community service, music, theater, and politics as well as fraternities, sororities, and major-related clubs that provide opportunities for students to organize career-related events. Each term the College hosts lectures, concerts, poetry readings, art exhibits, plays, and nationally recognized speakers. UC also offers a broad selection of Division III intercollegiate athletic programs, plus options for intramural and club sports.

CONTACT INFORMATION

Mr. Patrick Quinn, Vice President for Undergraduate Admissions

☎ 315-792-3006 or toll-free 800-782-8884

- **Enrollment:** *2,981*
- **Selectivity:** *moderately difficult*
- **Test scores:** *ACT—over 18, 84.3%; SAT—critical reading over 500, 36.49%; SAT—math over 500, 47.69%*
- **Application deadline:** *Rolling (freshmen), rolling (transfer)*
- **Expenses:** *Tuition $30,890; Room & Board $11,934*

F. Eugene Romano Hall, Phase I of Utica College's Science and Technology Complex.

A longstanding Vanderbilt tradition, the 12th Man Tailgate sees new 'Dores rush Dudley Field prior to each season's first home game.

VANDERBILT
UNIVERSITY

NASHVILLE, TENNESSEE
www.vanderbilt.edu/
facebook.com/vanderbilt

In 1873, on the heels of the Civil War, Commodore Cornelius Vanderbilt donated a million dollars to found the university that now bears his name, with the hope that it would "contribute to strengthening the ties which should exist between all sections of our common country." Today, Vanderbilt enrolls some of the most talented students from all over the United States and the world and challenges them daily to expand their intellectual horizons.

Vanderbilt's interdisciplinary approach to education allows students to take a variety of courses outside of their main focus of study. Vanderbilt is a medium-sized university that includes four undergraduate schools and six graduate and professional schools. The university provides an 8:1 student-faculty ratio, over 120 research centers, and a strong focus on the undergraduate academic experience.

Known for its gorgeous 330-acre, national arboretum campus, Vanderbilt provides a variety of housing options for students—traditional dorms, apartments, houses, and suites. The Martha Rivers Ingram Commons consists of ten residential houses built or renovated in 2008, and it houses all 1,600 first-year students and 10 faculty Heads of House. The new College Halls, to be opened in fall 2014, will provide an additional upperclassman living/learning community.

Vanderbilt students can take their pick of the more than 400 organizations on campus. From the Momentum Dance Group to intramural sports and from fraternities/sororities to Alternative Spring Break, Vanderbilt students are highly involved on campus. Student athletes compete in the Southeastern Conference. Varsity teams for both men and women include basketball, cross-country, golf, and tennis. Men also compete in baseball and football, and women compete in bowling, lacrosse, soccer, swimming, and track and field.

The Ingram Commons Center includes a new dining area with study space, a post office, and an exercise facility. The Sarratt Student Center houses a newly expanded dining hall, cinema, pub,

coffee shop, art gallery, student-run television studio, and plenty of meeting space. Facilities at the Student Recreation Center include gymnasiums, an indoor swimming pool, squash and racquetball courts, a rock climbing wall, an indoor suspended track, and a weight room.

Vanderbilt University is located in Nashville, the capital of Tennessee. Known as Music City, USA, Nashville has more than 1.6 million residents and hosts over 20,000 live music performances every year. The greater Nashville area is home to two major-league professional sports teams, eighty-one parks and more than 30,000 acres of lakes.

Iconic Kirkland Hall, Vanderbilt's oldest building, stands as a symbol of Commodore pride throughout the four seasons.

- **Enrollment:** *12,859*

- **Selectivity:** *most difficult*

- **Test scores:** *ACT Middle 50%: 31–34; SAT (Critical Reading & Math) Middle 50%: 1380–1550*

- **Application deadline:** *11/1 (Early Decision I, freshman), 1/3 (Early Decision II and Regular Decision, freshmen), 3/15 (transfer)*

- **Expenses:** *Tuition $41,088; Room & Board $13,818*

CONTACT INFORMATION

John O. Gaines, Director of Undergraduate Admissions

☎ 615-936-2811 or toll-free 800-288-0432

🖳 admissions@vanderbilt.edu

Vaughn College's campus is in Queens, New York, minutes from Manhattan.

VaughnCollege
of aeronautics and technology

FLUSHING, NEW YORK

http://www.vaughn.edu

Vaughn College of Aeronautics and Technology, founded in 1932, is a private, four-year college committed to providing students with the education and skills needed to achieve success in engineering, technology, management, and aviation. Adjacent to LaGuardia Airport, Vaughn is a high-quality institution where students experience personal attention as they progress through academic course work.

In 2004, the College of Aeronautics became Vaughn College. The name reflects Vaughn's aviation heritage as well as its future as an expanding institution, with new programs such as a Bachelor of Science in mechatronic engineering and a master's-level management offering. The College's population of more than 1,600 and its low 16:1 student-faculty ratio ensure a personalized learning environment. More than 95 percent of Vaughn College graduates are employed or continue their education within one year of obtaining their degrees.

The College's New York City location offers opportunities with an array of technology, manufacturing, and aviation companies. The cultural, spiritual, and physical needs of the students are met by the outstanding facilities of New York City. Restaurants are accessible, and hospitals and other medical facilities are among the best in the world. New York City's museums focus on arts, natural history, science, and world civilization.

The College awards the Associate of Applied Science (A.A.S.) degree in 6 programs. The Bachelor of Science (B.S.) degree is available in 11 programs. A non-degree course of study in air traffic control through the Federal Aviation Administration's Air Traffic Collegiate Training Initiative (AT-CTI) Program is available. The College is one of 36 institutions nationwide to offer this program.

Vaughn's laboratories offer hands-on experience that helps qualify students for employment upon graduation. From the mechatronics laboratory to the CATIA/NASTRAN computer center, the College is committed to providing students with the knowledge and tools they are likely to need and find in today's businesses. The College's $1-million flight simulator center includes a Canadair regional jet trainer and two Redbird simulators. A partnership with Redbird Flight Simulations enables students to pursue FAA flight certifications and ratings at Redbird's facility in San Marcos, Texas.

Vaughn is nearing the construction phase of a new library that will provide students and faculty with a one-stop location for research materials, academic support services, and technology support. Scheduled to open in 2013, it triples the size of the current facility and is part of a more than $30-million renovation of Vaughn's campus planned over the next several years.

CONTACT INFORMATION

Mr. Vincent M. Papandrea, Associate Vice President

☎ 718-429-6600 Ext. 167

🖥 vincent.papandrea@vaughn.edu

- **Enrollment:** *1,680*
- **Selectivity:** *moderately difficult*
- **Test scores:** *ACT—over 18, 100%; SAT— critical reading over 500, 47%; SAT—math over 500, 79%*
- **Application deadline:** *Rolling (freshmen), rolling (transfer)*
- **Expenses:** *Tuition $17,675; Room & Board $10,600*

Students receive valuable flight training in Vaughn College's state-of-the-art simulator lab.

St. Thomas of Villanova Church is a historic campus landmark and an iconic symbol of Villanova University's unique Augustinian Catholic heritage.

VERITAS UNITAS CARITAS
1842

VILLANOVA
UNIVERSITY
IGNITE CHANGE. GO NOVA.

VILLANOVA, PENNSYLVANIA
www.villanova.edu/
https://www.facebook.com/VillanovaU

Villanova University's Augustinian Catholic intellectual tradition is the cornerstone of an academic community that was founded in 1842 by the Order of Saint Augustine. Here, students learn to think critically, act compassionately, and succeed while serving others. Villanova prepares students to become ethical leaders who create positive change everywhere life takes them.

The strength of the Villanova experience comes largely from the University's welcoming community. All members are united by a shared responsibility to uphold the ideals of Saint Augustine and let the principles of truth, unity, and love guide their lives. The Villanova community helps students grow intellectually, professionally, and spiritually, while challenging them to reach their full potential.

The University's rigorous academic experience, rooted in the liberal arts, forms an environment in which students and professors are partners in learning. The Villanova community is dedicated to providing a personalized experience that fosters every student's intellectual and spiritual well-being. As part of their education, students are encouraged to enrich their own lives by working for those in need. Through academic and service programs, students use their knowledge, skills, and compassion to better the world around them.

There are more than 10,000 undergraduate, graduate, and law students in the University's five colleges—the College of Liberal Arts and Sciences, the Villanova School of Business, the College of Engineering, the College of Nursing, and the Villanova University School of Law. These colleges are the setting for an experience that develops both the heart and the mind, and creates the atmosphere where students are called to ignite change.

Villanova University's 260-acre campus is located in a suburban community, 12 miles west of Philadelphia, Pennsylvania.

CONTACT INFORMATION

Mr. Michael Gaynor, Director of University Admission

☎ 610-519-4000

📧 gotovu@villanova.edu

- **Enrollment:** *10,467*
- **Selectivity:** *very difficult*
- **Test scores:** *ACT—over 18, 99.8%; SAT—critical reading over 500, 95.61%; SAT—math over 500, 97.54%*
- **Application deadline:** *11/1 Early Action; 1/7 (Regular Decision), 6/1 (transfer)*
- **Expenses:** *Average tuition (2012–13) $42,150; Room & Board $11,370*

Students seeking a study break gather on Mendel Field for a friendly game of flag football.

Webb is all about hands-on engineering.

Webb Institute

GLEN COVE, NEW YORK
http://www.webb-institute.edu

Webb Institute, over 120 years old and the only college devoted to naval architecture and marine engineering in the United States, is located in Glen Cove on the picturesque north shore of Long Island, about 30 miles from New York City, Webb Institute seeks to attract able students who are interested in engineering and can recognize that the design and construction of ships of all types, and in their motive power, is engineering to the max.

All of the students admitted to Webb receive four-year, full-tuition scholarships. The only costs to students are for room, board and books. Though the enrollment is small, the student body is made up of students who come from all over the country to study at Webb.

The aim of Webb is to educate its students generally, while simultaneously providing professional competence in naval architecture and marine engineering. The degree Webb confers is a Bachelor of Science in Naval Architecture and Marine Engineering.

Webb can boast of 100 percent placement of its graduates every year since it was founded—an amazing record. How Webb does this is by combining two academic semesters each year with an eight-week internship program for all students introducing students to the marine industry right from freshman year on through graduation. Students get paid experience working in shipyards, going to sea, and working in design offices and research firms all around the United States and overseas. Students are also given time to attend major industry conferences and professional society meetings throughout the year.

The student-faculty ratio is an enviable 7 to 1. Webb has no teaching assistants and no big lecture hall classrooms. In fact, classrooms serve as the students' design studios and

are open 24 hours a day, as is the rest of this Honor Code campus.

The wireless campus is a 26-acre estate and mansion located right on the water, with boating facilities, an athletic field, tennis courts, and access to the local YMCA. Webb fields intercollegiate teams in sailing, soccer, basketball, tennis, and volleyball. Proximity to New York City permits many cultural and artistic experiences, and back on campus, there is opportunity to sing with the chorus or be part of the theater group

CONTACT INFORMATION

Mr. William Murray, Director of Enrollment Management

☎ 516-671-2213

🖳 admissions@webb-institute.edu

- **Enrollment:** *81*
- **Selectivity:** *most difficult*
- **Test scores:** *SAT—critical reading over 500, 100%; SAT—math over 500, 100%*
- **Application deadline:** *10/15 (Early Decision), 2/15 (freshmen & transfer students)*
- **Expenses:** *Tuition $0; Room & Board $13,200*

Webb is located right on the shoreline of Long Island Sound.

The Quad is a beautiful, park-like gathering space for faculty and staff members.

WESTERN CONNECTICUT STATE UNIVERSITY

DANBURY, CONNECTICUT
www.wcsu.edu/

Western Connecticut State University (WestConn) provides its students with a high-quality education and a memorable campus experience—all at an affordable cost. With programs in the arts and sciences, business, and professional studies, this accredited university offers degrees through its five progressive schools. The most popular majors include communication, theater arts, education, business, justice and law administration, music, and nursing.

The Ancell School of Business offers the Master of Business Administration, Master of Health Administration, and Master of Science in justice administration. The School of Arts and Sciences offers the Master of Arts in biological and environmental sciences, earth and planetary sciences, English, history, and mathematics; the Master of Fine

Arts is offered in professional writing. The School of Professional Studies offers the Master of Science in counselor education, elementary education, nursing, and secondary education; also offered is WestConn's Doctor of Education (Ed.D.) in instructional leadership. WestConn's newly formed School of Visual and Performing Arts offers the Master of Fine Arts in visual arts and the Master of Music Education.

The University also is rich with a number of learning and social activities beyond the classroom. Students run academic clubs and fraternities, publish an award-winning newspaper and yearbook, and operate a radio station. They stage theater and musical productions, participate in cooperative education and internship programs, and administer their own campus government association. The University provides services for learning-disabled students, study abroad, a University Scholars program, and international students.

A variety of NCAA Division III men's and women's sports are represented on campus. Students enjoy intramural sports and a premier recreation center that includes a swimming pool, an indoor track, and weight-lifting machines. The campus also features a child-care center, a counseling center, and campus ministries.

WestConn offers two campuses in Danbury, in the heart of western Connecticut, as well as a satellite campus in Waterbury. Danbury is a major city in the foothills of the Berkshire Mountains, just 65 miles north of Manhattan and 50 miles west of Hartford. In Danbury, the 34-acre Midtown campus has an interesting mix of old and new architecture, and it offers easy access to entertainment, restaurants, and shopping. The 364-acre Westside campus is ideal for hikers and nature buffs who want to explore the outdoors while enjoying state-of-the-art facilities. The WestConn at-Waterbury campus offers a convenient location closer to the center of the state, with the same level of excellent service.

CONTACT INFORMATION

Office of University Admissions
☎ 203-837-9000 or toll-free
   877-837-WCSU
💻 admissions@wcsu.edu

- **Enrollment:** *6,407*
- **Selectivity:** *moderately difficult*
- **Test scores:** *SAT—critical reading over 500, 51.2%; SAT—math over 500, 47.7%*
- **Application deadline:** *Rolling (freshmen), rolling (transfer)*
- **Expenses:** *Tuition $7909; Room only $5898*

Fairfield Hall is a residence hall on the university's historic midtown campus.

William Peace University students develop an appreciation for lifelong learning, pursuing meaningful careers and building skills for ethical citizenship.

WILLIAM PEACE
UNIVERSITY
Your Success. Our Mission.

EST. 1857

RALEIGH, NORTH CAROLINA
http://www.peace.edu

William Peace University is a four-year private university located in downtown Raleigh, North Carolina. The University has made bold strides to meet the challenges of higher education in the 21st century, and it offers innovative academic programs rooted in the liberal arts tradition to prepare students for careers in the organizations of tomorrow. William Peace University students develop an appreciation for lifelong learning, pursue meaningful careers, and build skills for ethical citizenship. The institution was founded in 1857 and named for founding benefactor William Peace.

Bachelor of Arts degrees are offered in biology, communication, education, English, liberal studies, political science, pre-law, psychology, simulation and game design, and theatre. In addition, Bachelor of Science degrees are offered in biology and business administration. William Peace University also offers a Bachelor of Fine Arts degree in musical theatre, and several minors and concentrations in fields such as anthropology, global studies, graphic design, religion, and Spanish.

A new core curriculum includes courses in personal financial management, media literacy, and four years of writing courses within the English department. Students are also required to take a series of three classes focusing on career and professional development and an academic internship related to their major.

Academic and dormitory facilities are networked with wireless Internet service. Computer laboratories, the library, and the student publications area are equipped with state-of-the-art computer hardware and software. Other specialized computer laboratories are available in the biology, chemistry, media, theatre, and visual communication departments. The recital hall and theater host a multitude of performances, plays, exhibits, and speaker series.

WPU hosts athletic teams in basketball, cross-country, golf, soccer, softball, tennis, and volleyball (baseball will be added by 2014). There are more than 30 student-led clubs, organizations, and publications, and students complete thousands of hours of community service every year.

WPU is located in downtown Raleigh. If you don't feel like walking, a step away is a stop for the R-Line, a free bus service in the downtown area that connects students to restaurants as well as retail and entertainment venues. The State Capitol, Legislative Building, State Library, North Carolina Symphony, and several museums lie within a few blocks of the campus.

Raleigh is consistently ranked in the top for its green space and cultural performance, as well as being a top technology town and the hottest job market for young adults. On average, 90 percent of William Peace University graduates find jobs or are enrolled in graduate school within a year of graduation.

CONTACT INFORMATION

Office of Admissions
☎ 919-508-2214 or toll-free 800-PEACE-47
💻 Admissions@peace.edu

William Peace University provides a liberal arts–based higher education, with innovative academic programs that prepare students for the future.

Dance is one of the many forms of self expression we offer students at Wilson College. Choose from theatre, music, drawing, painting, photography...be creative. Be you!

WILSON COLLEGE

1869

WITH CONFIDENCE

CHAMBERSBURG, PENNSYLVANIA

www.wilson.edu

www.facebook.com/WilsonCollege

Since 1869, Wilson College graduates have excelled in their chosen fields, including prominent positions in business, education, government, law, medicine, veterinary science, and research. Students earn degrees from 30 majors, 18 areas of concentration, and 39 minors. Pre-professional programs are offered in Health Sciences, Law, Medicine, and Veterinary Medicine. The most popular majors include Veterinary Medical Technology, Equestrian Studies, Business, Education, and English. A 3+1 option allows students to earn a bachelor's degree and a Master of Arts (M.A.) degree in humanities. Most majors require internships or capstone projects, and all majors in the sciences require a three-semester research project—something that sets Wilson graduates apart from the average biology or chemistry major. Whether students are interested in an exciting internship, pursuing honors classes, or studying elephants in South Africa, Wilson provides outstanding opportunities that expand their horizons.

Wilson offers many clubs and activities, including NCAA Division III athletics and IHSA Equestrian teams.

Wilson is proud of its exceptional Penn Hall Equestrian Center, the base for its equestrian programs. The state-of-the-art equestrian center includes two indoor riding arenas featuring shadow-less lighting and sand/sawdust footing. The center also houses an outdoor arena with racetrack sand footing, three pristine barns with 72 stalls, 20 acres of fenced paddocks and pastures, and plenty of space for outdoor riding. Horse board is available.

Those who want to explore sustainability in food production, energy, transportation, land stewardship, and community awareness find opportunities for practical learning at the Fulton Center for Sustainable Living.

With state of the art class-room, laboratory and research spaces, the Harry R. Brooks Complex for Science, Mathematics and Technology enhances teaching and learning and the practice of science at the undergraduate level. The building has transformed the campus and is changing the lives of Wilson's students and faculty.

Wilson College guarantees on-campus housing all four years; students can even have their own single room. Students can have cars on campus, and laundry is free. The campus shuttle takes students to local shopping areas.

Wilson College is located on 300 acres in the historic small city of Chambersburg, Pennsylvania. Located along the Interstate 81 corridor approximately 17 miles from the Maryland border, Wilson is 1 hour from Harrisburg; 2 hours from Baltimore and Washington, D.C.; 3 hours from Philadelphia and Pittsburgh; and 4 hours from New York City. The campus, with its gracious lawns,

mature trees, and rolling hills, is on the National Register of Historic Places as an historic district.

- **Enrollment:** *746*
- **Selectivity:** *moderately difficult*
- **Application deadline:** *Rolling (freshmen), rolling (transfer)*
- **Expenses:** *Tuition $28,745; Room & Board $10,148*

CONTACT INFORMATION

Admissions Office
☎ 717-262-2002 or toll-free
    800-421-8402
🖳 admissions@wilson.edu

Twilight on the campus green is accented by the warm glow of the lights in the John Stewart Memorial Library.

Taking the SAT

TIPS AND PRACTICE FOR THE SAT

JUST HOW IS THE SAT USED FOR COLLEGE ADMISSIONS

The explicitly stated purpose of the SAT is to predict how students will perform academically as first-year college students. But the more practical purpose of the SAT is to help college admissions officers make acceptance decisions. When you think about it, admissions officers have a difficult job, particularly when they are asked to compare the academic records of students from different high schools in different parts of the country taking different classes. It's not easy to figure out how one student's grade point average (GPA) in New Mexico correlates with that of another student in Florida. Even though admissions officers can do a good deal of detective work to fairly evaluate candidates, they benefit a great deal from the SAT. The SAT provides a single, standardized means of comparison. After all, virtually every student takes the SAT, and the SAT is the same for everyone. It doesn't matter whether you hail from New York, North Dakota, or New Mexico.

So the SAT is an important test. But it is not the be-all, end-all. Keep it in perspective! It is only one of several important pieces of the college admissions puzzle. Other factors that weigh heavily into the admission process include GPA, difficulty of course load, level of extracurricular involvement, and the strength of the college application itself.

WHEN YOU SHOULD TAKE THE SAT

When you decide which schools you're going to apply to, find out if they require the SAT. Most do! Your next step is to determine when they need your SAT scores. Write that date down. That's the one you *really* don't want to miss.

You do have some leeway in choosing your test date. The SAT is typically offered on one Saturday morning in October, November, December, January, March (or April, alternating), May, and June. Check the exact dates to see which ones meet your deadlines. To do this, count back six weeks from each deadline, because that's how long it takes Educational Testing Service (ETS) to score your test and send out the results.

What if you don't know which schools you want to apply to? Don't panic! Even if you take the exam in December or January of your senior year, you'll probably have plenty of time to send your scores to most schools.

When you plan to take the SAT, select a test date that works best with your schedule. Ideally, you should allow yourself at least two to three months to prepare. Many students like to take the test in March of their junior year. That way, they take the SAT several months before final exams, the prom, and end-of-the-year distractions. Taking the test in March can give you early feedback as to how you're scoring. If you are dissatisfied with your scores, there is ample opportunity to take the test again in the spring or following fall. But there's a chance that your schedule might not easily accommodate a March testing. Maybe you're involved in a winter sport or school play that will take too much time away from SAT studying. Maybe you have a family reunion planned over spring break in March. Or maybe you simply prefer to prepare during a different time of year. If that's the case, just pick another date.

HOW YOUR SCORES ARE REPORTED

After you have taken the SAT, ETS scores your test and creates a score report. At the time of registration, you can pick four colleges or universities to also receive your score report. ETS will send your scores to these four schools for free. Within nine days of taking the test, you can change your school selection. If you want to send more than four reports or change your mind more than nine days after your test date, you will have to pay for it.

If you decide to take the SAT more than once, ETS offers you the option to decide which scores to send to the schools you've picked—scores from one, several, or all test dates. You may only designate the test date or dates for your score reports; you cannot designate individual test sections. In other words, if you take the SAT in October, December, and March, you cannot pick the Verbal score from October, Math score from December, and Essay score from March and tell ETS to send those results to the schools of your choice. You can only choose whether ETS should send your complete results from one, two, or all three test dates.

If you choose not to take advantage of this option, ETS will send all of your scores to the schools you've selected. However, no score reports will ever be sent without your specific consent. ETS will send e-mail reminders to you and your counselor, asking which scores you want to send, so you have time to make a decision at the time you take the SAT. You can find more information about this and how colleges and universities use your score reports on the Web site www.collegeboard.com.

THE SAT FORMAT AND SCORING

The SAT consists of sections on mathematical reasoning, critical reading, and writing. There are eight sections that count toward your accumulated score and one—the wild card—that does not. The wild card, formally known as the experimental, section can be math, critical reading, or writing. This is the part of the test where ETS—the company that writes the SAT—tries out questions that might be used on future tests. Even though the wild card section doesn't count toward your score, you won't know which section it is. ETS does this on purpose. It knows that if you knew which section didn't count, you probably wouldn't try your hardest on it. So you'll have to do your best on all the sections.

The sections are timed to range from 20 to 35 minutes. The whole test, including the experimental section, takes 3 hours and 45 minutes. Don't worry. There are breaks. The following chart gives you an idea of what to expect. Note that the order of the sections will vary and are mixed so that you may have a math section followed by a critical reading section followed by a writing section. You won't have all the math sections grouped together and then both writing sections

On the SAT, all questions count the same. You won't get more points for answering a really difficult math question than you will get for answering a very simple sentence completion question. Remember that when you're moving through the test. The more time you spend wrestling with the answer to one "stumper," the less time you have to whip through several easier questions. Don't spin your wheels by spending too much time on any one question. Give it some thought, take your best shot, and move along.

TIP: Always cross out answer choices that you are eliminating. If you find that you can't decide on an answer and have to move on, you won't have to waste time reading all the answer choice again if you have time to come back.

Question Sets Usually Go from Easiest to Most Difficult

A question set is one set of similar questions within the larger math, critical reading, or writing sections. Except for the reading passages in the critical reading section, SAT questions follow the pattern of easiest to hardest. Work your way through the earlier, easier questions as quickly as you can. That way you'll have more time for the later, more difficult ones.

But two words of caution: First, what may be easy to the test-writer may not be to you. Don't panic if Question 3 seems hard. Try to work through it, but don't spend too much time on it if it's a topic such as factoring that has just never been easy for you to understand. Second, work quickly but carefully. Don't work so fast that you make a silly mistake and lose a point that you should have aced.

You Can Set Your Own Speed Limit

All right, how will you know what your speed limit is? Use practice tests to check your timing. If you've answered most of the questions in the time limit but have a lot of incorrect answers, you'd better slow down. On the other hand, if you are very accurate in your answers but aren't answering every question in a section, you can probably pick up the pace a bit.

It's Smart to Keep Moving

Don't spend too much time on any one question before you've tried all the questions in a section. There may be questions later on in the test that you can answer easily, and you don't want to lose points just because you didn't get to them.

The Easy Answer Isn't Always Best

Are you at the end of a section? Remember, that's where you'll find the hardest questions, which means that the answers are more complex. Look carefully at the choices and really think about what the question is asking.

You Don't Have to Read the Directions

Yes, that's right—you don't have to read the directions. By the time you actually sit down to take the SAT, you should have taken numerous practice tests and read those SAT directions multiple times. So when the exam clock starts ticking, don't waste time rereading directions you already know. Instead, go directly to Question 1.

You're Going to Need a Watch

If you're going to pace yourself, you need to keep track of the time—and what if there is no clock in your room or if the only clock is out of your line of vision? That's why it's a good idea to bring a watch to the test. A word of warning: Don't use a watch alarm or your watch will end up on the proctor's desk.

GETTING READY: THE NIGHT BEFORE AND THE DAY OF THE TEST

On the night before taking the SAT, you should lay out the following items before you go to bed:

- **Registration ticket:** Unless you are taking the test as a standby tester, you should have received one of these in the mail.
- **Identification:** A driver's license is preferable, but your school ID with a picture will certainly do.
- **Pencils:** Make sure you bring at least three number 2 pencils; those are the only pencils that the machines can read.
- **Calculator:** Bring the calculator with which you're most comfortable. Don't pack a scientific or graphing calculator if you're unfamiliar with how it works. And don't take any calculator that beeps, produces a paper

tape, makes any noise at all, or that is a part of a computer or other device. You won't be allowed to use such a calculator on the SAT.

- **Layered clothing:** You never know what the temperature of the test-taking room will be. By dressing in layers, you can adapt to either a warm or a cold room.
- **Wristwatch:** Your classroom should have an operational clock, but if it doesn't, you want to be prepared. Again, don't wear a watch that beeps, unless you can turn off the alarm function.
- **Snack:** You're not allowed to eat in the room during the test, but you are given a 5- to 10-minute break. So be armed with a fortifying snack that you can eat quickly in the hallway.

Make sure you allow enough time to arrive at the test site at least 15 minutes before the 8 a.m. start time. You don't want to raise your level of anxiety by having to rush to get there.

In the morning, take a shower to wake up and then eat a sensible breakfast. If you are a person who usually eats breakfast, you should probably eat your customary meal. If you don't usually eat breakfast, don't gorge yourself on test day, because it will be a shock to your system. Eat something light (like a granola bar and a piece of fruit) and remember to pack that snack!

SIMULATE TEST-TAKING CONDITIONS

Practice exams, like Peterson's *Master the SAT*, help you prepare for the experience of taking a timed, standardized test. They can help improve your familiarity with the SAT, reduce your number of careless errors, and increase your overall level of confidence. To make sure that you get the most out of this practice, you should do everything in your power to simulate actual test-taking conditions. Here are some expert suggestions for simulating testing conditions when you work through your SAT practice exams.

Find a Block of Time

Because the SAT is administered in one long block of time, the best way to simulate test-taking conditions is to take an entire practice exam in one sitting.

This means that you should set aside $3\frac{1}{2}$ hours of consecutive time to take the practice tests.

If you find it difficult to find that amount of quiet time at home, maybe take the test in the library. If you decide to take a test at home, be sure to turn off the ringer on all nearby house phones, turn off your cell phone or put it in another room, and ask your parents to please keep your siblings away from where you're taking your practice test.

Work at a Desk and Wear a Watch

Don't take a practice test while you are lounging on your bed. Clear off enough space on a desk or table to work comfortably. Wear a watch to properly administer the sections under timed conditions. Or use a timer. Most sections of the SAT are 25 minutes. The time for each section is marked on the section, so check the beginning of each section, and set your timer or your watch for that amount of time.

You are not allowed to explore other sections on the test while you are supposed to be working on a particular one. So when you take your practice tests, don't look ahead or back. Take the full time to complete each section.

Practice on a Weekend Morning

Since the SAT is typically administered at 8:30 a.m. on Saturday (or Sunday for religious observers), why not take the exam at the exact same time on a weekend morning? You should be most energetic in the morning anyway. If you are not a morning person, now is a good time to become one since that's when you'll have to take the actual SAT! When you take the practice test, allow yourself two breaks. Give yourself a 5-minute break after Section 3 to run to the bathroom, eat a snack, and resharpen your pencils. After Section 6, give yourself a 1-minute stretch break. During this time on SAT day, you are not allowed to leave the room or speak with anyone. To simulate this, stand up after Section 6, take a minute to collect your thoughts, and then proceed to Section 7.

BASIC STEPS FOR SOLVING SENTENCE COMPLETION QUESTIONS

- The sentence completion questions are arranged in order from easiest to most difficult.

- Sentence completion questions test your vocabulary and your reading comprehension skills by presenting sentences with one or two blanks and asking you to choose the best words to fill the blanks.

- In general, you follow these six steps to answer sentence completion questions:

  1 Read the sentence carefully.

  2 Think of a word or words that will fit the blank(s) appropriately.

  3 Look through the five answer choices for that word(s). If it's not there, move on to step 4.

  4 Examine the sentence for clues to the missing word.

  5 Eliminate any answer choices that are ruled out by the clues.

  6 Try the ones that are left and pick whichever is best.

- Eliminate choices that are illogical or grammatically incorrect, and use both words within a two-word choice to test for the best response.

- Try to spend no more than 45 to 50 seconds on any one sentence completion question.

BASIC STEPS FOR SOLVING READING COMPREHENSION QUESTIONS

To answer critical reading questions, follow these four steps:

1 Read the introduction, if one is provided. Don't zoom past the introductory paragraph because it can be very helpful to you. It might provide some important background information about the passage, or it might set the stage so you know what you're reading about.

2 Read the passage. Try to pick up main ideas, but don't get bogged down in the factual trivia. After all, you won't even be asked about most of the material in the passage!

3 Read the questions and their answer choices. Go back into the passage to find answers, and answer every question you can. Remember, all the answers are somewhere in the passage, so go back and reread any sections that will help you!

4 For any question you're not sure of, eliminate obviously wrong answers and take your best guess from the choices that are left.

Do the Critical Reading Questions Last

The verbal section of the SAT also contains sentence completions. Because the critical reading questions require the most time to complete, you should save these questions for last.

Answer All of the Questions Before You Move on to the Next Passage

There won't be time to go back to these passages at the end of this section, so answer every question that you can about the passage before moving on. If you skip a question and try to come back to it later, you might have to reread the whole passage to find the answer—and you'll be out of time. Just guess if you have to, but finish all the questions that you can before you move on to the next passage.

Remember That the Questions Follow the Order of the Passage

The questions are like a map to the passage—their order follows the order of the information in the passage. For a long passage, the first questions refer to the early part of the passage, and later questions refer to later parts of the passage. If there are two long passages, the first questions are for Passage 1, the next for Passage 2, and the last questions refer to both. This arrangement is true for short passages as well. In a single short passage, the questions will follow the order of the information in the passage. For paired short passages there will be four questions. Each passage may have one or two questions, and the final one or two questions will ask about the relationship between the two short passages. Regardless of how the four questions are apportioned between the two passages, any questions about an individual passage will ask for information in the order in which it was discussed.

Handle Those Double Passages One Passage at a Time

Since the questions are arranged like a map, take advantage! Read Passage 1 and answer the questions that relate to Passage 1. Then read Passage 2 and answer the questions that relate to Passage 2. Finally, answer the comparative questions. In this way, you won't have to read too much at once, and you won't confuse the message of Passage 1 with that of Passage 2.

Don't Panic When You Read an Unfamiliar Passage

The passages are supposed to be unfamiliar. In their attempt to be fair, the test-makers purposely choose passages that are from the darkest recesses of the library. This helps make sure that no test-taker has ever seen them before. Remember, you're not being tested on your knowledge of the topic, but on how well you do the following:

- Figure out the meaning of an unfamiliar word from its context
- Determine what an author means by noting certain words and phrases
- Understand the author's assumptions, point of view, and main idea
- Analyze the logical structure of a piece of writing

Remember That Everything You Need to Know Is Right There in Front of You

The introductory paragraph and the passage have all the information you'll need to answer the questions. Even if the passage is about the price of beans in Bulgaria or the genetic makeup of a wombat, don't worry. It's all right there on the page.

Start with the Short Passages and with those Passages That Interest You

A point is a point. It doesn't matter if the point comes from correctly answering a question about the longest passage or the shortest. Check the short passages and the paired short passages first. If the topics seem familiar, or at least not mind-numbing, start with them. Then try the long passages. If you can find some long passages that interest you, whether they're fiction, science, or whatever, start with those and work your way down to the ones that you think will be hardest for you. If the style and subject matter appeal to you, you'll probably go through a passage more quickly and find the questions easier to deal with.

Highlight Important Information as You Read the Passages

It pays to be an active reader. When you read, actively use your pencil to underline important names, dates, and facts. Bracket the main idea. Circle the supporting details. The questions are likely to be about the most important information in a passage. If you've highlighted those pieces of information, you'll be able to find them easily when you need them to answer the questions.

Don't Get Bogged Down in the Details

You don't have to understand every bit of information. You just have to find the information you need to answer the questions. Don't waste time trying to analyze technical details or information not related to a question.

Don't Confuse a "True" Answer with a "Correct" Answer

The fact that an answer choice is true doesn't mean it's right. What does that mean? It means that a certain answer choice may be perfectly true—in fact, all of the answer choices may be true. But the *right* answer must be the correct answer to the question that's being asked. Only one of the answer choices will be correct and, therefore, the right choice. Read carefully—and don't be fooled!

- All of the information you need is right in the passage.
- Read the introduction, if one is provided.
- Read the passage without getting bogged down in details.
- Read the questions and their answer choices. Go back into the passage to find answers.
- Critical reading questions follow the order of information in the passage. They are not arranged in order of difficulty.
- Answer every question for a passage before starting the next passage.
- For any question you're not sure of, eliminate obviously wrong answers and take your best guess.

BASIC STRATEGIES FOR ANSWERING THE MULTIPLE-CHOICE WRITING QUESTIONS

NOTE

If you skip a question, be sure that you skip the answer oval on the answer sheet.

The different multiple-choice question types will be in separate sections. You won't find improving paragraph questions mixed in with identifying sentence errors, but here are a few basic strategies that will help with any of the three question types.

For identifying sentence errors and improving sentences, read each sentence twice before you do anything else.

Try to find the error or improve the sentence yourself before looking at the answer choices.

Look for errors based on level of difficulty. Check for errors in the following:

- Capitalization and punctuation
- Grammar
- Tenses, usage, parallel structure, and redundancy

Pace yourself. If you have no idea how to answer a question within a few seconds, circle it in your test booklet and move on.

If you have some idea about an answer but aren't sure enough to fill in an answer oval, put an "X" next to the question and move on.

Don't expect to be able to go back to a lot of questions once you've been through the section, so if you know something about a question and can eliminate at least one answer, GUESS.

STRATEGIES FOR ANSWERING IDENTIFYING SENTENCE ERRORS QUESTIONS

Unlike most of the SAT, for the Identifying Sentence Error questions, you are looking for what's wrong in the sentences, not what's right. Use the following six strategies to help you find the error:

1. Read the sentence carefully—twice.
2. As you read, listen for any awkward or strange-sounding word or phrase.

3 If you can't hear the mistake, check to see what kinds of words and phrases are underlined. Sentence errors often involve wrong tenses, incorrect subject-verb agreement, and incorrect agreement between pronoun and antecedent.

4 Cross out any of the answer choices that you know are correct. Remember, you are looking for what's wrong.

5 Check the remaining choices to see if they are correct.

6 If you have ruled out all the answer choices except E, *No error,* choose it.

STRATEGIES FOR ANSWERING IMPROVING SENTENCES QUESTIONS

Use the following six basic steps to answer improving sentences items:

1 Read the entire sentence. Don't try to save time by reading only the underlined part. You may think that it sounds correct until you fit it into the rest of the sentence.

2 Errors in this section often involve verbs, pronoun reference mistakes, incorrect comparisons, and errors in standard English usage.

3 If the underlined portion sounds incorrect to you, substitute answers (B) through (E) into the sentence. Don't just substitute choice (B), decide it's correct, fill in the oval, and move on. Try all the answer choices—unless you read an answer choice and find that it has an error in it.

4 Cross out each answer choice that has an error in it.

5 Cross out each answer choice that is not the best substitution in the sentence. An answer may be correctly written but not fit the answer very well. You are looking for the *best* answer.

6 If the sentence sounds correct to you, then choose answer choice (A), which repeats the underlined portion.

STRATEGIES FOR ANSWERING IMPROVING PARAGRAPH QUESTIONS

There are two ways to approach improving paragraph questions. One way is to read the questions first and then the paragraph. The other way is to read the paragraph first and then the questions.

Reading the Essay First

Reading is really not the right word. You will be skimming the essay for general meaning. You won't be looking for errors, awkwardness, or redundancies, but for what the essay is about, how it's organized, and what its purpose is. Then you can either reread the essay more slowly, looking for problems before you begin to answer questions, or you can go right to answering questions and reread parts of the essay only as needed to find an answer.

Reading the Questions First

When you read the questions, read just the questions. Don't spend time on the answers at this point. You want to find out how many questions you have to answer for this passage, what kind of questions they are (main idea, revision, sentence combining, sentence purpose, and so on), and which paragraph has the most questions. You will want to read that paragraph with particular care.

Once you have read the questions, skim the essay to get an overall idea of what it is about and how it is organized. Jot question numbers in the margin next to information that will help you answer particular questions. If you can't remember question numbers, make notes such as "to persuade" for author's intent and "chrono" for type of organization. Once you've read through the essay, go back and answer the questions.

A CLOSER LOOK AT THE ESSAY QUESTION

The essay section of the SAT is 25 minutes long. In this time, you need to read the essay prompt, choose a position, and plan and write your essay. It doesn't need to be—and isn't supposed to be—a final, polished version. The high school and college English teachers who will score your essay are trained to view the essays as first drafts. They will be assessing your essay and hundreds of others against a rubric that guides them to look at the essays holistically. They are reading for an overall general impression of your writing abilities.

You will be given one essay prompt and asked to write a persuasive essay in response. You won't have a choice of questions to answer. This is good because it saves you time, as you don't have to decide which one to choose. The essay prompt sets out an issue and a question, which asks whether you agree or disagree with the issue as stated.

Once you have figured out your response, then you can begin your planning. You don't need any specific subject-area knowledge to write your essay. The purpose of the essay is to demonstrate for the readers that you can develop a thesis, support it with examples, and present a conclusion that accurately describes your point of view on the topic.

THE SCORING RUBRIC FOR THE SAT ESSAY

The SAT essay is scored from 1 to 6, with 6 being the highest score. Two readers assess your essay and the scores are combined, so your final score will range somewhere between 2 and 12. If the scores from the two readers differ by more than one point, a third scorer will read the essay. The two closest scores will then be used.

All of the scorers read the essays against the same rubric developed by the College Board and the Educational Testing Service, which administers the SAT. This rubric guides the scorers in considering overall impression, development, organization, diction, sentence structure, grammar, usage, and mechanics. The score guidelines are similar to the following:

Essay Scoring 6 (Outstanding)

- *Overall impression:* develops a point of view with clarity and insight; uses excellent critical thinking in presenting the viewpoint; uses appropriate supporting examples, reasoning, and details
- *Organization:* is well organized with a clear focus; coherent; clear and orderly progression of ideas

- *Diction:* uses appropriate, varied, and accurate vocabulary for interest and clarity
- *Sentence structure:* varies sentence structure
- *Grammar, usage, mechanics:* is almost free of grammar, usage, and mechanics errors

Essay Scoring 5 (Effective)

- *Overall impression:* develops viewpoint effectively; uses strong critical thinking in presenting viewpoint; most examples, reasons, and details are appropriate
- *Organization:* is well organized and focused; coherent; progression of ideas present
- *Diction:* demonstrates skill in the use of appropriate language
- *Sentence structure:* varies sentence structure
- *Grammar, usage, mechanics:* is mostly free of grammar, usage, and mechanics errors

Essay Scoring 4 (Competent)

- *Overall impression:* develops viewpoint; shows competent critical thinking; provides adequate support through the use of examples, reasons, and details
- *Organization:* is mostly organized and focused; coherent for the most part; has some clear progression of ideas
- *Diction:* is inconsistent in the use of appropriate vocabulary; is generally adequate
- *Sentence structure:* uses some varied sentence structure
- *Grammar, usage, mechanics:* makes some grammar, usage, and mechanics errors

Essay Scoring 3 (Inadequate)

- *Overall impression:* develops a point of view; shows some use of critical thinking; may be inconsistent in reasoning; may provide insufficient support
- *Organization:* shows limited organization or some lack of focus; some lack of coherence or progression of ideas

- *Diction:* shows some facility in language use; uses weak or inappropriate vocabulary
- *Sentence structure:* uses little sentence variety; may have problems in use of sentence structures
- *Grammar, usage, mechanics:* shows a number of grammar, usage, and mechanics errors

Essay Scoring 2 (Limited)

- *Overall impression:* develops a vague or limited viewpoint; weak critical thinking; uses inappropriate supporting evidence or too few examples to make the points
- *Organization:* poor or unfocused; serious weaknesses in coherence or progression of ideas
- *Diction:* shows little facility with language; limited word choice; inappropriate vocabulary
- *Sentence structure:* has numerous errors in sentence structure
- *Grammar, usage, mechanics:* has numerous errors in grammar, usage, and mechanics that interfere with meaning

Essay Scoring 1 (Fundamentally Flawed)

- *Overall impression:* has no point of view on the issue or offers little or no support for the point of view
- *Organization:* lacks organization or focus; incoherent; no progression of ideas
- *Diction:* has basic errors in the use of vocabulary
- *Sentence structure:* has serious problems with sentence structure
- *Grammar, usage, mechanics:* has numerous errors in grammar, usage, and mechanics interfering with meaning

Note that a score of 0 will be given if an essay is not based on the writing prompt.

A LOOK AT THE SAT MATH SECTION

The questions in each multiple-choice math section are arranged from easiest to most difficult. The questions don't stick to one content area. They jump around from algebra to geometry to arithmetic to data analysis to statistics and back to algebra in no particular pattern.

SAT multiple-choice math is easier than the math tests you take in class because the answers are right there in front of you. As you know from other standardized tests, multiple-choice tests always give you the answer. You just have to figure out which answer is the correct one. So even if you aren't sure and have to guess, you can use estimating to narrow your choices and improve your odds.

QUESTION FORMAT FOR SAT MATH

On the SAT, each set of multiple-choice math questions starts with directions and a reference section that look like this:

Directions: Solve the following problems using any available space on the page for scratchwork. On your answer sheet, fill in the choice that best corresponds to the correct answer.

Notes: The figures accompanying the problems are drawn as accurately as possible unless otherwise stated in specific problems. Again, unless otherwise stated, all figures lie in the same plane. All numbers used in these problems are real numbers. Calculators are permitted for this test.

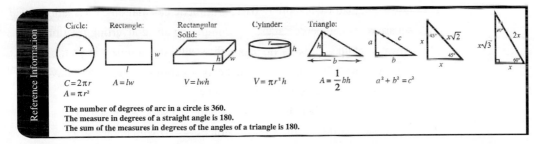

The number of degrees of arc in a circle is 360.
The measure in degrees of a straight angle is 180.
The sum of the measures in degrees of the angles of a triangle is 180.

The information in the reference section should all be familiar to you from your schoolwork. Know that it's there in case you need it. But remember: the formulas themselves aren't the answers to any problems. You have to know when to use them and how to apply them.

Some multiple-choice questions are straight calculations, while others are presented in the form of word problems. Some include graphs, charts, or tables that you will be asked to interpret. All of the questions have five answer choices. These choices are arranged in order by size from smallest to largest or occasionally from largest to smallest.

TIP

For multiple-choice math questions, circle what's being asked so that you don't pick a wrong answer by mistake. That way, for example, you won't pick an answer that gives perimeter when the question asks for an area.

SOLVING MULTIPLE-CHOICE MATH QUESTIONS

These five steps will help you solve multiple-choice math questions:

1 Read the question carefully and determine what's being asked.

2 Decide which math principles apply and use them to solve the problem.

3 Look for your answer among the choices. If it's there, mark it and go on.

4 If the answer you found is not there, recheck the question and your calculations.

5 If you still can't solve the problem, eliminate obviously wrong answers and take your best guess.

A Few More Helpful Tips

- Use a calculator when doing basic arithmetic calculations, calculating square roots and percentages, and comparing and converting fractions.
- Always set up your work on paper, then enter the numbers in your calculator; that way, if your calculation becomes confused, you don't have to try to replicate your setup from memory.
- The question number shows how hard the question is (on a 1 to 25 scale).
- Work backward from the answer choices—start with choice (C).
- Try to work with numbers instead of letters. This will help you avoid unnecessary algebraic calculations.
- Figures in the math section are always drawn to scale unless you see a warning. So use your eye as an estimator if you need to.

WHY GRID-INS ARE EASIER THAN YOU THINK

Grid-ins are officially named "student-produced responses," because you have to do the calculations and find the answer on your own; there are no multiple-choice answers to choose from. Many students are intimidated by grid-ins. Don't be! Grid-in questions test the exact same mathematical concepts as the multiple-choice questions. The only difference is that there are no answer choices to work with.

The grid-in questions are in a section of their own, and they're arranged in order of difficulty from easy to hard.

On the SAT, each set of grid-in questions starts with directions that look approximately like this:

Directions: Solve each of these problems. Write the answer in the corresponding grid on the answer sheet and fill in the ovals beneath each answer you write. Here are some examples.

Note: Either format is correct.   **Note:** Either position is correct.

1. Write your answer in the boxes at the top of the grid. Technically, this isn't required by the SAT, but it does give you something to follow as you fill in the ovals. Do it—it will help you.

2. Mark the corresponding ovals, one per column. The machine that scores the test can only read the ovals, so if you don't fill them in, you won't get credit. Just entering your answer in the boxes is not enough!

3. Start in any column. You can start entering your answer in any column, if space permits. Unused columns should be left blank; don't put in zeroes. Look at this example.

4. Work with decimals or fractions. For example, an answer can be expressed as $\frac{3}{4}$ or as .75. You don't have to put a zero in front of a decimal that is less than 1. Just remember that you have only four spaces to work with and that a decimal point or a fraction slash uses up one of the spaces.

5. Express mixed numbers as decimals or improper fractions. A mixed number has to be expressed as a decimal or as an improper fraction. If you tried to grid $1\frac{3}{4}$, it would be scored as $\frac{13}{4}$, which would give you a wrong answer. Instead, you could grid the answer as 1.75 or as $\frac{7}{4}$.

The above answers are acceptable.

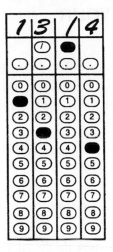

The above answer is unacceptable.

6 If more than one answer is possible, grid any one. Choose one and grid it.

For example, if a question asks for a prime number between 5 and 13, the answer could be 7 or 11. Grid 7 or grid 11, but **don't** put in both answers.

TOP 10 STRATEGIES TO RAISE YOUR SAT SCORE

When it comes to taking the SAT, some test-taking skills will do you more good than others. There are concepts you can learn and techniques you can follow that will help you do your best. Here's our pick for the top 10 strategies to raise your score:

1. **Create a study plan and follow it.** The right SAT study plan will help you get the most out of this book in whatever time you have.

2. **Don't get stuck on any one question.** Since you have a specific amount of time to answer questions, you can't afford to spend too much time on any one problem.

3. **Learn the directions in advance.** If you already know the directions, you won't have to waste your time reading them. You'll be able to jump right in and start answering questions as soon as the testing clock begins.

4. **For the Essay, it's important to develop your ideas and express them clearly, using examples to back them up.** Your essay doesn't have to be grammatically perfect, but it does have to be focused and organized.

5. **For the Writing multiple-choice questions, think about the simplest, clearest way to express an idea.** If an answer choice sounds awkward or overly complicated, chances are good that it's wrong.

6. **For Sentence Completions, as you read, try to predict what word should go in each blank.** Sometimes you can guess the meaning of one blank, but not the other. In that case, scan the answer choices, look for a word that's similar to the one you've predicted, and then eliminate the answer choices that don't match up.

7. **For Reading Comprehension questions, skim the passage to see what it's about.** Don't worry about the details; you can always look them up later if you need to. Look for the main ideas, and then tackle the questions that direct you straight to the answer by referring you to a specific line in the passage. If you have time afterward, you can try solving the harder questions.

8. **For the Math multiple-choice questions, you're allowed to use a calculator, but it won't help you unless you know how to approach the problems.** If you're stuck, try substituting numbers for variables. You can also try plugging in numbers from the answer choices. Start with the middle number. That way, if it doesn't work, you can strategically choose one that's higher or lower.

9. **For the math grid-ins, you come up with the answer and fill it into a grid.** Unlike the multiple-choice questions, you won't be penalized for wrong answers, so make your best guess even if you're not sure.

10. **Finally, relax the night before the test.** Don't cram. Studying at the last minute will only stress you out. Go to a movie or hang out with a friend—anything to get your mind off the test!

Next, you'll find some sample Practice Test questions, followed by detailed answer explanations, from *Peterson's Master the SAT*. It's not a full practice test, but we hope it will give you a taste of the type of questions you are likely to find on the exam. The editors of Peterson's wish you much success.

Essay • 25 Minutes

Directions: Think carefully about the statement below and the assignment that follows it.

There is an old saying, "The squeaky hinge gets the grease." If you do not make your needs known and heard in our society, you will not succeed in having them satisfied.

Assignment: What is your opinion of the idea that assertiveness is necessary in order to have issues acted upon? Plan and write an essay that develops your ideas logically. Support your opinion with specific evidence taken from your personal experience, your observations of others, or your reading.

STOP

END OF SECTION 5. IF YOU HAVE ANY TIME LEFT, GO OVER YOUR WORK IN THIS SECTION ONLY. DO NOT WORK IN ANY OTHER SECTION OF THE TEST.

Section 2

Directions: Each of the following questions consists of an incomplete sentence followed by five words or pairs of words. Choose that word or pair of words that when substituted for the blank space or spaces, best completes the meaning of the sentence and mark the letter of your choice on your answer sheet.

In view of the extenuating circumstances and the defendant's youth, the judge recommended __________.

(A) conviction

(B) a defense

(C) a mistrial

(D) leniency

(E) life imprisonment

The correct answer is (D).

1. An audience that laughs in all the wrong places can __________ even the most experienced actor.

(A) disparage
(B) allay
(C) disconcert
(D) upbraid
(E) satiate

2. Their assurances of good faith were hollow; they __________ on the agreement almost at once.

(A) conferred
(B) expiated
(C) recapitulated
(D) obtruded
(E) reneged

3. If we _____ our different factions, then together we can gain the majority in the legislature.
   (A) amalgamate
   (B) manifest
   (C) preclude
   (D) alienate
   (E) deviate

4. The Eighteenth Amendment, often called the Prohibition Act, _____ the sale of alcoholic beverages.
   (A) prolonged
   (B) preempted
   (C) sanctioned
   (D) proscribed
   (E) encouraged

5. The police received a(n)_____ call giving them valuable information, but the caller would not give his name out of fear of _____.
   (A) private .. impunity
   (B) anonymous .. reprisals
   (C) professional .. dissension
   (D) enigmatic .. refusal
   (E) adamant .. transgression

6. A person who is _____ is slow to adapt to a new way of life.
   (A) nonchalant
   (B) intractable
   (C) rabid
   (D) insolent
   (E) doughty

7. Though they came from _____ social backgrounds, the newly married couple shared numerous interests and feelings.
   (A) desultory
   (B) obsolete
   (C) malleable
   (D) disparate
   (E) deleterious

8. The _____ was a _____ of gastronomic delights.

    (A) internist .. progeny

    (B) gourmet .. connoisseur

    (C) scientist .. facilitator

    (D) xenophobe .. promoter

    (E) tyro .. master

9. Mrs. Jenkins, upon hearing that her arm was broken, looked _____ at the doctor.

    (A) jovially

    (B) plaintively

    (C) fortuitously

    (D) serendipitously

    (E) opportunely

Directions: Each passage below is followed by a set of questions. Read each passage, then answer the accompanying questions, basing your answers on what is stated or implied in the passage and in any introductory material provided. Mark the letter of your choice on your answer sheet.

QUESTIONS 10 AND 11 ARE BASED ON THE FOLLOWING PASSAGE.

    Edouard Manet was one of the foremost painters of the mid and late nineteenth century. Although he was a friend of the Impressionists, he never became one of them. He chose not to exhibit with them in an effort to remain fixed in the public's mind as the finest painter of the
5 era. While experimental in his style and techniques, he did not go as far as Impressionists such as Degas and Pissaro or his sister-in-law Berthe Morisot. Manet's paintings, however, served as a model for younger painters looking for different ways to capture light, movement, detail, and color. Manet himself had studied earlier painters and owed much
10 to the Spanish, Italian, and Dutch masters.

10. The purpose of the passage is to

    (A) describe the difference between Manet's work and that of the Impressionists.

    (B) discuss Manet's ego.

    (C) discuss Manet's legacy to later painters.

    (D) discuss Manet's relation to Impressionism.

    (E) explain why Manet chose not to exhibit with the Impressionists.

11. The phrase "did not go as far as Impressionists" (lines 5–6) means that
    (A) Manet was less creative.
    (B) Manet did not travel as much as the Impressionists in looking for subjects.
    (C) Manet's works were more traditional than those of the Impressionists.
    (D) the Impressionists exhibited more than Manet did.
    (E) Manet was less interested in public opinion.

QUESTIONS 12 AND 13 ARE BASED ON THE FOLLOWING PASSAGE.

This, then, is . . . the duty of the man of wealth: first, to set an example of modest, unostentatious living, shunning display or extravagance; to provide moderately for legitimate wants of those dependent upon him; and after doing so to consider all surplus revenues which come to
5 him simply as trust funds, which he is called upon to administer, and strictly bound as matter of duty to administer in the manner which, in his judgment, is best calculated to produce the most beneficial results for the community—the man of wealth thus becoming the mere agent and trustee for his poorer brethren, bringing to their service his superior
10 wisdom, experience, and ability to administer, ...

—Andrew Carnegie,
The Gospel of Wealth

12. The word *unostentatious* (line 2) means
    (A) not pretending.
    (B) stable.
    (C) not showy.
    (D) real.
    (E) lacking in luster.

13. The passage implies that the author believes that
    (A) wisdom comes with wealth.
    (B) wealthy men are wise.
    (C) the wealthy and the poor are locked in a battle for the resources of wealth.
    (D) the poor are not able to take care of themselves.
    (E) the wealthy need to step in to help the poor.

The Great Famine, which occurred in Ireland between 1845–1848, affected the country so profoundly that today, more than 100 years later, it is still discussed both in Irish-American communities in the United States and in Ireland. The passage presents a timeline of the famine and some of the events leading up to it.

During the mid-1840s, from 1845–1848, the potato crop in Ireland failed, creating a famine that ravaged the population. This event, the Great Famine, was one of the most significant events in the 8000-year history of this island nation, and the effects of it continue to haunt the
5 Irish, both those who still live in Ireland and those who live in the United States. The most immediate effect of the famine was the dramatic decline in the Irish population—either through death from starvation and disease or through emigration to other countries.

In Ireland, the potato had historically been the mainstay of the
10 diet of a large proportion of the rural population. Highly nutritional, the potato was easy to plant and easy to harvest. If a family of six had one acre of land, it could grow a potato crop that would feed them for almost a year. However, dependence on one crop had its downside as well. Potatoes could not be stored for long, and farmers who had grown
15 so accustomed to dealing with this one crop neglected to plant other crops as a hedge against possible failures.

Rapid population increases in the years preceding the Great Famine had created a country whose expanding population was often poverty-stricken. Expanding population, coupled with landowners' lack
20 of responsibility toward tenant-farmers, led to a system where tenant-farmers frequently subdivided their land so that they could gain a bit of rent themselves. Consequently, the rural areas were dotted with small plots of land, most of which were used for potato farming. Prior to the famine, urban areas in Ireland were also experiencing economic distress
25 because of a decline in Irish industry that resulted in unemployment and poverty in cities such as Dublin.

In 1845, the year the famine began, a good potato crop was expected, so it came as a great surprise when nearly half of the crop of the country failed because of a blight that had come from North America. This
30 particular blight was unusual inasmuch as when the potato was dug from the ground, it appeared to be healthy; it was only after a day or two that the potato began to rot.

Despite the fact that only half the crop failed in 1845, starvation and disease plagued the entire country because many starving people,
35 some of whom were infected with contagious diseases, roamed the countryside looking for food and spreading disease. Then, in 1846, the crop failed completely. In 1847, there was another partial failure,

but because people had eaten their seed potatoes in 1846, the crop was
much smaller in 1847. Then again in 1848, the crop failed completely.

40   As if the crop failures were not enough, other factors affected
the seriousness of the situation. Various contagious diseases such as
typhus, dysentery, and several different types of fever spread rapidly.
Landlords evicted tenant-farmers, and the government did very little
to provide relief. Nor did it help that the winter of 1846–1847 was one
45 of the coldest on record.

When the famine was over in 1849, a cholera epidemic struck
Ireland, so that by 1850 the country found its population reduced from
8.5 million to 6.5 million. One million people had died from disease
and starvation, and one million had left Ireland for Britain, Europe, or
50 North America.

The results of the Great Famine were profound. Farming in
Ireland changed from a one-crop economy to an agricultural economy
that included livestock and other crops, such as grains. The seeds of
animosity toward Great Britain, which had not helped the Irish in their
55 time of need, were sown. And a pattern of emigration was established
that lasts until today.

14. The word *ravaged* (line 2) means

(A) pillaged.

(B) devastated.

(C) wasted.

(D) sacked.

(E) assisted.

15. According to the passage, the potato became a staple of the Irish diet for all
of the following reasons EXCEPT

(A) it was filled with nutrients.

(B) it was easy to plant.

(C) it was easy to harvest.

(D) the soil was good for potatoes.

(E) one acre could support a whole family.

16. The passage implies that

(A) dependence on one crop was sensible.

(B) the potato was not the only crop in Ireland.

(C) the dependence on one crop had no downside.

(D) the Irish were a happy people.

(E) dependence on one crop was dangerous.

17. According to the passage, rural life in the years before the Great Famine can best be described as
    (A) prosperous.
    (B) declining in population.
    (C) harsh.
    (D) decreasing in tenant-farmers.
    (E) expanding in farm size.

18. Irish farmers tended to subdivide their farms repeatedly because
    (A) the farms were getting too large.
    (B) they had big families.
    (C) it was easier to farm a smaller plot.
    (D) they needed rent payments.
    (E) they wanted to diversify their crops.

19. The word *blight* (line 29) means
    (A) curse.
    (B) disease.
    (C) injury.
    (D) omen.
    (E) impairment.

20. Disease plagued the Irish during the famine because
    (A) the potato was diseased.
    (B) immigrants brought disease.
    (C) starving Irish carried disease from place to place.
    (D) living conditions were not sanitary.
    (E) they were not prepared.

21. All of the following were results of the famine EXCEPT that the Irish
    (A) emigrated to new lands.
    (B) began to raise livestock.
    (C) were no longer dependent on one crop.
    (D) became independent from Great Britain.
    (E) became angered at the British.

STOP

END OF SECTION. IF YOU HAVE ANY TIME LEFT, GO OVER YOUR WORK IN THIS SECTION ONLY. DO NOT WORK IN ANY OTHER SECTION OF THE TEST.

Section 3

20 Questions • 25 Minutes

Directions: Solve the following problems using any available space on the page for scratchwork. On your answer sheet, fill in the choice that best corresponds to the correct answer.

Notes: The figures accompanying the problems are drawn as accurately as possible unless otherwise stated in specific problems. Again, unless otherwise stated, all figures lie in the same plane. All numbers used in these problems are real numbers. Calculators are permitted for this test.

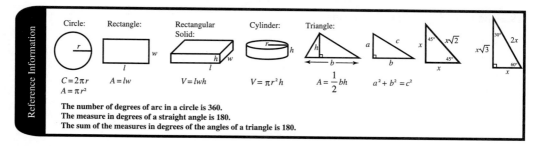

Circle: $C = 2\pi r$, $A = \pi r^2$

Rectangle: $A = lw$

Rectangular Solid: $V = lwh$

Cylinder: $V = \pi r^2 h$

Triangle: $A = \frac{1}{2}bh$, $a^2 + b^2 = c^2$

The number of degrees of arc in a circle is 360.
The measure in degrees of a straight angle is 180.
The sum of the measures in degrees of the angles of a triangle is 180.

1. Jamal bought two dozen apples for $3. At this rate, how much will 18 apples cost?

   (A) $1.20
   (B) $2.25
   (C) $2.50
   (D) $2.75
   (E) $4.50

2. What is $\frac{1}{10}\%$ of $\frac{1}{10}$ of 10?

   (A) 0.000001
   (B) 0.00001
   (C) 0.0001
   (D) 0.001
   (E) 0.01

3. If T is the set of all integers between 10 and 99 that are perfect squares, and S is the set of all integers between 10 and 99 that are perfect cubes, how many elements are there in the set $S \cap T$?

(A) 0

(B) 1

(C) 2

(D) 7

(E) 8

4. What is the fifth term of the geometric sequence whose first term is 3 and whose common ratio is 2?

(A) 16

(B) 24

(C) 32

(D) 48

(E) 96

5. The numbers v, w, x, y, and z are five consecutive integers. If $v < w < x < y < z$, and none of the integers is equal to 0, what is the value of the average (arithmetic mean) of the five numbers divided by the median of the five numbers?

(A) 0

(B) 1

(C) 2.5

(D) 5

(E) It cannot be determined from the information given.

6. If a cubic inch of metal weighs 2 pounds, a cubic foot of the same metal weighs how many pounds?

(A) 8

(B) 24

(C) 96

(D) 288

(E) 3456

7. If the number of square inches in the area of a circle is equal to the number of inches in its circumference, what is the diameter of the circle in inches?

(A) 4

(B) π

(C) 2

(D) $\dfrac{\pi}{2}$

(E) 1

8. John is now three times Pat's age. Four years from now John will be x years old. In terms of x, how old is Pat now?

(A) $\dfrac{x+4}{3}$

(B) $3x$

(C) $x + 4$

(D) $x - 4$

(E) $\dfrac{x-4}{3}$

9. When the fractions $\dfrac{2}{3}$, $\dfrac{5}{7}$, $\dfrac{8}{11}$, and $\dfrac{9}{13}$ are arranged in ascending order of size, what is the result?

(A) $\dfrac{8}{11}, \dfrac{5}{7}, \dfrac{9}{13}, \dfrac{2}{3}$

(B) $\dfrac{5}{7}, \dfrac{8}{11}, \dfrac{2}{3}, \dfrac{9}{13}$

(C) $\dfrac{2}{3}, \dfrac{8}{11}, \dfrac{5}{7}, \dfrac{9}{13}$

(D) $\dfrac{2}{3}, \dfrac{9}{13}, \dfrac{5}{7}, \dfrac{8}{11}$

(E) $\dfrac{9}{13}, \dfrac{2}{3}, \dfrac{8}{11}, \dfrac{5}{7}$

10. In a certain course, a student takes eight tests, all of which count equally. When figuring out the final grade, the instructor drops the best and the worst grades and averages the other six. The student calculates that his average for all eight tests is 84%. After dropping the best and the worst grades the student averages 86%. What was the average of the best and the worst test?

(A) 68

(B) 72

(C) 78

(D) 88

(E) It cannot be determined from the information given.

Student-Produced Response Questions

Directions: Solve each of these problems. Write the answer in the corresponding grid on the answer sheet and fill in the ovals beneath each answer you write. Here are some examples.

Answer: $\frac{3}{4} = .75$; **show answer either way**

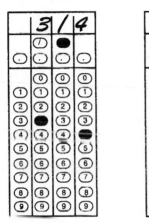

Note: A mixed number such as $3\frac{1}{2}$ must be gridded as 7/2 or as 3.5. If gridded as "3 1/2," it will be read as "thirty-one halves."

Answer: 325

Note: Either position is correct.

11. Jerry grew 5 inches in 2007 and 2 inches more in 2008 before reaching his final height of 5 feet 10 inches. What percentage of his final height did his 2007–2008 growth represent?

12. Seth bought $4\dfrac{5}{6}$ pounds of peanuts. He gave $\dfrac{1}{4}$ of his purchase to his sister. How many pounds of peanuts did Seth keep for himself?

13. If $p = 2r = 3s = 4t$, then $\dfrac{pr}{st} =$

14. $\sqrt{7+9+7+9+7+9+7+9} =$

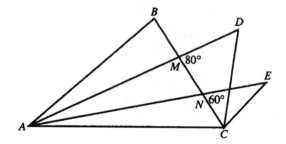

DA and EA trisect angle A.

15. In the figure above, if m∠DMC = 80° and m∠ENC = 60°, then angle BAC = (Do not grid the degree symbol.)

16. $\dfrac{\dfrac{7}{8}+\dfrac{7}{8}+\dfrac{7}{8}}{\dfrac{8}{7}+\dfrac{8}{7}+\dfrac{8}{7}} =$

17. The average of 8 numbers is 6; the average of 6 other numbers is 8. What is the average of all 14 numbers?

18. If the ratio of 4a to 3b is 8 to 9, what is the ratio of 3a to 4b?

19. Solve the following equation for x: $\dfrac{2x}{3} + \dfrac{1}{5} = 3$

20. If $f(x) = 3|x|^3$, what is the value of $f(-2)$?

STOP

END OF SECTION. IF YOU HAVE ANY TIME LEFT, GO OVER YOUR WORK IN THIS SECTION ONLY. DO NOT WORK IN ANY OTHER SECTION OF THE TEST.

Section 4

35 Questions • 25 Minutes

Directions: Some of the sentences below contain an error in grammar, usage, word choice, or idiom. Other sentences are correct. Parts of each sentence are underlined and lettered. The error, if there is one, is contained in one of the underlined parts of the sentence. Assume that all other parts of the sentence are correct and cannot be changed. For each sentence, select the one underlined part that must be changed to make the sentence correct and mark its letter on your answer sheet. If there is no error in a sentence, mark answer space E. No sentence contains more than one error.

Being that it's such a lovely day, we
    A   B

are having a difficult time concentrating on
    C   D

our assignment. No error
              E

The correct answer is (A).

1. The second speaker was the most amusing
                         A

    of the two, though he had little
           B   C

    of substance to add. No error
     D   E

2. Anyone dissatisfied with the board's
          A

    decision should make their objections
          B   C

    known. No error
   D   E

3. All that he added as extra equipment
        A

    on the new car was two speakers, a
          B   C

    cassette deck, and a retractable antenna.
        D

    No error
  E

4. She <u>owned</u> a small glass pyramid
        A
<u>and a crystal</u>, and she <u>claimed</u> <u>that it</u>
   B   C   D
had a mysterious healing power. <u>No error</u>
                             E

5. In making rounds, <u>the chief resident</u> in
                      A
the hospital <u>was always</u>
           B
<u>accompanied with</u> an <u>intern</u>. <u>No error</u>
     C   D   E

6. If it is in a <u>person's</u> best interest, <u>then</u>
              A   B
<u>she should</u> apply for a stipend as <u>soon as</u>
   C   D
possible. <u>No error</u>
          E

7. When the mirror <u>cracked</u> yesterday,
                A
<u>they got</u> very nervous <u>about</u> the bad luck
  B   C
<u>they may be</u> in for. <u>No error</u>
    D   E

8. <u>He tripped</u> on the rock and <u>fell,</u> <u>broke</u>
     A   B   C
his ankle <u>in the process</u>. <u>No error</u>
         D   E

9. <u>By changing</u> the combination, the
      A
locksmith was able <u>to provide</u> us with
               B
<u>peace of mind</u>, convenience,
    C
<u>and feeling safe</u> when we came home.
     D
<u>No error</u>
  E

10. Having studied your report carefully,
        A
I am convinced that neither of your
     B   C
solutions are correct. No error
        D   E

11. The fabric, even though it is not
              A
expensive, feels soft to the touch.
    B   C   D
No error
E

12. The major affects of the battle
       A
were made known to the
      B
military personnel, but they were not
      C
revealed to the media. No error
        D   E

13. There was, contrary to what you believe,
      A   B   C
many complaints about
            D
the poor service. No error
          E

14. The chart does appear to be larger
          A   B
than any chart in the room, although this
    C
may well be only an optical illusion.
                D
No error
E

15. Even a random sampling of the questions
       A
reveal that there is an emphasis on correct
   B   C   D
punctuation. No error
      E

16. He spoke <u>softly</u> and appealed to the
    A

audience, <u>using</u> such expressions <u>like</u>
    B   C

"for the common <u>welfare" and "to</u>
                    D

help the oppressed and homeless."
<u>No error</u>
    E

17. The leaders of the <u>movement</u> believed
                        A

<u>that</u> persuasion was a more <u>effective</u>
    B   C

means than <u>to use</u> force. <u>No error</u>
            D   E

18. <u>Thanks</u> <u>in large part</u> to an excellent <u>score</u>
    A   B   C

and <u>imaginary</u> staging, the musical had a
        D

successful run. <u>No error</u>
                    E

19. The influence of radio <u>on</u> American life
                            A

<u>during</u> the Depression years <u>were</u>
    B   C

<u>profound</u>. <u>No error</u>
    D   E

I have always enjoyed <u>singing as well as to dance</u>.

(A) singing as well as to dance

(B) singing as well as dancing

(C) to sing as well as dancing

(D) singing in addition to dance

(E) to sing in addition to dancing

The correct answer is (B).

20. In order to achieve the highest rating in the diving competition, <u>it is necessary to enter the water</u> with a minimal splash.
    (A) it is necessary to enter the water
    (B) of necessity you must necessarily enter the water
    (C) the water must, as is necessary, be entered
    (D) it is entering the water with necessity
    (E) necessarily you must be entered in the water

21. The ancient Egyptians built structures that still stand after 2500 <u>years, their accomplishments are a marvel to behold.</u>
    (A) years, their accomplishments are a marvel to behold.
    (B) years, their accomplishing marvels that are to be beheld.
    (C) years; and they have accomplished marvelous beholdings.
    (D) years; their accomplishments are a marvel to behold.
    (E) years, beholding their accomplishments is a marvel.

22. The contract that was made between the students and the teacher stated that the students would hand in homework <u>on the day it was scheduled to be.</u>

(A) on the day it was scheduled to be.

(B) on the scheduled day.

(C) in accordance with the planned scheduling.

(D) on the scheduled day that it was
to be.

(E) with the schedule that was
handed out.

23. The turnout for the game was very low, but <u>those in attending</u> enjoyed every minute of the contest.

(A) those in attending

(B) those in attendance

(C) those who were in attending

(D) the attendance of those who were there

(E) the people being in attendance

24. People are concerned about the nearby nuclear plant because it employs new technology and <u>that real estate prices will decrease.</u>

(A) that real estate prices will decrease.

(B) that the price of real estate will decrease.

(C) that the decrease will be in real estate.

(D) the decrease in real estate will happen.

(E) decreases the price of real estate.

25. <u>Several notes were sent by the principal of the school that</u> were concerned with vandalism in the gymnasium.

(A) Several notes were sent by the principal of the school that

(B) Several notes written by the principal of the school that

(C) The principal of the school sent several notes that

(D) The principal of the school in sending notes that

(E) Several of the notes sent that

26. Since no one bothered to bring a copy of the directions, <u>so they had no idea</u> how to put the tent together.

(A) so they had no idea

(B) they were having no idea

(C) they had no ideas on

(D) they had no idea

(E) their ideas were none on

27. When I mentioned that I was trying to learn a foreign language, <u>the professor recommended that I read comic books written in that language</u>.

    (A) the professor recommended that I read comic books written in that language
    (B) the professor made a recommendation that I be reading comic books that were written in that language
    (C) the professor, who was recommended, said to read comic books
    (D) the professor was recommended because he wrote comic books in that language
    (E) the professor recommended to me the reading of comic books

28. The stock market fell more than sixty points in <u>one day, this is a sure sign that</u> the economic recovery is not materializing.

    (A) one day, this is a sure sign that
    (B) one day, this sign is sure that
    (C) one day; notwithstanding the surety of the sign
    (D) one day and this was a sure sign when
    (E) one day, and this is a sure sign that

29. A fundamental difference between the two parties is reflected in their attitudes toward affirmative <u>action, one certainly strongly</u> endorses the concept while the other condemns it.

    (A) action, one certainly strongly
    (B) action, the stronger one certainly
    (C) action; one strongly
    (D) action which one, however strongly,
    (E) action, and one certainly strongly

Directions: Questions 30–35 are based on a passage that might be an early draft of a student's essay. Some sentences in this draft need to be revised or rewritten to make them both clear and correct. Read the passage carefully; then answer the questions that follow it. Some questions require decisions about diction, usage, tone, or sentence structure in particular sentences or parts of sentences. Other questions require decisions about organization, development, or appropriateness of language in the essay as a whole. For each question, choose the answer that makes the intended meaning clearer and more precise and that follows the conventions of Standard Written English.

(1) Hopefully the government of the United States will soon make sure that all their citizens are able to have good, affordable health care. (2) If legislation is enacted and national coverage is assured, we will truly be ready to enter a new age in America. (3) It will be one in which all people—rich or poor, working or unemployed—will be provided for when they are ill.

(4) The significance of a national health care plan cannot be over-stated. (5) Recently, for instance, my aunt and uncle were involved in an automobile accident. (6) Although their injuries were pretty serious, yet after some emergency treatment they didn't get a lot of medical attention. (7) Due to the fact that they didn't have much coverage. (8) So doctors and hospital staff didn't want to treat them. (9) It's hard to believe that good, hardworking people like my relatives, now they are being neglected by society.

(10) And this is only one example of a situation in which people without adequate protection are mistreated by the medical profession, there are many other stories that could be told. (11) For this reason, that's why I sincerely hope that our government will soon provide for all those needy people, like my aunt and uncle, who presently lack adequate health care coverage.

30. Which of the following is the best revision of the underlined portion of sentence (1) below?

Hopefully the government of the United States will soon make sure that all their citizens are able to have good, affordable health care.

(A) Hopefully the government of the United States will soon provide all citizens with
(B) It is hoped that the government of the United States will soon make sure that all its citizens are able to have
(C) Hopefully the government of the United States will soon make sure that all citizens would be able to have
(D) I hope that the government of the United States will soon make sure that all its citizens will be able to have
(E) I hope that the government of the United States soon makes sure that all their citizens would be able to have

31. Which of the following is the best way to combine sentences (2) and (3)?

(A) If legislation is enacted and national coverage is assured, we will truly be ready to enter a new age in America, being one in which all people, rich or poor, will be provided for when they are ill.

(B) If legislation is enacted and national coverage is assured, we will truly be able to enter a new age, one in which all Americans—rich or poor, working or unemployed—will be provided for when they are ill.

(C) If legislation is enacted and national coverage is assured, we will truly be ready to enter a new age in America, it will be one in which all people, rich or poor, working or unemployed, will be provided for when they are ill.

(D) If legislation is enacted then all people, no matter what their abilities will be provided for by their government at all times.

(E) If we enact legislation and assure national coverage, we will be able to enter a new age in America; in which all—rich or poor, working or unemployed—will be provided for when they are ill.

32. Which of the following is the best way to revise sentences (6), (7), and (8)?

(A) Although their injuries were serious, after some emergency treatment, they received very little medical attention. Since they did not have much coverage, doctors and hospital staff did not want to treat them.

(B) Although their injuries were serious, yet after some emergency treatment, they didn't get a lot of medical attention. Due to the fact they didn't have much coverage, doctors and hospital staff didn't want to treat them.

(C) Their injuries were pretty serious although after some emergency treatment they didn't get a lot medical attention, due to the fact that they didn't have much coverage. So doctors and hospital staff didn't want to treat them.

(D) Their injuries were pretty serious, yet after some emergency treatment they did not get much medical attention. Due to the fact that they did not have much coverage, so doctor and hospitals did not want to treat them.

(E) Although their injuries were serious, after some emergency treatment, they didn't get a lot of attention because of the fact that they didn't have much coverage so doctors and hospital staff didn't want to treat them.

33. Which of the following is the best revision of the underlined portion of sentence (9) below?

It's hard to believe that good, hard-working people like my <u>relatives, now they are being neglected by society.</u>

(A) relatives. Now they are being neglected by society.

(B) relatives and being neglected by society now.

(C) relatives are now being neglected by society.

(D) relatives and now they are being neglected by society.

(E) relatives have neglected society.

34. Which of the following is the reason sentence (10) should be revised?

(A) To provide another example

(B) To correct an error in usage

(C) To correct a sentence structure error

(D) To correct an error in verb agreement

(E) To correct a pronoun reference error

35. Which of the following is the best revision of the underlined portion of sentence (11) below?

<u>For this reason, that's why</u> I sincerely hope that our government will soon provide for all those needy people, like my aunt and uncle, who presently lack adequate health care coverage.

(A) Because this is why

(B) For this reason it is why

(C) Because of this reason is why

(D) This reason is why

(E) This is why

STOP

END OF SECTION 5. IF YOU HAVE ANY TIME LEFT, GO OVER YOUR WORK IN THIS SECTION ONLY. DO NOT WORK IN ANY OTHER SECTION OF THE TEST.

Section 5

15 Questions • 10 Minutes

Directions: The sentences below may contain problems in grammar, usage, word choice, sentence construction, or punctuation. Part or all of each sentence is underlined. Following each sentence you will find five ways of expressing the underlined part. Answer choice (A) always repeats the original underlined section. The other four answer choices are all different. You are to select the lettered answer that produces the most effective sentence. If you think the original sentence is best, choose (A) as your answer. If one of the other choices makes a better sentence, mark your answer sheet for the letter of that choice. Do not choose an answer that changes the meaning of the original sentence.

I have always enjoyed <u>singing as well as to dance</u>.

(A) singing as well as to dance

(B) singing as well as dancing

(C) to sing as well as dancing

(D) singing in addition to dance

(E) to sing in addition to dancing

The correct answer is (B).

1. <u>Recognizing the expense of the repairs,</u> the plumbing mishap created a great deal of consternation.
   - **(A)** Recognizing the expense of the repairs,
   - **(B)** Recognizing the expensive repairs,
   - **(C)** Recognizing that the repairs are expensive
   - **(D)** Due to the repairs are going to be expensive
   - **(E)** Recognizing the expense of the repairs, he noted that

2. <u>Seatbelts, while unquestionably a good idea, it's sometimes a nuisance to use them.</u>
   - **(A)** Seatbelts, while unquestionably a good idea, it's sometimes a nuisance to use them.
   - **(B)** Seatbelts, while unquestionably a good idea, are sometimes a nuisance.
   - **(C)** Seatbelts are unquestionably a good idea and also they are sometimes a nuisance.

(D) Seatbelts, while unquestionably a good idea, but sometimes a nuisance to use.

   (E) Seatbelts, while it's unquestionably a good idea to have them, it's sometimes a nuisance to use them.

3. Your application for a scholarship <u>arriving late, however: it will still be considered by the committee</u>.

   (A) arriving late, however; it will still be considered by the committee

   (B) arrived late, however the committee will consider it still

   (C) arrived late; however, the committee will still consider it

   (D) will be considered by the committee that arrived late

   (E) arriving late and is being considered by the committee

4. When I travel, <u>I most always enjoy seeing sights that differ from the typical tourist traps</u>.

   (A) I most always enjoy seeing sights that differ from the typical tourist traps

   (B) I almost always enjoy to see sights other than the typical tourist traps

   (C) I most always enjoy seeing sights that are different than the typical tourist traps

   (D) I almost always enjoy seeing sights that are different than the typical tourist traps

   (E) I almost always enjoy seeing sights that are different from the typical tourist traps

5. Unless treated and rewarmed, <u>hypothermia causes death</u>.

   (A) hypothermia causes death

   (B) death results from hypothermia

   (C) hypothermia kills

   (D) the victim of hypothermia will die

   (E) hypothermia will cause death

6. First choose a recipe; then <u>you should make a list of the ingredients needed</u>.

   (A) you should make a list of the ingredients needed

   (B) a list can be made of the ingredients needed

   (C) you can make a list of the ingredients needed

   (D) you should list the ingredients needed

   (E) make a list of the ingredients needed

7. Living in the city for the first time, the <u>traffic noise, she found, disrupted her sleep</u>.

    (A) the traffic noise, she found, disrupted her sleep

    (B) she found that the traffic noise disrupted her sleep

    (C) she found out how the traffic noise disrupted her sleep

    (D) her sleep, she found, was disrupted by the traffic noise

    (E) her sleep disrupted, she found, by traffic noise

8. Elgin called to find out <u>will you lend him your bicycle.</u>

    (A) will you lend him your bicycle.

    (B) will you lend him your bicycle?

    (C) did you lend him your bicycle.

    (D) will your bicycle be lent to him?

    (E) whether you will lend him your bicycle.

9. Few freshmen these days <u>are as ingenuous as him that first year</u>.

    (A) are as ingenuous as him that first year

    (B) were as ingenuous as him that first year

    (C) is as ingenuous as him that first year

    (D) are as ingenuous as he that first year

    (E) were as ingenuous as he that first year

10. Congress is expected to enact legislation soon that <u>will attempt to slow the rising trade deficit</u> that the U.S. is experiencing.

    (A) will attempt to slow the rising trade deficit

    (B) would attempt to slow the rising trade deficit

    (C) will slow the rising trade deficit

    (D) will attempt to slow the raising trade deficit

    (E) would attempt to slow the raising trade deficit

11. Listening to another student's question, I frequently discover <u>that they are confused about the same points that I am</u>.

    (A) that they are confused about the same points that I am

    (B) that they are as confused about the same points as I am

    (C) they are confused about the same points that I am

    (D) that I am not the only one confused about the same points

    (E) that he or she is confused about the same points that I am

12. <u>Noticing how close the other car was to him,</u> his hands began to shake and he broke out in a sweat.

    (A) Noticing how close the other car was to him,

    (B) Noticing how closely the other car was following him,

(C) When he noticed how close the other car was to him,

(D) After noticing how close the other car was to him,

(E) He noticed how close the other car was near to him,

13. The conditions of the contract <u>by which the strike has been settled has not yet been made public</u>.

   (A) by which the strike has been settled has not yet been made public

   (B) by which the strike has been settled have not yet been made public

   (C) by which the strike had been settled has not yet been made public

   (D) under which the strike has been settled has not yet been made public

   (E) that settled the strike has not yet been made public

14. Myths are often marked by <u>anthropomorphism, the concept where animals and inanimate forces are invested</u> with human characteristics.

   (A) anthropomorphism, the concept where animals and inanimate forces are invested

   (B) anthropomorphism— the concept—where animals and inanimate forces are invested

   (C) anthropomorphism, the concept, where animals and inanimate forces are invested

   (D) anthropomorphism, the concept by which animals and inanimate forces are invested

   (E) anthropomorphism, the concept that invests animals and inanimate forces

15. It is not <u>I to whom you should complain</u>.

   (A) I to whom you should complain

   (B) I, to whom you should complain

   (C) I who you should complain to

   (D) me whom you should complain to

   (E) me to whom you should complain

STOP

END OF SECTION 5. IF YOU HAVE ANY TIME LEFT, GO OVER YOUR WORK IN THIS SECTION ONLY. DO NOT WORK IN ANY OTHER SECTION OF THE TEST.

ANSWERS AND EXPLANATIONS

Section 1

Sample Essay 1

If you want something, you've got to ask for it, the old saying goes. It's not enough to wait quietly for someone to read your mind and satisfy your desires. Rather it is necessary to speak out and take action, to be the "squeaky hinge" that will get "the grease."

This concept is proven by the actions of a number of groups in our country. For instance, if the civil rights activists of the 1950s and 1960s had not made plenty of noise and demanded satisfaction of their legal rights, who knows how much progress would have been made in the area of human rights by now. Similarly, organizations that feed the homeless or that take care of the poor also must make enough political noise so that they will have access to government funds to continue their good work.

However, making too much noise can have a reverse effect. If the public's perception is that a person or group is complaining too much, or asking for too much, then that group may be acting in a counterproductive manner. So it is important to strike the proper balance.

With all the budgetary cuts on local, state, and federal levels, it is crucial for public interest groups to "squeak" for the "grease." Without attention from media and without money from private individuals or government sources, it is extremely difficult for organizations or agencies to exist and succeed.

Analysis of Essay 1

This is an excellent essay. It focuses clearly upon the topic and does not stray. The organization into four well-defined paragraphs is well handled. Both the first and last paragraphs cleverly make reference to words in the quotation (*squeaky hinge, squeak, grease*) so that the reader is always aware of the citation that is at the heart of the essay.

The punctuation is accurate. The vocabulary is mature. The content is well developed. The writer makes use of appropriate transitional phrases and words (*For instance, however*). The essay takes into account both the positive and negative aspects of the issue and then comes to a strong and valid conclusion. This is a well-written paper.

Sample Essay 2

It just doesn't pay to suffer in silence any more. If you keep still, no one will know you're around or if they do they will not care. If you have a complaint you have to yell or make noise. Then people will hear you and take action.

For example, I remember that my father once told me that he worked in a factory under very poor conditions and everyone felt that their had to be improvement so they went to the boss and gave him a list of there demands. They waited many weeks maybe even months and there was no results. Finally all the men got together and had a sit-in at the plant and they made a lot of noise and then the boss arrange for a meeting and even improved the problems.

Many of us were brought up and told to be polite and not to make trouble. We were told to listen to our parents and obey our teachers. But now we know that there are times when the people in authority can be wrong. Police make mistakes. Innocent people are sent to jail. And parents aren't always right either.

I think that the conclusion we have to come to is that if we want to get any action and make changes in the world or in our living conditions then we have to make a fuss and raise our voices. We see from our study of history and current events that it was only when people went out and took action that they were able to change their society and improve their living conditions because then people had to listen and hear what was said and they were force to take action and make changes.

Analysis of Essay 2

Although the essay shows a sense of organization (there are four paragraphs with a clear introduction and conclusion), there appears to be a lack of specific examples to substantiate arguments. Thus, in the final paragraph, the conclusion reached is that "it was only when people went out and took action that they were able to change their society . . . ." This statement is not followed by a specific example or even a historical allusion. Certainly the illustration of the factory workers in the second paragraph is valid and indicates that the writer is aware of the need for specifics.

There is a problem in tone. The second person "you" is used in the first paragraph and then abandoned. It would be preferable to use a third-person construction throughout the essay. Errors in technical English also detract. Omission of the final "d" in the past tense of verbs (*arrange, force*), errors of agreement (*everyone . . . they*), and spelling errors (*their* for *there*) also hurt the writing.

Section 2

1. C	7. D	12. C	17. C
2. E	8. B	13. B	18. D
3. A	9. B	14. B	19. B
4. D	10. D	15. D	20. C
5. B	11. C	16. E	21. D
6. B			

1. **The correct answer is (C).** Audience laughter at the wrong moment can easily *disconcert* (upset or confuse) an actor.

2. **The correct answer is (E).** Since the assurances of good faith were "hollow," it is not surprising that those who made them *reneged* on (went back on) their agreement.

3. **The correct answer is (A).** To win the majority, we must unite, or *amalgamate,* the different factions.

4. **The correct answer is (D).** A law known as the Prohibition Act would naturally be expected to *proscribe* (outlaw) something.

5. **The correct answer is (B).** A caller who will not give his name is by definition *anonymous*. Since he is giving information to the police, he may well fear *reprisals* (retaliation) by a criminal.

6. **The correct answer is (B).** An *intractable*, or stubborn, individual is likely to have trouble adapting to a new way of life. Choice (A), *nonchalant*, means unconcerned. Choice (C), *rabid*, means furious. Choice (D), *insolent*, means rude. And choice (E), *doughty*, means valiant.

7. **The correct answer is (D).** The key word *though* indicates that the word in the blank should be opposite in meaning from *shared*. The only choice that satisfies this condition is *disparate* (very different; having nothing in common).

8. **The correct answer is (B).** If you understand that *gastronomic* is an adjective having to do with eating, the only possible choice is (B). A *gourmet* (person who appreciates good food) is a *connoisseur*, or expert, in food.

9. **The correct answer is (B).** The phrase "her arm was broken" points to a negative word choice for this sentence. The only negative word is *plaintively*, which means *sadly*. All other choices are positive.

10. **The correct answer is (D).** Although the other answer choices are pieces of information stated or implied in the passage, the overriding purpose is to discuss the connection between Manet and the Impressionists.

11. **The correct answer is (C).** There is no reason to believe that the author means either choices (A) or (D), and the passage disproves choice (E). Choice (B) is too literal a reading of the word *far*.

12. **The correct answer is (C).** The prefix *un-* is a hint that the word means not or a lack of. Choice (A) is a distracter. A synonym for unostentatious is unpretentious, which is not the same as "not pretending."

13. **The correct answer is (B).** Choice (A) is the opposite of Carnegie's belief. Men are wealthy because they are wise, or wealth comes to the wise. Choice (E) may have confused you. This is not implied in the passage, but stated.

14. **The correct answer is (B).** While choices (A), (C), and (D) are all synonyms for *ravaged*, the context of the sentence supports the choice of *devastated*.

15. **The correct answer is (D).** Nowhere in the passage is the quality of the soil mentioned as a reason for the dependence on the potato as a staple.

16. **The correct answer is (E).** While not directly stated in the passage, the author certainly implies that the dependence on one crop was dangerous.

17. **The correct answer is (C).** The passage certainly describes Irish life as characterized by poverty and oppression from landlords, so *harsh* is the correct answer.

18. **The correct answer is (D).** The passage states that farmers were compelled to subdivide in order to make rent payments to their landlords.

19. **The correct answer is (B).** The best answer according to the context of the sentence is *disease*, particularly since in the sentence the word applies to the crop.

20. **The correct answer is (C).** While some of the other responses may be true, they are not stated in the passage.

21. **The correct answer is (D).** The Irish did not gain their independence during this period; no reference to Irish independence is made in the passage.

Section 3

1. B	5. B	9. D	13. 18	17. 60
2. D	6. E	10. C	14. 3	18. 8
3. B	7. A	11. 8.89	15. 360	19. 18
4. D	8. E	12. 95	16. 8	20. 6

Note: A ▣ following a math answer explanation indicates that a calculator could be helpful in solving that particular problem.

1. **The correct answer is (B).** Set up a proportion comparing apples to dollars.

$$\frac{\text{apples}}{\text{dollars}} \to \frac{24}{3} = \frac{18}{x}$$

$$8 = \frac{18}{x}$$

$$8x = 18$$

$$x = \frac{18}{8} = 2.25$$

2. **The correct answer is (D).** Rewrite $\frac{1}{10}$ as 0.1. Note that $\frac{1}{10}\% = 0.1\% = 0.001$. Therefore, $\frac{1}{10}\%$ of $\frac{1}{10}$ of $10 = 0.001 \times 0.1 \times 10 = 0.001$.

3. **The correct answer is (B).** Set $T = \{16, 25, 36, 49, 64, 81\}$ and set $S = \{27, 64\}$. The only element that these sets have in common is 64. Thus, $S \cap T = \{64\}$.

4. **The correct answer is (D).** Using the formula $a_n = a_1 \times r^{n-1}$, with $a_1 = 3, r = 2,$ and $n = 5$, determine that $a_5 = 3 \times 2^{5-1} = 3 \times 2^4 = 3 \times 16 = 48$.

5. **The correct answer is (B).** The average (arithmetic mean) of five consecutive integers is the number in the middle; therefore, the average is x. To find the median of five integers, arrange them in numerical order. The median will also be the number in the middle, x. Finally, note that x divided by x is equal to 1.

6. **The correct answer is (E).** One cubic foot equals 12^3 cubic inches, or 1728. Thus, one cubic foot of the metal would weigh 3456 pounds. ▣

7. **The correct answer is (A).** The area of the circle is πr^2 and the circumference is $2\pi r$. If the area equals the circumference, solve the equation $\pi r^2 = 2\pi r$, or $r = 2$. The diameter is $2r$, or 4 inches.

8. **The correct answer is (E).** Let's substitute J for John and P for Pat.

$(J$ is 3 times $P)$ $J = 3P$

$(J$ in four years$)$ $x = J + 4$

(substitute $3P$ for J) $x = 3P + 4$

$$x - 4 = 3P$$

$$\frac{x-4}{3} = P$$

You can also reason this way: If John will be x years old in 4 years, then he is $x - 4$ years old now. Since Pat's age is now one third of John's, Pat is now $\dfrac{x-4}{3}$ years old.

9. **The correct answer is (D).** Renaming the fractions as decimals, $\dfrac{2}{3} = 0.666\ldots$, $\dfrac{5}{7} = 0.7142\ldots$, $\dfrac{8}{11} = .7272\ldots$, and $\dfrac{9}{13} = 0.6923$. So the order is $\dfrac{2}{3}, \dfrac{9}{13}, \dfrac{5}{7}, \dfrac{8}{11}$.

10. **The correct answer is (C).** If the average for the eight tests is 84%, then the sum of the eight tests must be 8 times 84, or 672. For the six tests, the sum must be 6 times 86, or 516. The two dropped tests must have accounted for 156 points. 156 divided by 2 is 78.

11. **The correct answer is 8.89.**

$$\frac{\frac{-1}{3}}{3} - \frac{3}{\frac{-1}{3}} = \frac{-\frac{1}{3}}{3} - \frac{\frac{3}{1}}{-\frac{1}{3}}$$

$$= -\frac{1}{3}\left(\frac{1}{3}\right) - \frac{3}{1}\left(-\frac{3}{1}\right)$$

$$= -\frac{1}{9} + 9$$

$$= 8\frac{8}{9} = \frac{80}{9} = 8.89$$

12. **The correct answer is 95.** The sum of Dawn's scores for the first four tests is $80(4) = 320$.

$$\frac{320 + x}{5} = 83$$

$$320 + x = 415$$

$$x = 95$$

13. **The correct answer is 18.**

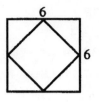

Area of a square = (side)² or $\dfrac{(\text{diagonal})^2}{2}$

Area of $ABCD$ = (side)² = 6² = 36

Area of $WXYZ = \dfrac{(\text{diagonal})^2}{2} = \dfrac{6^2}{2}$

Shaded area = 36 − 18 = 18

14. **The correct answer is 3.**

1 week = 7 days

1 day = 24 hours

1 hour = 60 minutes

$\dfrac{30,240}{7(24)(60)} = 3$

15. **The correct answer is 360.** The sum of the interior angles of a quadrilateral is 360°.

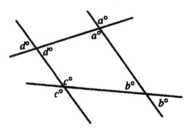

∴ $a + b + c + d = 360$.

16. **The correct answer is 8.**

Distance = rate × time

$360 = r(9)$

$40 = r$

If r were $40 + 5 = 45$

$d = rt$

$360 = 45t$

$t = 8$

17. The correct answer is 60.

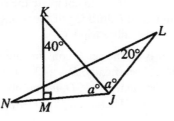

$$40 + 90 + a = 180$$
$$a = 50$$
$$\angle J = 2(50) = 100°$$
$$\angle N + \angle J + \angle L = 180°$$
$$\angle N + 100° + 20° = 180°$$
$$\angle N = 60°$$

18. The correct answer is 8.

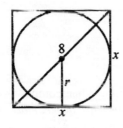

$$x^2 + x^2 = 8^2$$
$$2x^2 = 64$$
$$x = 4\sqrt{2}$$

The side of the square = $4\sqrt{2}$.

The radius of the circle = $\dfrac{1}{2}\left(4\sqrt{2}\right) = 2\sqrt{2}$.

$$A = \pi r^2$$
$$= \pi\left(2\sqrt{2}\right)^2 = 8\pi = a\pi \therefore a = 8$$

19. **The correct answer is 18.** There are 2 ways to complete the first leg of the trip. After this, there are 3 ways to complete the second leg of the trip, and then 3 ways to complete the third leg of the trip. Overall, there are $2 \times 3 \times 3 = 18$ ways to make the entire trip.

20. **The correct answer is 6.** The set D contains the numbers between 11 and 29 that are not prime. Specifically, $D = \{12, 14, 15, 16, 18, 20, 21, 22, 24, 25, 26, 27, 28\}$. Of the members of D, the numbers 12, 15, 18, 21, 24, and 27 are also multiples of 3. Therefore, $D \cap E = \{12, 15, 18, 21, 24, 27\}$.

Section 4

1. A	8. C	15. B	22. B	29. C
2. C	9. D	16. C	23. B	30. D
3. B	10. D	17. D	24. E	31. B
4. D	11. E	18. D	25. C	32. A
5. C	12. A	19. C	26. D	33. C
6. E	13. A	20. A	27. A	34. C
7. D	14. C	21. D	28. E	35. E

1. **The correct answer is (A).** When comparing only two persons or things, use the comparative forms *more* or *-er: more amusing or funnier.*

2. **The correct answer is (C).** A singular pronoun (*his* or *her*) is required to agree with the antecedent *Anyone.*

3. **The correct answer is (B).** The plural verb *were* is required to agree with the compound subject that follows.

4. **The correct answer is (D).** The plural pronoun *they* is required to agree with the plural antecedent, *a small glass pyramid and a crystal.*

5. **The correct answer is (C).** The correct idiomatic phrase is *accompanied by.*

6. **The correct answer is (E).** The sentence is correct.

7. **The correct answer is (D).** For correct sequence of tenses, the verb form *might* is required to follow *cracked* and *got.*

8. **The correct answer is (C).** The participle *breaking* is required to introduce the dependent clause.

9. **The correct answer is (D).** For parallel structure, the noun phrase *a feeling of safety* is required.

10. **The correct answer is (D).** The verb should be changed to *is* to agree with the singular subject *neither.*

11. **The correct answer is (E).** The sentence is correct.

12. **The correct answer is (A).** The correct word is *effects,* meaning *results.*

13. **The correct answer is (A).** The plural verb form *were* is required to agree with the plural subject, *complaints.*

14. **The correct answer is (C).** In this comparison, the correct phrase is "than any *other* chart."

15. **The correct answer is (B).** The singular subject, *sampling,* requires the third-person singular verb form, *reveals.*

16. **The correct answer is (C).** The correct idiomatic phrase is "such . . . *as.*"

17. **The correct answer is (D).** Use parallel forms for comparisons: *persuasion* was a more effective means than *force.*

18. **The correct answer is (D).** *Imaginary* means "existing in the imagination." The word needed here is *imaginative,* meaning "creative or original."

19. **The correct answer is (C).** The singular verb *was* is required to agree with the singular subject *influence.*

20. **The correct answer is (A).** The sentence is correct.

21. **The correct answer is (D).** The sentence contains two independent clauses. If there is not a connective, then the first clause must be followed by a semicolon.

22. **The correct answer is (B).** Choice (B) is more economical and does not end with the dangling infinitive *to be.*

23. **The correct answer is (B).** Although *in attending* might be acceptable in a different context, here the correct word is *attendance.*

24. **The correct answer is (E).** In order to keep the structure parallel, it is necessary to have a present-tense verb with an object.

25. **The correct answer is (C).** In the original sentence, it is difficult to be certain whether the school or the notes are concerned with vandalism.

26. **The correct answer is (D).** The word *so* has no function in the sentence.

27. **The correct answer is (A).** The sentence is correct.

28. **The correct answer is (E).** The original sentence would be acceptable if the comma were replaced by a semicolon. It is also acceptable to connect the clauses with *and.*

29. **The correct answer is (C).** The word *certainly* is unnecessary, and the clauses should be joined by a semicolon.

30. **The correct answer is (D).** To start the sentence with the adverb *hopefully* is poor since *hopefully* does not modify *government.* Therefore, choices

(A) and (C) are weak. Choice (B) is vague, and choice (E) has a problem of reference (*their* should be *its*). Choice (D) is best because the entire essay is written from the first-person point of view, and the pronoun is correct.

31. **The correct answer is (B).** Choice (A) is weak since the phrase *being one* is poor. Choice (C) contains a comma splice error following *America.* Choice (D) does not convey the sense of the original sentence. Choice (E) is poor since the semicolon following *America* is incorrect punctuation.

32. **The correct answer is (A).** The only choice that is clear and grammatically sound, with proper punctuation and good word choice, is choice (A).

33. **The correct answer is (C).** Choice (A) makes a fragment of the first part of the sentence, and choice (B) makes a fragment of the entire sentence. Choice (D), like the original sentence, includes the extra pronoun *they.* Choice (E) changes the meaning.

34. **The correct answer is (C).** The error in sentence (10) is a comma splice error. A comma cannot separate two main clauses. A period or a semicolon should be used after *profession.* This type of error is an error in sentence structure.

35. **The correct answer is (E).** The underlined portion is redundant, as are choices (A), (B), (C), and (D).

Section 5

1. E	5. D	9. D	13. B
2. B	6. E	10. A	14. D
3. C	7. B	11. E	15. A
4. E	8. E	12. C	

1. **The correct answer is (E).** As the sentence stands, there is a dangling participle (*recognizing*) so that the meaning conveyed is that the plumbing mishap recognized the expense of the repairs. A subject must be added in the main clause.

2. **The correct answer is (B).** The original includes the superfluous pronoun *it* and leaves *seatbelts* without a verb. Choices (D) and (E) do nothing to correct these problems. Choice (C) provides the verb needed to make a complete sentence, but it is awkward and wordy. Choice (B) is both correct and concise.

3. **The correct answer is (C).** When used as a conjunctive adverb, *however* is preceded by a semicolon and followed by a comma. In addition, a semicolon

is used to join closely related independent clauses. Choice (B) is a comma splice, choice (E) is a fragment, and choice (D) changes the meaning of the original sentence.

4. **The correct answer is (E).** The correct expressions are *almost always* (not *most always*) and *different from* (not *different than*).

5. **The correct answer is (D).** The *victim* is the one who must be treated and rewarmed. Only choice (D) correctly places the subject next to the phrase that modifies it.

6. **The correct answer is (E).** The original sentence shifts needlessly from the imperative (*choose*) to the indicative mood (*you should make*). Choices (C) and (D) do the same. Choice (B) shifts subjects (from *you* to a *list*). Choice (E) is consistent in both subject and mood.

7. **The correct answer is (B).** The original sentence says, in effect, that the *traffic noise* is living in the city. Choice (B) provides the correct subject for the introductory phrase and the rest of the sentence. Choice (C) uses *how* when logic calls for *that*. Choice (D) says that *her sleep* is living in the city. Choice (E) creates a series of introductory phrases with no main clause.

8. **The correct answer is (E).** There is a word missing in choice (A). The second clause (*will you . . . bicycle*), which is the object of *find out*, lacks a conjunction to link it to the main clause (*Elgin . . . out*). Only choice (E) provides this link in an indirect question.

9. **The correct answer is (D).** The verb is understood, so the phrase should read "as ingenuous as he (was) that first year."

10. **The correct answer is (A).** The sentence is correct.

11. **The correct answer is (E).** It is one student's question, so *he is* or *she is confused*, not *they are*.

12. **The correct answer is (C).** The sentence should be rephrased so that it does not seem as if *his hands* were *noticing*. Although choice (E) corrects the misplaced modifier, it creates a run-on sentence.

13. **The correct answer is (B).** The subject of the main clause is "conditions," a plural noun requiring a plural verb, "have been made." The subject of the subordinate clause is "strike," which requires a singular verb, "has been settled."

14. **The correct answer is (D).** A concept is not a place to be referred to as *where*. A concept is an idea, which is referred to by using such expressions as "according to which" or "by which."

15. **The correct answer is (A).** The sentence is correct.

WELCOME STUDENTS

WELCOME STUDE

WELCOME STUDENTS

Getting Into College

EXPLORING POSSIBLE CAREER PATHS IN HIGH SCHOOL

The word "career" has a scary sound to it when you're still in high school. Careers are for college graduates or those who have been in the workplace for years. But unless you grew up knowing for sure that you wanted to fly airplanes or be a botanist, what will you do? You'll be happy to know that interests you have now can very possibly lead to a college major or career. A job at a clothing store, for instance, could lead to a career designing clothes. Perhaps those hours you spend on your Xbox® video game system will lead to a career creating video games! Maybe you babysit and love being around kids, so teaching becomes an obvious choice. Perhaps cars fascinate you, and you find out you want to fix them for a living.

This chapter will show you how you can begin exploring your interests—sort of like getting into a swimming pool starting with your big toe, rather than plunging in. Vocational/career and tech-prep programs, summer jobs, and volunteering are all ways you can test various career paths to decide if you like them.

The Vocational/Career Education Path

If you're looking for a more real-world education, add yourself to the nearly 11 million youths and adults who are getting a taste of the workplace through vocational and career education programs offered in high schools across the nation. These programs are designed to help you develop competency in the skills you'll need in the workplace as well as in school.

What makes this kind of program different is that you learn in the classroom and in the "real world" of the workplace. Not only do you learn the academics in school, but you also get hands-on training by job shadowing, working under a mentor, and actually performing a job outside of school. Your interests and talents are usually taken into consideration, and you can choose from a variety of traditional, high-tech, and service industry training programs. Take a look at the following categories and see what piques your interest.

Agricultural education. These programs prepare students for careers in agricultural production, animal production and care, agribusiness, agricultural and industrial mechanics, environmental management, farming, horticulture and landscaping, food processing, and natural resource management.

Business education. Students prepare for careers in accounting and finance and computer and data processing as well as administrative/secretarial and management/supervisory positions in professional environments (banking, insurance, law, public service).

Family and consumer sciences. These programs prepare students for careers in child care, food management and production, clothing and interiors, and hospitality and facility care. Core elements include personal development, family life and planning, resource management, and nutrition and wellness.

Trade and industrial and health occupations. Students prepare for careers in auto mechanics, the construction trades, cosmetology, electronics, graphics, public safety, and welding. Health occupation programs offer vocational training for careers in dental and medical assisting, practical nursing, home health care, and medical office assisting.

Marketing education. These programs prepare students for careers in sales, retail, advertising, food and restaurant marketing, and hotel management.

Many vocational/career education programs are available; the kinds just listed represent only a few of the possibilities. To get more information about vocational education programs, call 202-245-7700, e-mail ovae@ed.gov, or visit the U.S. Department of Education, Office of Vocational and Adult Education Web site, www.ed.gov/about/offices/list/ovae/index.html.

The Tech-Prep Path

An even more advanced preparation for the workplace and/or an associate degree from a college is called tech-prep. It's an educational path that combines college-prep and vocational/technical courses of study.

During the sequence of courses, the focus is on blending academic and vocational/technical competencies. When you graduate from high school, you'll be able to jump right into the workforce or get an associate degree. But if you want to follow this path, you've got to plan for it starting in the ninth grade. Ask your guidance counselor for more information.

Using the Summer to Your Advantage

When you're sitting in class, a summer with nothing to do might seem appealing. But after you've downloaded and listened to all of your favorite new songs, aced all of your video games, hung out at the same old mall, and talked to your friends on the phone about being bored, what's left? How about windsurfing on a cool, clear New England lake? Horseback riding along breathtaking mountain trails? Parlez français in Paris? Trekking through spectacular canyon lands or living with a family in Costa Rica, Spain, Switzerland, or Japan? Exploring college majors or possible careers? Helping out on an archeological dig or community-service project? Along the way, you'll meet some wonderful people and maybe even make a couple of lifelong friends.

Interested? Get ready to pack your bags and join the 1 million kids and teens who will be having the summer of a lifetime at thousands of terrific camps, academic programs, sports clinics, arts workshops, internships, volunteer opportunities, and travel adventures throughout North America and abroad.

Oh, you don't have the money, you say? Not to worry. There are programs to meet every budget, from $50 workshops to $5000 world treks and sessions that vary in length from just a couple of hours to a couple of months.

Flip Burgers and Learn about Life

Many teenagers who are anxious to earn extra cash spend their summers in retail or food service since those jobs are plentiful. If you're flipping burgers or helping customers find a special outfit, you might think the only thing you're getting out of the job is a paycheck. Think again. You will be amazed to discover that you have gained far more.

Being employed in these fields will teach you how to get along with demanding (and sometimes downright unpleasant) customers, how to work on a team, and how to handle money and order supplies. Not only do summer jobs teach you life skills, they also offer ways to explore potential careers. What's more, when you apply to college or for a full-time job after high school graduation, the experience will look good on your application.

Sometimes, summer jobs become the very thing you want to do later in life. Before committing to a college major, summer jobs may give you the opportunity to try out many directions. Students who think they want to be engineers, lawyers, or doctors might spend the summer shadowing an engineer, being a gofer in a legal firm, or volunteering in a hospital.

Rather than grab the first job that comes along, find out where your interests are and build on what is natural for you. Activities you take for granted provide clues about your abilities. What about that bookcase you built? Or those kids you love to babysit? Same thing with that big party you arranged. The environments you prefer provide other hints, too. Perhaps you feel best in the middle of a cluttered garage instead of surrounded by people. That suggests certain types of jobs.

Getting a summer job while in high school is the first step in a long line of work experiences to come. And the more experience you have, the better you'll be at getting jobs all your life.

Try Your Hand at an Internship

Each year, thousands of interns work in a wide variety of places, including corporations, law firms, government agencies, media orga- nizations, interest groups, clinics, labs, museums, and historical sites.

How popular are internships? Consider the recent trends. In the early 1980s, only 1 in 36 students completed an internship or other experiential learning program. Compare this to a more recent study that found that 62 percent of college students had planned for a summer internship. And an increasing number of high school students are signing up for internships now, too.

THE EMPLOYER'S PERSPECTIVE

Employers consider internships a good option in both healthy and ailing economies. In healthy economies, managers often struggle to fill their positions with eager workers who can adapt to changing technologies. Internships offer a low-cost way to get good workers "into the pipeline" without offering them a full-time position up front. In struggling economies, on the other hand, downsizing often requires employers to lay off workers without thinking about who will cover their responsibilities. Internships offer an inexpensive way to offset position losses resulting from disruptive layoffs.

THE INTERN'S PERSPECTIVE

If you are looking to begin a career or supplement your education with practical training, internships are a good bet for several reasons.

1. **Internships offer a relatively quick way to gain work experience and develop job skills.** Try this exercise. Scan the Sunday want ads of your newspaper. Choose a range of interesting advertisements for professional positions that you would consider taking. List the desired or required job skills and work experiences specified in the ads. How many of these skills and experiences do you have? Chances are, if you are still in school, you don't have most of the skills and experience that employers require of their new hires. What do you do?

   The growing reality is that many entry-level positions require skills and experiences that schools and part-time jobs don't provide. Sure, you know your way around a computer. You have some customer service experience. You may even have edited your school's newspaper or organized your junior prom. But you still lack the relevant skills and on-the-job experiences that many hiring managers require. A well-chosen internship can offer a way out of this common dilemma by providing you job training in an actual career field. Internships help you take your existing knowledge and skills and apply them in ways that will help you compete for good jobs.

2. **Internships offer a relatively risk-free way to explore a possible career path.** Believe it or not, the best internship may tell you what you *don't* want to do for the next ten or twenty years. Think about it. If you put all your eggs in one basket, what happens if your dream job turns out to be the exact opposite of what you want or who you are? Internships offer a relatively low-cost opportunity to "try out" a career field to see if it's right for *you*.

3. **Internships offer real opportunities to do career networking and can significantly increase your chances of landing a good full-time position.** Have you heard the saying: "It's not what you know, but who you know"? The reality is that who you know (or who knows you) can make a big difference in your job search. Studies show that fewer than 20 percent of job placements occur through traditional application methods, including newspaper and trade journal advertisements, employment agencies, and career fairs. Instead, 60 to 90 percent of jobs are found through personal contacts and direct application.

4. **Career networking is the exchange of information with others for mutual benefit.** Your career network can tell you where the jobs are and help you compete for them. Isn't it better to develop your networking skills now, when the stakes aren't as high, than later when you are competing with everyone else for full-time jobs? The internship hiring process and the weeks you actually spend on the job provide excellent opportunities to talk with various people about careers, your skills, and ways to succeed.

Volunteering in Your Community

You've probably heard the saying that money isn't everything. Well, it's true, especially when it comes to volunteering and community service. There are a number of benefits you'll get that don't add up in dollars and cents but do add up to open doors in your future.

Community service looks good on a college application.
Admissions staff members look for applicants who have volunteered
and done community service in addition to earning good grades.
You could have gotten top grades, but if that's all that's on your application, you won't come across as a well-rounded person.

Community service lets you try out careers. How will you know
you'll like a certain type of work if you haven't experienced it? For
instance, you might think you want to work in the health-care field.
Volunteering in a hospital will let you know if this is really what you
want to do.

Community service is an American tradition. You'll be able to meet
some of your own community's needs and join with all of the people
who have contributed their talents to our country. No matter what your
talents, there are unlimited ways for you to serve your community. Take
a look at your interests, and then see how they can be applied to help
others.

Here are some ideas to get you started:

- ❑ **Do you like kids?** Volunteer at your local parks and recreation
  department, for a Little League team, or as a Big Brother or
  Sister.

- ❑ **Planning a career in health care?** Volunteer at a blood bank,
  clinic, hospital, retirement home, or hospice. There are also
  several organizations that raise money for disease research.

- ❑ **Interested in the environment?** Volunteer to assist in a recy-
  cling program. Create a beautification program for your school
  or community. Plant trees and flowers or design a community
  garden.

- ❑ **Just say no.** Help others stay off drugs and alcohol by volunteering at a crisis center, hotline, or prevention program. Help
  educate younger kids about the dangers of drug abuse.

- ❑ **Lend a hand.** Collect money, food, or clothing for the homeless. Food banks, homeless shelters, and charitable organizations need your help.

- ❑ **Is art your talent?** Share your knowledge and skills with youngsters, the elderly, or local arts organizations that depend on volunteers to help present their plays, recitals, and exhibitions.

- ❑ **Help fight crime.** Form a neighborhood watch or organize a group to clean up graffiti.

- ❑ **Your church or synagogue may have projects that need youth volunteers.** The United Way, your local politician's office, civic groups, and special interest organizations also provide exceptional opportunities to serve your community. Ask your principal, teachers, or counselors for additional ideas.

For more information on joining in the spirit of youth volunteerism, write to the Federal Citizen Information Center (FCIC), Pueblo, Colorado 81009, and request the *Catch the Spirit* booklet. Also check out the FCIC's Web site at www.pueblo.gsa.gov.

PLANNING YOUR EDUCATION

Non-planners see the words "plan" and "future" and say, "Yeah, yeah, I know." Meanwhile, they're running out the door for an appointment they were supposed to be at 5 minutes ago.

Unfortunately, when it comes time to really do something about those goals and future hopes, the non-planners often discover that much of what should have been done wasn't done—which is not good when they're planning their future after high school. What about those classes they should have taken? What about those jobs they should have volunteered for? What about that scholarship they could have had if only they'd found out about it sooner?

But there is hope for poor planners. Now that you've thought about the direction you might want to go after graduating, you can use this chapter to help you plan what you should be doing and when you should be doing it, while still in high school.

Regardless of what type of education you're pursuing after high school, here's a plan to help you get there.

Your Education Timeline

Use this timeline to help you make sure you're accomplishing everything you need to accomplish on time.

NINTH GRADE

- As soon as you can, meet with your guidance counselor to begin talking about colleges and careers.

- Make sure you are enrolled in the appropriate college-preparatory or tech-prep courses.

- Get off to a good start with your grades. The grades you earn in ninth grade may be included in your final high school GPA and class rank.

- College might seem a long way off now, but grades really do count toward college admission and scholarships.

- Explore your interests and possible careers. Take advantage of Career Day opportunities.

- Get involved in extracurricular activities (both school and non-school-sponsored).

- Talk to your parents about planning for college expenses. Continue or begin a savings plan for college.

- Look at the college information available in your counselor's office and school and public libraries. Use the Internet to check out college Web sites.

- Tour a nearby college, if possible. Visit relatives or friends who live on or near a college campus. Check out the dorms, go to the library or student center, and get a feel for college life.

- Investigate summer enrichment programs.

TENTH GRADE

Fall

- In October, take the Preliminary SAT/National Merit Scholarship Qualifying Test (PSAT/NMSQT) for practice. When you fill out your test sheet, check the box that releases your name to colleges so you can start receiving brochures from them.

- Ask your guidance counselor about the American College Testing program's PLAN® (Pre-ACT) assessment program, which helps determine your study habits and academic progress and interests. This test will prepare you for the ACT next year.

- Take geometry if you have not already done so. Take biology and a second year of a foreign language.

- Become familiar with general college entrance requirements.

- Participate in your school's or state's career development activities.

Winter

🕐 Discuss your PSAT score with your counselor.

🕐 The people who read college applications aren't just looking for grades. Get involved in activities outside the classroom. Work toward leadership positions in the activities that you like best. Become involved in community service and other volunteer activities.

🕐 Read, read, read. Read as many books as possible from a comprehensive reading list.

🕐 Read the newspaper every day to learn about current affairs.

🕐 Work on your writing skills—you'll need them no matter what you do.

🕐 Find a teacher or another adult who will advise and encourage you to write well.

Spring

🕐 Keep your grades up so you can have the highest GPA and class rank possible.

🕐 Ask your counselor about postsecondary enrollment options and Advanced Placement (AP) courses.

🕐 Continue to explore your interests and careers that you think you might like.

🕐 Begin zeroing in on the type of college you would prefer (two-year or four-year, small or large, rural or urban).

🕐 If you are interested in attending a military academy, such as West Point or Annapolis, now is the time to start planning and getting information.

🕐 Write to colleges and ask for their academic requirements for admission.

🕐 Visit college campuses. Read all of the mail you receive from colleges. You may see something you like.

🕐 Attend college fairs.

- Keep putting money away for college. Get a summer job.

- Consider taking SAT Subject Tests in the courses you took this year while the material is still fresh in your mind. These tests are offered in May and June.

ELEVENTH GRADE

Fall

- Meet with your counselor to review the courses you've taken, and see what you still need to take.

- Check your class rank. Even if your grades haven't been that good so far, it's never too late to improve. Colleges like to see an upward trend.

- If you didn't do so in tenth grade, sign up for and take the PSAT/NMSQT. In addition to National Merit Scholarships, this is the qualifying test for the National Hispanic Recognition Program.

- Make sure that you have a social security number.

- Take a long, hard look at why you want to continue your education after high school so you will be able to choose the best college or university for your needs.

- Make a list of colleges that meet your most important criteria (size, location, distance from home, majors, academic rigor, housing, and cost). Weigh each of the factors according to their importance to you.

- Continue visiting college fairs. You may be able to narrow your choices or add a college to your list.

- Speak to college representatives who visit your high school.

- If you want to participate in Division I or Division II sports in college, start the certification process. Check with your counselor to make sure you are taking a core curriculum that meets NCAA requirements.

- If you are interested in one of the military academies, talk to your guidance counselor about starting the application process now.

Winter

- Collect information about college application procedures, entrance requirements, tuition and fees, room and board costs, student activities, course offerings, faculty composition, accreditation, and financial aid. The Internet is a good way to visit colleges and obtain this information. Begin comparing the schools by the factors that you consider to be most important.

- Discuss your PSAT score with your counselor.

- Begin narrowing down your college choices. Find out if the colleges you are interested in require the SAT, ACT, or SAT Subject Tests for admission.

- Register for the SAT and additional SAT Subject Tests, which are offered several times during the winter and spring of your junior year. You can take them again in the fall of your senior year if you are unhappy with your scores.

- Register for the ACT, which is usually taken in April or June. You can take it again late in your junior year or in the fall of your senior year, if necessary.

- Begin preparing for the tests you've decided to take.

- Have a discussion with your parents about the colleges in which you are interested. Examine financial resources, and gather information about financial aid.

- Set up a filing system with individual folders for each college's correspondence and printed materials.

Spring

- Meet with your counselor to review senior-year course selection and graduation requirements.

- Discuss ACT/SAT scores with your counselor. Register to take the ACT and/or SAT again if you'd like to try to improve your score.

- Discuss the college essay with your guidance counselor or English teacher.

- Stay involved with your extracurricular activities. Colleges look for consistency and depth in activities.

- Consider whom you will ask to write your recommendations. Think about asking teachers who know you well and who will write positive letters about you. Letters from a coach, activity leader, or an adult who knows you well outside of school (e.g., volunteer work contact) are also valuable.

- Inquire about personal interviews at your favorite colleges. Call or write for early summer appointments. Make necessary travel arrangements.

- See your counselor to apply for on-campus summer programs for high school students. Apply for a summer job or internship. Be prepared to pay for college applications and testing fees in the fall.

- Request applications from schools you're interested in by mail or via the Internet.

Summer

- Visit the campuses of your top five college choices.

- After each college interview, send a thank-you letter to the interviewer.

- Talk to people you know who have attended the colleges in which you are interested.

- Continue to read books, magazines, and newspapers.

- Practice filling out college applications, and then complete the final application forms or apply online through the Web sites of the colleges in which you're interested.

- Volunteer in your community.

- Compose rough drafts of your college essays. Have a teacher read and discuss them with you. Polish them, and prepare final drafts. Proofread your final essays at least three times.

- Develop a financial aid application plan, including a list of the aid sources, requirements for each application, and a timetable for meeting the filing deadlines.

TWELFTH GRADE

Fall

- Continue to take a full course load of college-prep courses.

- Keep working on your grades. Make sure you have taken the courses necessary to graduate in the spring.

- Continue to participate in extracurricular and volunteer activities. Demonstrate initiative, creativity, commitment, and leadership in each.

- To male students: You must register for selective service on your eighteenth birthday to be eligible for federal and state financial aid.

- Talk to counselors, teachers, and parents about your final college choices.

- Make a calendar showing application deadlines for admission, financial aid, and scholarships.

- Check resource books, Web sites, and your guidance office for information on scholarships and grants. Ask colleges about scholarships for which you may qualify.

- Give recommendation forms to the teachers you have chosen, along with stamped, self-addressed envelopes so your teachers can send them directly to the colleges. Be sure to fill out your name, address, and school name on the top of the form. Talk to your recommendation writers about your goals and ambitions.

- Give School Report forms to your high school's guidance office. Fill in your name, address, and any other required information. Verify with your guidance counselor the schools to which transcripts, test scores, and letters are to be sent. Give your counselor any necessary forms at least two weeks before they are due or whenever your counselor's deadline is, whichever is earlier.

- Register for and take the ACT, SAT, or SAT Subject Tests, as necessary.

- Be sure you have requested (either by mail or online) that your test scores be sent to the colleges of your choice.

- Mail or send electronically any college applications for early decision admission by November 1.

- If possible, visit colleges while classes are in session.

- If you plan to apply for an ROTC scholarship, remember that your application is due by December 1.

- Print extra copies or make photocopies of every application you send.

Winter

- Attend whatever college-preparatory nights are held at your school or by local organizations.

- Send midyear grade reports to colleges. Continue to focus on your schoolwork!

- Fill out the Free Application for Federal Student Aid (FAFSA) and, if necessary, the PROFILE®. These forms can be obtained from your guidance counselor or go to www.fafsa.ed.gov/ to download the forms or to file electronically. These forms may not be processed before January 1, so don't send them before then.

- Submit any remaining applications and financial aid forms before winter break. Make sure you apply to at least one college that you know you can afford and where you know you will be accepted.

- Meet with your counselor to verify that all forms are in order and have been sent out to colleges.

- Follow up to make sure that the colleges have received all application information, including recommendations and test scores.

Spring

- Watch your mail between March 1 and April 1 for acceptance notifications from colleges.

- Watch your mail for notification of financial aid awards between April 1 and May 1.

- Compare the financial aid packages from the colleges and universities that have accepted you.

- Make your final choice, and notify all schools of your intent by May 1. If possible, do not decide without making at least one campus visit. Send your nonrefundable deposit to your chosen school by May 1 as well. Request that your guidance counselor send a final transcript to your college in June.

- Be sure that you have received a FAFSA acknowledgment.

- If you applied for a Pell Grant (on the FAFSA), you will receive a Student Aid Report (SAR) statement. Review this notice, and forward it to the college you plan to attend. Make a copy for your records.

- Complete follow-up paperwork for the college of your choice (scheduling, orientation session, housing arrangements, and other necessary forms).

Summer

- Receive the orientation schedule from your college.

- Get housing assignment from your college.

- Obtain course scheduling and cost information from your college.

- Congratulations! You are about to begin the greatest adventure of your life. Good luck.

Classes to Take if You're Going to College

Did you know that classes you take as early as the ninth grade will help you get into college? Make sure you take at least the minimum high school curriculum requirements necessary for college admission.

Even if you don't plan to enter college immediately, take the most demanding courses you can handle. Talk with your guidance counselor to select the curriculum that best meets your needs and skills.

Of course, learning also occurs outside of school. While outside activities will not make up for poor academic performance, skills learned from jobs, extracurricular activities, and volunteer opportunities help you become a well-rounded student and can strengthen your college or job application.

GETTING A HEAD START ON COLLEGE COURSES

You can take college courses while still in high school so that when you're in college, you'll be ahead of everyone else. The formal name is "postsecondary enrollment." (In Texas, the formal names are "dual credit"—academic credit and articulated credit—and "Tech-Prep.") What it means is that some students can take college courses and receive both high school and college credit for the courses taken. It's like a two-for-one deal!

Postsecondary enrollment is designed to provide an opportunity for qualified high school students to experience more advanced academic work. Participation in a postsecondary enrollment program is not intended to replace courses available in high school but rather to enhance the educational opportunities available to students while in high school. There are two options for postsecondary enrollment:

Option A: Qualified high school juniors and seniors take courses for college credit. Students enrolled under Option A must pay for all books, supplies, tuition, and associated fees.

Option B: Qualified high school juniors and seniors take courses for high school and college credit. For students enrolled under this option, the local school district covers the related costs, provided the student completes the selected courses. Otherwise, the student and parent are assessed the costs.

Certain preestablished conditions must be met for enrollment, so check with your high school counselor for more information.

6 Study Skills That Lead to Success

1. **Set a regular study schedule.** No one at college is going to hound you to do your homework. Develop the study patterns in high school that will lead to success in college. Anyone who has ever pulled an all-nighter knows how much you remember when you are on the downside of your fifth cup of coffee and no sleep—not much! Maintain steady and consistent study habits.

2. **Save everything.** To make sure your history notes don't end up in your math notebook and your English papers are not at the bottom of your friend's locker, develop an organized system for storing your papers. Stay on top of your materials, and be sure to save quizzes and tests. It is amazing how questions from a test you took in March can miraculously reappear on your final exam.

3. **Listen.** Teachers give away what will be on the test by repeating themselves. If you pay attention to what the teacher is saying, you will probably notice what is being emphasized. If what the teacher says in class repeats itself in your notes and in review sessions, chances are that material will be on the test. So listen.

4. **Take notes.** If the teacher has taken the time to prepare a lecture, then what he or she says is important enough for you to write down. Develop a system for reviewing your notes. After each class, rewrite them, review them, or reread them. Try highlighting the important points or making notes in the margins to jog your memory.

5. **Use textbooks wisely.** What can you do with a textbook besides lose it? Use it to back up or clarify information that you don't understand from your class notes. Reading every word may be more effort than it is worth, so look at the book intelligently. What is in boxes or highlighted areas? What content is emphasized? What do the questions ask about in the review sections?

6. **Form a study group.** Establish a group that will stay on task and ask one another the questions you think the teacher will ask. Compare notes to see if you have all the important facts. And discuss your thoughts. Talking ideas out can help when you have to respond to an essay question.

THE COLLEGE SEARCH

The Best Resources

There are thousands of colleges and universities in the United States, so before you start filling out applications, you need to narrow down your search. There are a number of sources that will help you do this.

YOUR GUIDANCE COUNSELOR

Your guidance counselor is your greatest asset in the college search process. He or she has access to a vast repository of information, from college bulletins and catalogs to financial aid applications. She knows how well graduates from your high school have performed at colleges across the country and has probably even visited many of the colleges to get some firsthand knowledge about the schools she has recommended. The more your guidance counselor sees you and learns about you, the easier it is for her to help you. So make sure you stop by her office often, whether it's to talk about your progress or just to say "hi."

YOUR TEACHERS

Use your teachers as resources, too. Many of them have had years of experience in their field. They have taught thousands of students and watched them go off to college and careers. Teachers often stay in contact with graduates and know about their experiences in college and may be familiar with the schools you are interested in attending. Ask your teachers how they feel about the match between you and your choice of schools and if they think you will be able to succeed in that environment.

YOUR FAMILY

Your family needs to be an integral part of the college selection process, whether they are financing your education or not. They have opinions and valuable advice. Listen to them carefully. Try to absorb all their information and see if it applies to you. Does it fit with who you are and what you want? What works and what doesn't work for you? Is some of what they say dated? How long ago were their experiences, and how relevant are they today? Take in the information, thank them for their concern, compare what they have said with the information you are gathering, and discard what doesn't fit.

COLLEGES AND UNIVERSITIES

Don't forget to go to college fairs. Usually held in large cities in the evening, they are free and sponsored by your local guidance counselors' association and the National Association of College Admission Counseling (NACAC). The admissions counselors of hundreds of colleges, vocational/career colleges, and universities attend college fairs each year. Whether your questions are as general as what the overall cost of education is at a particular institution or as specific as how many biology majors had works published last year, the admissions office works to assist you in locating the people who can answer your questions. Bring a shopping bag for all the information you will get.

Admissions officers also visit high schools. Don't forget to attend these meetings during your junior and senior years. In general, college admissions counselors come to a school to get a general sense of the high school and the caliber and personality of the student body. Although it is difficult to make an individual impression at these group sessions, the college counselors do take names on cards for later contact, and you will occasionally see them making notes on the cards when they are struck by an astute questioner. It is helpful to attend these sessions because consistent contact between a student and a college is tracked by colleges and universities. An admissions decision may come down to examining the size of your admissions folder and the number of interactions you have had with the school over time.

College and university brochures and catalogs are a good place to look, too. After reading a few, you will discover that some offer more objective information than others. You will also start to learn what information colleges think is essential to present. That's important. If one college's brochure does not present the same information as most of the other college brochures, you have to ask yourself why. What might this say about the college's academic offerings, athletic or extracurricular programs, or campus life? What does the campus look like? How is the campus environment presented in the brochure? The brochures should present clues to what schools feel are their important majors, what their mission is, and on which departments they are spending their budgets. Take the time to do these informational resources justice. They have a great deal to say to the careful reader.

A college's Web site can give you a glimpse of campus life that does not appear in the college's brochure and catalog. It is true that the virtual tour will show you the shots that the college marketing department wants you to see, highlighting the campus in the best light, but you can use the home page to see other things, too. Read the student newspaper. Visit college-sponsored chat rooms. Go to the department in the major you are investigating. Look at the Course Bulletin to see what courses are required.

Online Help

To help you find two-year and four-year colleges or universities, check out the following online resources for additional information on college selection, scholarships, student information, and much more.

The National Association for College Admission Counseling. This site offers information for professionals, students, and parents: www.nacacnet.org

U.S. Department of Education. This federal agency's National Center for Education Statistics produces reports on every level of education, from elementary to postgraduate. Dozens are available for downloading. You can find these and other links at http://nces.ed.gov.

Campus Visits

You've heard the old saying, "A picture is worth a thousand words." Well, a campus visit is worth a thousand brochures. Nothing beats walking around a campus to get a feel for it. Some students report that all they needed to know that they loved or hated a campus was to drive through it. Then there is the true story of the guy who applied to a school because it had a prestigious name. Got accepted. Didn't visit, and when he arrived to move into the dorms, discovered to his horror it was an all-male school. A visit would have taken care of that problem.

The best time to experience the college environment is during the spring of your junior year or the fall of your senior year. Although you may have more time to visit colleges during your summer off, your observations will be more accurate when you can see the campus in full swing. Open houses are a good idea and provide you with opportunities to talk to students, faculty members, and administrators. Write or call in advance to take student-conducted campus tours. If possible, stay overnight in a dorm to see what living at the college is really like.

Bring your transcript so that you are prepared to interview with admission officers. Take this opportunity to ask questions about financial aid and other services that are available to students. You can get a good snapshot of campus life by reading a copy of the student newspaper. The final goal of the campus visit is to study the school's personality and decide if it matches yours. Your parents should be involved with the campus visits so that you can share your impressions. Here are some additional campus visit tips:

- Read campus literature prior to the visit.
- Ask for directions, and allow ample travel time.
- Make a list of questions before the visit.
- Dress in neat, clean, and casual clothes and shoes.
- Ask to meet one-on-one with a current student.
- Ask to meet personally with a professor in your area of interest.
- Ask to meet a coach or athlete in your area of interest.
- Offer a firm handshake.
- Use good posture.
- Listen, and take notes.
- Speak clearly, and maintain eye contact with people you meet.

- ☑ Don't interrupt.

- ☑ Be honest, direct, and polite.

- ☑ Be aware of factual information so that you can ask questions of comparison and evaluation.

- ☑ Be prepared to answer questions about yourself. Practice a mock interview with someone.

- ☑ Don't be shy about explaining your background and why you are interested in the school.

- ☑ Ask questions about the background and experiences of the people you meet.

- ☑ Convey your interest in getting involved in campus life.

- ☑ Be positive and energetic.

- ☑ Don't feel as though you have to talk the whole time or carry the conversation yourself.

- ☑ Relax, and enjoy yourself.

- ☑ Thank those you meet, and send thank-you notes when appropriate.

After you have made your college visits, rank the schools in which you're interested. This will help you decide not only which ones to apply to, but also which one to attend once you receive your acceptance letters.

The College Interview

Not all schools require or offer an interview. However, if you are offered an interview, use this one-on-one time to evaluate the college in detail and to sell yourself to the admission officer. The following list of questions can help you collect vital information you will want to know.

- ☑ How many students apply each year? How many are accepted?

- ☑ What are the average GPA and average ACT or SAT score(s) for those accepted?

- How many students in last year's freshman class returned for their sophomore year?
- What is the school's procedure for credit for Advanced Placement high school courses?
- As a freshman, will I be taught by professors or teaching assistants?
- What is the ratio of students to instructors?
- When is it necessary to declare a major?
- Is it possible to have a double major or to declare a major and a minor?
- What are the requirements for the major in which I am interested?
- How does the advising system work?
- Does this college offer study abroad, cooperative programs, or academic honors programs?
- What is the likelihood, due to overcrowding, of getting closed out of the courses I need?
- What technology is available, and what are any associated fees?
- How well equipped are the libraries and laboratories?
- Are internships available?
- How effective is the job placement service of the school?
- What is the average class size in my area of interest?
- Have any professors in my area of interest recently won any honors or awards?
- What teaching methods are used in my area of interest (lecture, group discussion, fieldwork)?
- What percentage of students graduate in four years in my area of interest?

- ☑ What are the special requirements for graduation in my area of interest?

- ☑ What is the student body like? Age? Sex? Race? Geographic origin?

- ☑ What percentage of students live in dormitories? In off-campus housing?

- ☑ What percentage of students go home for the weekend?

- ☑ What are some of the regulations that apply to living in a dormitory?

- ☑ What are the security precautions taken on campus and in the dorms?

- ☑ Is the surrounding community safe?

- ☑ Are there problems with drug and alcohol abuse on campus?

- ☑ Do faculty members and students mix on an informal basis?

- ☑ How important are the arts to student life?

- ☑ What facilities are available for cultural events?

- ☑ How important are sports to student life?

- ☑ What facilities are available for sporting events?

- ☑ What percentage of the student body belongs to a sorority/fraternity?

- ☑ What is the relationship between those who belong to the Greek system and those who don't?

- ☑ Are students involved in the decision-making process at the college? Do they sit on major committees?

- ☑ In what other activities can students get involved?

- ☑ What percentage of students receive financial aid based on need?

- ☑ What percentage of students receive scholarships based on academic ability?

☑ What percentage of a typical financial aid offer is in the form of a loan?

☑ If a family demonstrates financial need on the FAFSA (and PROFILE®, if applicable), what percentage of the established need is generally awarded?

☑ How much did the college increase the cost of room, board, tuition, and fees from last year?

☑ Do opportunities for financial aid, scholarships, or work-study increase each year?

☑ When is the admission application deadline?

☑ When is the financial aid application deadline?

☑ When will I be notified of the admission decision?

☑ Is a deposit required and is it refundable?

Keep in mind that you don't need to ask all these questions—in fact, some of them may have already been answered for you in the catalog, on the Web site, on a campus tour, or in the interview. Ask only the questions for which you still need answers.

Should You Head for the Ivy League?

Determining whether to apply to one of the eight Ivy League schools is something about which you should think long and hard. Sure, it can't hurt to toss your application into the ring if you can afford the application fee and the time you'll spend writing the essays. But if you want to figure out if you'd be a legitimate candidate for acceptance at one of these top-tier schools, you should understand the type of student that they look for and how you compare. Take a look at these statistics:

- On average only 15 percent or fewer applicants are accepted at Ivy League colleges each year.

- Most Ivy League students have placed in the top 10 percent of their class.

- Because Ivy League schools are so selective, they want a diverse student population. That means they want students who represent not only the fifty states but also a wide selection of other countries.

- In 2012, Harvard University admitted 2,032 students, or 5.9 percent of its 34,302 applicants. (In 2011, Harvard admitted 6.17 percent of the 34,950 applicants.) According to officials, the 2012 applicant pool included 3,800 students who were ranked first in their high school classes.

- At Yale University, the 2012 acceptance rate, 6.82 percent, was lower than the 7.35 percent admitted in 2011. Of the 28,974 applicants, Yale admitted 1,975 in 2012. Approximately 1,000 students were on the 2012 waitlist, and of the 996 waitlisted in 2011, only 103 were accepted.

- At Princeton University, the 2012 acceptance rate was 7.86 percent. Princeton accepted 2,095 of the 26,664 students who applied. According to officials, the 2012 applicant pool was the second largest in the University's history.

- In 2012, fewer students applied to Columbia University, but a higher percentage of applicants were accepted. Of the 31,851 applicants in 2012, Columbia accepted 2,363 students—a 7.4 percent acceptance rate, compared to the 6.93 percent rate in 2011.

Being accepted at an Ivy League school is a process that starts in the ninth grade. You should select demanding courses and maintain good grades in those courses throughout all four years of high school. Get involved in extracurricular activities as well, and, of course, do well on your standardized tests. When it comes time to apply for college, select at least three schools: one ideal, one possible, and one shoe-in. Your ideal can be an Ivy League if you wish.

While the ultimate goal is to get the best education possible, students are sometimes more concerned about getting accepted than with taking a hard look at what a school has to offer them. Often, a university or college that is less competitive than an Ivy may have exactly what you need to succeed in the future. Keep that in mind as you select the colleges that will offer you what you need.

Minority Students

African American, Hispanic, Asian American, and Native American high school students have a lot of doors into higher education opening for them. In fact, most colleges want to respond to the social and economic disadvantages of certain groups of Americans. They want to reflect the globalization of our economy. They want their student populations to look like the rest of America, which means people from many different backgrounds and ethnic groups. You'll find that most colleges have at least one member of the admissions staff who specializes in recruiting minorities.

One of the reasons college admissions staff are recruiting minorities and want to accommodate their needs is because there are more minorities thinking of attending college—and graduating. Let's put some numbers to these statements. In its October 2010 *Minorities in Higher Education 2010—Twenty-Fourth Status Report,* the American Council on Education (ACE) found that between 1997 and 2007 minority enrollment at U.S. colleges and universities increased by 52 percent—from 3.6 million to 5.4 million. **Colleges and universities became more diverse during the past decade, with the minority share of the student body rising from 25 to 30 percent.**

ACADEMIC RESOURCES FOR MINORITY STUDENTS

In addition to churches, sororities and fraternities, and college minority affairs offices, minority students can receive information and assistance from the following organizations:

American Indian Higher Education Consortium (AIHEC)

AIHEC's mission is to support the work of tribal colleges and the national movement for tribal self-determination through four objectives: maintain commonly held standards of quality in American Indian education; support the development of new tribally controlled colleges; promote and assist in the development of legislation to support American Indian higher education; and encourage greater participation by American Indians in the development of higher education policy.

121 Oronoco Street
Alexandria, Virginia 22314
703-838-0400
www.aihec.org

ASPIRA

ASPIRA's mission is to empower the Puerto Rican and Latino community through advocacy and the education and leadership development of its youth.

1444 Eye Street, NW, Suite 800
Washington, D.C. 20005
202-835-3600
www.aspira.org

Gates Millennium Scholars (GMS)

The Gates Millennium Scholars, funded by a grant from the Bill & Melinda Gates Foundation, was established in 1999 to provide outstanding African American, American Indian/Alaska Natives, Asian Pacific Islander Americans, and Hispanic American students with an opportunity to complete an undergraduate college education in all discipline areas and a graduate education for those students pursuing studies in mathematics, science, engineering, education, or library science. The goal of GMS is to promote academic excellence and to provide an opportunity for thousands of outstanding students with significant financial need to reach their fullest potential.

P.O. Box 10500
Fairfax, Virginia 22031-8044
877-690-4677 (toll-free)
www.gmsp.org

Hispanic Association of Colleges & Universities (HACU)

The Hispanic Association of Colleges & Universities is a national association representing the accredited colleges and universities in the United States where Hispanic students constitute at least 25 percent of the total student enrollment. HACU's goal is to bring together colleges and universities, corporations, government agencies, and individuals to establish partnerships for promoting the developing Hispanic-serving colleges and universities; improving access to and the quality of postsecondary education for Hispanic students; and meeting the needs of business, industry, and government through the development and sharing of resources, information, and expertise.

8415 Datapoint Drive, Suite 400
San Antonio, Texas 78229
210-692-3805
www.hacu.net

Hispanic Scholarship Fund (HSF)

The Hispanic Scholarship Fund is the nation's leading organization supporting Hispanic higher education. HSF was founded in 1975 with a vision to strengthen the country by advancing college education among Hispanic Americans. In support of its mission, HSF provides the Latino community with college scholarships and educational outreach support.

55 Second Street, Suite 1500
San Francisco, California 94105
877-473-4636 (toll-free)
www.hsf.net

INROADS

INROADS is a national career-development organization that places and develops talented minority youth (African American, Hispanic American, and Native American) in business and industry and prepares them for corporate and community leadership.

10 South Broadway, Suite 300
St. Louis, Missouri 63102
314-241-7488
www.inroads.org

National Action Council for Minorities in Engineering (NACME)

NACME is an organization that aims to provide leadership and support for the national effort to increase the representation of successful African American, American Indian, and Latino women and men in engineering and technology and math- and science-based careers.

440 Hamilton Avenue, Suite 302
White Plains , New York 10601-1813
914-539-4010
www.nacme.org

National Association for the Advancement of Colored People (NAACP)

The purpose of the NAACP is to ensure the political, educational, social, and economic equality of all citizens; to achieve equality of rights and eliminate race prejudice among the citizens of the United States; to remove all barriers of racial discrimination through democratic processes; to seek enactment and enforcement of federal, state, and local laws securing civil rights; to inform the public of the adverse effects of racial discrimination and to seek its elimination; and to educate persons as to their constitutional rights and to take all lawful action to secure the exercise thereof, and to take any other lawful action in furtherance of these objectives, consistent with the efforts of the national organization.

4805 Mt. Hope Drive
Baltimore, Maryland 21215
877-NAACP-98 (toll-free)
www.naacp.org

The National Urban League

The National Urban League's Campaign for African American Achievement is a community-based movement that embodies the values of academic achievement, social development, and economic independence. Among children and youth, the Campaign strives to foster positive attitudes about academic achievement, consistent and enthusiastic participation in school, commitment to meeting and exceeding education standards, increased social polish and improved navigational skills, and a heightened sense of history, community, and self-worth.

120 Wall Street
New York, New York 10005
212-558-5300
www.nul.org

United Negro College Fund (UNCF)

The UNCF serves to enhance the quality of education by raising operating funds for its 39 member colleges and universities, providing financial assistance to deserving students, and increasing access to technology for students and faculty at historically black colleges and universities.

8260 Willow Oaks Corporate Drive
P.O. Box 10444
Fairfax, Virginia 22031-8044
800-331-2244 (toll-free)
www.uncf.org

Students with Disabilities Go to College

The Americans with Disabilities Act (ADA) requires educational institutions at all levels, public and private, to provide equal access to programs, services, and facilities. Schools must be accessible to students, as well as to employees and the public, regardless of any disability. To ensure such accessibility, they must follow specific requirements for new construction, alterations or renovations, academic programs, and institutional policies, practices, and procedures. Students with specific disabilities have the right to request and expect accommodations, including auxiliary aids and services that enable them to participate in and benefit from all programs and activities offered by or related to a school.

To comply with ADA requirements, many high schools and universities offer programs and information to answer questions for students with disabilities and to assist them both in selecting appropriate colleges and in attaining full inclusion once they enter college. And most colleges and universities have disabilities services offices to help students negotiate the system. When it comes time to apply to colleges, write to the ones that you're interested in to find out what kinds of programs they have in place. When it comes time to narrow down your choices, request a visit.

WHAT IS CONSIDERED A DISABILITY?

A person is considered to have a disability if he or she meets at least one of three conditions. The individual must:

1. have a documented physical or mental impairment that substantially limits one or more major life activities, such as personal self-care, walking, seeing, hearing, speaking, breathing, learning, working, or performing manual tasks; or

2. have a record of such an impairment; or

3. be perceived as having such an impairment.

Physical disabilities include impairments of speech, vision, hearing, and mobility. Other disabilities, while less obvious, are similarly limiting; they include diabetes, asthma, multiple sclerosis, heart disease, cancer, mental illness, mental retardation, cerebral palsy, and learning disabilities.

Learning disabilities refer to an array of biological conditions that impede a person's ability to process and disseminate information. A learning disability is commonly recognized as a significant deficiency in one or more of the following areas: oral expression, listening comprehension, written expression, basic reading skills, reading comprehension, mathematical calculation, or problem solving. Individuals with learning disabilities also may have difficulty with sustained attention, time management, or social skills.

If you have a disability, you will take the same steps to choose and apply to a college as other students, but you should also evaluate each college based on your special need(s). Get organized, and meet with campus specialists to discuss your specific requirements. Then, explore whether the programs, policies, procedures, and facilities meet your specific situation.

It is usually best to describe your disability in a letter attached to the application so the proper fit can be made between you and the school. You will probably need to have your psychoeducational evaluation and testing record sent to the school. Some colleges help with schedules and offer transition courses, reduced course loads, extra access to professors, and special study areas to help address your needs.

Remember, admission to college is a realistic goal for any motivated student. If you invest the time and effort, you can make it happen.

TIPS FOR STUDENTS WITH DISABILITIES

- ☑ Document your disability with letters from your physician(s), therapist, case manager, school psychologist, and other service providers.
- ☑ Get letters of support from teachers, family, friends, and service providers that detail how you have succeeded despite your disability.
- ☑ Learn the federal laws that apply to students with disabilities.
- ☑ Research support groups for peer information and advocacy.
- ☑ Visit several campuses.
- ☑ Look into the services available, the pace of campus life, and the college's programs for students with disabilities.
- ☑ Ask about orientation programs, including specialized introductions for, or about, students with disabilities.
- ☑ Ask about flexible, individualized study plans.
- ☑ Ask if the school offers technology such as voice synthesizers, voice recognition, and/or visual learning equipment to its students.
- ☑ Ask about adapted intramural/social activities.
- ☑ Ask to talk with students who have similar disabilities to hear about their experiences on campus.
- ☑ Once you select a college, get a map of the campus and learn the entire layout.

- If you have a physical disability, make sure the buildings you need to be in are accessible to you. Some, even though they comply with the ADA, aren't as accessible as others.

- Be realistic. If you use a wheelchair, for example, a school with an exceptionally hilly campus may not be your best choice, no matter what other accommodations it has.

APPLYING TO COLLEGE

Once your list is finalized, the worst part is filling out all the forms accurately and getting them in by the deadlines. Because requirements differ, you should check with all the colleges that you are interested in attending to find out what documentation is needed and when it is due.

What Schools Look for in Prospective Students

As if you were sizing up the other team to plan your game strategy, you'll need to understand what admissions committees want from you as you assemble all the pieces of your application.

Academic record. Admission representatives look at the breadth (how many), diversity (which ones), and difficulty (how challenging) of the courses on your transcript.

Grades. You should show consistency in your ability to work to your potential. If your grades are not initially good, colleges look to see that significant improvement has been made. Some colleges have minimum grade point averages that they are willing to accept.

Class rank. Colleges may consider the academic standing of a student in relation to the other members of his or her class. Are you in the top 25 percent of your class? Top half? Ask your counselor for your class rank.

Standardized test scores. Colleges look at test scores in terms of ranges. If your scores aren't high but you did well academically in high school, you shouldn't be discouraged. There is no set formula for admission. Even at the most competitive schools, some students' test scores are lower than you would think.

Extracurricular activities. Colleges look for depth of involvement (variety and how long you participated), initiative (leadership), and creativity demonstrated in activities, service, or work.

Recommendations. Most colleges require a recommendation from your high school guidance counselor. Some ask for references from teachers or other adults. If your counselor or teachers don't know you well, you should put together a student resume, or brag sheet, that outlines what you have done during your four years of high school.

College interview. An interview is required by most colleges with highly selective procedures.

Admission Procedures

Your first task in applying is to get application forms. That's easy. Nearly all applications are available online and are completed on the school's Web site. Admission information can be gathered from college representatives, catalogs, Web sites, and directories; alumni or students attending the college; and campus visits.

WHICH ADMISSION OPTION IS BEST FOR YOU?

One of the first questions you will be asked on applications for four-year colleges and universities is which admission option you want. What this means is whether you want to apply early action, early decision, deferred admission, regular admission, rolling admission, or other possible options.

Four-year institutions generally offer the following admissions options:

Early admission. A student of superior ability is admitted into college courses and programs before completing high school.

Early decision. A student declares a first-choice college, requests that the college decide on acceptance early (between November and January), and agrees to enroll if accepted. Students with a strong high school record who are sure they want to attend a certain school may want to consider early decision admission. (See "More on Early Decision" later on in this chapter.)

Early action. This is similar to early decision, but if a student is accepted, he or she has until the regular admission deadline to decide whether or not to attend.

Early evaluation. A student can apply under early evaluation to find out if the chance of acceptance is good, fair, or poor. Applications are due before the regular admission deadline, and the student is given an opinion between January and March.

Regular admission. This is the most common option offered to students. A deadline is set for when all applications must be received, and all notifications are sent out at the same time.

Rolling admission. The college accepts students who meet the academic requirements on a first-come, first-served basis until it fills its freshman class. No strict application deadline is specified. Applications are reviewed, and decisions are made immediately (usually within two to three weeks). This method is commonly used at large state universities, so students should apply early for the best chance of acceptance.

Open admission. Virtually all high school graduates are admitted, regardless of academic qualifications.

Deferred admission. An accepted student is allowed to postpone enrollment for a year.

If you're going to a two-year college, these options also apply to you. Two-year colleges usually have an "open-door" admission policy, which means that high school graduates may enroll as long as space is available. Sometimes vocational/career colleges are somewhat selective, and competition for admission may be fairly intense for programs that are highly specialized.

MORE ON EARLY DECISION

Early decision is a legally binding agreement between you and the college. If the college accepts you, you pay a deposit within a short period of time and sign an agreement stating that you will not apply to other colleges. To keep students from backing out, some colleges mandate that applicants' high school counselors cannot send transcripts to other institutions.

In many ways, early decision is a win-win for both students and colleges. Students can relax and enjoy their senior year of high school without waiting to see if other colleges have accepted them. And colleges know early in the year who is enrolled and can start planning the coming year.

When Is Early Decision the Right Decision?

For good and bad reasons, early decision is a growing trend, so why not just do it? Early decision is an excellent idea that comes with a warning. It's not a good idea unless you have done a thorough college search and know without a shred of doubt that this is the college for you. Don't go for early decision unless you've spent time on the campus, in classes and dorms, and you have a true sense of the academic and social climate of that college.

Early decision can get sticky if you change your mind. Parents of students who have signed agreements and then want to apply elsewhere get angry at high school counselors, saying they've taken away their rights to choose among colleges. They try to force them to send out transcripts even though their children have committed to one college. To guard against this scenario, some colleges ask parents and students to sign a statement signifying their understanding that early decision is a binding plan. Some high schools now have their own form for students and parents to sign acknowledging that they completely realize the nature of an early decision agreement.

The Financial Reason Against Early Decision

Another common argument against early decision is that if an institution has you locked in, there's no incentive to offer applicants the best financial packages. The consensus seems to be that if you're looking to play the financial game, don't apply for early decision.

However, some folks argue that the best financial aid offers are usually made to attractive applicants. In general, if a student receives an early decision offer, they fall into that category and so would get "the sweetest" financial aid anyway. That doesn't mean that there aren't colleges out there using financial incentives to get students to enroll. A strong candidate who applies to six or eight schools and gets admitted to all of them will look at how much money the colleges throw his or her way before making a decision.

Before You Decide...

If you're thinking about applying for early decision at a college, ask yourself these questions first. You'll be glad you did.

- ☑ Why am I applying early decision?
- ☑ Have I thoroughly researched several colleges, and do I know what my options are?
- ☑ Do I know why I'm going to college and what I want to accomplish there?
- ☑ Have I visited several schools, spent time in classes, stayed overnight, and talked to professors?
- ☑ Do the courses that the college offers match my goals?
- ☑ Am I absolutely convinced that one college clearly stands out above all others?

More Mumbo Jumbo

Besides confusing terms like deferred admission, early decision, and early evaluation, just discussed, you'll most likely stumble upon some additional terms that might be unfamiliar to you. Here, we explain a few more:

ACADEMIC CALENDAR

Traditional semesters. Two equal periods of time during a school year.

Early semester. Two equal periods of time during a school year. The first semester is completed before Christmas.

Trimester. Calendar year divided into three equal periods of time. The third trimester replaces summer school.

Quarter. Four equal periods of time during a school year.

4-1-4. Two equal terms of about four months separated by a one-month term.

ACCREDITATION

Accreditation is recognition of a college or university by a regional or national organization, which indicates that the institution has met its objectives and is maintaining prescribed educational standards. Colleges may be accredited by one of six regional associations of schools and colleges and by any one of the many national specialized accrediting bodies.

Specialized accreditation of individual programs is granted by national professional organizations. This is intended to ensure that specific programs meet or exceed minimum requirements established by the professional organization. States may require that students in some professions that grant licenses graduate from an accredited program as one qualification for licensure.

Accreditation is somewhat like receiving a pass/fail grade. It doesn't differentiate colleges and universities that excel from those that meet minimum requirements. Accreditation applies to all programs within an institution, but it does not mean that all programs are of equal quality within an institution. Accreditation does not guarantee transfer recognition by other colleges. Transfer decisions are made by individual institutions.

AFFILIATION

Not-for-profit colleges are classified into one of the following categories: state-assisted, private/independent, or private/church supported. The institution's affiliation does not guarantee the quality or nature of the institution, and it may or may not have an effect on the religious life of students.

State-assisted colleges and universities and private/independent colleges do not have requirements related to the religious activity of their students. The influence of religion varies among private/church-supported colleges. At some, religious services or study are encouraged or required; at others, religious affiliation is less apparent.

ARTICULATION AGREEMENT

Articulation agreements facilitate the transfer of students and credits among state-assisted institutions of higher education by establishing transfer procedures and equitable treatment of all students in the system.

One type of articulation agreement links two or more colleges so that students can continue to make progress toward their degree, even if they must attend different schools at different times. For example, some states' community colleges have agreements with their state universities that permit graduates of college parallel programs to transfer with junior standing.

A second type of articulation agreement links secondary (high school) and postsecondary institutions to allow students to gain college credit for relevant vocational courses. This type of agreement saves students time and tuition in the pursuit of higher learning.

Because articulation agreements vary from school to school and from program to program, it is recommended that students check with their home institution and the institution they are interested in attending in order to fully understand the options available to them and each institution's specific requirements.

CROSS-REGISTRATION

Cross-registration is a cooperative arrangement offered by many colleges and universities for the purpose of increasing the number and types of courses offered at any one institution. This arrangement allows students to cross-register for one or more courses at any participating host institution. While specific cross-registration program requirements may vary, typically a student can cross-register without having to pay the host institution additional tuition.

If your college participates in cross-registration, check with your home institution concerning any additional tuition costs and request a cross-registration form. Check with your adviser and registrar at your home institution to make sure that the course you plan to take is approved, and then contact the host institution for cross-registration instructions. Make sure that there is space available in the course you want to take at the host institution, as some host institutions give their own students registration priority.

To participate in cross-registration, you may need to be a full-time student (some programs allow part-time student participation) in good academic and financial standing at your home institution. Check with both colleges well in advance for all of the specific requirements.

The Complete Application Package

Freshman applications can be filed any time after you have completed your junior year of high school. Colleges strongly recommend that students apply by April (at the latest) of their senior year in order to be considered for acceptance, scholarships, financial aid, and housing. College requirements may vary, so always read and comply with specific requirements. In general, admission officers are interested in the following basic materials:

- A completed and signed application and any required application fee.

- An official copy of your high school transcript, including your class ranking and grade point average. The transcript must include all work completed as of the date the application is submitted. Check with your guidance counselor for questions about these items. If you apply online, you must inform your guidance counselor and request that he or she send your transcript to the schools to which you are applying. Your application will not be processed without a transcript.

- An official record of your ACT and/or SAT scores.

- Other items that may be required include letters of recommendation, an essay, the secondary school report form and midyear school report (sent in by your guidance counselor after you fill out a portion of the form), and any financial aid forms required by the college.

Make sure you have everything you need before you send out your application.

FILLING OUT THE FORMS

Filling out college applications can seem like a daunting task, but there are six easy steps to follow for the successful completion of this part of the process.

Step 1: Practice Copies

Make a photocopy of each application of each college to which you plan to apply. Since the presentation of your application may be considered an important aspect in the weighting for admission, you don't want to erase, cross out, or use white-out on your final application. Make all your mistakes on your copies. When you think you have it right, then transfer the information to your final original copy or go online to enter it on the college's electronic application. Remember, at the larger universities, the application packet may be the only part of you they see.

Step 2: Decide on Your Approach

What is it about your application that will grab the admission counselor's attention so that it will be pulled out of the sea of applications on his or her desk for consideration? Be animated and interesting in what you say. Be memorable in your approach to your application, but don't overdo it. You want the admissions counselor to remember you, not your Spanish castle made of popsicle sticks. Most importantly, be honest and don't exaggerate your academics and extra-curricular activities. Approach this process with integrity every step of the way. First of all, it is the best way to end up in a college that is the right match for you. Second, if you are less than truthful, the college will eventually learn about it. How will they know? You have to supply support materials to accompany your application—things like transcripts and recommendations. If you tell one story and they tell another, the admissions office will notice the disparity—trust us!

Step 3: Check the Deadlines

In September of your senior year, organize your applications in chronological order. Work on materials with the earliest due date first.

Step 4: Check the Data on You

You need to make sure that the information you will be sending to support your applications is correct. The first thing to double check is your transcript. This is an important piece because you must send a transcript with each application you send to colleges. Take a trip to the guidance office and ask for a "Transcript Request Form." Fill out the request for a formal transcript, indicating that you are requesting a copy for yourself and that you will pick it up. Pay the fee if there is one.

When you get your transcript, look it over carefully. It will be several pages long and will include everything from the titles of all the courses that you have taken since the ninth grade along with the final grade for each course and community service hours you have logged each year. Check the information carefully. It is understandable that with this much data, it is easy to make an input error. Because this information is vital to you and you are the best judge of accuracy, it is up to you to check it. Take any corrections or questions you have back to your guidance counselor to make the corrections. If it is a questionable grade, your counselor will help you find out what grade should have been posted on your transcript. Do whatever needs to be done to make sure your transcript has been corrected no later than October 1 of your senior year.

Step 5: List Your Activities

When you look through your applications, you will find a section on extracurricular activities. It is time to hit your computer again to prioritize your list of extracurricular activities and determine the best approach for presenting them to your colleges. Some students prepare a resume and include this in every application they send. Other students choose to develop an "Extracurricular, Academic, and Work Experience Addendum" and mark those specific sections of their application as "See attached Addendum."

If you are a powerhouse student with a great deal to say in this area, it will take time to prioritize your involvement in activities and word it succinctly yet interestingly. Put those activities that will have the strongest impact, show the most consistent involvement, and demonstrate your leadership abilities at the top of the list. This will take time, so plan accordingly. If you feel you have left out important information because the form limits you, include either an addendum or your resume as a back-up.

Step 6: Organize Your Other Data

What other information can you organize in advance of sitting down to fill out your applications?

The Personal Data Section

Most of this section is standard personal information that you will not have any difficulty responding to, but some items you will need to think about. For example, you may find a question that asks, "What special college or division are you applying to?" Do you have a specific school in mind, like the College of Engineering? If you are not sure about your major, ask yourself what interests you the most and then enter that college. Once you are in college and have a better sense of what you want to do, you can always change your major later.

The application will provide an optional space to declare ethnicity. If you feel you would like to declare an area and that it would work to your advantage for admission, consider completing this section of the application.

You are also going to need your high school's College Entrance Examination Board (CEEB) number. That is the number you needed when you filled out your test packets. It is stamped on the front of your SAT and ACT packets, or, if you go to the guidance department, they'll tell you what it is.

The Standardized Testing Section

Applications ask you for your test dates and scores. Get them together accurately. All your College Board scores should be recorded with the latest test results you have received. Your latest ACT record will only have the current scores unless you asked for all your past test results. If you have lost this information, call these organizations or go to your guidance department. Your counselor should have copies. Be sure the testing organizations are sending your official score reports to the schools to which you're applying. If you are planning to take one of these tests in the future, the colleges will want those dates, too; they will wait for those scores before making a decision. If you change your plans, contact the admissions office and provide the new dates or the reason for canceling.

The Senior Course Load Section

Colleges will request that you list your present senior schedule by semester. Set this information up in this order: List any AP or honors-level full-year courses first, as these will have the most impact. Then list other required full-year courses and then required semester courses, followed by electives. Make sure you list first-semester and second-semester courses appropriately. Do not forget to include physical education if you are taking it this year.

YOUR RECOMMENDATION WRITERS

Most schools will require you to submit two or three letters of recommendation from adults who know you well.

Guidance Counselor Recommendations

Nearly all colleges require a letter of recommendation from the applicant's high school guidance counselor. Some counselors will give students an essay question that they feel will give them the background they need in order to structure a recommendation. Other counselors will canvass a wide array of individuals who know a student in order to gather a broader picture of the student in various settings. No one approach is better than the other. Find out which approach is used at your school. You will probably get this information as a handout at one of those evening guidance programs or in a classroom presentation by your school's guidance department. If you are still not sure you know what is expected of you or if the dog has eaten those papers, ask your guidance counselor what is due and by what date. Make sure that you complete the materials on time and that you set aside enough of your time to do them justice.

Teacher Recommendations

In addition to the recommendation from your counselor, colleges may request additional recommendations from your teachers. Known as formal recommendations, these are sent directly to the colleges by your subject teachers. Most colleges require at least one formal recommendation in addition to the counselor's recommendation. However, many competitive institutions require two, if not three, academic recommendations. Follow a school's directions regarding the exact number. A good rule-of-thumb is to have recommendations from teachers in two subject areas (e.g., English and math).

Approach your recommendation writers personally to request that they write for you. They may agree. On the other hand, you may be met with a polite refusal on the order of "I'm sorry, but I'm unable to write for you. I've been approached by so many seniors already that it would be difficult for me to accomplish your recommendation by your due dates." This teacher may really be overburdened with requests for recommendations, especially if this is a senior English teacher, or the teacher may be giving you a signal that someone else may be able to write a stronger piece for you. Either way, accept the refusal politely, and seek another recommendation writer.

How do you decide whom to ask? Here are some questions to help you select your writers:

- How well does the teacher know you?

- Has the teacher taught you for more than one course? (A teacher who taught you over a two- to three-year period has seen your talents and skills develop.)

- Has the teacher sponsored an extracurricular activity in which you made a contribution?

- Do you get along with the teacher?

- Does the college/university indicate that a recommendation is required or recommended from a particular subject-area instructor?

- If you declare an intended major, can you obtain a recommendation from a teacher in that subject area?

Other Recommendation Writers

Consider getting recommendations from your employer, your rabbi or pastor, the director of the summer camp where you worked for the last two summers, and so on—but only if these additional letters are going to reveal information about you that will have a profound impact on the way a college will view your candidacy. Otherwise, you run the risk of overloading your application with too much paper.

WRITING THE APPLICATION ESSAY

Application essays show how you think and how you write. They also reveal additional information about you that is not in your other application material. Not all colleges require essays, and those that do often have a preferred topic. Make sure you write about the topic that is specified and keep to the length of pages or words. If the essay asks for 300 words, don't submit 50 or 500. Some examples of essay topics include:

Tell us about yourself. Describe your personality and a special accomplishment. Illustrate the unique aspects of who you are, what you do, and what you want out of life. Share an experience that made an impact on you, or write about something you have learned from your parents.

Tell us about an academic or extracurricular interest or idea. Show how a book, experience, quotation, or idea reflects or shapes your outlook and aspirations.

Tell us why you want to come to our college. Explain why your goals and interests match the programs and offerings of that particular school. This question requires some research about the school. Be specific.

Show us an imaginative side of your personality. This question demands originality but is a great opportunity to show off your skills as a writer. Start writing down your thoughts and impressions well before the essay is due. Think about how you have changed over the years so that if and when it comes time to write about yourself, you will have plenty of information. Write about something that means a lot to you, and support your thoughts with reasons and examples. Then explain why you care about your topic.

The essay should not be a summary of your high school career. Describe yourself as others see you, and use a natural, conversational style. Use an experience to set the scene in which you will illustrate something about yourself. For example, you might discuss how having a disabled relative helped you to appreciate life's simple pleasures. Or you may use your athletic experiences to tell how you learned the value of teamwork. The essay is your chance to tell something positive

FROM THE GUIDANCE OFFICE

Q: What's a big mistake high school athletes make when thinking about college?

A: Some athletes think that their athletic ability alone will get them a scholarship and do not believe that their academics must be acceptable. The Division I or II schools cannot offer scholarships if the student has not met the academic standards required by the school for admission. Our counselors start reminding students in the freshman year and every year after that the courses they take do make a difference in how colleges view their transcripts. Students can't start preparing in their senior year of high school.

Sue Bradshaw
Guidance Counselor
Sterling High School
Baytown, Texas

or enriching about yourself, so highlight an experience that will make the reader interested in you.

Outline in the essay what you have to offer the college. Explain why you want to attend the institution and how your abilities and goals match the strengths and offerings at the university. Write, rewrite, and edit. Do not try to dash off an essay in one sitting. The essay will improve with time and thought. Proofread and concentrate on spelling, punctuation, and content. Have someone else take a look at your essay. Keep copies to save after mailing, e-mailing, or uploading the original.

Admission officers look for the person inside the essay. They seek students with a breadth of knowledge and experiences, someone with depth and perspective. Inner strength and commitment are admired, too. Not everyone is a winner all the time. The essay is a tool you can use to develop your competitive edge. Your essay should explain why you should be admitted over other applicants.

As a final word, write the essay from the heart. It should have life but not be contrived or one-dimensional. Avoid telling them what they want to hear; instead, be yourself.

Special Information for Athletes

If you weren't a planner before, but you want to play sports while in college or go to college on an athletic scholarship, you'd better become a planner now. There are many regulations and conditions you need to know ahead of time so that you don't miss out on possible opportunities.

First, think about whether or not you have what it takes to play college sports. It's a tough question to ask, but it's a necessary one. In general, playing college sports requires both basic skills and natural ability, a solid knowledge of the sport, overall body strength, speed, and sound academics. Today's athletes are stronger and faster because of improved methods of training and conditioning. They are coached in skills and techniques, and they begin training in their sport at an early age. Remember, your talents will be compared with those from across the United States and around the world.

Second, know the background. Most college athletic programs are regulated by the National Collegiate Athletic Association (NCAA), an organization that has established rules on eligibility, recruiting, and financial aid. The NCAA has three membership divisions: Division I, Division II, and Division III. Institutions are members of one or another division according to the size and scope of their athletic programs and whether they provide athletic scholarships.

If you are planning to enroll in college as a freshman and you wish to participate in Division I or Division II athletics, you must be certified by the NCAA Eligibility Center (https://web1.ncaa.org/eligibilitycenter). The Center was established as a separate organization by the NCAA member institutions to ensure consistent interpretation of NCAA eligibility requirements for all prospective student athletes at all member institutions.

You should start the certification process when you are a junior in high school. Check with your counselor to make sure you are taking a core curriculum that meets NCAA requirements. Also, register to take the ACT or SAT as a junior. Submit your Student Release Form (available in your guidance counseling office) to the Center by the beginning of your senior year.

INITIAL ELIGIBILITY OF FRESHMAN ATHLETES FOR DIVISION I AND II

Students who plan to participate in NCAA Division I or II college sports must obtain the Student Release Form from their high school, complete it, and send it to the NCAA Eligibility Center. This form authorizes high schools to release student transcripts, including test scores, proof of grades, and other academic information, to the Center. It also authorizes the Center to release this information to the colleges that request it. The form and corresponding fee must be received before any documents will be processed. (Fee waivers are available in some instances. Check with your counselor for fee waiver information.)

Students must also make sure that the Center receives ACT and/or SAT score reports. Students can have score reports sent directly to the Center by entering a specific code (9999) printed in the ACT and SAT registration packets.

Once a year, high schools will send an updated list of approved core courses, which lists each course offering that meets NCAA core course requirements. The Center personnel will validate the form. Thereafter, the Center will determine each student's initial eligibility. Collegiate institutions will request information from the Center on the initial eligibility of prospective student-athletes. The Center will make a certification decision and report it directly to the institution.

Additional information about the Center can be found in the *Guide for the College-Bound Student-Athlete*, published by the NCAA. To get a copy of this guide, visit the NCAA Web site at www.ncaa.org.

NATIONAL ASSOCIATION OF INTERCOLLEGIATE ATHLETICS (NAIA) REGULATIONS

The National Association of Intercollegiate Athletics (NAIA) has different eligibility requirements for student-athletes. To be eligible to participate in intercollegiate athletics as an incoming freshman, two of the following three requirements must be met:

1. Have a minimum overall high school grade point average of 2.0 on a 4.0 scale.

2. Have a composite score of 18 or higher on the ACT or an 860 total score or higher on the SAT Critical Reading and Math sections.

3. Have a top-half final class rank in his or her high school graduating class.

Student-athletes must also have on file at the college an official ACT or SAT score report from the appropriate national testing center. Results reported on the student's high school transcript are not acceptable. Students must request that their test scores be forwarded to the college's admission office.

If you have additional questions about NAIA eligibility, contact them at:

NAIA
1200 Grand Boulevard
Kansas City, Missouri 64106-2304
816-595-8000
www.naia.org

Auditions and Portfolios

If you decide to study the arts, such as theater, music, or fine arts, you may be required to audition or show your portfolio to admissions personnel. The following tips will help you showcase your talents and skills when preparing for an audition or portfolio review.

MUSIC AUDITIONS

High school students who wish to pursue a degree in music, whether it is vocal or instrumental, typically must audition. If you're a singer, prepare at least two pieces in contrasting styles. One should be in a foreign language, if possible. Choose from operatic, show music, or art song repertories, and make sure you memorize each piece. If you're an instrumentalist or pianist, be prepared to play scales and arpeggios, at least one etude or technical study, and a solo work. Instrumental audition pieces need not be memorized. In either field, you may be required to do sight-reading.

When performing music that is sight-read, you should take time to look over the piece and make certain of the key and time signatures before proceeding with the audition. If you're a singer, you should bring a familiar accompanist to the audition.

"My advice is to ask for help from teachers, try to acquire audition information up front, and know more than is required for the audition," says one student. "It is also a good idea to select your audition time and date early."

"Try to perform your solo in front of as many people as you can as many times as possible," says another student. "You may also want to try to get involved in a high school performance."

Programs differ, so students are encouraged to call the college and ask for audition information. In general, music departments seek students who demonstrate technical competence and performance achievement.

Admission to music programs varies in degree of competitiveness, so you should audition at a minimum of three colleges and a maximum of five to amplify your opportunity. The degree of competitiveness also varies by instrument, especially if a renowned musician teaches a certain instrument. Some colleges offer a second audition if you feel you did not audition to your potential. Ideally, you will be accepted into the music program of your choice, but keep in mind that it's possible to not be accepted. You must then make the decision to either pursue a music program at another college or consider another major at that college.

DANCE AUDITIONS

At many four-year colleges, an open class is held the day before auditions. A performance piece that combines improvisation, ballet, modern, and rhythm is taught and then students are expected to perform the piece at auditions. Professors look for coordination, technique, rhythm, degree of movement, and body structure. The dance faculty members also assess your ability to learn and your potential to complete the curriculum. Dance programs vary, so check with the college of your choice for specific information.

ART PORTFOLIOS

A portfolio is simply a collection of your best pieces of artwork. A well-developed portfolio can help you gain acceptance into a prestigious art college and increase your chances of being awarded a scholarship in national portfolio competitions. The pieces you select to put in your portfolio should demonstrate your interest and aptitude for a serious education in the arts and should show diversity in technique and variety in subject matter. You may show work in any medium (oils, photography, watercolors, pastels, etc.) and in either black-and-white or color. Your portfolio can include classroom assignments as well as independent projects. You can also include your sketchbook.

Specialized art colleges request that you submit an average of ten pieces of art, but remember that quality is more important than quantity. The admission office staff will review your artwork and transcripts to assess your skill and potential for success. Some schools have you present your portfolio in person; however, some schools allow students to mail artwork if distance is an issue. There is no simple formula for success other than hard work. In addition, there is no such thing as a "perfect portfolio," nor any specific style or direction to achieve one.

Tips for Pulling Your Portfolio Together

- ☑ Try to make your portfolio as clean and organized as possible.

- ☑ It is important to protect your work, but make sure the package you select is easy to handle and does not interfere with the viewing of the artwork.

- ☑ Drawings that have been rolled up are difficult for the jurors to handle and view. You may shrink-wrap the pieces, but it is not required.

- ☑ Avoid loose sheets of paper between pieces. Always spray fixative on any pieces that could smudge.

- ☑ If you choose to mount or mat your work (not required), use only neutral gray tones, black, or white.

- ☑ Slides should be presented in a standard 8 x 11 plastic slide sleeve.

- ☑ Label each piece with your name, address, and high school.

THEATER AUDITIONS

Most liberal arts colleges do not require that students audition to be accepted into the theater department unless they offer a Bachelor of Fine Arts (B.F.A.) degree in theater. You should apply to the college of your choice prior to scheduling an audition. You should also consider spending a full day on campus so that you may talk with theater faculty members and students, attend classes, meet with your admission counselor, and tour the facilities.

Although each college and university has different requirements, you should prepare two contrasting monologues taken from plays of your choice if you're auditioning for a B.F.A. acting program. Musical theater requirements generally consist of one up-tempo musical selection and one ballad, as well as one monologue from a play or musical of your choice. The total of all your pieces should not exceed 5 minutes. Music for the accompanist, a resume of your theater experience, and a photo are also required.

Tips to Get You Successfully through an Audition

- ☑ Choose material suitable for your age.

- ☑ If you choose your monologue from a book of monologues, you should read the entire play and be familiar with the context of your selection.

- ☑ Select a monologue that allows you to speak directly to another person; you should play only one character.

- ☑ Memorize your selection.

- ☑ Avoid using characterization or style, as they tend to trap you rather than tapping deeper into inner resources.

WHAT TO EXPECT IN COLLEGE

No one can fill in all the details of what you'll find once you begin college. However, here's some information about a few of the bigger questions you might have, such as how to choose your classes or major and how you can make the most of your life outside the classroom.

Choosing Your Classes

College is designed to give you freedom, but at the same time, it teaches you responsibility. You will probably have more free time than in high school, but you will also have more class material to master. Your parents may entrust you with more money, but it is up to you to make sure there's enough money in your bank account when school fees are due. The same principle applies to your class schedule: You will have more decision-making power than ever, but you also need to know and meet the requirements for graduation.

To guide you through the maze of requirements, all students are given an adviser. This person, typically a faculty member, will help you select classes that meet your interests and graduation requirements. During your first year or two at college, you and your adviser will choose classes that meet general education requirements and select electives, or non-required classes, that pique your interests. Early on, it is a good idea to take a lot of general education classes. They are meant to expose you to new ideas and help you explore possible majors. Once you have selected a major, you will be given an adviser for that particular area of study. This person will help you understand and meet the requirements for that major.

In addition to talking to your adviser, talk to other students who have already taken a class you're interested in and who really enjoyed how a professor taught the class. Then try to get into that professor's class when registering. Remember, a dynamic professor can make a dry subject engaging. A boring professor can make an engaging subject dry.

As you move through college, you will notice that focusing on the professor is more important than focusing on the course title. Class titles can be cleverly crafted. They can sound captivating. However, the advice above still holds true: "Pop Culture and Icons" could turn out to be awful, and "Beowulf and Old English" could be a blast.

When you plan your schedule, watch how many heavy reading classes you take in one semester. You don't want to live in the library or the dorm study lounge. In general, the humanities, such as history, English, philosophy, and theology, involve a lot of reading. Math and science classes involve less reading; they focus more on solving problems.

Finally, don't be afraid to schedule a fun class. Even the most intense program of study will let you take a few electives. So take a deep breath, dig in, and explore!

Choosing Your Major

You can choose from hundreds of majors—from accounting to zoology—but which is right for you? Should you choose something traditional or select a major from an emerging area? Perhaps you already know what career you want, so you can work backward to decide which major will best help you achieve your goals.

If you know what you want to do early in life, you will have more time to plan your high school curriculum, extracurricular activities, jobs, and community service to coincide with your college major. Your college selection process may also focus upon the schools that provide strong academic programs in a certain major.

WHERE DO I BEGIN?

Choosing a major usually starts with an assessment of your career interests. Picture yourself taking classes, writing papers, making presentations, conducting research, or working in a related field. Talk to people you know who work in your fields of interest and see if you like what you hear. Also, try reading the classified ads in your local newspaper. What jobs sound interesting to you? Which ones pay the salary that you'd like to make? What level of education is required in the ads you find interesting? Select a few jobs that you think you'd like and then consult the following list of majors to see which major(s) coincide. If your area of interest does not appear here, talk to your counselor or teacher about where to find information on that particular subject.

MAJORS AND RELATED CAREERS

Agriculture

Many agriculture majors apply their knowledge directly on farms and ranches. Others work in industry (food, farm equipment, and agricultural supply companies), federal agencies (primarily in the Departments of Agriculture and the Interior), and state and local farm and agricultural agencies. Jobs might be in research and lab work, marketing and sales, advertising and public relations, or journalism and radio/TV (for farm communications media). Agriculture majors also pursue further training in biological sciences, animal health, veterinary medicine, agribusiness management, vocational agriculture education, nutrition and dietetics, and rural sociology.

Architecture

Architecture and related design fields focus on the built environment as distinct from the natural environment of the agriculturist or the conservationist. Career possibilities include drafting, design, and project administration in architectural, engineering, landscape design, interior design, industrial design, planning, real estate, and construction firms; government agencies involved in construction, housing, highways, and parks and recreation; and government and nonprofit organizations interested in historic or architectural preservation.

Area/Ethnic Studies

The research, writing, analysis, critical thinking, and cultural awareness skills acquired by area/ethnic studies majors, combined with the expertise gained in a particular area, make this group of majors valuable in a number of professions. Majors find positions in administration, education, public relations, and communications in such organizations as cultural, government, international, and (ethnic) community agencies; international trade (import-export); social service agencies; and the communications industry (journalism, radio, and TV). These studies also provide a good background for further training in law, business management, public administration, education, social work, museum and library work, and international relations.

Arts

Art majors most often use their training to become practicing artists, though the settings in which they work vary. Aside from the most obvious art-related career—that of the self-employed artist or craftsperson—many fields require the skills of a visual artist. These include advertising; public relations; publishing; journalism; museum work; television, movies, and theater; community and social service agencies concerned with education, recreation, and entertainment; and teaching. A background in art is also useful if a student wishes to pursue art therapy, arts or museum administration, or library work.

Biological Sciences

The biological sciences include the study of living organisms from the level of molecules to that of populations. Majors find jobs in industry; government agencies; technical writing, editing, or illustrating; science reporting; secondary school teaching (which usually requires education courses); and research and laboratory analysis and testing. Biological sciences are also a sound foundation for further study in medicine, psychology, health and hospital administration, and biologically oriented engineering.

Business

Business majors comprise all the basic business disciplines. At the undergraduate level, students can major in a general business administration program or specialize in a particular area, such as marketing or accounting. These studies lead not only to positions in business and industry but also to management positions in other sectors. Management-related studies include the general management areas (accounting, finance, marketing, and management) as well as special studies related to a particular type of organization or industry. Management-related majors may be offered in a business school or in a department dealing with the area in which the management skills are to be applied. Careers can be found throughout the business world.

Communication

Jobs in communication range from reporting (news and special features), copywriting, technical writing, copyediting, and programming to advertising, public relations, media sales, and market research. Such positions can be found at newspapers, radio and TV stations, publishing houses (book and magazine), advertising agencies, corporate communications departments, government agencies, universities, and firms that specialize in educational and training materials.

Computer, Information, and Library Sciences

Computer and information science and systems majors stress the theoretical aspects of the computer and emphasize mathematical and scientific disciplines. Data processing, programming, and computer technology programs tend to be more practical; they are more oriented toward business than to scientific applications and to working directly with the computer or with peripheral equipment. Career possibilities for computer and information science majors include data processing, programming, and systems development or maintenance in almost any setting: business and industry, banking and finance, government, colleges and universities, libraries, software firms, service bureaus, computer manufacturers, publishing, and communications.

Library science gives preprofessional background in library work and provides valuable knowledge of research sources, indexing, abstracting, computer technology, and media technology, which is useful for further study in any professional field. In most cases, a master's degree in library science is necessary to obtain a job as a librarian. Library science majors find positions in public, school, college, corporate, and government libraries and research centers; book publishing (especially reference books); database and information retrieval services; and communications (especially audiovisual media).

Education

Positions as teachers in public elementary and secondary schools, private day and boarding schools, religious and parochial schools, vocational schools, and proprietary schools are the jobs most often filled by education majors. However, teaching positions also exist in noneducational institutions, such as museums, historical societies, prisons, hospitals, and nursing homes, as well as jobs as educators and trainers in government and industry. Administrative (nonteaching) positions in employee relations and personnel, public relations, marketing and sales, educational publishing, TV and film media, test development firms, and government and community social service agencies also tap the skills and interests of education majors.

Engineering and Science Technology

Engineering and science technology majors prepare students for practical design and production work rather than for jobs that require more theoretical, scientific, and mathematical knowledge. Engineers work in a variety of fields, including aeronautics, bioengineering, geology, nuclear engineering, and quality control and safety. Industry, research labs, and government agencies where technology plays a key role, such as in manufacturing, electronics, construction communications, transportation, and utilities, hire engineering as well as engineering technology and science technology graduates regularly. Work may be in technical activities (research, development, design, production, testing, scientific programming, or systems analysis) or in nontechnical areas where a technical degree is needed, such as marketing, sales, or administration.

Family and Consumer Sciences and Social Services

Home economics encompasses many different fields—basic studies in foods and textiles as well as consumer economics and leisure studies—that overlap with aspects of agriculture, social science, and education. Jobs can be found in government and community agencies (especially those in education, health, housing, or human services), nursing homes, child-care centers, journalism, radio/TV, educational media, and publishing. Types of work also include marketing, sales, and customer service in consumer-related industries, such as food processing and packaging, appliance manufacturing, utilities, textiles, and secondary school home economics teaching (which usually requires education courses).

Majors in social services find administrative positions in government and community health, welfare, and social service agencies, such as hospitals, clinics, YMCAs and YWCAs, recreation commissions, welfare agencies, and employment services.

Foreign Language and Literature

Knowledge of foreign languages and cultures is increasingly recognized as important in today's international world. Language majors possess a skill that is used in organizations with international dealings as well as in career fields and geographical areas where languages other than English are prominent. Career possibilities include positions with business firms with international subsidiaries; import-export firms; international banking; travel agencies; airlines; tourist services; government and international agencies dealing with international affairs, foreign trade, diplomacy, customs, or immigration; secondary school foreign language teaching and bilingual education (which usually require education courses); freelance translating and interpreting (high level of skill necessary); foreign language publishing; and computer programming (especially for linguistics majors).

Health Professions

Health professions majors, while having a scientific core, are more focused on applying the results of scientific investigation than on the scientific disciplines themselves. Allied health majors prepare graduates to assist health professionals in providing diagnostics, therapeutics, and rehabilitation. Medical science majors, such as optometry, pharmacy, and the premedical profession sequences, are, for the most part, preprofessional studies that comprise the scientific disciplines necessary for admission to graduate or professional school in the health or medical fields. Health service and technology majors prepare students for positions in the health fields that primarily involve services to patients or working with complex machinery and materials. Medical technologies cover a wide range of fields, such as cytotechnology, biomedical technologies, and operating room technology.

Administrative, professional, or research assistant positions in health agencies, hospitals, occupational health units in industry, community and school health departments, government agencies (public health, environmental protection), and international health organizations are available to majors in health fields, as are jobs in marketing and sales of health-related products and services, health education (with education courses), advertising and public relations, journalism and publishing, and technical writing.

Humanities (Miscellaneous)

The majors that constitute the humanities (sometimes called "letters") are the most general and widely applicable and the least vocationally oriented of the liberal arts. They are essentially studies of the ideas and concerns of human kind. These include classics, history of philosophy, history of science, linguistics, and medieval studies. Career possibilities for humanities majors can be found in business firms, government and community agencies, advertising and public relations, marketing and sales, publishing, journalism and radio/TV, secondary school teaching in English and literature (which usually requires education courses), freelance writing and editing, and computer programming (especially for those with a background in logic or linguistics).

Law and Legal Studies

Students of legal studies can use their knowledge of law and government in fields involving the making, breaking, and enforcement of laws; the crimes, trials, and punishment of law breakers; and the running of all branches of government at local, state, and federal levels. Graduates find positions of all types in law firms, legal departments of other organizations, the court or prison system, government agencies (such as law enforcement agencies or offices of state and federal attorneys general), and police departments.

Mathematics and Physical Sciences

Mathematics is the science of numbers and the abstract formulation of their operations. Physical sciences involve the study of the laws and structures of physical matter. The quantitative skills acquired through the study of science and mathematics are especially useful for computer-related careers. Career possibilities include positions in industry (manufacturing and processing companies, electronics firms, defense contractors, consulting firms); government agencies (defense, environmental protection, law enforcement); scientific/technical writing, editing, or illustrating; journalism (science reporting); secondary school teaching (usually requiring education courses); research and laboratory analysis and testing; statistical analysis; computer programming; systems analysis; surveying and mapping; weather forecasting; and technical sales.

Natural Resources

A major in the natural resources field prepares students for work in areas as generalized as environmental conservation and as specialized as groundwater contamination. Jobs are available in industry (food, energy, natural resources, and pulp and paper companies), consulting firms, state and federal government agencies (primarily the Departments of Agriculture and the Interior), and public and private conservation agencies. See the "Agriculture" and "Biological Sciences" sections for more information on natural resources–related fields.

Psychology

Psychology majors involve the study of behavior and can range from the biological to the sociological. Students can study individual behavior, usually that of humans, or the behavior of crowds. Students of psychology do not always go into the obvious clinical fields, the fields in which psychologists work with patients. Certain areas of psychology, such as industrial/organizational, experimental, and social, are not clinically oriented. Psychology and counseling careers can be in government (such as mental health agencies), schools, hospitals, clinics, private practice, industry, test development firms, social work, and personnel. The careers listed in the "Social Sciences" section are also pursued by psychology and counseling majors.

Religion

Religion majors are usually seen as preprofessional studies for those who are interested in entering the ministry. Career possibilities for religion also include casework, youth counseling, administration in community and social service organizations, teaching in religious educational institutions, and writing for religious and lay publications. Religious studies also prepare students for the kinds of jobs other humanities majors often pursue.

Social Sciences

Social sciences majors study people in relation to their society. Thus, social science majors can apply their education to a wide range of occupations that deal with social issues and activities. Career opportunities are varied. People with degrees in the social sciences find careers in government, business, community agencies (serving children, youth, and senior citizens), advertising and public relations, marketing and sales, secondary school social studies teaching (with education courses), casework, law enforcement, parks and recreation, museum work (especially for anthropology, archaeology, geography, and history majors), preservation (especially for anthropology, archaeology, geography, and history majors), banking and finance (especially for economics majors), market and survey research, statistical analysis, publishing, fundraising and development, and political campaigning.

Technologies

Technology majors, along with trade fields, are most often offered as two-year programs. Majors in technology fields prepare students directly for jobs; however, positions are in practical design and production work rather than in areas that require more theoretical, scientific, and mathematical knowledge. Engineering technologies prepare students with the basic training in specific fields (e.g., electronics, mechanics, or chemistry) that are necessary to become technicians on the support staffs of engineers. Other technology majors center more on maintenance and repair. Work may be in technical activities, such as production or testing, or in nontechnical areas where a technical degree is needed, such as marketing, sales, or administration. Industries, research labs, and government agencies in which technology plays a key role—such as in manufacturing, electronics, construction, communications, transportation, and utilities—hire technology graduates regularly.

STILL UNSURE?

Relax! You don't have to know your major before you enroll in college. More than half of all freshmen are undecided when they start school and prefer to get a feel for what's available at college before making a decision. Most four-year colleges don't require students to formally declare a major until the end of their sophomore year or beginning of their junior year. Part of the experience of college is being exposed to new subjects and new ideas. Chances are your high school never offered anthropology. Or marine biology. Or applied mathematics. So take these classes and follow your interests. While you're fulfilling your general course requirements, you might stumble upon a major that appeals to you, or maybe you'll discover a new interest while you're volunteering or participating in other extracurricular activities. Talking to other students might lead to new options you'll want to explore.

CAN I CHANGE MY MAJOR IF I CHANGE MY MIND?

Choosing a major does not set your future in stone, nor does it necessarily disrupt your life if you need to change your major. However, there are advantages to choosing a major sooner rather than later. If you wait too long to choose, you may have to take additional classes to satisfy the requirements, which may cost you additional time and money.

The Other Side of College: Having Fun!

There is more to college than writing papers, reading books, and sitting through lectures. Your social life plays an integral part in your college experience.

MEETING NEW PEOPLE

The easiest time to meet new people is at the beginning of something new. New situations shake people up and make them feel just uncomfortable enough to take the risk of extending their hand in friendship. Fortunately for you, college is filled with new experiences. There are the first weeks of being the newest students. This can be quickly followed by being a new member of a club or activity. And with each passing semester, you will be in new classes with new teachers and new faces. College should be a time of constantly challenging and expanding yourself, so never feel that it is too late to meet new people.

But just how do you take that first step in forming a relationship? It's surprisingly easy. Be open to the opportunities of meeting new people and having new experiences. Join clubs and activities. Investigate rock-climbing. Try hip-hop. Write for the school paper. But most of all, get involved.

CAMPUS ACTIVITIES

College life will place a lot of demands on you. Your classes will be challenging. Your professors will expect more from you. You will have to budget and manage your own money. But there is a plus side you probably haven't thought of yet: college students do have free time.

The average student spends about 3 hours a day in class. Add to this the time you will need to spend studying, eating, and socializing, and you will still have time to spare. One of the best ways to use this time is to participate in campus activities.

Intramural Sports

Intramurals are sports played for competition between members of the same campus community. They provide competition and a sense of belonging without the same level of intensity in practice schedules. Anyone can join an intramural sport. Often there are teams formed by dormitories, sororities, or fraternities that play team sports such as soccer, volleyball, basketball, flag-football, baseball, and softball. There are also individual intramural sports such as swimming, golf, wrestling, and diving. If you want to get involved, just stop by your school's intramural office.

Student Government

Student government will be set up in a way that is probably similar to your high school. Students form committees and run for office. However, student government in college has more power than in high school. The officers address all of their class's concerns directly to the President of the college or university and the Board of Trustees. Most student governments have a branch responsible for student activities that brings in big name entertainers and controversial speakers. You may want to get involved to see how such contacts are made and appearances negotiated.

Community Service

Another aspect of student life is volunteering, commonly called community service. Many colleges offer a range of opportunities. Some allow you to simply commit an afternoon to a cause, such as passing out food at a food bank. Others require an ongoing commitment. For example, you might decide to help an adult learn to read every Thursday at 4 p.m. for three months. Some colleges will link a service commitment with class credit. This will enhance your learning, giving you some real-world experience. Be sure to stop by your community service office and see what is available.

Clubs

There are a variety of clubs on most college campuses spanning just about every topic you can imagine. Amnesty International regularly meets on most campuses to write letters to help free prisoners in foreign lands. Most college majors band together in a club to discuss their common interests and career potential. There are also clubs that are based on the use of certain computer software or that engage in outdoor activities like sailing or downhill skiing. The list is endless. If you cannot find a club for your interest, consider starting one of your own. Stop by the student government office to see what rules you will need to follow. You will also need to find a location to hold meetings and post signs to advertise your club. When you hold your first meeting, you will probably be surprised at how many people are willing to take a chance and try a new club.

Greek Life

A major misconception of Greek life is that it revolves around wild parties and alcohol. In fact, the vast majority of fraternities and sororities focus on instilling values of scholarship, friendship, leadership, and service in their members. From this point forward, we will refer to both fraternities and sororities as fraternities.

Scholarship

A fraternity experience helps you make the academic transition from high school to college. Although the classes taken in high school are challenging, they'll be even harder in college. Fraternities almost always require members to meet certain academic standards. Many hold mandatory study times, keep old class notes and exams on file for study purposes, and make personal tutors available. Members of a fraternity have a natural vested interest in seeing that other members succeed academically, so older members often assist younger members with their studies.

Friendship

Social life is an important component of Greek life. Social functions offer an excellent opportunity for freshmen to become better acquainted with others in the chapter. Whether it is a Halloween party or a formal dance, there are numerous chances for members to develop poise and confidence. By participating in these functions, students enrich friendships and build memories that will last a lifetime. Remember, social functions aren't only parties; they can include such activities as intramural sports and Homecoming.

Leadership

Because fraternities are self-governing organizations, leadership opportunities abound. Students are given hands-on experience in leading committees, managing budgets, and interacting with faculty members and administrators. Most houses have as many as ten officers, along with an array of committee members. By becoming actively involved in leadership roles, students gain valuable experience that is essential for a successful career. Interestingly, although Greeks represent less than 10 percent of most undergraduate student populations, they often hold the majority of leadership positions on campus.

Service

According to the North-American Interfraternity Council, fraternities are increasingly involved in philanthropies and hands-on service projects. Helping less fortunate people is a major focus of Greek life. This can vary from work with Easter Seals, blood drives, and food pantry collections to community upkeep, such as picking up trash, painting houses, or cleaning up area parks. Greeks also get involved in projects with organizations such as Habitat for Humanity, the

American Heart Association, and Children's Miracle Network. By being involved in philanthropic projects, students not only raise money for worthwhile causes, they also gain a deeper insight into themselves and their responsibility to the community.

Roommates

When you arrive on campus, you will face a daunting task: to live peacefully with a stranger for the rest of the academic year.

To make this task easier, most schools use some type of room assignment survey. This can make roommate matches more successful. For example, two people who prefer to stay up late and play guitar can be matched, while two people who prefer to rise at dawn and hit the track can be a pair. Such differences are easy to ask about on a survey and easy for students to report. However, surveys cannot ask everything, and chances are pretty good that something about your roommate is going to get on your nerves.

In order to avoid conflict, plan ahead. When you first meet, work out some ground rules. Most schools have roommates write a contract together and sign it during the first week of school. Ground rules help eliminate conflict from the start by allowing each person to know what is expected. You should consider the following areas: privacy, quiet time, chores, and borrowing.

When considering privacy, think about how much time alone you need each day and how you and your roommate will arrange for private time. Class schedules usually give you some alone time. Be aware of this; if your class is cancelled, consider going for a cup of coffee or a browse in the bookstore instead of immediately rushing back to your room. Privacy also relates to giving your roommate space when he or she has had a bad day or just needs time to think. Set up clear hours for quiet time. Your dorm may already have some quiet hours established. You can choose to simply reiterate those or add additional time. Just be clear.

Two other potentially stormy issues are chores and borrowing. If there are cleaning chores that need to be shared, make a schedule and stick to it. No one appreciates a sink full of dirty dishes or a dingy shower. Remember the golden rule: do your chores as you wish your roommate would. When it comes to borrowing, set up clear rules. The safest bet is to not allow it; but if you do, limit when, for how long, and what will be done in case of damage.

Another issue many students confront is whether or not to live with a best friend from high school who is attending the same college. Generally, this is a bad idea for several reasons. First, you may think you know your best friend inside and out, but you may be surprised by his or her personal living habits. There is nothing like the closeness of a dorm room to reveal the annoying routines of your friend. Plus, personalities can change rapidly in college. Once you are away from home, you may be surprised at how you or your friend transforms from shy and introverted to late night partygoer. This can cause conflict. A final downfall is that the two of you will stick together like glue in the first few weeks and miss out on opportunities to meet other people.

Armed with this information, you should have a smooth year with your new roommate. But just in case you are the exception, most colleges do allow students who absolutely cannot get along to move. Prior to moving, each student must usually go through a dispute resolution process. This typically involves your Resident Adviser, you, and your roommate trying to work through your problems in a structured way.

Living with a roommate can be challenging at times, but the ultimate rewards—meeting someone new, encountering new ideas, and learning how to compromise—will serve you well later in life. Enjoy your roommate and all the experiences you will have, both good and bad, for they are all part of the college experience.

Commuting from Home

For some students, home during the college years is the same house in which they grew up. Whether you are in this situation because you can't afford to live on campus or because you'd just rather live at home with your family, some basic guidelines will keep you connected with campus life.

By all means, do not just go straight home after class. Spend some of your free time at school. Usually there is a student union or a coffee shop where students gather and socialize. Make it a point to go there and talk to people between classes. Also, get involved in extracurricular activities, and visit classmates in the dorms.

If you drive to school, find other students who want to carpool. Most schools have a commuters' office or club that will give you a list of people who live near you. Sharing a car ride will give you time to talk and form a relationship with someone else who knows about the challenges of commuting.

Commuters' clubs also sponsor a variety of activities throughout the year—give them a try! Be sure also to consider the variety of activities open to all members of the student body, ranging from student government to community service to intramural sports. You may find this takes a bit more effort on your part, but the payoff in the close friendships you'll form will more than make up for it.

What If You Don't Like the College You Pick?

In the best of all worlds, you compile a list of colleges, find the most compatible one, and are accepted. You have a great time, learn a lot, graduate, and head off to a budding career. However, you may find the college you chose isn't the best of all worlds. Imagine these scenarios:

- Halfway through your first semester of college, you come to the distressing conclusion that you can't stand being there for whatever reason. The courses don't match your interests. The campus is out in the boonies, and you don't ever want to see another cow. The selection of extracurricular activities doesn't cut it.

- You have methodically planned to go to a community college for two years and move to a four-year college to complete your degree. Transferring takes you nearer to your goal.

- You thought you wanted to major in art, but by the end of the first semester, you find yourself more interested in English lit. Things get confusing, so you drop out of college to sort out your thoughts and now you want to drop back in, hoping to rescue some of those credits.

HOMESICKNESS

Homesickness in its most basic form is a longing for the stuff of home: your parents, friends, bedroom, school, and all of the other familiar people and objects that make you comfortable. But on another level, homesickness is a longing to go back in time. Moving away to college forces you to take on new responsibilities and begin to act like an adult. This can be scary.

While this condition is often described as a "sickness," no pill will provide a quick fix. Instead, you need to acknowledge that your feelings are a normal reaction to a significant change in your life. Allow yourself to feel the sadness of moving on in life and be open to conversations about it that may crop up in your dorm or among your new friends. After all, everyone is dealing with this issue. Then, make an effort to create a new home and a new life on campus. Create new habits and routines so that this once-strange place becomes familiar. Join activities and engage in campus life. This will help you to create a feeling of belonging that will ultimately be the key to overcoming homesickness.

- You didn't do that well in high school—socializing got in the way of studying. But you've wised up, have gotten serious about your future, and two years of community college have brightened your prospects of transferring to a four-year institution.

Circumstances shift, people change, and, realistically speaking, it's not all that uncommon to transfer. Many people do. The reasons why students transfer run the gamut, as do the institutional policies that govern them. The most common transfers are students who move from a two-year to a four-year university or the person who opts for a career change midstream.

If your plan is to attend a two-year college with the ultimate goal of transferring to a four-year school, you'll be pleased to know that the increased importance of the community college route to a bachelor's degree is recognized by all segments of higher education. As a result, many two-year schools have revised their course outlines and established new courses in order to comply with the programs and curricular offerings of the universities. Institutional improvements to make transferring easier have also proliferated at both the two- and four-year levels. The generous transfer policies of the Pennsylvania, New York, and Florida state university systems, among others, reflect this attitude; these systems accept all credits from students who have graduated from accredited community colleges.

If you are interested in moving from a two-year college to a four-year school, the sooner you make up your mind that you are going to make the switch, the better position you will be in to transfer successfully (that is, without having wasted valuable time and credits). The ideal point at which to make such a decision is before you register for classes at your two-year school; a counselor can help you plan your course work with an eye toward fulfilling the requirements needed for your major course of study.

Naturally, it is not always possible to plan your transferring strategy that far in advance, but keep in mind that the key to a successful transfer is preparation, and preparation takes time—time to think through your objectives and time to plan the right classes to take.

Here are some commonly asked questions—and their answers:

QUESTION: Do students who go directly from high school to a four-year college do better academically than transfer students from community colleges?

ANSWER: On the contrary: some institutions report that transfers from two-year schools who persevere until graduation do better than those who started as freshmen in a four-year college.

QUESTION: Why is it so important that my two-year college be accredited?

ANSWER: Four-year colleges and universities accept transfer credits only from schools formally recognized by a regional, national, or professional educational agency. This accreditation signifies that an institution or program meets or exceeds a minimum level of educational quality necessary for meeting stated educational objectives.

QUESTION: What do I need to do to transfer?

ANSWER: First, send for your high school and college transcripts. Having chosen the school you wish to transfer to, check its admission requirements against your transcripts. If you find that you are admissible, file an application as early as possible before the deadline. Part of the process will be asking your former schools to send official transcripts to the admission office— not the copies you used in determining your admissibility.

Plan your transfer program with the head of your new department as soon as you have decided to transfer. Determine the recommended general education pattern and necessary preparation for your major. At your present school, take the courses you will need to meet transfer requirements for the new school.

QUESTION: What qualifies me for admission as a transfer student?

ANSWER: Admission requirements for most four-year institutions vary. Depending on the reputation or popularity of the school and program you wish to enter, requirements may be quite selective and competitive. Usually, you will need to show satisfactory test scores, an academic record up to a certain standard, and completion of specific subject matter.

Transfer students can be eligible to enter a four-year school in a number of ways: by having been eligible for admission directly upon graduation from high school, by making up shortcomings in grades (or in subject matter not covered in high school) at a community college, or by satisfactory completion of necessary courses or credit hours at another postsecondary institution. Ordinarily, students coming from a community college or from another four-year institution must meet or exceed the receiving institution's standards for freshmen and show appropriate college-level course work taken since high school. If necessary, students can also present proof of proficiency through results on the General Educational Development (GED) test.

QUESTION: Is it possible to transfer courses from several different institutions?

ANSWER: Institutions ordinarily accept the courses that they consider transferable, regardless of the number of accredited schools involved. However, there is the danger of exceeding the maximum number of credit hours that can be transferred from all other schools or earned through credit by examination, extension courses, or correspondence courses. The limit placed on transfer credits varies from school to school, so read the catalog carefully to avoid taking courses you won't be able to use. To avoid duplicating courses, keep attendance at different campuses to a minimum.

QUESTION: Which is more important for transfer—my grade point average or my course completion pattern?

ANSWER: Some schools believe that your past grades indicate academic potential and overshadow prior preparation for a specific degree program. Others require completion of certain introductory courses before transfer to prepare you for upper-division work in your major. In any case, appropriate course selection will cut down the time to graduation and increase your chances of making a successful transfer.

WHO WANTS TO BE A COLLEGE SCHOLARSHIP MILLIONAIRE?

There are high school seniors around the country who are becoming rich beyond their wildest dreams even before stepping inside the hallowed halls of higher education. These college upstarts are not start-up kings and queens, ala Mark Zuckerberg of Facebook fame. But they may be just as innovative. They're a part of small, but growing, elite—the College Scholarship Millionaire Club.

The concept of earning a million dollars for college sounds like the premise of a television game show. And to be honest, such a goal remains incredibly lofty for some and downright impossible for others. But what was once a fantasy of every would-be college student is now fast becoming a reality for those willing to work incredibly hard to make it happen.

So just what is the College Scholarship Millionaire Club? It's a group of students who have won $1 million or more in scholarship commitments from universities and colleges and private scholarship funds. The definition should clue you in on at least one prerequisite for joining this club—you have to apply for scholarships—A LOT OF THEM. Still, a quick analysis of some college scholarship millionaires and how they secured their awards can offer any pre-college student great advice on how to get the most out of their scholarship application season.

While there is no sure fire way to ensure that you earn big bucks in the college scholarship process, anyone promising that is just running a scam, there are steps you can take to increase your odds of having a big scholarship haul. Here are some valuable tips:

Make High-Achieving a Group Sport

More than a decade ago James Ralph Sparks, a calculus teacher at Whitehaven High School (WHS), in Memphis, Tennessee, wanted to find a way to get more of his students into college. Back in 2002, the public school located on Elvis Presley Blvd., wasn't exactly known for its academic aptitude. Back then, graduating seniors were bringing in less than $5 million in scholarship offers for the entire school. But Sparks felt the school could do better. So he created a competition. The 30+ club was the first weapon in the battle to get students more money for college there was only one criterion for membership: a 30 or more on the ACT. By encouraging students to score high on the national standardize test, Sparks ensured that his students would be in the running for top scholarships. Students who achieved entrance into the club had their scholarship offer letters and scores posted on bulletin boards in the school.

But Sparks wasn't finished. He created the Fortune 500 club, providing exclusive membership only to students who could achieve more than $100,000 in scholarships. The combination of the 30+ club and the Fortune 500 club helped to spur students to achieve. The WHS graduating senior class brought in more than $30 million in scholarship offers in 2010–11.

Apply, Apply, and Apply Again

Another facet of the Whitehaven High School's scholarship program was playing the odds. Anyone who has guided students through a college scholarship application understands that the process can become a numbers game. The more applications you complete, the better your chances of securing a scholarship. While the average high school student applies for two to three scholarships, WHS' millionaire club members applied for ten times that number—about thirty or forty.

Become a Super College Candidate

By now everyone applying to college knows you have to do more than get good grades to stand out. If you want to rise to the top of the scholarship heap you're going to have to be extraordinary. You can't just volunteer at your local soup kitchen—that's a given. You might have to start your own soup kitchen to be considered above your peers. To be a part of the million-dollar scholarship club, you're going to have to go above and beyond to pull down that six-figure college gift.

So let's break down what it takes to be a million-dollar scholar:

- **Start early.** It's never too early to research scholarship opportunities as well as plan your scholarship strategy. Practice writing your personal statement, essay, interviewing skills, and so on to get yourself acquainted with the scholarship process.

- **Make applying a group sport.** Everyone loves a good competition, and it seems earning scholarship money is no exception. At Whitehaven High School, teachers publicly list the scholarship earnings of students with more than $100,000. WHS also has a scoreboard in front of its school that highlights scholarship amounts, not just football scores.

- **Don't forget the academics.** Many scholarships have an academic threshold, so you want to make sure to get above that to open more opportunities. Generally, a 30 or more on the ACT and a 1300 or more on the SAT are good baselines to put you in the scholarship category.

- **Keep Your Options Open.** There are critics who say that applying for scholarships you have no intention of using is not appropriate. But how do you know where you want to go until you figure out how to pay for it? Don't pigeon-hole yourself into one option. If you don't get your first-choice, you'll at least have something to fall back upon.

- **Be sincere.** You may think it's all about the numbers, but you become a million-dollar scholar through authenticity not fakery. Apply to scholarships that fit your passion, purpose, and educational prowess. And apply to schools you actually want to attend. Applying for scholarships and grants take time, and you don't want to waste it on pipe dreams.

WINNING THE SCHOLARSHIP WITH A WINNING ESSAY

Who knew it was going to be this hard?

You've already dealt with SO much: the SAT, doing community service, excelling in your AP class, etc. Convincing your parents that you will be fine 1,500 miles from home and that each and every one of those college application fees are, yes, absolutely necessary!

And now in front of you—the scholarship essay.

Much as you may feel like, c'mon, I'm worth it, just give me the scholarship money, we all know it just doesn't work like that. Because you know what—lots of students are worth it! And lots of students are special, just like you! And where does that leave a scholarship selection committee in deciding to whom their money should be awarded? Yes, now you are catching on—they will pour over everyone's scholarship essay.

So, first and foremost, write your scholarship essay in a way that makes it easy for the scholarship-awarding committees to do their job! It's almost like a partnership—you show them (in 500 words, more or less) why YOU ARE THE MOST WORTHY RECIPIENT, and they say, thank you, you are right, here is a scholarship for you and everyone wins! Easy, right?

Sorry, It Really Isn't That Easy

What? You are still sitting there in front of a blank computer screen with nary a thought or sentence? Understood. It's really not that easy. That, too, is part of the point.

No doubt that your GPA, SAT scores, volunteer efforts, leadership roles, and community service are immensely important, but again, you must remember that, during the process of selecting an award recipient, pretty much all the applicants are going to be stellar on some level. And so the scholarship-awarding committee uses your essay to see what sets you apart from the crowd. They are looking for a reason to select you over everyone else.

Your scholarship essay serves many purposes. You have to convince the scholarship-awarding committee you are able to do the following:

- Effectively communicate through the written word

- Substantiate your merit and unique qualities

- Follow directions and adhere to guidelines

A winning scholarship essay can mean up to tens of thousands of dollars for your college education, so let's get started on putting that money in YOUR hands!

Effective Written Communication

BE PASSIONATE

Let's face it—you have already written lots of essays. And, we won't tell, but most were probably about topics that were as interesting to you as watching paint dry, right? But you plowed through them and even managed to get some good grades along the way. You may think about just "plowing through" your scholarship essay the same way—mustering up the same amount of excitement you feel when you have to watch old home videos of your dad on his summer camping trips. But that would be a huge mistake!

An important feature of all winning essays is that they are written on subjects about which the author is truly passionate. Think about it— it actually takes a good bit of effort to fake passion for a subject. But when you are genuinely enthusiastic about something, the words and thoughts flow much more easily and your passion and energy naturally shine through in your writing. Therefore, when you are choosing your scholarship essay topic, be sure it is something you truly care about and can show your affinity for—keeping both you and your reader interested and intrigued!

BE POSITIVE

You've probably heard the expression: "If you don't have anything nice to say, don't say anything at all." Try to steer clear of essays that are too critical, pessimistic, or antagonistic. This doesn't mean that your essay shouldn't acknowledge a serious problem or that everything has to have a happy ending. But it does mean that you should not just write about the negative. If you are writing about a problem, you need to present solutions. If your story doesn't have a happy ending, write about what you learned from the experience and how you would do things differently if faced with a similar situation in the future. Your optimism is what makes the scholarship-awarding committee excited about giving you money to pursue your dreams. Use positive language and be proud to share yourself and your accomplishments. Everyone likes an uplifting story and even scholarship judges want to feel your enthusiasm and zest for life.

BE CLEAR AND CONCISE

Don't fall into the common essay-writing trap of using general statements instead of specific ones. All scholarship judges read at least one essay that starts with "Education is the key to success." And that means nothing to them. What does mean something is writing about how your tenth grade English teacher opened your eyes to the understated beauty and simplicity of haiku—how less can be more—and how that then translated into you donating some of your old video games to a homeless shelter, where you now volunteer once a month. That's powerful stuff! It's a very real story, clearly correlating education to a successful outcome. Focusing on a specific and concise example from your life helps readers relate to you and your experiences. It also guarantees you bonus points for originality!

EDIT AND PROOFREAD AND THEN EDIT AND PROOFREAD

There is an old saying: "Behind every good writer is an even better editor." Find people (friends, siblings, coaches, teachers, guidance counselors) to read your essay, to provide feedback on how to make it better, and to edit it for silly, sloppy mistakes. Some people will read your essay and find issues with your grammar. Others will read your essay and point out how one paragraph doesn't make sense in relation to another paragraph. Some people will tell you how to give more examples to better make your point. All of those people are giving you great information, and you need to take it all in and use it to your advantage! However, don't be overwhelmed by it, and don't let it become all about what everyone else thinks. It's your essay and your thoughts—the goal of editing and proofreading is to clean up the rough edges and make the entire essay shine!

And when you do get to that magical point where you think "DONE!"—instead, just put the essay aside for a few days. Come back to it with an open mind and read, edit, and proofread it one last time. Check it one last time for spelling and grammar fumbles. Check it one last time for clarity and readability (reading it out loud helps!). Check it one last time to ensure it effectively communicates why you are absolutely the winning scholarship candidate!

Your Unique Qualities

It's one thing to help out at the local library a few hours a week; it's a completely different thing if you took it upon yourself to suggest, recruit, organize, and lead a fundraising campaign to buy 10 new laptops for kids to use at the library!

And don't simply rattle off all your different group memberships. Write about things you did that demonstrate leadership and initiative within those groups—did you recruit new members or offer to head up a committee or find a way for the local news station to cover your event or reach out to another organization and collaborate on an activity? Think about your unique qualities and how you use them to bring about change.

A SLICE OF YOUR LIFE

While one goal of your essay is surely to explain why you should win the scholarship money, an equally important goal is to reveal something about you, something that makes it easy to see why you should win. Notice we said to reveal "something" about you and not "everything" about you. Most likely, the rest of the scholarship application gathers quite a bit of information about you. The essay is where you need to hone in on just one aspect of your unique talents, one aspect of an experience, one aspect of reaching a goal. It's not about listing all your accomplishments in your essay (again, you probably did that on the application). It's about sharing a slice of your life—telling your story and giving your details about what makes YOU memorable.

YOUR ACCOMPLISHMENTS, LOUD AND PROUD

Your extracurricular activities illustrate your personal priorities and let the scholarship selection committee know what's important to you. Being able to elaborate on your accomplishments and awards within those activities certainly bolsters your chances of winning the scholarship. Again, though, be careful to not just repeat what is already on the application itself. Use your essay to focus on a specific accomplishment (or activity or talent or award) of which you are most proud.

Did your community suffer through severe flooding last spring? And did you organize a clothing drive for neighbors who were in need? How did that make you feel? What feedback did you get? How did it inspire your desire to become a climatologist?

Were school budget cuts going to mean the disbanding of some after-school clubs? Did you work with teachers and parents to write a proposal to present to the school board, addressing how new funds could be raised in order to save the clubs? How did that make you feel? What feedback did you get? How did it inspire you to start a writing lab for junior high kids?

You have done great things—think about that one special accomplishment and paint the picture of how it has made you wiser, stronger, or more compassionate to the world around you. Share the details!

BUT DON'T GO OVERBOARD

A five-tissue story may translate into an Oscar-worthy movie, but rarely does it translate into winning a scholarship. If your main reason for applying for the scholarship is that you feel you deserve the money because of how much suffering you have been through, you need a better reason. Scholarship selection committees are not really interested in awarding money to people with problems; they want to award money to people who solve problems. While it's just fine to write about why you need the scholarship money to continue your education, it's not fine for your essay to simply be a laundry list of family tragedies and hardships.

So, instead of presenting a sob story, present how you have succeeded and what you have accomplished despite the hardships and challenges you faced. Remember that everyone has faced difficulties. What's unique about you is how YOU faced your difficulties and overcame them. That is what makes your essay significant and memorable.

Following Directions

DOES YOUR ESSAY REALLY ANSWER THE QUESTION?

Have you ever been asked one question but felt like there was another question that was really being asked? Maybe your dad said something like, "Tell me about your new friend." But what he really meant to ask you was, "Tell me about your new friend. Do his lip rings and tattoos mean he's involved in things I don't want you involved in?"

The goal of every scholarship judge is to determine the best applicant out of a pool of applicants who are all rather similar. Pay attention and you'll find that the essay question is an alternate way for you to answer the real question the scholarship-awarding committee wants to ask. For instance, an organization giving an award to students who plan to study business might ask, "Why do you want to study business?" But their real underlying question is, "Why are you the best future business person to whom we should give our money?" If there is a scholarship for students who want to become doctors, you can bet that 99 percent of the students applying want to become doctors. And if you apply for that scholarship with an essay simply delving into your lifelong desire to be a potter, well, that doesn't make you unique, it makes you pretty much unqualified for that opportunity. Be sure to connect your personal skills, characteristics, and experiences with the objectives of the scholarship and its awarding organization.

DOES YOUR ESSAY THEME TIE IN?

Let's say that you are applying for a community service-based award and, on the application, you go ahead and list all the community service groups you belong to and all the awards you have won. But in your essay, you write about how homeless people should find a job instead of sitting on street corners begging for money. Hey—everyone is entitled to their opinion, but would you agree that there is some sort of disconnect between your application and your essay? And no doubt you have made the scholarship-awarding committee wonder the same thing.

So how do you ensure your essay doesn't create a conflicting message? You need to examine the theme of your essay and how it relates both to your application and the reason the scholarship exists in the first place. If the scholarship-funding organization seeks to give money to someone who wants a career in public relations and your essay focuses on how you are not really a "people person," well, you can see how that sends a mixed message to your reader.

Think about it this way: The theme of your essay should naturally flow around the overarching purpose or goal of the organization awarding the scholarship money. Once you have clarified this nugget, you can easily see if and how your words tie in to the organization's vision of whom their scholarship winner is.

THREE MORE PIECES OF ADVICE

1. **Follow the essay length guidelines closely.** You certainly don't want your essay disqualified simply because it was too long or too short!

2. **The deadline is the deadline.** A day late and you could certainly be more than a dollar short in terms of the award money that isn't going to be awarded to you if your application is not received by the due date. Begin the essay writing process well in advance of the scholarship deadline. Writing and editing and rewriting takes time so you should probably allow yourself at least 2 weeks to write your scholarship essay.

3. **Tell the truth.** No need to say anything further on that, right? Right.

TWEET FOR DOLLARS: USE YOUR FINGERTIPS & SOCIAL MEDIA TO PAY FOR COLLEGE

By Felecia Hatcher, Author of *The C Student's Guide to Scholarships*

The biggest question you may have right now is where do I find the money? What if I told you that you could find thousands of scholarship dollars and opportunities by using your computer and your cell phone and thumbs!

It's said that over 1 billion dollars in scholarships goes un-awarded each year. You may think that colleges and scholarship committees are intentionally hiding the money. I promise you that they are not trying to hide the money from you; in fact, they are actually starting to use social media to get the information directly to you. Currently, there are thousands of social media sites on the Internet, and these sites could possibly bring you one step closer to paying for college. Keep reading to find out how you can use social media and crowd sourcing sites to great creative with your search—and not only think outside the box but also think outside the application.

Twitter™:

Twitter allows you to get short messages of 140 characters or less in real time. The one thing that is great about Twitter is that it has a search bar that allows you to search for tweets from anyone or any entity that belongs to the social network. By using special keywords in the search bar, you should be able to find scholarship information and direct links to scholarship applications, about which the scholarship organizations have tweeted.

Go to the search bar in Twitter and type in the following keywords:

"Scholarship Deadline"
"Scholarship+ [Your State]"
"Scholarship PDF"
"Scholarship Deadline http"

Google It!

I jokingly tell people that I feel like I can rule the world with my iPhone and Google. Need a restaurant recommendation? Google it! Need to research the best place to get school supplies for a project? Google it! Need to find money for your college? Google it! Yes, believe it or not, it may be just that simple. But in order to not be bombarded with thousands of useless results, you must use the right keywords. Here is a short list of some keyword combinations that will yield some great results in your scholarship search.

You can use the same search terms previously used for your Twitter searches for Google as well as the following:

Scholarship+ 2012
Scholarship+2013
Scholarship+ Deadline+ Current Month
Scholarship+ [Your City]
Scholarship+ [your race/ethnicity/religion]
Scholarship+ [Your Talent]

You can also replace the word "Scholarship" with grant or fellowship.

Crowd Funding

So, you applied for a huge scholarship and you didn't win that big $25,000 scholarship. Don't despair—put the power of your network of family, friends, and social media followers to work, and create your own scholarship through crowd funding! With crowd funding, you can get 5,000 strangers to donate $5 each, which equals $25,000 … right? No, I'm not talking about standing on a busy corner and playing your guitar. Web sites like Paypal.com, Indiegogo.com, YouCaring. com, PeerBacker.com, and even a brand new tuition exclusive site Scholar.com allow you to reach out to your friends and family or total strangers; pitch your need through a profile, pictures, and compelling video; and creatively fundraise your way to funding your college education.

Tips to Help you Maximize your Chances of Getting Funding

Tell a Compelling Story: Scholarship committees know that you need money, that's a given. But you want to captivate the committee with an exciting story that will keep them reading and opening up their wallets with each word. Tell them who you are and what makes you and your needs different from other students. Most importantly, tell them why they should care enough to part with their money. Get Creative!

Create an exciting profile: Photos and video go a long way when you are creating profiles on crowd funding sites or even on an application that asked for additional information. Take the time to capture great pictures that really let your personality shine. There are an increasing number of applications asking for video submissions. This is your time to shine, so take out your camera and start shooting testimonials from teachers, coaches, and guidance counselors raving about how fabulous you are instead of (or in addition to) submitting the traditional recommendation letter. Pictures and video paint the best picture and makes the need *real*.

Don't be afraid to ask for help: Let me put it frankly, You only get what you ask for! Networks like Facebook®, Twitter™, LinkedIn, and YouCaring.com allow you to amplify your message, so put the message out there. If you don't ask for the help and let everyone know then you can't expect anyone to help you.

So, the next time your parents tell you to get off Facebook or Twitter or put down your phone, tell them that you are searching for scholarship dollars.

Clean Up Your Act: How to Spruce Up your Internet and Social Media Presence to Wow Scholarship Judges

Social media is a huge part of today's social realm. There is a good chance that you probably communicate with your friends on Facebook and Twitter more then you do in person. While these social networks are great for connecting with friends and family, and even meeting new people, they can hurt your scholarship efforts if you are not careful. Having this information in mind, set aside some time before, or directly after, you mail out that first scholarship application to investigate and (if necessary) clean up your online presence.

Are you wondering why this is necessary? You may think that your Facebook page has nothing to do with your scholarship application. Well, if these are your thoughts, you are unfortunately very wrong. There's an excellent chance that a scholarship organization will spend time searching for you on the Internet. If you're shuddering at the thought of the scholarship committee members seeing anything on your page, follow these tips for "scrubbing" your Web reputation squeaky clean:

1. **Google yourself.** Search for every possible variation of your name on Google. If anything unbecoming pops up in the search results, do what you can to have it taken down.

2. **Check your social media sites.** This includes Facebook, LinkedIn, Twitter, Flickr, Tublr, Wordpress, and so on. Make sure all the content on these sites is dignified and academic, meaning that it's serious and grammatically correct. It would be wise to include blog posts about social issues, quotes from famous people you admire, poetry you've written (not including dirty limericks), etc. Your social media pages need to present you as being "smart," "mature," and "hardworking." If it doesn't do those things, then clean up your page, and replace it with content that does. This doesn't mean that you have to be boring; just be cautious of how everything you post on the Internet *looks* because it's like a tattoo—once it is posted, it can not be erased.

3. **Web pages that can't be scrubbed should be hidden.** Try to use nicknames when creating your social profiles, and always use the highest privacy settings so that people must be approved in order to see the page. After doing these things, you should still log out and check what information appears on your default profile page. If a picture that depicts you partying or anything else that would

be unflattering to a scholarship committee appears, log back in, and replace it with something else.

4. **Take those videos off YouTube.** Do this right now. You know which ones we mean.

5. **Remain vigilant.** Just because you cleaned up your Web presence today, it doesn't mean it will be clean as a whistle next week. Be aware of what others are posting and tagging with your name. Some search engines allow you to set up "alerts" to warn you every time your name shows up on the Web. We recommend using this to your full extent.

6. **Check your voicemail.** This is of the utmost importance. If you have an inappropriate ring-back tone or voicemail greeting, you need to either replace it with something professional and appropriate, or kiss your scholarship chances goodbye.

WHAT TO DO IF YOU DON'T WIN A SCHOLARSHIP, GRANT, OR PRIZE

More than 20 million students will enroll in the nation's colleges and universities this year, and you can bet nearly all of them will be vying for the more than $4 billion in private scholarship money that's available. In fact, 85 percent of all first-time undergraduate students attending a four-year college receive some type of financial aid—including scholarships, grants, awards, and student loans.

Yet, even though billions of dollars are out there for the grasping, the average scholarship award is just $2815. That's only going to put a minor dent in the $20,000 annual price tag for in-state tuition, room, and board at a public four-year institution ($39,800 for private). So, unless you started working as a toddler, you're going to have to do something spectacular to avoid buckling under a mountain of student loan debt to get your degree.

Applying for grants and private scholarships is a given. But what if your living room table is filling up with denial letters? What do you do then? Well, the first thing is not to panic. There are plenty of ways to pay for college without going into an enormous amount of debt. Here are some tips and suggestions that will help you to formulate a back-up plan if, by some miracle, you miss out on the college scholarship lottery.

If at First You Don't Succeed

A rejection letter doesn't mean no, it really means, "Not right now." There is nothing wrong with applying for a private scholarship, fellowship or grant again, even if you've been rejected. Just think, you'll have a leg up on everyone who is coming to the competition cold, as you've been there before. Before you dust off your essay from last year and shove it into an envelope this year, be sure to contact the organization and ask for feedback.

Sure, some may not be willing to speak to you, but you have nothing to lose by trying. Often the best advice comes from the unlikeliest places, and asking pointed, mature questions about why your first application failed can only serve you in your college money hunt. In addition, the counsel might help you to improve an application for another organization. So follow up on those who've said no—you never know what kind of great tips and suggestions they will have for you. Here are some questions you may ask when you seek feedback:

- Did my application get rejected because of a procedural mistake? Did I mess up the application process? Did I meet the deadline? Were all my documents included?

- Was my personal statement/essay well done? How could it have been improved?

- Could you give me suggestions on how best to apply for your scholarship again?

Note: You, of course, can't do any of this if you waited until the last minute to fill out your scholarship application, so it pays to start your quest for college treasure early.

You Can Apply for Scholarships While in College

Even if you've already started your college career with your scholarship coffers empty and your student loan debt toppling over, do not fret. You can still apply for grants, scholarships, and programs that do not require you go into debt while you're attending school. Many scholarships are not automatically renewed, and if students do not apply for them, there may be more cash for you. Create an application cycle for every year you attend school. You never know what opportunity you may be missing if you do not at least try to apply while attending school.

Work Now, Not Later

It used to be that flipping burgers at the local fast-food joint was the way most college students paid for college. And to be sure that option is still open. But the recent technology boom fueled by the monetization of the Internet has allowed even the youngest among us to become entrepreneurs. From teen-age search engine app maker Nick D'Alosio, who has raised capital from one of China's billionaires, to the pre-adolescent Mallory Kiveman, who invented a lollipop to cure the hiccups, the spirit of innovation runs deep among the young. Use technology to start your version of a lemonade stand, and you may make enough in your senior year to pay for college and beyond. Technology has allowed people to think better, smarter, and bigger than ever before. As you're working on that latest science project, think about ways to monetize it. It could be your ticket to a full-ride to college.

Don't Leave Money on the Table

Did you know that only 1 in 10 undergraduate students receive a scholarship award? This isn't because there aren't enough scholarships available. On the contrary, millions of dollars in scholarship money go unclaimed because students do not apply for them. Instead, 9 out of 10 students borrowed an average of $63,400 to complete their degrees, according to the National Center for Education Statistics.

Yes, that's right. College students, desperate to incur massive amounts of debts forget to apply for grants, miss deadlines and sloppily fill out scholarship applications to ensure they get rejected and leave money on the table. You, of course, would never do that. But some people will.

Do not be one of those people. Make sure you are taking advantage of all your opportunities to gain debt-free money for college. In addition, to applying for private scholarships make sure you go beyond the Federal Pell Grant. Remember, there are state grants, local grants, need-based grants, merit grants, and college university grants that are available for students. Be sure to check with your admitting institution to make sure you haven't overlooked grants—many of which are automatically offered to students regardless of income.

Practice Some Altruism

There are still some programs that will help pay for your college education as long as you commit to do public service. From AmeriCorps, which defrays college costs for students who work for nonprofits or in high-need areas to the newly minted Public Service Loan Forgiveness Program, which will wipe out federal loan debt for individuals who, after October 2007, work full-time in government or nonprofit jobs, there are dozens of programs that will lower your college costs in exchange for public service. Even top-tier universities such as Harvard and Princeton are offering free tuition (Harvard for just one year) for students who choose to work in public service careers. There are loan forgiveness programs for virtually every public service profession from state-appointed prosecutors, teachers, primary-care doctors, and law enforcement officers; members of the armed forces; nurses and health-care workers; and even Peace Corps volunteers. But beware—the programs have strict guidelines, and you may need to consult a tax advisor.

Here are some contacts for programs that pay down college costs for volunteerism or public service:

AmeriCorps

More than 75,000 adults work with thousands of nonprofits around the country providing tutoring, mentoring, housing management, and a host of other services to the disadvantaged through AmeriCorps. In exchange they receive money to pay for college or graduate school, or they obtain forgiveness on student loans plus a pay check.

AmeriCorps

1201 New York Avenue, NW
Washington, DC 20525
Phone: 202-606-5000
TTY: 800-833-3722 (toll-free)
www.americorps.gov

National Health Service Corps

The National Health Service Corps awards scholarships to students who are pursuing careers in primary care. Students must be pursuing degrees in medicine, dentistry, nursing, and physician assistant studies.

National Health Corps

Phone: 800-221-9393 (toll-free)
http://nhsc.hrsa.gov

Public Service Loan Forgiveness

Congress created the Public Service Loan Forgiveness Program in 2007 as an incentive for people to enter fields that focused on public service. The beneficial program offers qualified borrowers the opportunity to have their federal loans forgiven if they work in certain public service areas.

Learn more at: www.studentaid.gov.

Notes

Notes

Notes

Notes

Notes

Notes

Notes

Notes

Notes

Notes

Notes